FS.192

FOOD SECURITY IN SUB-SAHARAN AFRICA

Dedicated to Sir Hans Singer, on the occasion of his
ninetieth birthday on 29 November 2000.

FOOD SECURITY IN
SUB-SAHARAN AFRICA

Edited by

Stephen Devereux
and
Simon Maxwell

ITDG
PUBLISHING
London

UNIVERSITY OF NATAL PRESS
Pietermaritzburg
South Africa

Published by:
ITDG Publishing
103-105 Southampton Row, London WC1B 4HL, UK
www.itdgpublishing.org.uk

Published in South Africa by:
University of Natal Press
Private Bag X01
Scottsville 3209
www.unpress.co.za

First published in 2001 by ITDG Publishing
Reprinted in 2003

ISBN 1 85339 523 4 (ITDG Publishing)
ISBN 1 86914 027 3 (University of Natal Press)

© Institute of Development Studies 2001

A catalogue record for this book is available from the British Library.

ITDG Publishing is the publishing arm of the
Intermediate Technology Development Group.
Our mission is to build the skills and capacity of people
in developing countries through the dissemination of
information in all forms, enabling them to improve the
quality of their lives and that of future generations.

Typeset by J&L Composition, Filey, North Yorkshire
Printed in Great Britain by Bell & Bain Ltd., Glasgow

Contents

Acknowledgements

This book would not have been possible without the stimulating interactions and mutual learning that the contributing authors enjoyed with over one hundred participants on the study course 'Food Security in Africa: Policy, Planning and Interventions', which was held at IDS Sussex in five rounds between 1991 and 1997, under the direction of Susanna Moorehead (then Susanna Davies), Margie Buchanan-Smith, Simon Maxwell and Stephen Devereux.

In the process of converting 'Food Security in Africa' course modules into chapters for this book, invaluable research assistance was provided by Naomi Hossain on the 'Food Security and the Environment' chapter and on the food aid section of the 'Transfers and Safety Nets' chapter, also by Gareth Williams on the Tanzanian case study in the 'Food Marketing' chapter. Bob Baulch thanks Jonathan Kydd and Scott Pearson for commenting on early versions of the 'Food Marketing' chapter.

The editors are particularly grateful to Jane Kennan, who apart from co-authoring one chapter also provided substantive inputs to several others, and copy-edited the first draft of the manuscript. A special vote of thanks is reserved for Jenny Edwards, who chased the authors for missing references and the editors for missing deadlines, and who gamely took on responsibility for compiling disparate texts into a perfectly formatted manuscript.

Chapter 2 and Chapter 11 are versions of articles published in *Food Policy*, Vol 21(2), 1996, pp 155–170, Simon Maxwell, 'Food security: a postmodern perspective', and Vol 22 (6), 1997, pp 515–531, Simon Maxwell, 'Implementing the World Food Summit Plan of Action: Organisational issues in multisectoral planning' respectively, reprinted here with permission from Elsevier Science. Finally, the editors acknowledge the contribution of the Department for International Development (DFID), which provided financial support towards research assistance and publishing costs.

The publishers would like to thank Nick Robinson and Panos Pictures for permission to use the cover photograph.

Boxes

Figures

Tables

Acronyms

AAF-SAP	African Alternative Framework for Structural Adjustment Programme
ACC/SCN	United Nations Administrative Committee on Co-ordination – Sub-Committee on Nutrition
ACP	African, Caribbean and Pacific
ADB	African Develoment Bank
ADLI	Agricultural Development Led Industrialization
AHFSI	Aggregate Household Food Security Index
AMIS	Agricultural Market Information System
AMS	Aggregate Measure of Support
APPER	African Priority Programme for Economic Recovery
BMI	Body Mass Index
BULOG	Badan Urusan Logistik
CAP	Common Agricultural Policy
CDF	Comprehensive Development Framework
CFS	Crop Forecast Survey
CGIAR	Consultative Group on International Agricultural Research
CILSS	Comité permanent Inter-états pour la Lutte contre la Sécheresse dans le Sahel
CNWs	Community Nutrition Workers
CSO	Central Statistical Office
DES	Dietary Energy Supply
EC	European Community
ECA	Economic Commission for Africa
EDF	European Development Fund
EU	European Union

EWS	Early Warning System
FAC	Food Aid Convention
FAO	Food and Agriculture Organization (of the United Nations)
FEWS	Famine Early Warning System (USAID)
FIVIMS	Food Insecurity and Vulnerability Information and Mapping Systems
FSIS	Food Security Information Systems
FSR	Farming Systems Research
GATT	General Agreement on Tariffs and Trade
GDP	Gross Domestic Product
GIEWS	Global Information and Early Warning System (FAO)
GM	Genetically Modified
GNP	Gross National Product
GSP	Generalized System of Preferences
HDI	Human Development Index
HEM	High Energy Milk
HFA	Height-For-Age
IADP	Integrated Area Development Programme
ICAFE	Costa Rican Coffee Institute
ICN	International Conference on Nutrition
IDT	International Development Targets
IEFR	International Emergency Food Reserve
IFAD	International Fund for Agricultural Development
IFPRI	International Food Policy Research Institute
IGADD	Intergovernmental Authority on Drought and Development
ILO	International Labour Organization
IMF	International Monetary Fund
IRD	Integrated Rural Development
ISNAR	The Institute for Strengthening Agricultural Research
IT	Information Technology
IUCN	World Conservation Union
MCH	Mother and Child Health

MFN	Most Favoured Nation
MSNP	Multi-Sectoral Nutrition Planning
MUAC	Mid-Upper-Arm Circumference
NCHS	National Center for Health Statistics
NGO	Non-Governmental Organization
NIE	New Institutional Economics
NMC	National Milling Corporation (Tanzania)
OAU	Organization of African Unity
OECD	Organisation for Economic Co-operation and Development
ORS	Oral Rehydration Salts
PADEP	Peasant-Area Development Projects
PRA	Participatory Rural Appraisal
PTA	Preferential Trade Area
RaFSA	Rapid Food Security Assessment
RNIS	Reports on the Nutrition Situation of Refugees and Displaced Persons
SADC	Southern Africa Development Community
SADCC	Southern Africa Development Coordination Conference
SCF-UK	Save the Children Fund United Kingdom
S-C-P	Structure–Conduct–Performance
SGR	Strategic Grain Reserve
SIP	Sector Investment Programme
SSA	Sub-Saharan Africa
SWAP	Sector Wide Approach
TNC	Transnational Corporation
UN	United Nations
UNDP	United Nations Development Programme
UNHCR	United Nations High Commissioner for Refugees
UNICEF	United Nations Children's Fund
USA	United States of America
USAID	United States Agency for International Development
VAM	Vulnerability Assessment and Mapping

WCED	World Commission on Environment and Development
WFA	Weight-For-Age
WFC	World Food Council
WFH	Weight-For-Height
WFI	World Financial Institution
WFP	World Food Programme
WFS	World Food Summit
WHO	World Health Organization
WTO	World Trade Organization

Introduction

Stephen Devereux and Simon Maxwell

Sub-Saharan Africa (SSA) is the only region in the world currently facing widespread chronic food insecurity as well as persistent threats of famine. Why is this so, and what can be done? This book addresses these questions by bringing together eleven perspectives on Africa's food security problems, from the analysis of causes to planning of policy interventions. In keeping with current thinking on the complex nature of food insecurity, a variety of disciplinary perspectives is drawn upon, from agricultural economics to nutrition.

A feature of many contributions to this book is the way in which our deepening theoretical and empirical understanding of food insecurity has generated increasingly sophisticated analytical frameworks and policy recommendations. Every chapter reflects an evolution of thinking that has permeated all dimensions of food security analysis and policy making. Perhaps most significantly, food insecurity is no longer seen simply as a failure of *agriculture* to produce sufficient food at the *national* level, but instead as a failure of *livelihoods* to guarantee access to sufficient food at the *household* level. This recognition is evident in two of the three conceptual shifts identified in Chapter 1, in the discussion of 'food security' *versus* 'livelihoods' in Chapter 3 on livelihoods, and in the paradigm shift described in Chapter 5 on famine, from supply-side to demand-side theories.

As with all paradigm shifts, this evolution of the food security discourse has often been highly contentious, and in many arenas the debate has become unnecessarily polarized. Currently, in the analysis of both chronic food insecurity (undernutrition) and acute food insecurity (famine) a consensus appears to be emerging whereby the contributions of limited food *availability* and restricted *access* to food are both recognized. Food insecurity in Africa is a product of low agricultural production plus low incomes, not one or the other alone, and is a consequence of policy failure as well as institutional failure. Similarly, Chapter 6 on food marketing notes that the crude policy dichotomy of 'state or market' has been widely rejected as excessively ideological, and current initiatives are focused instead on finding the appropriate mix of complementary roles between public and private actors. Even in more technical aspects of food security, such as nutrition, an initial preoccupation with protein energy malnutrition has been superseded by a holistic view that incorporates micronutrient deficiencies.

The Sixth World Food Survey, published by FAO in 1996, estimated that more than 840 million people were undernourished in 1992. A growing proportion of these people – 26 per cent in 1992, up from 11 per cent in 1971 – live in Africa (FAO 1996), due to a combination of deteriorating food security in that continent and improvements elsewhere (notably South and East Asia). This depressing statistic, together with recurrent famines in the Horn and the constant threat of food crises triggered by conflict or drought in other parts of Africa, make a convincing case for continuing to prioritize food insecurity in its own right. Food insecurity is not merely a subset of poverty. Food crises and chronic hunger have not been eradicated, despite dramatic improvements during the twentieth century in agricultural productivity, transport and communications infrastructure, and international humanitarianism.

Africa's persistent vulnerability is arguably due as much to a failure of understanding as to a failure of interventions. The objective of this book is to contribute towards an improved understanding of Africa's food security problems, in order to inform the design of more effective strategies and policies. The starting point for this improved understanding, in our view, is an acceptance of the following propositions:

1 That hunger and poverty in Africa must now be seen as the most urgent and intractable problem facing those concerned with development in the twenty-first century: poverty and food security are increasingly 'Africanized'.
2 That a precondition for tackling poverty in Africa lies in improving the production, marketing and consumption of food: national and household food security must be at the heart of poverty reduction.
3 That food security policy faces unprecedented challenges associated with a range of internal and external influences on Africa: from the impact of new technology, conflict and HIV/AIDS, to the effects of globalization on trading options in the agricultural sector.
4 That food security management in Africa requires better collaboration across sectors, disciplines and institutions: food security is too important and too complex to be left to specialist ministries such as Agriculture.
5 That the problems and failures of the past should not lead to pessimism and cynicism about the future. Africans themselves are confident that the resources of the continent can be harnessed to achieve food security and poverty reduction, and so are we. The challenge is to put the right institutions and policies in place, nationally and internationally.

Each of these propositions challenges both accepted ways of thinking and the ways that governments and donors work. Yet poverty is a long-standing phenomenon in Africa; food security is now a well-established field of study; many of the external and internal shocks facing Africa are neither new nor unpredictable; integrated planning is not unknown; and food security plans have been developed for most the countries of sub-Saharan Africa. Why, then, are we calling for a renewed focus on food security and for innovative approaches to food security planning? The reasons relate directly to the five propositions set out above.

First, poverty and hunger are getting worse in Africa, but better almost everywhere else. Data prepared for the World Development Report 2000–1 show that nearly half the population of SSA is living below the international poverty line of US$1 per day. This proportion has failed to fall over time, and is higher than for any other region. In East Asia, for example, the proportion living below $1 per day fell from 27 per cent in 1987 to 15 per cent in 1998, in South Asia from 45 to 40 per cent. In SSA, the proportion remained unchanged at 46 per cent, and, because of population growth, the number of poor Africans rose, from 217 million in 1987 to 291 million in 1998 (World Bank 2000). Child malnutrition has also risen, both in numbers and in proportionate terms. Data from the UN show that the proportion of underweight children in SSA increased from 26 per cent in 1980 to 28.5 per cent in 2000; with population increase, this meant a rise in absolute numbers from 22 million to 38 million children (ACC/SCN 2000).

To make things worse, the long-term outlook for SSA is not encouraging. Inequality is the highest in the world (with an average Gini coefficient of 0.51), population will increase by as much as 70 per cent by 2020 – even allowing for HIV/AIDS – and economic growth rates will not be sufficient to reduce poverty substantially. The US Department of Agriculture recently predicted that 60 per cent of the population of SSA will be consuming less than the minimum nutritional requirement by 2009 (USDA 1999). The International Food Policy Research Institute (IFPRI) estimates that child malnutrition will rise by 30 per cent by 2020 (Pinstrup-Andersen et al. 1999). The international community has committed itself to halve both poverty and undernutrition by 2015: on present trends, neither of these targets will be met in sub-Saharan Africa.

As poverty worsens – and this is our second point – food becomes more important than ever. This is self-evident in contexts of heightened vulnerability, for example among refugees or internally displaced people (more than 20 million of whom are in Africa) who have lost their access to food. More generally, though, a defining characteristic of the poor is that they spend most of their income on food, or expend most of their time and energy on producing food for subsistence. As millions of Africans become poorer, so the severity of their food insecurity intensifies, and they become trapped in the debilitating struggle simply to find adequate food for survival.

There is much more to tackling hunger than simply producing more food. An individual's access to food can derive from his or her own production, but food can equally be acquired by purchase, exchange or gift. Today, the majority of the poor in Africa are smallholders with some capacity to produce food – though whether they are always wise to depend on farming for their food needs is a matter for debate, and a topic that is explored in later chapters. Many of the rural poor, however, are effectively landless, and some of Africa's poorest citizens live in urban areas rather than rural villages. Increasingly, the poor in Africa will become alienated from the land. How they acquire food will then be a matter for urbanization and employment strategies, social security policy, infrastructure development, and a plethora of food-related policies concerned with international trade, internal food marketing and subsidy programmes, and emergency relief. This increasingly complex reality demands increasingly complex, multisectoral food security policies.

Of course, agriculture will remain a core sector for food security – as a source of food, but also of employment, raw materials, foreign exchange, and other resources essential for economic development. In Africa, there are strong linkages between agricultural performance and the health of the broader economy. Agriculture still accounts for a quarter of Gross Domestic Product (GDP) in sub-Saharan Africa, and thus remains one of the primary motors of growth and poverty reduction. Contrary to some pessimistic beliefs, food production has increased in Africa – by over a quarter in the last two decades. This increase has not, however, been as fast as in other regions, and has not been fast enough to prevent food imports rising and *per capita* food availability falling. IFPRI estimate that imports will rise further – from 10 million tonnes in 1995 to nearly 14 million tonnes in 2020 – a rise that would be higher still if Africa could afford to buy all the food it needs (Pinstrup-Andersen et al. 1999).

As consumers, producers, traders, and planners think about food security, they face new challenges – and this is our third point. The future will not be like the past, in several ways.

- First, the level and intensity of shocks may well be increasing. Africa is all too familiar with the devastating impact that war, drought or floods can have on national food systems and on the livelihoods of the poor. In the last two decades, internal conflicts have erupted in no fewer than 28 African countries, while many (often the same) countries have suffered the severest consequences of climatic aberrations – droughts in the Horn in 1984/5 and southern Africa in 1991/2, floods in Mozambique in early 2000. Global warming analysts predict increased climatic variability and increased incidence of extreme weather events, and some climatologists foresee lower rainfall trends for much of Africa. Similarly, although some observers believe that outbreaks of genocidal violence in several African states may recede into history as a post-cold war settlement slowly emerges, others fear that a 'culture of violence' is becoming endemic: an inevitable consequence of rising poverty and inequality, unresolved ethnic tensions and the easy availability of weapons.

- Second, globalization offers opportunities, but also risks, to Africa. The importance of trade in the global economy is growing fast – trade is currently growing at three times the rate of GDP – and this should be good news for small, open, trade-dependent economies (as many African economies are). Africa, however, is not benefiting from the boom. It is poorly represented in new manufacturing sectors, and, since 1960, its share of world agricultural exports has fallen from over 10 per cent to under 4 per cent. There are success stories to report – for example, the horticultural export industry in Kenya – but typically these are niche markets whose profits are accruing to relatively few African farmers. Wider replication will need better and more stable economic policies and more investment in infrastructure and in training. Africa must also equip itself to participate in the current round of trade talks on agricultural liberalization: better access to Northern markets is a tempting prize.

- Third, new technology will transform agriculture in the years to come. It is well known that Africa lags behind other regions in the adoption of 'old' technology, particularly irrigation, fertilizer and improved varieties – the classic elements of the Green Revolution. This is partly because land has not historically been a scarce resource in much of Africa, so that these land-enhancing innovations have been of lower priority for African farmers. Land is becoming increasingly scarce, however, which will encourage the adoption of high input, high output technology. The future also holds the prospect of a new, 'doubly green' revolution (Conway 1997): higher yielding, but also more friendly to the environment, exploiting the benefits of genetic modification but paying more attention to water conservation, the maintenance of soil fertility, and the use of information technology to conserve resources and improve efficiency.

- Finally, urbanization will pose dramatic new challenges to food security planners in Africa. The proportion of Africa's population living in cities has doubled, from 15 per cent in the 1960s to over 30 per cent today, and Africa has the world's highest rates of urban population growth (4.3 per cent in 1995, followed by Latin America at 2.3 per cent and Asia at 2.2 per cent (United Nations 1996)). IFPRI estimates that for the developing world as a whole, urban populations will overtake rural populations before 2020 (Pinstrup-Andersen et al. 1999). A new kind of food system will be needed, no longer concentrating on meeting local subsistence needs, but instead supplying cheap, safe food to cities, in an integrated supply and distribution chain. Market integration, in economies where weak and segmented markets have been a causal factor in many food crises, will become a crucial element of urban and rural food security.

The challenges are not straightforward. Our fourth question, then, is about how planners can deal with these questions. Will a new planning paradigm be needed? Food security is, by definition, a multisectoral issue. Yet, despite recent initiatives such as the World Bank's 'Comprehensive Development Framework', governments and donors continue to programme resources and deliver services vertically, through sector ministries. 'SWAPs' and 'SIPs' (Sector-Wide Approaches and Sector Investment Programmes), for example, are currently being designed and implemented throughout Africa, but these mechanisms attempt to coordinate and focus efforts within – rather than across – sectors. Successive generations of food security planners can testify to the difficulties of multisectoral planning (this topic is taken up explicitly in this book's final chapter). The potential for conflict between ministries is large, and special measures are needed to reach jointly owned decisions. On the other hand, many countries have devised integrated 'Food Security and Nutrition Action Plans'; Ethiopia has established a 'Food Security Unit' in each of its regions; and Save the Children Fund (UK) has appointed 'food economists' to its national offices in several African countries. In this area, as in others, food security may offer positive lessons for wider development objectives, such as the preparation of 'Poverty Reduction Strategy Papers'.

From this observation comes our final theme, which is that there are many optimistic features of the food security debate, which need to be heard more widely. The tendency to generalize about 'sub-Saharan Africa' as a whole obscures the fact that some African countries have performed well in recent decades, repudiating the view that there is something peculiar about Africa that leads African countries to perform badly. Botswana is much cited as an example of a country that has grown consistently fast for many years. Botswana has benefited greatly from substantial income from diamond mining, but it has also been well served by economic policies that have ensured that these revenues were well used. There are other success stories to report: FAO reports that ten countries in SSA are reducing the prevalence of hunger fast enough to reach the international development target (IDT) of halving hunger by 2015, with West African countries being star performers. For example, Ghana reduced undernourishment between 1980 and 1996 more rapidly than any other country in the world, largely as a result of rapid economic growth and increased yields for food staples: calorie availability rose from 1790 calories per day to over 2600 (FAO 1999, p. 24).

The Botswana and Ghana examples illustrate that effective policies are available to Africa and to the international community; and that these can make a real difference to the food security of the poor. Our approach in this book is to argue from both theory and evidence, and to combine a historical perspective with an understanding of contemporary realities in Africa. Our perspective is thus one that favours evidence-based policy.

In Chapter 1, Simon Maxwell traces **The Evolution of Thinking about Food Security** both conceptually and chronologically. Three fundamental shifts in food security thinking since the 1970s are identified: at the *level of analysis*, from the global and national to the household and individual; in the *scope of analysis*, from a narrow 'food first' perspective to a broader 'livelihoods' perspective, and in the *assessment* of food (in)security, from objective (measured) indicators to subjective (self-reported) perceptions. These shifts also reflect trends in general development thinking over this period, from supply-side to demand-side analyses, and from quantitative to qualitative and participatory methodologies. Maxwell disaggregates the period since the 1974 World Food Conference, when food security thinking and policy in the present era effectively began, into five half-decade phases. To some extent the conceptual shifts reflect conditions of the period: thus, the food supply focus that dominated the 1970s was a logical response to the 'world food crisis' and the African famines early in the decade. In the 1980s, growing concerns about the social costs of structural adjustment, together with the acceptance of Amartya Sen's 'entitlement approach' to famine analysis, saw a growing awareness of the demand-side of food security, a focus on access to food and a recognition that food insecurity is a consequence of household-level poverty as much as inadequate food production or availability at the national level. In the early 1990s, food security was displaced in the international development discourse by poverty reduction. But in the last few years of the century, especially since a commitment was made at the World Food Summit in 1996 to halve the numbers of hungry people by the year 2015, food security reasserted itself as a global policy concern.

Simon Maxwell next examines **Agricultural Issues in Food Security** in some detail, because of the centrality of agriculture to food production, rural livelihoods and the national economy throughout SSA, and because of the failure of agriculture to deliver food security to the population of many African countries over a long time period. Food production per capita has fallen steadily in SSA since the 1970s, *contra* global trends. At the same time, the scope for policy support to agriculture has been steadily eroded by structural adjustment programmes that insist on less government intervention in the productive sectors. Nonetheless, a number of key planning arenas remain, many of these requiring choices to be made between contested alternative strategies. Two of these are the 'cash crop debate' and the decision to invest in high potential or low potential agricultural areas. These choices are contingent on broader government strategy, which can be reduced to one of three alternatives: growth first, food first, or food security first. Prioritizing economic growth would imply a focus on cash crops and high potential areas, with food insecurity problems being solved by 'trickle down' effects plus redistribution. A 'food first' strategy requires a concentration on food crop production and intensification in high potential areas. Finally, adopting a 'food security' focus suggests allocating resources either to food crops or cash crops, according to comparative advantage, while protecting chronically food insecure households by investing in marginal areas.

Agriculture might be the most important contributor to national and household food security in Africa, but it is not the only source of food and income. In Chapter 3 on **Household Food and Livelihood Security**, Jeremy Swift and Kate Hamilton point out that households throughout rural Africa follow highly diversified livelihood portfolios, as a logical response to the risks and uncertainty associated with rainfall dependent activities such as farming and pastoralism. Despite the well documented resilience and adaptability of pastoralism, conflict and market dependence are threatening this way of life in all of Africa's dryland regions. Swift and Hamilton also emphasize another often neglected correlate of food insecurity in Africa: urban poverty. Although urban residents derive most of their food from the market, a common response to unemployment and low incomes is urban farming, or alternatively, maintaining farms in the rural areas. This chapter highlights the growing significance of rural–urban linkages in livelihood diversification. More generally, Swift and Hamilton draw on the 'sustainable livelihoods' framework to argue for a broader conceptual approach to understanding food security in Africa. Sustainable livelihoods can be achieved only if the institutions that govern livelihoods are favourable, which includes not only government policies and donor/NGO interventions, but local rules and norms around common property resource management, as well as control and allocation of resources between genders and generations within households.

In her analysis of the complex links between **Food Security and the Environment** in Chapter 4, Susanna Moorehead tackles the perception that environmental awareness often conflicts with the needs of people such as farmers and pastoralists who derive their living directly from the environment. This conflict is neither necessary nor inevitable, Moorehead argues, and the fashionable notion of 'sustainable livelihoods' reconciles the needs of people to earn a living from the environment with the imperative to conserve and regenerate the natural resource base. True, for the rural poor, trade-offs must sometimes be made between immediate subsistence needs and long-term environmental sustainability. But environmentally damaging behaviour, such as overgrazing and deforestation, reflects not ignorance or mismanagement, but poverty. Besides, many counter-examples to the 'conventional myths' exist, such as Machakos District in Kenya and the 'forest–savannah mosaic' in Guinea, where the poor actively enhance their environments through soil conservation techniques and reforestation. A community-based political ecology approach to the food security/environment relationship is advocated. Policy makers must understand the ways in which people interact with their environments before designing policies that can successfully address both sets of needs.

Moving from chronic food insecurity to food crises, Stephen Devereux's chapter on **Famine in Africa** traces the shifts in thinking about famines over time, some of which reflect in magnified form the general shifts in food security thinking identified above. Famine was originally seen as an 'act of God' or 'nature', but is now understood as an 'act of man'; famines used to be seen as abnormal *events* but are increasingly recognized as *processes* associated with poverty and heightened vulnerability; famine was thought to be caused by a lack of food (supply failure), but is now analysed in terms of lack of *access* to food (demand failure). The chapter reviews and critiques the main theories of famine causation, including climatic theories (drought, flood, climate change), Malthusianism (overpopulation relative to food supplies), market failure (trader speculation or hoarding of food), and Sen's 'entitlement approach' (famine as a failure at the household level to acquire sufficient food through production plus purchases plus gifts). The complexity of contemporary food crises means that famines can no longer be attributed to a single causal factor, but instead reflect systemic failures of food production, trade and aid. Although the logistical problems around redistributing food from surplus to deficit areas have virtually been eradicated, political failures – especially civil war – mean that famines can and still do occur. In Africa famines are increasingly related to war, not drought, and millions of refugees and internally displaced people are highly vulnerable to food insecurity.

One of the explanations given for famines is market failure, and in Chapter 6 Bob Baulch analyses the crucial role of **Food Marketing** in food security, particularly in non-emergency contexts. This issue has been at the forefront of food security policy debates since the 1980s, as governments across Africa have struggled to find the optimal balance between public and private sector actors – or parastatals *versus* private traders. A careful examination of the justifications for government intervention in food markets – e.g. to stabilize food prices and supplies through 'buffer stock' management to protect the food security of poor consumers – is balanced against the efficiency gains from competitive market forces. Baulch argues for a compromise between those who argue for state control and those who advocate full market liberalization. Parastatals should neither monopolize food marketing nor be closed down. Rather, government should intervene only where household food security is threatened because of market failures (e.g. dramatic price seasonality), and the private sector should otherwise be encouraged to flourish. A case study of agricultural marketing in Tanzania illustrates the potential gains from radical but not total market liberalization. The parastatal and the private sector have achieved a harmonious relationship whereby the government agency supports and complements private trading activities.

Chapter 7 by Christopher Stevens and Jane Kennan on **Food Aid and Trade** addresses one of the thorniest issues in national food security policy – the 'self-sufficiency debate'. Should a poor country strive to grow all the food it needs to maintain independence from unpredictable world markets, or should it specialize in producing 'cash crops' and other goods for export, and use its export earnings to import food? The answer lies in a combination of international trade theory (comparative advantage, terms of trade) and the unique portfolio of resources (natural, human and infra-structural) that each country possesses. Analysis of empirical data reveals that Africa is highly dependent on food imports (both commercial and aid) and that export crop prices have been subjected to large cyclical swings, both favourable and unfavourable, which have been responsible for uncertainty and insecurity. In general, however, terms of trade have tended to move favourably for African producers, partly because of preferential agreements with European Union (EU) importers and partly because of increasing exports of high-value (e.g. horticultural) produce. The chapter also assesses the likely impacts on food security of the rapidly changing international trade regime – the creation of the World Trade Organization, tariffication, cuts in producer and export subsidies. Although the net impact of these indicators of globalization are uncertain, low-income food deficit countries (most of which are in SSA), are highly vulnerable to food price rises because of their food import dependence, and to measures that threaten their preferential status with large trading blocs like the EU.

In Chapter 8, Stephen Devereux considers the role of **Food Security Information Systems** in predicting and helping to prevent famines, as well as in monitoring food insecurity in non-emergency contexts. This chapter examines the evolution of early warning systems (EWS) from their exclusive focus on supply issues through to incorporation of demand factors (access variables). The level of data collection and analysis has evolved from the original national level to now include decentralized and regional data in some areas. The information collected by typical early warning systems is outlined together with their constraints. The Food Balance Sheet approach is critiqued with an example from Zambia which illustrates its limitations. Institutional and political constraints on the use of early warning information are outlined and recommendations are made on methods for improvement. Food security information systems (FSIS) are defined separately from EWS and are discussed in detail with special attention given to their conceptual base and existing food security indices. The issues of vulnerability and sub-national food security monitoring are addressed with the Food Economy approach being described as an innovative model. The important role of market information systems in FSIS is highlighted with a discussion on how these have been realized in the field. The need for greater sharing of information and capacity building within African institutions are stressed as essential for sustainable information systems within these countries.

Nutrition status is the primary outcome indicator for food security assessment. Helen Young's chapter on **Nutrition and Intervention Strategies** offers an accessible introduction to one of the more technical areas in this book, explaining the jargon, concepts and assessment methodologies, and providing a number of illustrative case studies from nutrition surveys and interventions in a variety of emergency and non-emergency situations throughout Africa. The chapter emphasizes the scale and depth of the nutrition crisis in SSA, where nutritional indicators have deteriorated during the 1990s and where droughts and complex political emergencies continue to produce recurrent outbreaks of hunger and starvation. The multi-sectoral approach to nutrition planning which followed the 1974 World Food Conference, and UNICEF's conceptual framework of the underlying causes of malnutrition and mortality, both recognized that malnutrition is an outcome of many interrelated problems, inadequate food intake and disease being just the triggers. More recently, community-based approaches have tended to replace multi-sectoral approaches, in line with trends throughout development practice towards decentralization and participation. While this chapter is positive about the conceptual and methodological advances in thinking about and delivering nutrition programmes, it recognizes that the solutions lie in tackling the root causes of food insecurity. To some extent, any nutrition intervention that is not preventative – such as the immunization of children – no matter how successful it is, implies a prior failure of food security planning and policy.

An important policy question for food security planning concerns the choice of interventions. **Transfers and Safety Nets** (Chapter 10) were the third prong of the 'New Poverty Agenda' as set out in the World Bank's *World Development Report 1990*, but this phrase applies to many forms of assistance to the poor, the food insecure, and other vulnerable groups. In his chapter on the role of transfers and safety nets for addressing food insecurity, Stephen Devereux examines the case for and against various food-related interventions, including price subsidies and seasonal price stabilization, public works programmes (food-for-work and cash-for-work), and supplementary feeding programmes. Identifying beneficiaries of transfer programmes is often problematic, and this chapter evaluates the pros and cons of alternative targeting mechanisms: means testing (individual assessment of applicants' income), demographic criteria (where eligibility is determined by age, sex, or disability), and self-targeting (as on public works programmes, where the work requirement and low wages discourage the non-needy). Another problematic area is the evaluation of transfers and safety net programmes. Evaluations of food security interventions such as supplementary feeding and school feeding programmes have often yielded disappointing results in terms of nutritional impacts, but these may reflect the complex and multi-dimensional nature of food insecurity, rather than intrinsic failures of project design. Although targeted interventions can address specific food problems, effective solutions require holistic food security programmes that address the root causes of chronic food insecurity.

In the book's final chapter, Simon Maxwell explores **Organizational Issues in Food Security Planning**, drawing on the theory of organizations to illustrate the complexity of multisectoral planning which a multidimensional issue like food security requires. Maxwell develops a fictional scenario in which two food security planners struggle to coordinate policies across the Ministries of Agriculture, Health and Commerce, and between their national government and the international donors and financial institutions. Maxwell argues that many difficulties could be overcome with an understanding of alternative organizational cultures and structures, and with a shift within bureaucracies from a 'role' culture towards a 'task' culture. The chapter concludes by drawing lessons for food security planning from previous initiatives in multisectoral planning, such as integrated rural development programmes, farming systems research, and multisector nutrition planning.

Amartya Sen once remarked that the purpose of studying famine is to contribute to its eradication. Despite the great technological achievements of the twentieth century, food insecurity in Africa – including famine – remains stubbornly uneradicated. It is the ambition of all our contributors that this volume contributes, in some small measure, to the achievement of enhanced food security in sub-Saharan Africa.

CHAPTER ONE

The Evolution of Thinking about Food Security

Simon Maxwell

FOOD SECURITY HAS been in the public eye for a long time. The biblical story of Joseph at the Pharaoh's court, predicting seven years of plenty followed by seven years of famine, is an early example of food security planning in practice. Some years later, the Israelites fleeing the Pharaoh through the desert were provided with manna from heaven – this has been cited by Professor Sir Hans Singer as an early example of food aid. More prosaically, many current food security problems have historical antecedents. For example, Julius Caesar struggled with the spiralling cost of food subsidies in ancient Rome, and counted it something of a triumph to have reduced the number of people receiving free grain to a mere 150 000 (cited in Tannehill 1988, p. 71).

In more recent history, food security began to make a serious impact on the development debate in the 1970s and has rarely been out of the limelight since. However, it must also be acknowledged that interest in food security has waxed and waned over time, partly in response to the evolution of thinking about development more widely, and partly because of changes in the nature of the food problem in the real world. At the same time, there have been changes in thinking about food security itself, principally a gradual shift away from concern with issues of global and national food supply, towards the issue of household and individual access to food. More recently, however, this particular pendulum has begun to swing back again, with renewed interest in food supply – this question is discussed in more detail in Chapter 2.

The two tendencies we have identified – for interest in food security to wax and wane, and for the pendulum to swing from supply issues to consumption issues – can be depicted as the two axes of a diagram, as in Figure 1.1. The horizontal axis indicates the extent to which food security has had a high or low profile. The vertical axis indicates whether the main focus of attention had been on the production or the consumption side.

FOOD SECURITY: A CLOSER LOOK AT THREE PARADIGM SHIFTS

We can develop the schematic representation in Figure 1.1 by looking at the conceptual development of thinking about food security, and then by relating this to particular historical phases. In broad terms, the history of thinking about food security since the World Food Conference in 1974 can be conceptualized as consisting of three important and overlapping paradigm shifts (Maxwell 1996). The shifts are reflected in successive definitions of the term, of which thirty or so are listed as examples in Box 1.1.[1] The three shifts are:

- from the global and the national to the household and the individual;
- from a 'food first' perspective to a livelihood perspective;
- from objective indicators to subjective perception.

FROM THE GLOBAL AND THE NATIONAL TO THE HOUSEHOLD AND THE INDIVIDUAL

The World Food Conference defined food security as:

availability at all times of adequate world supplies of basic food-stuffs ... to sustain a steady expansion of food consumption ... and to offset fluctuations in production and prices (UN 1975).

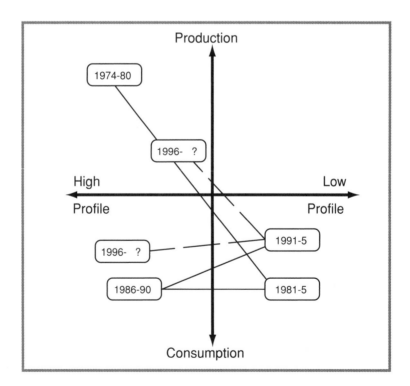

Figure 1.1   The evolution of thinking about food security

Box 1.1   Definitions of food security and insecurity, 1975–1991

1   'Availability at all times of adequate world supplies of basic food-stuffs …, to sustain a steady expansion of food consumption … and to offset fluctuations in production and prices' (UN 1975).
2   'A condition in which the probability of a country's citizens falling below a minimal level of food consumption is low' (Reutlinger and Knapp 1980).
3   'The ability to meet target levels of consumption on a yearly basis' (Siamwalla and Valdes 1980).
4   'Everyone has enough to eat at any time – enough for life, health and growth of the young, and for productive effort' (Kracht 1981).
5   'The certain ability to finance needed imports to meet immediate targets for consumption levels' (Valdes and Konandreas 1981).
6   'Freedom from food deprivation for all of the world's people all of the time' (Reutlinger 1982).
7   'Ensuring that all people at all times have both physical and economic access to the basic food they need' (FAO 1983).
8   'The stabilization of access, or of proportionate shortfalls in access, to calories by a population' (Heald and Lipton 1984).
9   'A basket of food, nutritionally adequate, culturally acceptable, procured in keeping with human dignity and enduring over time' (Oshaug 1985, in Eide et al. 1985).
10 'Access by all people at all times to enough food for an active and healthy life' (Reutlinger 1985).
11 'Access by all people at all times to enough food for an active, healthy life' (World Bank 1986).
12 'Always having enough to eat' (Zipperer 1987).
13 'An assured supply and distribution of food for all social groups and individuals adequate in quality and quantity to meet their nutritional needs' (Barraclough and Utting 1987)
14 'Both physical and economic access to food for all citizens over both the short and the long run' (Falcon et al. 1987).
15 'A country and people are food secure when their food system operates efficiently in such a way as to remove the fear that there will not be enough to eat' (Maxwell 1988).
16 'Adequate food available to all people on a regular basis' (UN World Food Council 1988).
17 'Adequate access to enough food to supply energy needed for all family members to live healthy, active and productive lives' (Sahn 1989).
18 'Consumption of less than 80% of WHO average daily caloric intake' (Reardon and Matlon 1989).

19 'The ability ... to satisfy adequately food consumption needs for a normal and healthy life at all times' (Sarris 1989).
20 'Access to adequate food by and for households over time' (Eide 1990).
21 'Food insecurity exists when members of a household have an inadequate diet for part or all of the year or face the possibility of an inadequate diet in the future' (Phillips and Taylor 1990).
22 'The ability ... to assure, on a long-term basis, that the food system provides the total population access to a timely, reliable and nutritionally adequate supply of food' (Staatz 1990).
23 'The absence of hunger and malnutrition' (Kennes 1990).
24 'The assurance of food to meet needs throughout every season of the year' (UNICEF 1990).
25 'The inability ... to purchase sufficient quantities of food from existing suppliers' (Mellor 1990).
26 'The self-perceived ability of household members to provision themselves with adequate food through whatever means' (Gillespie and Mason 1991).
27 '(Low) risk of on-going lack of access by people to the food they need to lead healthy lives' (Von Braun 1991).
28 'A situation in which all individuals in a population possess the resources to assure access to enough food for an active and healthy life' (Weber and Jayne 1991).
29 'Access to food, adequate in quantity and quality, to fulfil all nutritional requirements for all household members throughout the year' (Jonsson and Toole 1991).
30 'Access to the food needed for a healthy life for all its members and ... not at undue risk of losing such access' (ACC/SCN 1991).
31 'Enough food available to ensure a minimum necessary intake by all members' (Alamgir and Arora 1991).
32 'The viability of the household as a productive and reproductive unit (not) threatened by food shortage' (Frankenberger and Goldstein 1991).

A statement in these terms leads inexorably to a focus on supply, to a concern with national self-sufficiency and to proposals for world food stocks or import stabilization schemes. Indeed, these concerns were reflected in the early literature on food security (e.g. Valdes 1981). It was clear from the outset, however, that widespread hunger could, and often did, co-exist with adequate food supply at the national and international levels.

Amartya Sen (1981) has been credited with initiating the paradigm shift that moved this issue of access to food to centre stage. However, the idea was already commonplace in nutrition planning and had been amply demonstrated in field studies (Berg 1973; Joy 1973; Levinson 1974; Kielman et al. 1977).

As a result, it has been impossible since the early 1980s to speak credibly of food security as being a problem of food supply, without at least making reference to the importance of access and entitlement. In practice, it has been more usual to define food security as being first and foremost a problem of access to food, with food production at best a route to entitlement, either directly for food producers or indirectly by driving market prices down for consumers.

Ambiguities remain, however, particularly about whether the unit of analysis should be the individual or the household. While one school of thought has focused on the household as the unit of analysis for food security (Sahn 1989; Swift 1989; Eide 1990; Frankenberger and Goldstein 1991), another has placed intra-household power and resource allocation issues in the front line of analysis and focused instead on individual food security (Reutlinger 1985; Gittinger et al. 1990). The first school certainly recognizes the importance of intra-household issues: indeed, its concern is often specifically with mother and child health. However, the difference lies in whether intra-household issues are treated as within the domain of food security or as more appropriate to a discussion of caring capacity and health conditions (Jonsson and Toole 1991) – the United Nations Children's Fund (UNICEF) model of the causes of under-nutrition is relevant here (see Chapter 9).

Recent research favours the view that access to food by individuals in a household is pervasively linked to the control they have over household resources and the access they have to household income (Hart 1986; Evans 1991; Kabeer 1991, 1995). The implications for food security can be substantial: in urban Brazil, for example, the impact of unearned income on child survival is twenty times greater if it is controlled by mothers (Thomas 1991).

Following this logic, most current definitions of food security begin with individual entitlement, though recognizing the complex inter-linkages between the individual, the household, the community, the nation and the international economy. Thus, the most-cited definition of food security is taken from a World Bank policy study, published in 1986: 'Food security is access by all people at all times to enough food for an active, healthy life' (World Bank 1986, p. 1).

Here the stress is on individual access, in all seasons and all years; and to enough food not just for survival, but for active participation in society. The World Bank draws an important distinction between chronic and transitory food insecurity. The former is long-term and the latter temporary.

FROM A FOOD FIRST PERSPECTIVE TO A LIVELIHOOD PERSPECTIVE

The second paradigm shift is from a food first perspective to a livelihood perspective, and beyond that to a preoccupation with the long-term resilience of livelihoods. Whereas the first shift took place largely in the period 1975–85, the second occurred mainly after 1985, stimulated by observation of the African famine of 1984–5.

The conventional view of food security was of food as a primary need, a lower-order need in Maslow's (1954) hierarchy. The view was well expressed by Hopkins, who argued that:

> food security stands as a fundamental need, basic to all human needs and the organisation of social life. Access to necessary nutrients is fundamental, not only to life per se, but also to stable and enduring social order (1986, p. 4).

In recent years, however, the assumptions underlying this view have been questioned. It has been recognized that food, especially short-term nutritional intake, is only one of the objectives people pursue. Thus, de Waal found that in the 1984–5 famine in Darfur, Sudan, people chose to go hungry to preserve assets and future livelihood: 'people are quite prepared to put up with considerable degrees of hunger, in order to preserve seed for planting, cultivate their own fields or avoid having to sell an animal' (de Waal 1991, p. 68). Furthermore, 'avoiding hunger is not a policy priority for rural people faced with famine' (de Waal 1991). Others have similar findings, particularly in the context of analysing the sequence of coping or adaptive strategies people follow in times of drought (Corbett 1988; Frankenberger and Goldstein 1991; Davies 1993).

In part, these findings reflect an issue of time preference: people going hungry now, in order to avoid going (more) hungry later. However, there is a broader issue of livelihood at stake, in which objectives other than nutritional adequacy are pursued (Chambers 1988a, p. 1; Davies 1996). Davies has pointed to these differences in a diagram reproduced as Table 1.1.

The management of risk and vulnerability are central here, as people try to achieve secure and sustainable livelihoods (Chambers 1988b, 1997). Thus Oshaug (1985, p. 5–13) has argued that:

> a society which can be said to enjoy food security is not only one which has reached [a] food norm ... but which has also developed the internal structures that will enable it to sustain the norm in the face of crises threatening to lower the achieved level of food consumption.

Oshaug identified three kinds of household:

- *enduring households*, which maintain household food security on a continuous basis;
- *resilient households*, which suffer shocks but recover quickly;
- *fragile households*, which become increasingly insecure in response to shocks.

Similar approaches are found elsewhere (Benson et al. 1986; Barraclough and Utting 1987) and have been extended with the addition of 'sensitivity', a measure of the extent of change following a shock (Blaikie and Brookfield

Table 1.1 Differences between a narrow 'food-first' approach and a wide 'sustainable livelihood' approach to household food security

Livelihood	'Food-first' approach	'Sustainable livelihood' approach
Objective	Access to food	Secure and sustainable livelihood
Point of departure	Failure to subsist	Success in feeding, living
Priorities	Food at the top of a hierarchy of needs	food one part of a jig-saw of livelihood needs
Time preferences	Food needs met before and in preference to all others	Food needs met to the extent possible given immediate and future livelihood needs
Entitlements	Narrow entitlement base (current and past consumption)	Broad entitlement base (includes future claims, access to common property resources, etc.)
Vulnerability	Lack or want of food	Defencelessness, insecurity, exposure to risk, shocks and stress
Security	Opposite of vulnerability is enough food, irrespective of the terms and conditions on which it is acquired	Opposite of vulnerability is security
Vulnerable groups	Based on social, medical criteria	Also based on economic, cultural criteria
Coping strategies	Designed to maximize immediate consumption	Designed to preserve livelihoods
Measuring and monitoring	Present and past consumption	Livelihood security and sustainability
Relationship to food security and environment	Degrade environment to meet immediate food needs	Preserve environment to secure future

Source: Davies 1996

1987; Bayliss-Smith 1991). The interaction between resilience and sensitivity provides a strong framework for the analysis of food insecurity over time, with the most food insecure households characterized by high sensitivity and low resilience (Swift 1989; Davies 1996). This framework is discussed more fully in Chapter 4.

The upshot of these ideas is a view of food security which identifies liveli-hood security as a necessary and often sufficient condition for food secu-rity (Maxwell 1988 and 1991, p. 22) and which focuses on the long-term viability of the household as a productive and reproductive unit (Franken-berger and Goldstein 1991).

FROM OBJECTIVE INDICATORS TO SUBJECTIVE PERCEPTION

The third shift is from an objective to a subjective approach. In the poverty literature there has been a long-standing distinction between 'the conditions of deprivation', referring to objective analysis, and 'feelings of deprivation', related to the subjective (Townsend 1974), and this has been picked up in the literature on rural poverty. Kabeer (1988), for example, identifies lack of self-esteem as an element of poverty, and Chambers (1989) talks similarly of self-respect. In the food security discussion, the paradigm shift is more recent.[2]

Conventional approaches to food security have relied on objective meas-urement: 'target' levels of consumption (Siamwalla and Valdes 1980); con-sumption of less than 80 per cent of World Health Organization (WHO) average required daily calorie intake (Reardon and Matlon 1989); or, more generally, a timely, reliable and nutritionally adequate supply of food (Staatz 1990). Definitions couched in these terms present problems, for two main reasons.

First, the notion of nutritional adequacy is itself problematic. For any individual, nutritional requirement is a function of age, health, size, work-load, environment and behaviour (Payne and Lipton 1994). Estimates of calorie requirements for average adults and children with average activity patterns in average years are subject to constant revision (Payne 1990). Adding adaptation strategies complicates the calculation. Estimating pre-cise calorie needs for different groups in the population is therefore diffi-cult. Indeed, in a strong statement on this subject, Pacey and Payne (1985, p. 70–1) have concluded that all estimates of nutritional requirements have to be treated as value judgements:

> Something which is specifically excluded ... is the notion of an 'optimum' state of nutritional health, achievement of which might be the criterion for a requirement leve ... Any views of 'desirable' or 'optimal' food intakes for human individuals or groups can only be value judgements.

If this is true, questions arise about who is to make the value judgements for individuals, households, communities or nations – a parallel discussion to the question asked in participatory research, 'whose knowledge counts?' (Chambers 1979). There must be a predisposition to believe that the judge-ment of the food insecure themselves is to be weighted disproportionately in this process.

A second problem arises because qualitative aspects are omitted from the kind of quantitative measures listed earlier. The issues include technical food quality (EC 1988; Bryceson 1990), consistency with local food habits (Oomen 1988), cultural acceptability and human dignity (Oshaug 1985; Eide et al. 1985, 1986), even autonomy and self-determination (Barraclough and Utting 1987; Barraclough 1991). The implication is that nutritional adequacy is a necessary but not sufficient condition for food security.

These ideas suggest that it is not just the quantity of food entitlement that matters, but also its 'quality'. Measurement questions again arise: how are the different aspects to be measured and weighted? Are there trade-offs between them? And who decides?

Problems of this kind have led some observers to stress the subjective dimension of food security. Thus, Maxwell (1988, p. 10, emphasis added) defines food security as follows:

> *A country and people are food secure when their food system operates in such a way as to remove the fear that there will not be enough to eat. In particular, food security will be achieved when the poor and vulnerable, particularly women and children and those living in marginal areas, have secure access to the food they want.*

This emphasis on subjective assessment is only beginning to be seen in data collection and evaluation (Frankenberger 1992, p. 96ff). Questions about perceptions of food problems have been asked in the Indian National Sample Survey, and research in the USA has attempted to develop indicators for subjective aspects of food insecurity, including lack of choice, feelings of deprivation and food acquisition in socially unacceptable ways (Radimer et al. 1992). There have been parallel advances in poverty work, where participatory methods have enabled the subjective perceptions of poor people themselves to be given greater weight (Chambers 1997).

The aggregate effect of these three paradigm shifts is a significant change in the food security agenda since the mid-1970s. Instead of a discussion concerned largely with national food supply and price, we find one concerned with the complexities of livelihood strategies in difficult and uncertain environments, and with understanding how people themselves respond to perceived risks and uncertainties. The new agenda has profound implications for the treatment of food security:

> *flexibility, adaptability, diversification and resilience are key words. Perceptions matter. Intra-household issues are central. Importantly ... food security must be treated as a multi-objective phenomenon, where the identification and weighting of objectives can only be decided by the food insecure themselves (Maxwell and Smith 1992, p. 4)*

FIVE PHASES OF FOOD SECURITY POLICY AND PRACTICE

The application of the changing ideas just reviewed has evolved in five main phases. Box 1.2 shows some of the milestones marking this evolution.

Box 1.2	Initiatives related to food security in Africa, 1967–96

1967	•	African Development Bank (ADB) established
	•	First Food Aid Convention (FAC)
1971	•	Establishment of Consultative Group on International Agricultural Research (CGIAR)
1973	•	Establishment of Comité permanent Inter-états pour la Lutte contre la Sécheresse dans le Sahel (Permanent Inter-state Committee for the struggle against drought in the Sahel) (CILSS)
	•	African Development Fund set up within ADB
1974	•	World Food Conference
	•	Universal declaration on the eradication of hunger and malnutrition
	•	World Food Council (WFC) established
	•	Food and Agriculture Organization (FAO) Committee on World Food Security established
1975	•	FAO Global Information and Early Warning System (GIEWS) established
	•	International Emergency Food Reserve (IEFR)
1976	•	Club du Sahel established in the Organisation for Economic Co-operation and Development (OECD)
1977	•	International Fund for Agricultural Development (IFAD) set up
	•	CILSS Strategy for Development and Drought Control (revised 1980, 1985)
1978	•	FAO Regional Food Plan for Africa
1979	•	CILSS/Club du Sahel Colloquium on Cereal Policies, Nouakchott
1980	•	Southern Africa Development Co-ordination Conference (SADCC) established
	•	Food Aid Convention enlarged to 7.6 million tonnes
	•	Organization of African Unity (OAU) Lagos plan of action
	•	Establishment of Preferential Trade Area (PTA)
1981	•	European Community 'Plan of Action to combat hunger in the world' and initiation of food strategies in four African countries
	•	International Monetary Fund (IMF) compensatory financing facility extended to cereals
1983	•	Broadened concept of food security adopted by FAO
1984	•	Lomé III Convention gives central place to food security

1985	●	Africa's Priority Programme for Economic Recovery
	●	United Nations (UN) Programme for African Economic Recovery and Development
	●	United States Agency for International Development (USAID) Famine Early Warning System (FEWS) established
	●	World food security compact (FAO)
1986	●	Mindelo colloquium on cereal policies (CILSS)
1986	●	Intergovernmental Authority on Drought and Development (IGADD) established in the Horn of Africa
	●	Special session of UN General Assembly on Africa's economic and social crisis
1987	●	Mandate of FAO food security assistance service broadened to focus more on national policy
1988	●	World Bank task force report 'The Challenge of Hunger in Africa: A Call to Action', and initiation of World Bank food security studies in Africa
1989	●	Initiation of FAO food security planning in four African countries
	●	Bellagio declaration: ending half the world's hunger by the year 2000
	●	WFC Cairo declaration and programme of co-operative action
	●	African alternative framework for structural adjustment programme for socio-economic recovery and transformation (AAF-SAP) Economic Commission for Africa (ECA)
1990	●	IGADD food security strategy adopted in Kampala
	●	Food Aid Charter for the countries of the Sahel
	●	World Summit for Children (UNICEF)
	●	Adoption by UN General Assembly of International Development Strategy for the 1990s
1991	●	World Bank/World Food Programme (WFP) joint report, 'Food Aid in Africa: An Agenda for the 1990s'
1992	●	International Conference on Nutrition
	●	UN Department of Humanitarian Affairs established
1993	●	World Bank Conference on Overcoming Global Hunger
1994	●	General Agreement on Tariffs and Trade (GATT) Uruguay Round finalized at Marrakesh
1995	●	Food Aid Convention renewed with new lower limit of 5.36 million tonnes
	●	World Bank Strategy for Reducing Poverty and Hunger
1996	●	World Food Summit

1974–80: GLOBAL FOOD SECURITY

The first phase began with the world food crisis of 1972–4, and lasted until about 1980. The crisis was characterized by famine in parts of Africa, particularly the Sahel and the Horn. However, the most notable and unusual feature was a doubling of international grain prices, caused largely by harvest failure in, and grain imports by, the Soviet Union. This was an issue of global food security, and one that could not be tackled by existing institutional arrangements. As ODI (1997) have noted:

> from 1945 until the early 1970s, US food surpluses had, in effect, been the guarantor of world food security. The massive food aid to India during its drought crisis of 1965–66 is a good example. Then the US abdicated this solo role by its prioritisation of commercial sales to the then USSR and its explicit use of food as a political weapon. By 1974 ... there was a considerable institutional gap to be filled.

In 1974, the World Food Conference recognized the global problem. It paid due attention to the question of hunger and malnutrition, but focused attention on global production, trade and stocks. The World Food Council was established, to monitor world food availability. The FAO set up a committee on World Food Security, and (in 1975) the GIEWS. In subsequent years, the Food Aid Convention was strengthened, and the IMF compensatory financing facility was extended to cereals. All these measures served to set in place an international regime in which the supply of food, and the ability of countries to acquire it, were essential features.

It was ironic that this period of thinking and action on food security at a global level coincided with one in which poverty and distribution were being given much greater attention in international discourse on development. The President of the World Bank, Robert McNamara, gave a famous speech on poverty to the Annual Meeting of the Bank and Fund in Nairobi in 1973. *Redistribution with Growth* was published in 1974 (Chenery et al. 1974). The concept of 'basic needs' was adopted by the International Labour Organization (ILO) in 1976. This was the era of integrated rural development, basic needs projects, and employment missions. There was something of a mismatch between food security and wider development thinking.

1981–5: FOOD ENTITLEMENT AND STRUCTURAL ADJUSTMENT

In academic thinking about food security, however, questions of poverty and access began to feature more prominently in the second half of the 1970s, first in the nutrition literature and then more widely. It was clear that food production on its own did not assure consumption, and that people needed access to food. The second period of thinking about food security, running from about 1981 to 1985, was marked by the acceptance of this idea. Amartya Sen's (1981) book, *Poverty and Famines*, codified the idea of 'food entitlement', and was influential in moving discussion forward. In

1981, the European Community launched its 'Plan of Action to Combat Hunger in the World', which resulted in the preparation of pioneering food strategies in four African countries (Kenya, Mali, Rwanda and Zambia). In 1983, FAO adopted a new and broader concept of food security, which gave prominence to access, alongside production and stability of food supply. And the World Bank sponsored influential research, by Shlomo Reutlinger and others, which helped to redefine the focus of food security.

Unfortunately, all this activity in the first half of the 1980s coincided with the beginning of the structural adjustment crisis, in which poverty reduction and basic needs were made subordinate to the need for debt management, fiscal balance, macroeconomic stability, and internal and external liberalization. Thus, food security concepts had improved, needs had increased as a result of structural adjustment, but the possibilities for practical action had diminished.

1986–90: THE GOLDEN AGE

In the third phase, the situation changed, for two reasons. First, and very dramatically, the African famine of 1984–5 gave renewed impetus to action on hunger and its causes. Second, world attention was drawn to the social costs of structural adjustment, particularly by UNICEF in its work on *Adjustment with a Human Face*, formally published in 1987 (Cornia et al.). As Robert Hindle noted in 1990, in an article on World Bank food security policy, the topic gained prominence at this time, partly because food security was a proxy for poverty. Thus, a celebrated World Bank study, 'Poverty and Hunger: Issues and Options for Food Security', was published in 1986, and followed two years later by the report of a task force, entitled 'The Challenge of Hunger in Africa: A Call to Action'. This report provided a platform for many World Bank food security studies in Africa in the second half of the 1980s. Other donors were also active. In 1987, FAO had broadened the mandate of its Food Security Assistance Service to encompass national planning reviews, and the organization launched its own food security studies at country level. The European Commission (EC), similarly, continued to commission country food strategies. Many countries in Africa were privileged to host food security studies by all three of these organizations.

There was also a great deal of academic work on food security during this period. One landmark was the publication of *Hunger and Public Action*, by Jean Drèze and Amartya Sen (1989). This introduced the key distinction between entitlement promotion – helping people to secure entitlement to food in the long term; and entitlement protection – providing a safety net against shocks.

1991–5: POVERTY, NOT FOOD SECURITY

The second half of the 1980s have been described as the golden age of food security analysis. This was short-lived, however. Again, action in the international arena coincided with changes in the real world and inaugurated a fourth phase. Internationally, the main event was the publication in 1990 of the World Bank's *World Development Report* on poverty. This was followed by a Poverty Handbook and by a Policy Directive on Poverty. Taken together, these initiatives brought poverty reduction back to the front of the development stage, and displaced food security. Despite the strong degree of overlap between poverty and food security, many donors abandoned or down-graded food security studies and programmes in favour of poverty assessments and poverty reduction programmes.

The drift away from a focus on food security was aided by the change in the nature of famines, which had begun in the 1980s but became more evident in the 1990s. Whereas African famines had traditionally been caused by drought, those of the 1990s were far more likely to be associated with war (see Chapter 5). Indeed, where drought did occur, as in Southern Africa in 1992, it seemed to be managed with reasonable efficiency. It was war that caused large-scale suffering and death: in Somalia, Liberia, Angola, Southern Sudan, and Rwanda. Here, the problem was not really one of food security policy per se, but rather one of managing food supplies in complex political emergencies characterized by social and policy breakdown. Thus, to the extent that food security was prominent in this phase, the agenda was to do with codes of conduct for relief, linking relief and development, and rehabilitation, usually in war zones.

Needless to say, hunger did not disappear during this fourth phase. More than 800 million people remained undernourished, with many more vulnerable to short-term shocks in their ability to acquire food. Nor did hunger disappear entirely from the agenda. The World Summit for Children in 1990 and the International Conference on Nutrition in 1992 both helped to keep nutrition issues in the public eye. The World Bank hosted an international conference in 1993 on Actions to Reduce Hunger Worldwide, and followed this up with a new Strategy for Reducing Poverty and Hunger, published in 1995.

1996 ... : WHERE NEXT?

Nevertheless, it took another rise in food prices, and renewed concern about the ability of the world to feed itself, before food security again came to the forefront. Thus, in the mid-1990s, a fifth phase began which is still continuing. Here the future of food security policy has been very much in play. Will the agenda shift back to the Malthusian concerns of the 1970s,[3] with a focus on food production, often in high-potential areas? Or will the concern with consumption and access, which has marked food security policy since the late 1970s, be sustained? These questions underpinned debate at the World Food Summit, convened by FAO and held in Rome in November 1996.

The World Food Summit agenda was fiercely contested. The negotiators had a difficult balancing act to perform, beset on all sides by strident interest groups concerned with bio-diversity, genetic manipulation, globaliza-tion, trade liberalization, and the importance of political change. NGOs, commercial interests, academics and pressure groups all vied for attention, with each other, with the negotiators and with the public.

In the event, the Declaration and Plan of Action (FAO 1996a) were remarkably well-balanced. The extreme Malthusians were seen off. A mis-placed emphasis on food self-sufficiency was avoided. The human right to food was acknowledged. And a balance was struck between high- and low-potential areas.

The difficulty with the Summit documentation lay in the lack of firm commitments and actions. Only one commitment – to reduce chronic under-nutrition by half by 2015 – was made, and that was recycled in weak-ened form from earlier meetings, such as the International Conference on Nutrition in 1992 (FAO/WHO 1992). It is interesting to compare the single target of the World Food Summit (WFS) with the more ambitious targets of the International Conference on Nutrition (ICN) and the earlier World Summit for Children, some of which are reproduced in Box 1.3.

Nevertheless, the preparations for the World Food Summit generated a great deal of useful analysis in the form of background papers (FAO 1996b). The final Plan of Action also provides a useful framework for discussion on food security issues. There were seven commitments, listed in Box 1.4. These cover poverty reduction, sustainable agricultural and rural develop-ment, access to food, fair trade and disaster preparedness. A procedure has been set in place for countries to prepare national action plans, and for progress to be monitored through the FAO Committee on Food Security.

CONCLUSION

As we have seen, the history of thinking about food security since the 1970s has been characterised by progressive conceptual development, as well as by a plethora of international initiatives.

Box 1.5 provides a current consensus statement on food security in Africa. The strategy recognizes the primacy of household and individual food insecurity, and offers prescriptions in the fields of production, mar-keting and consumption. It also contains entries on an appropriate inter-national environment, and on the process of food security planning.

Box 1.3   Goals for the Millennium

Nutrition goals of the World Summit for Children (1990)

1 Reduction in severe, as well as moderate, malnutrition among children under 5 by half of 1990 levels.
2 Reduction of the rate of low birth weight (2.5 kg or less) to less than 10 per cent.
3 Reduction of iron deficiency anaemia in women by one-third of the 1990 levels.
4 Virtual elimination of iodine deficiency disorders.
5 Virtual elimination of vitamin A deficiency and its consequences, including blindness.
6 Empowerment of all women to breast-feed their children exclusively for four to six months and to continue breast-feeding, with complementary food, well into the second year.
7 Growth promotion and its regular monitoring to be institutionalized by all countries by the end of the 1990s.
8 Dissemination of knowledge and supporting services to increase food production to ensure household food security.

Goals of the International Conference on Nutrition (1992)

1 To eliminate:
   ● famine and famine-related deaths;
   ● starvation and nutritional deficiency diseases in communities affected by natural and man-made disasters; and
   ● iodine and vitamin A deficiencies.
2 To reduce substantially:
   ● starvation and widespread chronic hunger;
   ● undernutrition, especially among children, women and the aged;
   ● other important micronutrient deficiencies, including iron;
   ● diet-related communicable and non-communicable diseases; and
   ● inadequate sanitation and poor hygiene, including unsafe drinking water.

Box 1.4   World Food Summit, 13–17 November 1996: plan of action

The member states have agreed the following seven commitments as a Plan of Action.

1 Ensuring an enabling political, social and economic environment designed to create the best conditions for the eradication of poverty and for durable peace, based on full and equal participation of women and men, which is most conducive to achieving sustainable food security for all.
2 Implementing policies aimed at eradicating poverty and inequality and improving physical and economic access by all, at all times, to sufficient, nutritionally adequate and safe food and its effective utilization.
3 Pursuing participatory and sustainable food, agriculture, fisheries, forestry and rural development policies and practices in high and low potential areas, which are essential to adequate and reliable food supplies at the household, national, regional and global levels, and combat pests, drought and desertification, considering the multi-functional character of agriculture.
4 Ensuring that food, agricultural trade and overall trade policies are conducive to fostering food security for all through a fair and market-oriented world trade system.
5 Preventing and preparing for natural disasters and man-made emergencies and meeting transitory and emergency food requirements in ways that encourage recovery, rehabilitation, development and a capacity to satisfy future needs.
6 Promoting optimal allocation and use of public and private investments to foster human resources, sustainable food, agriculture, fisheries and forestry systems, and rural development, in high and low potential areas.
7 Implementing, monitoring, and following up this Plan of Action at all levels in cooperation with the international community.

Box 1.5   Food security in Africa: a consensus strategy

1   A primary focus on supplying vulnerable people and households with secure access to food: individual and household needs take precedence over issues of national food self-sufficiency or self-reliance.

2   The overwhelming necessity for peace and physical security, given that war is the single greatest cause of famine in Africa.

3   The importance of economic growth: poor rural and urban people need secure and sustainable livelihoods, with adequate incomes and reasonable buffers against destitution; poor nations need buoyant economies and adequate foreign earnings, in order to provide jobs, acquire agricultural inputs and, where necessary, purchase food.

4   Within agriculture, growth strategies are needed which lay particular emphasis on generating jobs and incomes for the poorest groups, including those in resource-poor and environmentally degraded areas. Agriculture and rural development strategies should usually favour labour-intensity, though recognizing that some groups, especially female-headed households, may be short of labour and require more capital to increase productivity.

5   A balance between food and cash crops is the best route to food security, following the principle of long term comparative advantage rather than of self-sufficiency for its own sake. However, the potential income gains from cash cropping should not be sought at the expense of measures to reduce risk, through diversification; and policies are required which maximize the benefits of cash cropping to the poor.

6   Efficient food marketing is needed, to store and distribute food, at reasonable prices, to all parts of the country in all seasons and in all years. In the long term, the private sector may acquire and redistribute food surpluses over time and space, efficiently, competitively and without excess profit. However, the state retains a key role, as catalyst of the private sector, as buyer and seller of last resort and as controller of relief buffer stocks.

7   More effective and efficient safety nets need to be established, by strengthening community institutions, introducing new targeted food and nutrition interventions, and improving famine preparedness and response, especially at the local level. Improved targeting can limit the cost of these social security interventions, especially where the target group is small relative to the population and where administrative costs can be contained, for example by geographical or self-targeting approaches.

8   Famine preparedness is a critical need in many countries, involving not just early warning, which is often adequate, but also improved capacity

to respond. Possible measures include early decisions of when to import food, small, locally-based stocks of food for relief distribution, relief works that can be activated quickly, special programmes for vulnerable group feeding, early water and health interventions, and special programmes for rehabilitation.

9   Strong international support will be essential, through a more favourable trading environment, debt relief and greater and better-focused aid flows. Food aid can play an important part, but needs to be integrated more closely with financial aid and linked more closely to food security efforts, for example by better management of counterpart funds.

10   Finally, food security planning should follow a 'process' rather than a 'blueprint' approach, with large-scale decentralization, a bias to action over planning, the encouragement of risk-taking and innovation, and the fostering of task cultures, not role cultures, in multi-disciplinary and multi-sectoral planning teams.

Sources: World Bank 1988; Drèze and Sen 1989; Huddleston 1990; Maxwell 1992; von Braun et al. 1992

CHAPTER TWO

Agricultural Issues in Food Security

Simon Maxwell

AGRICULTURE IS AT the heart of food security. This is not only for the obvious reason that the agricultural sector – taken in its widest sense to include pastoral production, forest products and fisheries – is the only source of the food we need. It is also because of the multiple roles played by the agricultural sector as a source of employment and livelihood, and as one of the main motors of economic activity. It is the purpose of this chapter to lay out these roles, and to explore the complementarities and potential conflicts between them.

THE IMPORTANCE OF AGRICULTURE IN AFRICA

Policy makers in Africa have long recognized the importance of the agricultural sector to the continent. For example, the Lagos Plan of Action, adopted by the Organization of African Unity (OAU) in 1980, identified food security as one of the main priorities, and called for a target rate of growth of 4 per cent *per annum* in the agricultural sector. In 1985, the OAU African Priority Programme for Economic Recovery (APPER) called for African governments to devote up to 25 per cent of government budgets to the agricultural sector. These aspirations were carried over into the 1990s, and are reflected, for example, in the background documents for the World Food Summit in 1996 (FAO 1996).

There are two reasons why African policy makers have laid special emphasis on agriculture. The first is the relative importance of the sector in sub-Saharan Africa (SSA), compared with most other regions. Table 2.1 shows that the sector employs a greater share of the labour force than in any other region, apart from East Asia and the Pacific (which is dominated by China). It also shows that agriculture accounts for a greater share of Gross Domestic Product (GDP) than in any region except for South Asia (where India, Pakistan and Bangladesh are the most populous countries). Any sector which employs over two-thirds of the labour force and accounts for one-fifth of the economy is bound to play a central part in economic and social policy making.

The second reason for according special importance to agriculture in SSA is the widespread perception that the sector has underperformed. The growth rate in the 1990s averaged only 2.1 per cent, less than that achieved

Table 2.1   The importance of agriculture in Sub-Saharan Africa

	SSA		E. Asia and Pacific		South Asia		Latin America and Caribbean		High-income economies	
	Male	Female	M	F	M	F	M	F	M	F
% labour force in agriculture (1994)	65	75	62	72	59	75	29	12	6	4
Agriculture as a share of GDP (% 1995)	20		18		30		10		2	
Agricultural growth rate 1990–96 (% p.a.)	2.1		4.0		3.0		2.5		0.8	

Source: World Bank 1998

in the two Asian regions where agriculture plays a comparable role. Over a longer time period, the production deficit is not so pronounced. The data for agricultural and food production given in the first part of Figure 2.1 show that Africa has not lagged markedly behind the world as a whole. However, the data clearly reveal another problem. The *per capita* graphs in Figure 2.1 show that agriculture and food production for the world as a whole have both increased since 1970 – but in Africa have fallen by something like a quarter. It is not surprising, then, to find that food imports to Africa have risen sharply, from around 8 million tonnes in 1980, to nearly 12 million tonnes in 1994. At the same time, African agriculture has been notoriously volatile, subject to major shocks caused by erratic rainfall. The food supply and entitlement crises of 1972 and 1984–5 in the Sahel and the Horn, the Southern African drought of 1992 and the Mozambique floods of 2000, are all good examples of this phenomenon.

It is dangerous to generalize about African agriculture, however. Some countries are more dependent on agriculture than others, and some have agricultural sectors that have demonstrated robust performance over several decades. For example, in 1995 agriculture accounted for half or more of GDP in Burundi, Ethiopia, Tanzania and Uganda – but for 10 per cent or less in Botswana, Congo and Lesotho. Similarly, and contrary to the regional trend, some countries (Benin, Guinea-Bissau, Tanzania) appear to have achieved rates of growth well ahead of the Lagos targets. Statistics often need to be treated with great caution in Africa, but the point remains that policy analysts, especially outsiders, too often fall into the trap of assuming that Africa is homogeneous.

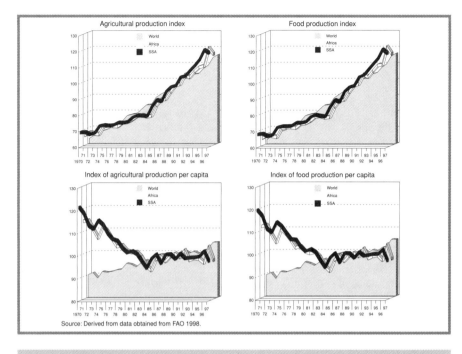

Figure 2.1   World and African agricultural and food production indices, 1970–97 (1989–91=100)

Another important source of heterogeneity must be noted, which is that Africa contains a bewildering variety of farming and other agricultural systems, each associated with its own form of social organization and its own mode of production. Ruthenberg (1980) provides the classic introduction to farming systems, ranging from extensive slash and burn in tropical rainforest, through arable farming at different levels of intensity of land use, to irrigated agriculture and plantations. In Africa, too, pastoralism is an important source of livelihood. In all these systems women play a large part in agricultural production. A casual look at any country in SSA will show a great variety of farming systems and output mixes.

CHOICES IN AGRICULTURAL STRATEGY

The heterogeneity of African agriculture helps to illustrate an important point about planning for this important sector. Planning is about choosing, and Box 2.1 illustrates some of the choices to be made. Should the food security planner advocate large farms or small farms? Capital intensive or labour intensive methods of production? Food crops or cash crops? Investment in high-potential or low-potential areas? Sometimes, agricultural choices like these can be avoided. Perhaps peace, or economic liberalization, or increased investment, will be good for all the component parts of

---

Box 2.1   Choices in agricultural strategy

Large farms	Small farms
Extensive	Intensive
Capital intensive	Labour intensive
Food crops	Cash crops
Trade	Self-sufficiency
High-potential areas	Low-potential areas
Production growth	Production stability
Free market	State control

---

an agricultural sector. More often, however, there will be trade-offs to consider. If funds are limited, a road built in one district to connect a producing area to its market must mean that somewhere else a road cannot be built. Each investment has an 'opportunity cost', the value of the money spent elsewhere. Similarly, each farming decision precludes alternatives: a field planted to coffee trees cannot thereafter be used to grow maize.

It might be argued that choosing has become more difficult since the era of structural adjustment, as many of the instruments hitherto deployed to intervene in domestic economies have become redundant. That the scope for policy intervention has now narrowed is certainly true. Parallel exchange rates, exchange controls, directed investment, agricultural parastatals, state farms – all these are out of fashion. Structural adjustment in SSA has been associated with large-scale liberalization and with a reduction in the role of the state. Market-determined prices, the removal of quantitative restrictions and the promotion of private sector operations are central to structural adjustment approaches. It might seem that the scope for policy has disappeared.

Food security planners should not despair, however. It is still possible to influence the direction of the agricultural sector, and to sharpen the choices listed in Box 2.1. Governments can set the incentive and regulatory framework within which producers make production decisions. They can also influence the economic environment through judicious use of the government budget. In the first category, we might put interventions such as land tenure reform, the legislation governing co-operatives, or investment codes governing the actions of foreign multi-nationals. In the latter, we would expect to find all the traditional agricultural programmes pursued by government: agricultural research, seed production, extension, support to infrastructure and marketing, sometimes subsidies for inputs or outputs.

Public expenditure is an especially important lever. Few countries have reached the OAU target, that 25 per cent of government budgets should be devoted to agriculture. Indeed, FAO (1995) reports that, for developing countries as a whole, expenditure on agriculture in the 1980s represented only 7–8 per cent of all public expenditure. FAO also concludes that 'the level of public spending on agriculture has fallen in recent years' (FAO 1996, p. 20). This has been exacerbated by a parallel fall in the share of agriculture in external funding. In constant price terms, total commitments of external assistance to agriculture fell from US$9.7 billion in 1981 (1985 constant dollars) to only US$6.0 billion in 1993, a fall of almost 40 per cent. One of the main objectives of the World Food Summit was to highlight this trend and to provide a framework within which it might be reversed.

Whether or not resources can be provided, it is the task of the food security planner to seek 'room for manoeuvre', both in the management of public expenditure and in the incentive and regulatory framework. To this end, the planner needs to understand in more detail how the agricultural sector contributes to food security, and how the sector can be stimulated to contribute more. It is to this that we now turn. We begin with a more detailed analysis of the different roles of the agricultural sector, and then turn to examples of practical policy issues that need to be decided.

CHANGING THINKING ABOUT AGRICULTURE

THE SIX CONTRIBUTIONS OF THE AGRICULTURAL SECTOR

We saw in Table 2.1 that agriculture accounts for some 20 per cent of GDP in SSA, and that it employs over two-thirds of the labour force. However, these data provide only a partial perspective on the contribution of agriculture to growth and food security. Building on the pioneering work of Johnston and Mellor (1961) and Nicholls (1964), we can identify six different contributions that the agricultural sector can make to food security, namely, agriculture as:

- food;
- livelihood;
- a market;
- raw materials;
- foreign exchange;
- surplus.

The first contribution that agriculture makes is to the supply of food. Despite the alarming trends illustrated in Figure 2.1, the agricultural sector in Africa provides by far the greatest part of the food that Africans eat. Import dependency is higher in the cereal sector than for root crops and other starchy staples, but even here the dependency ratio (imports/total consumption) is less than 15 per cent. In 1995, for example, cereal imports into SSA were 12 million tonnes, but production was close to 80 million tonnes. For some years, and in some countries, the dependency ratio is higher, and it needs to be noted that the degree of self-sufficiency achieved is at relatively low levels of consumption. Nevertheless, the achievement of African farmers in feeding their people should not be underestimated.

Agriculture is also a major source of livelihood, generating employment, as we have seen, for over two-thirds of the labour force in SSA. Some of these jobs are in food production, but many are not – or, at least, not in those sectors of food production which provide the basic staples. Thus, tea, coffee, cocoa, as well as non-traditional crops like cut flowers, are all major employers and generators of livelihood in SSA, sometimes on large plantations, but often also on small-holdings. Indeed 'cash crops', including non-food crops like cotton and sisal, are often more labour-intensive per unit area than food crops. An International Food Policy Research Institute (IFPRI) study of the commercialization of agriculture in ten countries, six of them in SSA, found significant employment effects (von Braun and Kennedy 1994). Note that in this discussion it is important to talk not about 'jobs', but rather about 'livelihoods', reflecting the tendency of the poor to derive income from diverse sources. Agriculture can provide livelihoods in the physical production process, but also in the supply of inputs and the processing and marketing of outputs.

Agriculture also contributes in a number of ways to employment and growth in other sectors. It provides a market, both directly for inputs, machinery and processing equipment, and indirectly by virtue of the expenditure of agricultural workers. It provides raw materials for nascent industry, for example textiles. And it generates foreign exchange, which can be used to purchase capital equipment and intermediate goods for the agricultural sector.

For all these reasons, a healthy agricultural sector is an essential foundation for non-agricultural growth. Agricultural and national growth rates are often highly correlated. This is partly a statistical artefact, because agriculture accounts for such a large part of the economy in SSA. However, it also reflects an underlying economic symbiosis, in which growth in one sector feeds off another. Mellor, in particular, has emphasized the inter-dependence between sectors (Mellor 1976; 1995). Many countries have set out to exploit the opportunities. For example, Ethiopia has adopted a strategy of Agricultural Development Led Industrialization (ADLI). Similarly, Kenya has committed itself to a policy of industrialization from an agricultural base.

A final contribution of the agricultural sector, especially for low-income countries where the sector is dominant, is that it provides the most important, sometimes the only real, source of savings or investible surplus needed for growth. Farmers save and invest in their own communities. In rare cases, their cash savings may be mobilized by the banking system for investment elsewhere. More commonly, however, governments look to the agricultural sector as a source of tax revenue to fund the public budget.

Taxes may be raised explicitly or implicitly. Explicit taxes on agriculture might include land taxes, a crop tax or an export levy, as well as business taxes on commercial farms or plantations. In general, governments in Africa have found it difficult to tax farmers directly, especially in the peasant sector. However, many countries have implemented export taxes, and have often maintained export crop parastatals for precisely this purpose. In recent years, export taxes have been frowned upon, because they create disincentives to producers. Indeed, the removal of farmer taxation was one of the main planks of structural adjustment in the 1980s. Farm incomes have usually benefited, but the public finances have not. Tanzania is just one case where the removal of an export tax (on coffee) caused a large shortfall in government revenue.

Where explicit taxes have proved economically difficult or politically contentious, governments have often resorted to implicit taxes. For example, currency over-valuation, a frequent occurrence in Africa before structural adjustment led to the deregulation of foreign exchange markets, had the effect of holding down prices received by exporters, and of making it more difficult for local producers to compete against imports. Similarly, export restrictions, often introduced in the name of food security, have the effect of keeping domestic food prices below those that would otherwise pertain. A major argument of the 'urban bias' school (Lipton 1977) was that terms of trade between agriculture and industry were biased against agriculture as a form of taxation, though this argument has been contentious (Jamal and Weeks 1993).

Agriculture, then, plays different roles and can help to meet different objectives. An immediate question arises, however, about possible trade-offs. Is agriculture a positive sum game in which food, livelihood, foreign exchange and taxation objectives can all be met simultaneously? Or is there some competition between objectives? For example, does commitment to the objective of producing more food, in order to meet domestic demand, mean that it becomes impossible to maximize foreign exchange earnings by producing more cash crops for export? Under certain conditions, as we shall see, it may indeed be possible to achieve these two objectives simultaneously. However, under normal circumstances, resources are scarce and there will be choices to be made. Though the potential trade-offs are often swept under the carpet when food security plans are being prepared (Heald and Lipton 1984), the job of the food security planner is precisely to make the choices explicit.

THE EVOLUTION OF THINKING ABOUT AGRICULTURE

It is interesting to see how the choices have been made in African agriculture over the years. There have been significant shifts of emphasis. These reflect changing thinking about agriculture, but also a changing situation on the ground.

A historical perspective is given by Delgado (1995) who identifies dominant paradigms of agricultural development from the colonial era to the mid-1990s. He describes growth and industrialization as being the primary objectives of the early phase of commercialization via cash cropping, with equity considerations appearing in the 1970s and conservation in the 1990s. Intermediate stages include emphasis on basic human needs in the 1970s, and a series of paradigms related to structural adjustment in the 1980s, including a regional integration paradigm focusing on food supply, and a school Delgado describes as 'supply shifters', principally concerned with non-price interventions like research, roads, input supplies and water control.

A simplified chronology is presented in Table 2.2, to make the point that thinking about agriculture has almost always reflected thinking about development more generally. The period since the Second World War can be broken down roughly into decade-long periods, in which thinking about agriculture and, accordingly, the priority given to different agricultural objectives, has differed substantially.

In the 1950s, the dominant development paradigm focused on growth through industrialization. It was rooted theoretically in the Lewis model of 'economic development with unlimited supplies of labour', and found expression in developing countries in national plans like that of India, where the Mahalanobis model emphasized industry at the expense of agriculture. In these models, the rural sector was seen principally as a source of labour and of surplus to finance industrialization. It was a place where the 'reserve army' of the unemployed could engage in subsistence agriculture until its labour was required in more productive sectors.

With this world view, little attention was given to agricultural development, and the primary focus of rural intervention was on community development, that is largely on social welfare interventions. The community development movement, which had its origin in the United States of America (USA), reached its apogee during the 1950s (Holdcroft 1984).

Table 2.2 The evolution of thinking about agriculture: 1950s–1990s

Period	Dominant development paradigm	Agricultural strategy
1950s	Growth through industrialization	Community development
1960s	Growth through industry and agriculture	Green Revolution
1970s	Redistribution with growth and basic needs	Integrated rural development
1980s	Structural adjustment	NGOs/emergency relief
1990s	Poverty reduction	Small-scale credit/linking relief and development

In the 1960s, the dominant development paradigm changed, largely as a result of the thinking about agriculture already referred to (Johnston and Mellor 1961; Nicholls 1964; Johnston 1970). The emphasis was still on growth of national income (as a reading of one of the main development manifestos of the period, the Pearson Commission report (1969), makes clear) but it was seen that agriculture could contribute to growth. A more positive attitude was greatly assisted by the spread of the Green Revolution, first in Mexico and then in South Asia. This demonstrated that agricultural productivity would increase rapidly if the right combination of seeds, inputs and water control was provided. It led many governments and aid donors to finance special programmes for agriculture in high-potential areas – the Integrated Area Development Programme (IADP) in India was a good example of the breed.

It was not long after the Pearson report that observers began to criticize patterns of development for neglecting poverty and unemployment. In the early 1970s, attention began to move away from Gross National Product (GNP) *per capita* as a measure of development, towards more complex indicators which took poverty into account. Much of the impetus for this move came from a series of International Labour Organization (ILO) employment missions, in Kenya, Colombia and Sri Lanka among others, which raised the profile of unemployment, underemployment and the role of the informal sector. Redistribution became an important theme, captured in the title of the seminal work by Chenery et al. in 1974, *Redistribution with Growth*. Many aid programmes began to take poverty more seriously – a good example was Britain, which published a White Paper in 1975 called 'More Aid for the Poorest'. The concern with poverty led to a better understanding of basic needs and to multi-sectoral programmes designed to operate across a range of productive and non-productive sectors.

The rural development counterpart of this new wave of activity took the form of integrated rural development projects, which grew rapidly during the 1970s. The Kenya Special Rural Development Programme was an example, but there were many others in Africa, especially in the second half of the decade. These programmes were characteristically donor funded and had a large multi-sectoral remit. Organizationally, they presented many difficulties, as discussed in more detail in Chapter 11.

The basic needs approach was dealt a body blow by the second oil crisis in 1979, and by the subsequent recession and fall in commodity prices. The financial austerity which followed was a principal cause of the debt crisis; but it also highlighted the difficulty of funding the recurrent costs of large social programmes like those launched under a basic needs or integrated rural development banner. It seemed that too much attention had been paid to the question of how to divide the cake, and not enough to that of how to make the cake bigger.

There was thus both a practical reason and a theoretical underpinning for new thinking in development, and this rapidly developed as a neo-liberal, structural adjustment paradigm. From an official perspective, production was once more the dominant objective, but this time government intervention was to be kept to a minimum. Poverty was not entirely neglected, however, and non-governmental organizations (NGOs) were encouraged to fill the vacuum left by donors and states. Indeed, many NGOs continued to try to fund integrated rural development programmes during the 1980s.

The other dominant feature of the 1980s, especially in Africa, was the impact of drought and the consequent rapid rise in emergency relief needs. Indeed, as we have seen in the previous chapter, the 1984–5 drought was largely responsible for giving a new impetus to food security planning in Africa in the second half of the 1980s. As the pendulum began to swing away from structural adjustment, *Adjustment With A Human Face* (Cornia et al. 1987) became a primary concern.

The 1990s saw another sea change, with the publication of the World Bank's *World Development Report* on poverty in 1990, and the first of UNDP's *Human Development Reports*. These two together helped to redefine the development paradigm, putting poverty reduction back at the centre of the argument. To this end, the World Bank advocated a three-pronged strategy of:

- labour-intensive growth;
- human capital development through the provision of health and education;
- safety nets to guard against destitution.

Since the majority of the poor live in rural areas, this turned the spotlight back onto agriculture and rural development. There was little enthusiasm for the large-scale integrated rural development programmes that had characterized the 1970s, but small-scale credit programmes became popular, following the Grameen Bank model. In areas where emergency relief had become almost continuous, there was a wave of interest in using this flow of resources to help reduce vulnerability and encourage faster development: this became known as *Linking Relief and Development* (Buchanan-Smith and Maxwell 1994).

The chronology in Table 2.2 is obviously an over-simplification. In particular, it leaves out of the account the radical critiques of the dominant ideology, notably those concerned with capitalist inter-relationships and dependency on a world scale. Nevertheless, the chronology illustrates the parallel evolution of dominant development paradigms and thinking about agriculture; and also serves to make the point that different possible objectives of agriculture have been prominent at different times. It is also interesting that there is a certain circularity to the progress of thinking about agriculture, with the community development ethos of the 1950s very much reflected in the emphasis on NGOs in the 1980s; and the emphasis on production of the Green Revolution period echoed in the emphasis on credit in the 1990s.

In any case, the evolution of theory reinforces the point about trade-offs in agricultural strategy. We can learn more about this by looking in more detail at some of the choices that food security planners must make.

FOOD SECURITY ISSUES IN AGRICULTURAL DEVELOPMENT

It is impossible in this short chapter to deal with all of the choices food security planners face in the agricultural sector. Instead, we focus on three:

- the currently prominent question of whether the world can feed itself in the century to come;
- investment in high- and low-potential areas;
- the choice between food crops and cash crops.

In taking these three issues, the intention is not only to highlight the issues themselves, but also to explore a pragmatic way of approaching them which can then be transferred elsewhere. Thus, there is nothing here about land tenure, mechanization, paradigms of agricultural research, or any other of a dozen crucial topics.

CAN THE WORLD FEED ITSELF?

A topic which generates heated debate is whether the world will be able to produce enough food to feed a growing population in the twenty-first century. Optimists point to past successes stemming from the Green Revolution, and to the potential implicit in new agricultural technologies such as genetic engineering. Pessimists point to problems with the sustainability of current agricultural production, and to the relentless increase of 90 million people a year in the world population. How this debate is resolved has important implications for national agricultural policy.

At first sight, the record of the past provides ample grounds for optimism. As Table 2.3 shows, the population of the world increased by more than two-thirds (from 3.1 billion to 5.3 billion) in the thirty years from the early 1960s to the early 1990s. During the same period, however, cereal production more than doubled, production *per capita* increased by nearly a quarter, and the daily *per capita* supply of calories (from all sources) increased from 2300 to over 2700. And, remarkably, food prices halved in real terms. Part of this fall can be explained by the impact of subsidies, particularly in the USA and Europe, but nevertheless world agriculture can claim a remarkable success over the past generation.

These successes are not accidental. They have been won by large investment in agricultural research and production. In most regions of the world, increased production has been obtained by intensifying production and increasing yields (Figure 2.2). In Asia, for example, the average yield of

Table 2.3   World food availability and prices, 1961–3 and 1990–2

	1961–3	1990–2
World population	3.1 billion	5.3 billion
World production of cereals *per annum* (million tonnes)	900	1900
Cereal production per head *per annum*	290 kg	358 kg
Daily *per capita* calorie supply	2300	2710
Index of world food prices (1961–63 = 100)	100	47

Source: FAO

wheat rose from 0.5 tonnes per hectare in 1960 to over 3 tonnes by 1990; for rice the increase was from under 2 tonnes to over 3.5.

Concerns about sustainability

Despite these successes, there are enough straws in the wind to indicate that past successes may not be sustainable. Underlying global success are marked regional inequalities, indications of high environmental cost, and concerns about the future progress of technical change.

In regional terms, the main features of recent food production trends have been over-production in developed countries and production short-falls, especially in *per capita* terms, in Africa. In Europe and the USA, protection of agriculture and subsidies to exports have encouraged rapid intensification of production, with high levels of chemical use and frequent extension of cereal cropping onto unsuitable land. In Africa, by contrast,

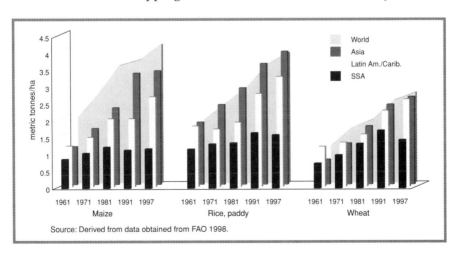

Source: Derived from data obtained from FAO 1998.

Figure 2.2   Regional yields: wheat, rice and maize, various years

rapid population growth has been associated with a decline in food production *per capita*, of 15 per cent between 1970 and 1990. Cereal yields in Africa average around 1 tonne per hectare, against a global average of almost 3 tonnes per hectare. Whereas calorie availability per day in North America exceeded 3400 in the late 1980s, in Africa it was over 40 per cent less, at just over 2000.

Whether food production can continue to outstrip population is also problematic. In the past decade, the rate of growth of food production has slowed and food availability per head has stagnated. It may even have declined. Thus rice yields in Asia increased by 2.9 per cent a year from the mid-1970s to the early 1980s, but by only 1.9 per cent a year for the rest of the decade (Figure 2.2). World grain production per head peaked at 380 kg *per annum* in 1985 and was down to 350 kg by 1993. The reductions in agricultural protection approved by the General Agreements on Tariffs and Trade (GATT) agreement in 1994 could mean further reductions in the rate of growth of agricultural output in Europe and the USA. Meanwhile, world population is increasing by 90 million each year, requiring an extra 30–40 million tonnes of grain a year, more if incomes rise and consumption, especially of grain-fed meat and dairy products, increases.

Projections

The likely evolution of supply and demand to 2010, 2020 or even beyond has been the subject of intensive study and modelling by research groups at FAO (Alexandratos 1995), the World Bank (Crosson and Anderson 1992; Mitchell and Ingco 1993) and under the umbrella of IFPRI's imaginative 20/20 project (Islam 1995; Rosegrant et al. 1995; Pinstrup-Anderson et al. 1999), as well as by independent analysts (e.g. Dyson 1996). There is a consensus in these studies that growth in world food production over the next two decades will be sufficient to keep up with growth in population and increased demand for food, provided that sufficient investments are made in research and infrastructure (see Chapter 7, Table 7.2).

In global terms, the current consensus is that world agricultural production will grow more slowly than in the past, so that the availability of food *per capita* is unlikely to rise significantly. This reflects the slow growth of effective demand, especially in developing countries.

Within this broadly positive global picture there will be regional inequalities, however. In developing countries, annual growth in food production is likely to be slower than the increase in consumption, so that imports will rise significantly, up to fourfold in SSA and tenfold in South Asia.

As in the recent past, the main source of projected growth for agricultural production will be further intensification (double cropping, reduced fallows and higher yields), rather than expansion onto new lands: probably two-thirds of the increase will result from intensification. Lack of water is likely to be a serious, even binding constraint, and the expansion of irrigated areas will be limited by the high costs of irrigation and environmental problems. In general, the environmental costs of agricultural production are likely to rise sharply.

To illustrate the sensitivity of these conclusions under different assumptions, Table 2.4 presents data on *per capita* food availability for 1990 and 2020 under various scenarios considered by IFPRI. This shows *per capita* food availability for a set of baseline assumptions with regard to population, economic growth, and the growth of area and productivity, compared with alternative options involving lower population growth, higher or lower investment in agriculture, slower or more rapid growth in the world economy, and full trade liberalization. The results show that world food availability is expected to increase somewhat in all scenarios, for both developed and developing countries. SSA, however, shows little improvement unless population growth can be curbed or the rate of food production growth increased.

As a final footnote on the projections, it is of course important to keep them constantly under review. There are great uncertainties with regard to economic growth, the rate of decline of population increase, and technical progress in agriculture. Furthermore, changes in large countries, especially China, could upset projections. For example, if China were to become a large importer, this would have a proportionate effect on world prices. Some observers think that this will happen (Brown and Kane 1994). Others (e.g. Dyson 1996; Pinstrup-Anderson et al. 1999) are more optimistic about the scope for production increases in China.

Ways forward

However accurate the projections turn out to be, it is clear that large increases in food production will be required in the decades to come. These can be achieved in different ways. Pretty et al. (1996) have identified five competing schools of thought on agriculture and food security (see Box 2.2).

- environmental pessimists;
- business-as-usual optimists;
- industrialized world to the rescue;
- new modernists;
- sustainable intensification.

The greatest contrast is between 'new modernists', who believe that growth in production can be achieved through high external-input farming, through a new Green Revolution on high-potential land; and the 'sustainable intensification' school, which would focus resources on low-input agriculture, often in lower-potential areas. Pretty et al. believe firmly in the sustainable option, particularly because of its impact on food security. They conclude that:

Table 2.4   *Per capita* food availability (kilocalories per day), 1990 and 2020: various scenarios

Region/country	1990	2020				
		Baseline	Low population growth[a]	Low investment/ slow growth[b]	High investment/ rapid growth[c]	Trade liberaliza-tion[d]
World	2773	2895	2987	2758	3032	2897
Developed countries	3353	3532	3613	3492	3599	3512
Developing countries	2500	2821	2916	2662	2978	2836
Asia	2500	3034	3136	2851	3225	3083
China	2667	3408	3457	3271	3616	3420
South Asia	2297	2640	2778	2425	2831	2711
Bangladesh	1978	2170	2363	1881	2350	2557
India	2332	2692	2814	2490	2886	2736
Pakistan	2370	2584	2758	2382	2753	2573
Other South Asian countries	2239	2565	2686	2328	2787	2532
Southeast Asia	2555	2840	2914	2712	2953	2853
Latin America and the Caribbean	2722	3026	3135	2878	3185	2963
Sub-Saharan Africa	2053	2135	2219	2021	2227	2093
West Asia and North Africa	2988	3114	3267	2943	3234	3081

Notes:
(a) The low population-growth scenario reflects the low-variant population-growth projections of the United Nations.
(b) The low-investment/slow-growth scenario simulates the combined effect of a 25 per cent reduction in non-agricultural income growth rates and reduced investment in agricultural public research and social services.
(c) The high-investment/rapid-growth scenario simulates a 25 per cent increase in non-agricultural income growth and higher investment in agricultural research and social services.
(d) The trade liberalization scenario simulates full removal of tariffs and subsidies.
Source: Rosegrant et al. 1995

a shift towards more intensive, sustainable forms of agriculture can make a sub-stantial positive contribution to food security – not only through its ability to con-tribute to sustainable intensification of production, but also through an emphasis on improving people's ability to acquire food (Pretty et al. 1996, p. 16).

The international agricultural research system has also heeded the call to combine greater agricultural productivity with greater attention to environmental sustainability. An external 'vision panel' appointed by the Consultative Group on International Agricultural Research (CGIAR) in 1994 called for a 'doubly-green' or 'super-green' revolution:

the agricultural research challenge for the future is complex and demanding. Research must continue to assist the intensification of high-potential areas, albeit on a more environment-friendly basis. At the same time, more research will be needed in lower-potential areas where rural poverty and associated resource degradation is and will increasingly be concentrated. ... In effect we require a revolution that is even more productive than the first Green Revolution and even more 'green' in terms of conserving natural resources and the environment. A doubly-green or super-green revolution. Over the next three decades it must aim to:

- *repeat the successes of the Green Revolution*
- *on a global scale*
- *in many diverse localities and*
- *be equitable-sustainable*
- *and environmentally-friendly*

(Conway et al. 1994, p. 38)

Thus, both independent observers and official bodies have put food security high on the list of priorities in agricultural development strategies.

INVESTMENT IN HIGH- OR LOW-POTENTIAL AREAS

Planning is about choosing. And in the agricultural and rural sectors, a key choice is about the balance to be struck between high- and low-potential areas. Should resources be concentrated in flat areas, well-watered and well-served by infrastructure? Or should they be directed instead to marginal agricultural environments, often poorly connected to national road networks? At first sight, the answer appears self-evident: returns will be higher by definition in high-potential areas. In practice, however, the issue is more complicated: for example, poor people may be concentrated in low-potential areas, and may not benefit from investment elsewhere. Similarly, there may be valuable environmental externalities to investment in low-potential areas, for example the protection of hillside watersheds.

The choices to be made are real. Any country which has experienced an intensive area development programme, or a crash programme to increase

---

Box 2.2   Five competing schools of thought on agriculture and
food security

1 *Environmental pessimists*. This group, with prominent adherents in the
   official aid circles and the international agricultural research agencies,
   contends that ecological limits to growth are being approached and will
   either soon be passed or have already been reached. Following a neo-
   Malthusian argument, these *'environmental pessimists'* claim that populations continue to grow too rapidly, while yields of major staple crops
   have declined and will continue to slow, or even fall in future. They argue
   that, given the current state of knowledge, no new technological break-
   throughs are likely; and that some agroecological systems have been too
   thoroughly degraded to recover. Solving these problems means making
   population control the first priority.
2 *Business-as-usual optimists*. This group, with a strong belief in the power
   of the market, argues that supply will always meet increasing demand,
   and so recent growth in aggregate food production will continue. These
   'business-as-usual optimists' expect that innovations in biotechnology
   will sustain the growth in food output. In many countries, however, it is
   also expected that the area under cultivation will expand dramatically –
   some estimates put the increase at an extra 79 million hectares in sub-
   Saharan Africa alone by 2020.
3 *Industrialized world to the rescue*. This predominantly northern-based
   group with ties to the agrochemical industry asserts that, for a variety of
   ecological, institutional and political economic reasons, developing countries will never be able to feed themselves. This group insists that the
   looming food gap will have to be filled by modernized agriculture based
   in the North. By increasing production in large, mechanized operations,
   this will force smaller and more 'marginal' farmers to go out of business,
   so taking the pressure off natural resources, which can then be conserved
   in protected areas and wilderness reserves. The large producers will then
   be able to trade their food with those who need it, or have it distributed
   by international agencies to provide famine relief or food aid.

The two remaining groups believe that significant biological yield increases
are possible on existing agricultural land. They are, however, fundamentally
divided over what is the most appropriate approach to achieve these
increases.

4 *New modernists*. This group, led by the partnership of the Sasakawa and
   Global 2000 Foundations, claims that food growth can only come
   through high external-input farming, either on existing Green Revolution
   lands or on the 'high-potential' areas that were missed by the past 30

years of agricultural development. These *'new modernists'* argue that farmers simply use too few artificial fertilizers, pesticides, high-yielding seed varieties and other external inputs, which are the only way to improve yields and reduce pressure on natural habitats. They also contend that high-input agriculture is more environmentally sustainable than low-input agriculture, as the latter requires the intensive use of local resources which may be degraded in the process.

5. *Sustainable intensification.* This group advances arguments in favour of the sustainable intensification of agricultural production, on the grounds that sustainable growth is possible in currently unimproved or degraded areas whilst at the same time protecting or even regenerating natural resources. Those advocating *'sustainable intensification'* point to recent empirical evidence from both the North and the South to argue that low-input (but not necessarily zero-input) agriculture can be highly productive, provided farmers participate fully in all stages of technology development and extension. They maintain that this evidence indicated that changes in the productivity of agricultural and pastoral lands is as much a function of human capacity and ingenuity as it is of biological and physical processes.

Source: Pretty et al. 1996

food production, will know that such programmes concentrate public resources in favoured areas – and that the opportunity cost consists of less attention being paid to low-potential areas. A particularly clear example is provided by Ethiopia in the late 1980s. Here, extension workers were withdrawn from low-potential areas on the margins of the central highlands in order to concentrate extension on areas identified for agricultural intensification under the Peasant-Area Development Projects (PADEP). These PADEP areas also benefited from agricultural research, fertilizer supply and infrastructure development. Low-potential areas did not receive the same level of investment. Instead, the strategy was one of small-scale development work by NGOs, supplemented by relief to mitigate the worst effects of neglect (Belshaw 1990).

The choice between high- and low-potential areas has become prominent in the debate about agriculture and rural development, reflecting the tension between two competing narratives about the world food problem (Maxwell 1996). Those who see the problem as one of producing enough food to feed the world's growing population will tend to favour support to productivity-enhancing investment in high-potential areas. By contrast, those who see the problem as one of tackling rural poverty and hunger will tend to favour investments which support livelihoods in low-potential areas (Pretty 1995). We are immediately reminded that there are multiple objectives in the rural sector: growth, poverty reduction, and environmental sustainability, to name but three.

The World Food Summit acknowledged the debate, and called for a balance between high- and low-potential areas (FAO 1996). Given the Malthusian tenor of much of the analysis preceding the summit, which might have indicated a focus on food production in high-potential areas, this was an important acknowledgement of multiple objectives. For example, the detailed Plan of Action adopted by the Summit noted that:

> most of the increases in food output of (low income food deficit) countries, and of more developed regions, are expected to come from areas which have the agro-climatic potential to generate sufficient surpluses in economically and environmentally sound conditions ... In marginal areas ... with lower-potential and fragile environments, there is also a need to increase food production through the provision of inputs and appropriate technology to reduce rural migration, but this should be based on sustainable management of resources and environment (FAO 1996, p. 14).

Table 2.5 summarizes the main arguments in the debate. In favour of investment in high-potential areas it can be argued that the rate of return is higher, that flows of people or money will equalize incomes across regions, and that the fiscal benefits are substantial. Furthermore, there are many poor people living in high-potential areas. In favour of investment in low-potential areas it can be argued that: the concentrations of poverty are higher here; high returns can be obtained from 'niche' investments in wadis or valley bottoms, or from non-marginal investments in major roads; there are significant environmental externalities; and there will be savings on

Table 2.5   Investment in high- and low-potential areas

Why invest in high-potential areas?	Why invest in low-potential areas?
1 Higher rate of return means more output, faster growth, more jobs, less poverty.	1 Low-potential areas can be transformed into high-potential areas with the right investment.
2 Labour migration will reduce pressure in low-potential areas.	2 There are pockets of high potential even in otherwise low-potential areas.
3 Remittances will reduce poverty in low-potential areas.	3 Investment in low-potential areas saves on relief costs.
4 Greater tax revenue means better funding for social security programmes in low-potential areas.	4 Investment in low-potential areas has environmental externalities.
5 'Poverty' is significant in high-potential areas.	5 It is more effective to tackle poverty in low-potential areas directly.

relief costs if the poor in low-potential areas are assisted to become self-reliant.

It should be noted that the way we have formulated the argument focuses attention on intra-country questions. Our main concern will be with high- and low-potential regions or districts within countries. There is, of course, an international dimension to the debate, as in the proposition that Holland, say, has higher potential than Burkina Faso. This has been an important strand in the debate about global food security, with some believing that resources should be concentrated in high-potential countries in the North: Pretty et al. (1996, p. 4) describe the position as 'industrialized world to the rescue'. We return to this question later.

What are high- and low-potential?

To take the arguments further, we need to start by exploring the terms 'high-' and 'low-potential'. The main use of the terms has been in the agricultural arena, with a technical and ecological focus.

Most of the agricultural development literature makes reference to two distinct land categories, usually 'high-potential' and 'low-potential'. However, alternatives include: 'high-input' and 'low-input' agriculture, 'green revolution' and 'low resource or resource poor' agriculture, 'advanced agricultural' and 'marginal areas', 'irrigated' and 'rainfed' areas, 'high-input favourable' and 'more marginal' environments, and 'high-production' and 'low-production' areas.

Other nomenclature has a decidedly practical focus, such as the distinction between 'areas with a high probability of early visible success' and 'more difficult situations'.

A general characterization would see high-potential areas as irrigated areas or areas of reliable rainfall, which have usually adopted modern technologies and have adequate physical and marketing infrastructure; low-potential areas would then be areas that are ecologically variable, more remote, less politically visible or influential, subject to high rainfall variability, with concentrated poverty, livelihoods heavily dependent on natural resources, and poor physical and social infrastructure. There is a substantial technical literature on land classification, suitability for crop production and yield potential; Alexandratos (1995) summarizes the procedures and findings. He shows that once high- and low-potential areas have been identified, it is possible to say something about the populations living in those areas. This has been attempted by Leonard (1989), with the results shown in Table 2.6. The table shows that 83 per cent of the world's poorest were estimated to live in rural areas, and that 55 per cent of this total was estimated to live in low-potential areas. The majority of the poor, and of the poor living in low-potential areas, are to be found in Asia.

Table 2.6   Poverty in high- and low-potential areas

Region	Number of the poorest people[a] in region (millions)	Location			
		Rural		Urban	
		High agricultural potential	Low agricultural potential	Squatter settlements	Other urban
All developing countries	778	277	370	100	31
Asia (including China and the Near East)	546	198	265	62	21
Sub-Saharan Africa	156	69	71	9	7
Latin America	78	12	35	28	3

Note:
(a) Defined as the poorest 20 per cent among the total population of all developing countries.
Source: Leonard 1989, p. 20

In a recent contribution, Conway (1997) has drawn on Leonard's analysis, to characterize the low-potential problem as follows:

> *The majority of the rural poor live in areas that are resource poor, highly hetero-geneous, and risk prone. They inhabit the impoverished lands of north-east Brazil, the low rainfall savannas and desert margins of the Sahel, the outer islands of the Philippines and Indonesia, the shifting deltas of Bangladesh, and the highlands of northern South Asia and the Andes of Latin America. The worst poverty is often located in arid or semi-arid zones or in steep hill-slope areas that are ecologically vulnerable. There the poor are isolated in every sense. They have meagre holdings or access to land, little or no capital and few opportunities for off-farm employment. Labour demand is often seasonal and insecure, Extension services are few and far between, and research aimed specifically at their needs is sparse.*

Some of the same aspects in the distinction between 'resource-rich' and 'resource-poor' families are shown in Table 2.7.

A practical case

There are examples to support both sides of the argument about investment in high- or low-potential areas (as in the case of the cash crop versus food crop debate – see next section). A practical example of how the choice might be worked out is whether it is sensible to divert investment resources from high- to low-potential areas in order to 'drought-proof'

Table 2.7   Characteristics of resource-rich and resource-poor areas

	Resource-rich family (RRF)	Resource-poor family (RPF)
Agroecological features:		
Topography	Flat, sometimes terraced	Often undulating and sloping
Soils	Deep, fertile, no constraints	Shallow, infertile, often severe constraints
Macro and micro deficiency	Occasional	Quite common
Plot size and nature	Large, small bunds	Small, irregular bunds larger where present
Hazards	Few, usually controllable	More common – floods, droughts, animals grazing crops etc.
Irrigation	Usually available	Often non-existent
Size of management unit	Large or medium, contiguous	Small, often scattered and fragmented
Diseases, pests, weeds	Controlled	Crops vulnerable to infestation
Social and economic features:		
Access to seeds, fertilizers, pesticides and other purchased inputs	High, reliable	Low, reliable
Seeds used	Purchased, high quality	Own seed
Access to credit	Good access	Poor access and seasonal shortages of cash when most needed
Irrigation, where facilities exist	Controlled by farmer or by others on whom he can rely	Controlled by others, less reliable
Labour	Hired, few constraints	Family, constraining at seasonal peaks
Prices	Lower than RPF for inputs; higher than RPF for outputs	Higher than RRF for inputs; lower than RRF for outputs
Appropriateness of technology generated on research experiment stations for the receiving environment	High	Low

Source: Chambers and Ghildyal 1985, p. 21

areas of low-potential and help to save on future relief costs. The argument here is about the opportunity cost of investing in high-potential areas, i.e. the cost of accepting a lower rate of return; and about whether this cost is justified by savings on future relief operations. The calculation requires information about the relative cost effectiveness of investments in different areas, and about the frequency and cost of drought emergencies (see Box 2.3).

Of course, the calculation in Box 2.3 is only illustrative. The rate of return differential would be lower if the cost of drought-proofing households were lower, droughts more frequent than three years in ten, or the relief cost higher. Figure 2.3 explores some of these questions in switching curve analysis, which shows how the choice between investment in high- or low-potential areas depends on (a) the frequency of drought and (b) the cost of relief. In the bottom left-hand corner of the figure, where drought is infrequent and relief costs low, other things being equal, investment in high-

---

Box 2.3   Investment in high- or low-potential areas?

Say that household income in a low-potential area is US$200 per year, and needs to be doubled to provide sufficient insurance against drought. Say also that the rate of return on investment in a low potential area is 5 per cent, compared with 10 per cent in a high-potential area. It would therefore take an investment of US$4000 in the low-potential area to raise the income of a household sufficiently to avoid the need for relief. Say that the cost of relief is US$50 per person and that there are six people in the household, giving a relief cost in drought years of US$300 per household. And say that there are three bad years in ten.
Then:

- Option A might be to invest US$4000 in the high-potential area, generate additional income of $400 per year, and spend US$300 twice in ten years to pay for relief;
- Option B might be to invest US$4000 in the low-potential area, generate an additional US$200 per year, and have no relief costs.

On these assumptions, which are not implausible for Ethiopia, the internal rate of return is higher for investment in high-potential areas, at 7 per cent compared with 5 per cent, despite the additional expenditure on relief and even when the three drought years occur at the worst possible time, at the beginning of each decade. This suggests a predisposition not to invest in low-potential areas.

Source: Maxwell and Lirenso 1994

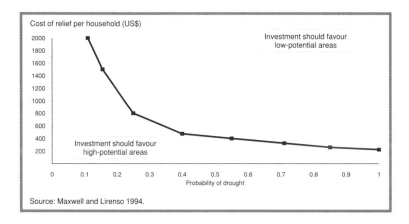

Figure 2.3 Switching curve for investment, with regard to drought frequency and relief cost

potential areas has a higher benefit:cost ratio. Conversely, in the top right-hand corner, where drought is more frequent and relief costs high, investment in low-potential areas is more profitable.

A simple cost–benefit calculation provides only a first cut at these issues, and a more sophisticated analysis is required to examine linkage effects. Similarly, there are other factors to take into account, including inter-regional equity. The point is not to draw a definitive conclusion, but to suggest that it is necessary to review the opportunity costs of different policies.

More generally, Maxwell (1996) has suggested that an appropriate agricultural strategy will be one that combines investment in both high- and low-potential areas, but with emphasis for public investment on low-potential areas where private resources are harder to mobilize. He calls this strategy 'Walking On Two Legs, But With One Leg Longer Than The Other'. He argues that:

> if the high potential strategy is pursued, it is clear that growth will be faster. But it can plausibly be argued that if that route is followed, the impact on food security will be less. A second kind of strategy, a food security strategy, will certainly produce more food, but growing food does not necessarily generate the jobs or livelihoods to reduce poverty. Neither strategy is sufficient on its own (Maxwell 1996, p. 96).

CASH CROPS VERSUS FOOD CROPS

The debate about food crops and cash crops is highly charged in Africa. On the one hand, proponents see cash cropping as a route to growth, diversification and prosperity for all. On the other, opponents see it as the manifestation of dependency, underdevelopment and immiserization. The debate has been especially acrid in food deficit countries, where the image of food shortage and starvation is contrasted with agricultural products being shipped abroad to the tables of the rich in developed countries. Here, then, is a central question facing food security planners. Are cash crops good for food security? Perhaps more to the point, under what conditions are cash crops good for food security? And how can the incentive and regulatory framework or the public expenditure budget be modified to enlarge the benefits while minimizing the costs?

We need to start answering these questions by clarifying the terminology, since the term 'cash crop' is used in different ways. It can refer to an export crop, a non-staple crop, or even any crop (or livestock product) sold. There is no right or wrong definition, but anyone participating in the argument should choose a definition and stick to it. Here, we use the term to refer to any crop that is sold. At the household level, therefore, the term will refer to any marketed surplus. At the national level, it will refer to export agriculture.

To further clear the decks, we should also note that cash cropping need not necessarily be competitive with other agricultural activities. Indeed, the evidence is that food cropping and export cash cropping often grow or decline together (von Braun and Kennedy 1994). This may be because the policy environment which favours one set of crops also favours the other. It may be because the money earned from one crop is used to buy inputs for another (e.g. coffee earnings used to buy fertilizer for the maize). Or it may be because two crops are technically complementary in a farming system: for example, food and cash crops may be inter-cropped in the same field so as to maximize the return to land. In this example, maize can be planted between the bushes in a young coffee plantation.

Cash crops: the arguments

Nevertheless, there may be conflict between food and cash crops, and it then becomes necessary to explore the arguments in more detail. They can be presented briefly under the headings of: growth, income distribution, food security, dependency, and the environment.

As far as growth is concerned, the argument in favour of cash crops is that they:

- allow farmers and countries to exploit comparative advantage, and thereby maximize income;
- generate an investible surplus which helps to maximize growth, again for both farmers and nations;
- generate linkages, both upstream to the supply of inputs and downstream through the use of products, which again generate growth and livelihoods.

Spooner (1988) talks about the 'economic transformation' made possible by cash crops.

Against this, the critics of cash cropping, particularly in the 'food-first' school (George 1976; Lappe and Collins 1979, 1986) argue that comparative advantage is a poor guide to agricultural investment. Not only is comparative advantage often the product of past investment or institutional relationships, it is also highly sensitive to current cost structures and exchange rates. Furthermore, the long-term decline in the prices received for many agricultural export commodities means that comparative advantage may be a short-lived phenomenon. Critics also charge that the alleged benefits of cash cropping are often leached out of local or even national economies by erroneous pricing policies or the repatriation of profits by foreign companies.

This last point leads immediately to the distributional argument about cash crops. Here, proponents argue that cash cropping can be a vehicle for small-farm development. The riposte of the other side is that cash cropping has often been associated with plantations or large farms, and that there are insurmountable barriers preventing small farmers from participating fully. In the short term, they may not have access to capital, technical skills or the markets necessary to participate in cash cropping. In the longer term, they may lose out because the initial profits of the first individuals to move into cash cropping are used to acquire more land or adopt new and more competitive technologies.

The arguments are similar when it comes to food security, but an important gender consideration must be included. If cash crops are good for the incomes of the poor, and if they enable poor families to spread their risks (both production risk and marketing risk), then it might be expected that food security will be improved. However, cash cropping may result in a different allocation of resources within the household, so that the access to food of different individuals is altered. For example, it is frequently alleged that an increase in cash cropping tends to increase male control over household resources, and that this reduces the access to food of women and children. Only if cash cropping can be controlled by women, the argument goes, will it be good for food security and nutrition within the household.

Turning to dependency, the main argument is that reliance on markets makes producers, whether household or nations, vulnerable to competition, price variability and physical controls affecting market access. Dependency is thus undesirable in itself, but also increases risk.

Finally, there is an argument about cash crops and the environment. Critics argue that cash crops are associated with monoculture, reducing biological diversity and often exposing land to higher degrees of erosion. The prevalence of cash cropping also increases the pressure on land and increases pollution (and health damage) by pesticides. On the other hand, defenders of cash crops argue that many cash crops in practice act to protect the environment, by providing tree cover and by encouraging good standards of husbandry.

These arguments, and others (Maxwell and Fernando 1989) provide a framework of analysis – in effect, a set of questions that can be asked of national or household cash crop experience. The evidence, of course, is mixed: there are cases to support every point of view.

Cash crops: the evidence

A few summary points are worth making, however. First, the importance of cash cropping to the economies of African countries should not be underestimated. Data assembled by Maxwell and Fernando (1989) showed that cash crops were important in terms of area, share of agricultural output exported, share of agricultural exports in total exports, and agricultural exports as a proportion of GDP. For example, over one-third of countries had more than 30 per cent of crop land under cash crops, taking 'cash crops' as crops that require substantial off-farm processing, that are usually exported, or usually marketed domestically. Similarly, agricultural exports accounted for over 80 per cent of all exports in something like two-thirds of African countries.

Table 2.8 provides data on the contribution of cash crop exports to GDP in 1992 for 76 countries in low-, lower-middle- and upper-middle-income countries, in Africa and other regions. This shows that cash crop exports accounted for less than 5 per cent in GDP in something like half the cases considered. However, the figure exceeded 10 per cent for nearly one country in five and in four cases (some 5 per cent of the total) exceeded 20 per cent of GDP. In most countries, it is hard to imagine the economy or the population prospering without a substantial contribution from cash crops. Can Ethiopia, Kenya or Uganda prosper without the contribution of coffee? Can Malawi or Zimbabwe prosper without tobacco, or Namibia without livestock?

On the central question of agricultural commercialization and nutrition,

Table 2.8   Other primary commodity exports in GDP, 1992

OPC/GDP	Low-income countries		Lower-middle-income countries		Upper-middle-income countries		Total	
(%)	Number	%	Number	%	Number	%	Number	%
0–5	17	52	14	50	10	67	41	54
6–10	7	21	11	39	3	20	21	28
11–20	7	21	1	4	2	13	10	13
20+	2	6	2	7	0	0	4	5
Total	33	100	28	100	15	100	76	100

Source: World Bank 1994

the most detailed case studies are reported by von Braun and Kennedy (1994). This research, carried out by IFPRI, examined the effects of commercialization in 11 different sites, ranging from export vegetable production in Guatemala, through dairy development in India, to sugar in Kenya and the Philippines. The main findings on the production, employment and income effects of the seven African case studies are summarized in Table 2.9. In general, and certainly in the African cases, commercialization took place with no significant cost in terms of subsistence food production. Further, in most cases, employment increased, and so did income. For example, the adoption of potato production for sale in Rwanda increased labour hiring by 64 person-days per hectare. In Zambia, household labour input went up by 46 per cent in areas adopting new maize technology. Income also increased.

Whether an increase in income also results in an increase in the nutritional status of individuals in the household is another matter. Theory would suggest a number of leakages between income and nutritional status, as a result of non-food expenditure, improvement to the quality of the diet, changes to the distribution of food within the household, and constraints imposed by the health care environment or time available for childcare. In fact, von Braun and Kennedy found that in all the study areas, except in Kenya, cash crops had a positive significant effect on the nutritional status of children. There was no significant negative effect in any of the study countries. However, the net nutritional effect of an increase in income was modest, because of the leakages identified, except in very poor households.

Table 2.10 summarizes their results. It shows that a 10 per cent increase in the income of poor households (those with a *per capita* income of US$100 *per annum* or less) translates to only a 1.1 per cent improvement in children's nutritional status (measured as weight for age) in Guatemala and the Philippines, 1.9 per cent in The Gambia, but 2.5 per cent in Rwanda and as much as 4.9 per cent in Malawi. At the upper level, these are attractive figures. Even at the lower level they indicate that cash cropping has positive effects.

There is other evidence to support the proposition that cash cropping can be good for the poor. The case of small-scale tea growing in Kenya is frequently cited, and, from outside Africa, Ellis provides a convincing description of beneficial small-scale sugar farming in Fiji (Ellis 1988). He attributes the success to the employment intensity of the industry, to its small-farm structure and to the prohibition of mechanical cane harvesting technology. In addition, small farmers are helped by the high proportion of total export revenue retained, and by the efficiency of the sugar industry, largely influenced by farmer interests.

There are, of course, counter examples, in both traditional and non-traditional export crops. In Central America, for example, Thrupp (1995) has reviewed the impact of non-traditional exports like fruit, flowers and vegetables. She recognizes the potential benefits, but also draws attention

Table 2.9 Impacts of agricultural commercialization in Africa

Country	Commercialization scheme	Main subsistence crops/ commercial crops	Did subsistence food production decline?	Did employment increase?	Did income increase?
Kenya	South Nyanza Sugar Company	Maize/sugarcane	No. Participants devoted as much land to food crops as sugar farmers. New entrants even increased subsistence income.	Information not available.	Yes significantly, for both new tenants and sugar farmers.
Kenya	Two rice schemes: Ahero Irrigation Scheme and West Kano Irrigation Scheme	Maize, sorghum/ rice, sugarcane	Yes, for those tenants who reside at the schemes, but not for non-resident tenants who have access to much more land.	Information not available.	Yes, for individual rice growers and non-resident tenants, but not for non-rice growers and residents. Controlling for household size, there were barely any differences among the four groups.
Rwanda	Potato production in the Gishwati forest area	Peas, beans, sweet potatoes, maize, sorghum/ potatoes, tea	No, no change in crop composition as modern potato production production exclusively.	Yes, significantly. Sixty-four man-days of wage labour hired per hectare per season.	Yes, to some extent. But income control within the household affected as men's greater.

Country	Project	Crops		Labour	Income
Zambia	Technological change in maize	Maize, sorghum, finger millet/hybrid maize	Information not available. Note, though, that only those farmers who could expand cultivated area beyond subsistence food requirements adopted hybrid maize.	Yes, household labour input up to 46 per cent in high-adopting areas for both males and females.	Yes, significantly. *Per capita* income about 25 per cent higher in adopting households.
Malawi	Commercialization of maize and tobacco	Maize, legumes/maize, tobacco	No, strong desire to produce as much maize as possible for food-security reasons. On average, tobacco did not displace maize.	Information not available.	Yes, but with wide variations. Income of tobacco specialists much higher than that of small tobacco households slightly less than that of non-tobacco households.
Sierra Leone	Bo-Pujehun Rural Development Project–Tree Crop Promotion	Upland rice, vegetables, roots/coffee, cocoa, oil palm	Not clear, less food crop area is cultivated but land productivity is much higher, which may offset the area substitution effects.	Information not available.	No, in fact, it was about 12 per cent lower among new adopters, and about the same for established plantation farmers and subsistence farmers.
The Gambia	Jahally-Pacharr Smallholder Rice Project	Millet, sorghum, rice/rice under modern irrigation, groundnuts	No, new rice technology increased rice yields substantially.	Yes, a 56 per cent increase.	Yes, for households as a whole, but women generally benefited less than men.

Source: Von Braun and Kennedy 1994

Table 2.10   Elasticities of children's nutritional status wth respect to income

Country	Elasticity
Guatemala	0.11
Philippines	0.11
Kenya	n.s.
Rwanda	0.25
Malawi	0.49
The Gambia	0.19

Note: 'n.s.' = not statistically significant.
Source: von Braun and Kennedy 1994

to socio-economic inequalities associated with these high-technology crops, and to the negative environmental impacts.

Cash crop policy

Various authors have attempted to distinguish between positive and negative cases by generating guidelines for cash crop policy. Thus, Maxwell and Fernando (1989) offer six sets of policies designed to maximize the benefits of cash cropping for the poor. These are reproduced in Box 2.4.

Thrupp, too, has identified six strategic principles, listed in Box 2.5 as a 'summary of strategic principles to guide policies and actions for sustainable agricultural development'.

Finally, and with specific reference to nutrition outcomes, Longhurst (1988) has produced a set of best and worst case scenarios for cash cropping, summarized in Table 2.11. This identifies the physical, household organization and regional or national policy characteristics of different cash crop enterprises, and indicates which are good for food security and which bad. For example, a 'good' cash crop is a food crop which generates several marketable products, has a short maturation period and can be processed locally under the control of both men and women. It has a regular income flow and high employment potential. Longhurst cites groundnuts in The Gambia as a good example which meets these criteria.

All these sets of guidelines and checklists suggest a way forward, which is to identify systematically which features of an existing or proposed cash cropping enterprise are beneficial to the poor and which are inimical. The question to ask about each of the negative effects is how it can be reversed, for example by a change in the regulatory environment or by a change in taxation. Similarly, how can the beneficial effects be enhanced or protected?

Box 2.4   Principles for cash crop policy

1 The need to assess the dynamic, long-term costs and benefits of different cash crops, taking account of both comparative advantage and potential linkages to the rest of the economy.
2 Because the prediction of dynamic comparative advantage is difficult and uncertain and because, in the short-term, revenues fluctuate widely for individual crops, diversification is almost certainly an important policy objective. This applies both at the national level and at the household level.
3 The question of overall growth strategies is crucial. The main value of cash cropping lies not in short-term income gains but in long-term surplus generation and growth through linkages. Cash crop policy needs to make sure that both are maximized, controlling profit repatriation, avoiding diversification to luxury consumption, whether public or private, and maximizing linkages through the encouragement of local input supply, downstream processing and domestic consumption.
4 An important and simultaneous part of the growth strategy should be attention to the distributional consequences of cash cropping, particularly in order to secure access by the poor and by women to the cash crop sector, both as producers and as labour. This requires policy on land tenure, on mechanization, on supply of credit and inputs and on access to markets. Cash crop policy needs to be consistent with rural development policy generally.
5 Cash crop policy needs to be closely related to food policy. The expansion of cash crops is likely to lead to a decline in nutritional standards unless food systems are developed to provide adequate supplies of food at appropriate prices throughout the year.
6 Finally, cash cropping, as all agricultural development, needs to pay attention to environmental questions and to be promoted in a sustainable form.

Source: Maxwell and Fernando 1989

CONCLUSION

Agriculture is important: there is no doubt about that. 'Getting agriculture moving' was the cry in the 1960s (Mosher 1966), and remains a laudable objective in 2000. However, our discussion of some current debates in agriculture has shown that a simple battle-cry is not enough. There are choices to be made in agriculture, as in other sectors.

The methodology we have used bears repeating. It is to approach

---

Box 2.5   A summary of strategic principles to guide policies and actions for sustainable agricultural development

1 Promote participatory approaches, focusing on the inclusion of poor farmers and workers in agricultural development decision making and in socio-economic opportunities.
2 Build a policy environment to mitigate/avoid adverse impacts of Non-Traditional Agro-Exports (NTAEs) and to support and multiply sustainable and equitable patterns of trade and agricultural development.
3 Promote and develop sustainable agricultural technologies, stressing Integrated Pest Management (IPM), organic practices, and diversity, through changes by all actors in the production-market chain.
4 Build a better balance in policy attention to local vs. export production, placing priority on alleviating hunger and fulfilling local food security needs.
5 Increase the empowerment and status of poor producers and workers in production and marketing, to overcome market barriers and to promote equitable alternatives.
6 Increase information on the market conditions and impacts of agro-exports, and improve access to such information to a wide audience of interested people.

Source: Thrupp 1995

debates in agricultural policy from a pragmatic, non-ideological perspective. By exploring debates from different perspectives, it is possible to tease out the many different factors impacting on food security, and then to sketch out scenarios which are more or less favourable to the poor and food insecure. Within this policy space, it is then possible to identify changes to the incentive and regulatory framework, or to public expenditure, which will increase the flow of benefits to the poor. This approach gave us a useful way into debates about agricultural output mixes, the geographical distribution of agricultural investment, and the focus on agricultural reforms.

In conclusion, though, it remains important to emphasize that different strategies of agricultural development help to achieve different objectives. Table 2.12 was prepared for a discussion in Ethiopia, but has relevance across SSA. It illustrates the extent to which three different agricultural strategies help to achieve five different policy objectives. In Ethiopia – and in many low-income food deficit countries in SSA – governments are

Table 2.11 Characteristics of cash crops for 'bad' and 'good' outcomes

Characteristics	Bad	Good
A *Physical*		
Composition	Non-food	Food
Marketable products	One	Several
Maturation period	Long	Short
Within the farming system	Competitive	Complementary
Processing	Not done locally	Locally done
B *Household Organization*		
Gender control	Men	Men and women
Income flow	Lumpy	Spread out
Impact on landless and off-farm industries	None	Some
C *Regional or national policy*		
Marketing outlet	One	Several
Research and extension	Focused on crop	Recognizes farming system
Food markets	Poorly integrated	Well integrated
Incentive price impact	Disruptive	Recognizes multi-products of farm

Source: Longhurst 1988

concerned with growth and poverty reduction. However, they are also concerned with the problem of food aid dependence, and are anxious to reduce food imports, increase commercial import capacity and reduce the need for food aid. The food aid objective has become more acute as food aid supplies have declined in recent years.

In order to achieve these multiple objectives, governments essentially have three agricultural strategies at their disposal.

- *A growth-first strategy.* This will probably concentrate agricultural investment, research and extension on high-potential areas, where returns are highest; and, within these areas, on the crops which display comparative advantage. These may be food crops, but may not. The government will take complementary measures to ensure a favourable climate for agricultural investment and will take steps to facilitate agricultural marketing.
- *A food-first strategy.* This will again concentrate on maximizing output, mostly in high-potential areas. But in this case there will be a marked bias to food production. This will mean directing public

Table 2.12 The impacts of alternative agricultural strategies

Agricultural development strategy	Growth	Impact on poverty reduction	Food import reduction	Commercial import capacity	Reduction in food aid need
Growth first	High	Medium	Medium	High	Medium
Food first	Medium	Low	High	Medium	Low
Food-security first	Low	High	Low	Low	High

investment, research and extension to food crops, even when these do not necessarily have a short- or long-term comparative advantage. For example, cereals might be favoured at the expense of coffee or tea, leaving these latter crops to stagnate (relatively) or to finance their own research and infrastructure development.

● *A food-security-first strategy.* In this case, the priority is to improve the ability of poor people to acquire food by production, purchase, exchange or gift – in other words, to focus on food entitlement rather than food production. Since most poor people in SSA are in rural areas, this will inevitably mean a strong focus on agriculture and rural development. However, resources are more likely to be directed to low-potential areas, to minimizing poor people's exposure to risk by helping to stabilize inter-annual fluctuations in food production, and to crops which increase income, regardless of whether these are food or cash crops.

The point about these three strategies is that each will contribute in different ways to the objectives set by government. Thus, a growth-first strategy will, by definition, make the greatest impact on growth in the medium term. However, it may contribute less to poverty reduction and to the reduction in food imports. By contrast, a food-first strategy will have its greatest impact on the food import reduction objective, and may also contribute to commercial import capacity. However, it will have an opportunity cost in terms of growth, and may do little for poverty reduction if capital-intensive methods in high-potential areas are chosen. A food-security-first strategy will focus on poverty reduction and should, therefore, have a high impact on the need for emergency relief. However, it may have an opportunity cost in terms of growth. It may not, of course, if high return investments can be found in low-potential areas where poor people are concentrated.

CHAPTER THREE

Household Food and Livelihood Security

Jeremy Swift and Kate Hamilton

AGRICULTURE IS CENTRAL to household food security and rural livelihoods in Africa. But this is not the end of the story. Agriculture is not the only, in many cases not even the main, source of food and income. This chapter extends the argument of the previous chapter by considering those people for whom farming plays a less important role (notably pastoralists and town dwellers), analyses the main causes of food insecurity in such cases, and argues that an approach based on livelihood systems makes analysis easier and policies more comprehensive.

CHARACTERISTICS OF FOOD INSECURE ENVIRONMENTS IN DRYLAND AFRICA

Food insecurity at household level arises from several causes, and is most devastating when more than one cause occurs together. In Africa, environmental risk is the most common trigger for episodes of acute household food insecurity; drought is the most common form of environmental risk in most areas, although disease (notably rinderpest, which decimated East African livestock herds at the end of the nineteenth century) formerly played a similar role, and could again, as the AIDS pandemic shows. Market risk, due to poor spatial arbitrage, low demand and a lack of economies of scale, can create chronic food insecurity in isolated areas, and can magnify food insecurity stemming initially from drought. Poverty creates food insecurity, worsens existing types and levels of food insecurity, and may also be a consequence of food insecurity. Conflict, within and between states, can create food insecurity in even the most food secure economies, but is especially damaging in places already predisposed to food insecurity for other reasons. The maps of recent conflicts and famines in Africa now overlap to a significant degree.

THE CHALLENGE OF RISKY ENVIRONMENTS

The naturally most food insecure environments in Africa are the arid and semi-arid zones, where drought is a major recurring risk. Drought was originally seen as an exception: an unpredictable disruption of 'normal' rainfall patterns. Recent research on dryland ecological dynamics challenges this view and instead makes climatic uncertainty the norm. Such a view also leads to new ways of thinking about the behaviour of dryland inhabitants.

Recent research in ecology (Behnke et al. 1993; Scoones 1995) starts from the observation that dryland ecological processes are driven not so much by the classic biological feedback mechanisms of the more humid environments, but by processes which often stem from episodic events originating outside the local ecological environment. Drought is the most important of these, but forest or grassland fire, animal disease and many others can play a similar role.

In such environments, uncertainty is the key constraint to which farmers and herders must adapt. Production, whether of crops or livestock, depends less on a fine and cumulative adjustment of inputs to a given set of environmental circumstances than on the ability to be flexible, to adapt to changes as they occur, and to spread risks. Successful households in these more dynamic environments are those who are able to diversify economic activities, to use different ecological niches (such as different micro-habitats), economic contexts (such as accessing a new set of markets), social networks and political jurisdictions (such as moving across an international frontier). Mobility (including the migrations of herders with their animals, and the wage labour migration of individuals) is one key to survival, the ability to build up a variety of forms of social capital (to be called upon in a crisis) is another.

CONFLICT

Ecological uncertainty is not the only source of risk in such dynamic environments. Conflict has become a critical influence on food security. Conflict has grown rapidly in Africa in the last three decades, and is now widespread in the arid and semi-arid areas, as well as some humid zones (Swift 1996; Kratli and Swift 1999).

Conflict has multiple actors, causes, links to the wider world, and outcomes. Interstate conflicts over such issues as sovereignty are highly damaging to the food security of the inhabitants of the disputed zones, but are less common than local conflicts along ethnic, political or economic lines, over issues such as access to land, water, or mineral resources. The main immediate protagonists of such conflicts are the farmers or herders directly involved, or the inhabitants of mineral-rich areas, but there are always wider circles of actors, including business people, politicians, the security forces, and mercenaries employed by both sides.

Conflict is increasingly linked both to domestic political issues around territorial political representation and to ethnic identity, and has become more commercial as all aspects of conflict are influenced by the market: the labour market for hired fighters, the weapons market, and markets for looted commodities such as livestock. Analysts increasingly view local conflicts not as irrational outbreaks of extreme violence but as a process in which there are winners and losers, and which may be extremely rational from the point of view of the winners who usually include business people, politicians and soldiers (de Waal 1996; Keen 1997; but see Cliffe and Luckham 1999 for a less functionalist view).

Whatever the cause, such local conflicts have drastic consequences for food security (Kratli and Swift 1999). Direct economic outcomes include:

- destruction or theft of livestock and other property;
- price changes for basic commodities (price increases where looted livestock or cereals are moved away from the affected area, price falls in areas where they are sold);
- closure of markets, with further knock-on effects on availability and prices of staple foods and livestock;
- induced sales of assets such as livestock at low prices;
- loss of access to farm land, pasture or water;
- long term changes in the productivity of pasture land (for example undergrazing and bush encroachment in insecure areas, and over-grazing as animals crowd into secure areas);
- destitution and displacement (75 per cent of people in three refugee camps in Turkana, north Kenya, in the late 1980s, apparently dis-placed by drought, reckoned that conflict was a significant factor in their displacement, and 47 per cent saw it as the main cause (McCabe 1990);
- new processes of accumulation – for example of weapons, livestock, water points, land, labour – which alter traditional relations of power and authority.

Social and political outcomes of conflict include increasing political margin-alization of conflict areas within the state, a loss of legitimate political authority, and a breakdown of local ethnic or community relations. Social capital, in the sense of networks of trust and accepted authority, is often a casualty of conflict, and the opponent's social capital is increasingly a specific target of warring parties. Women and children are particularly vulnerable to conflict.

The impact of conflict on food security is multi-faceted. At household level, it may be seen as a cause of unpredictable risk, analogous to risk of drought and other environmental risks. In practice, conflict often overlaps with and is a cause of extreme food insecurity (see Chapter 5).

Pastoralists are the main inhabitants of the vulnerable dry areas, and pastoral areas are often the theatre for violent conflict. The following sec-tion looks at the special characteristics of pastoral food insecurity, and also at urban food insecurity, which has often been ignored in the food security literature.

HOUSEHOLD STRATEGIES FOR ACHIEVING FOOD SECURITY IN PASTORAL AND URBAN AREAS

PASTORALISM

In drier areas, a common form of economic diversification by households in response to increasing risk and variability is to add livestock to the farming portfolio, with the number of livestock and their role in the household economy generally increasing with greater aridity. This creates a range of livelihood adaptations involving animals, from simply keeping a few animals around the house, through separate but parallel or integrated agro-pastoral operations, to several distinctive and specialist pastoral livelihood systems. The proportion of gross household income derived from the livestock operation allows a simple classification of livelihood systems into pastoral (more than 50 per cent), agro-pastoral (10–50 per cent), and agricultural (less than 10 per cent).

One of the advantages of animals in ecologically risky and variable environments is their mobility, which allows them to move away from places that don't have pasture and water, towards places that do. Such movements range in distance from a few kilometres in a year to many hundred, and in predictability from daily displacement of the animals around a village, through regular use of the same pastures each year at a given moment in the annual cycle, to movements which are completely contingent on highly variable environmental conditions and are rarely the same from one year to another. The distance moved in a year, and the unpredictability of the yearly movement cycle, tend to increase with increasing aridity and the increasing unpredictability which accompanies it. On such moves, the animals may be accompanied by a single herder (or be in the care of a hired, non-household, worker), or be accompanied by the entire family. Mobility of animals is not only a response to variable natural resource availability. It can also be a response to changing market opportunities, to new social or political alliances, or to conflict. Mobility gives households with sufficient animals much greater flexibility to respond to threats of all sorts, and is often an essential condition of livelihood security in the drylands.

Substantial economic dependence on livestock has important consequences for food security. On the positive side, it gives households the flexibility to move away from problems of all sorts, which contributes to household food security. On the negative side, it creates new sorts of vulnerabilities for pastoral households. Two of the most important are the timing of seasonal economic and nutritional stresses, and the increased dependence on market exchange for acquiring staple foods.

Seasonal food security stresses occur at different times of the year for farmers and herders in the same or neighbouring environments. Taking the example of a dry environment with a single rainfall peak, a typical pattern of farmer food insecurity is shown in Figure 3.1a. The rainy season occupies around a third of the year, with a peak agricultural labour period starting before the start of the rains and continuing until harvest. Food is scarcest, and food insecurity highest, in the mid- to late-rainy season. Maximum food availability, and lowest food insecurity, occurs after harvest.

The herder pattern, shown in Figure 3.1b, is very different. The period of hardest work starts in the dry season (when watering animals is a back-breaking task), and continues until early in the rainy season, when most young animals have been born. Labour demands then slack off, at a time when agricultural work remains high for several more months. This is also the time when milk becomes available, and may provide an important source of food for two or three months, making this late rainy season and immediate post rainy season the most food secure time for pastoralists.

Figure 3.1 shows how, within the same or neighbouring environments, food insecurity crises will occur at very different times of year for farmers (mid- to late-rainy season) and herders (mid- to late-dry season). In each livelihood system, the period of maximum food insecurity coincides with the period of highest labour demand.

A second type of food security vulnerability typical of a pastoral economy concerns market dependence. A pastoral or agro-pastoral livelihood does not necessarily mean that households are directly dependent on livestock for food. Although in a few East African pastoral groups, including for example some Maasai and the Turkana, milk from the household's own cattle was until recently the source of between half and two-thirds of calorie intake, and meat and blood for perhaps another 10 per cent, in most pastoral livelihood systems milk is responsible for between a third and a half of calorie intake (Swift et al. 1990). Most of the rest of calorie intake comes from consumption of staple cereals. Although agro-pastoralists grow a substantial part of these cereals themselves, pastoralists obtain them mostly through market purchase. The proportion of food energy intake originating in a market transaction has most probably increased for all categories of pastoralist in the last two or three decades.

Dependence on the market for a substantial part of daily calorie intake makes pastoralists vulnerable to changing prices of the products they sell – live animals, milk, animal products like hides, skins and wool – and the cereals they buy. These pastoral terms of trade are volatile. They vary seasonally, driven by a combination of:

- cereal prices which change in response to such supply-side factors as the success of the harvest, remaining farmer and trader stocks, prospects for the current cropping season, and demand-side factors which include urban and pastoral needs, and
- livestock prices which change according to such supply-side factors as the success of the breeding season, alternative sources of pastoral nutrition, herd-owners' expectations about pasture availability in the

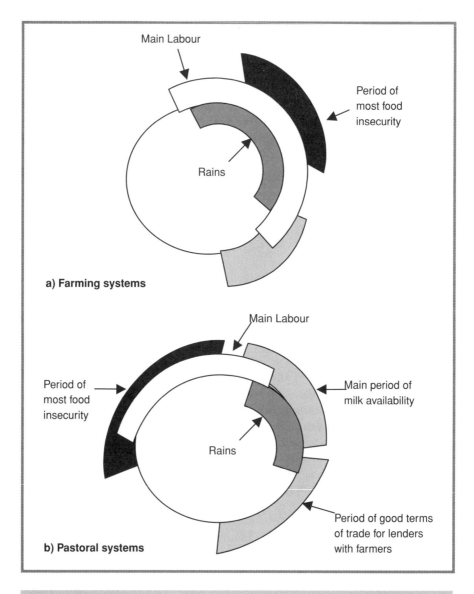

Figure 3.1   Seasonal patterns of food insecurity in agricultural and pastoral household economies

forthcoming dry season, and demand-side factors such as seasonal liveweight and condition of the animals, and cash incomes of purchasers such as farmers and urban people.

Pastoral terms of trade also vary in characteristic ways during drought (and to a lesser extent animal disease epidemic) years (Downing et al. 1989). In drought years, farmers have less disposable income, and traders and other purchasers are unwilling to buy animals in poor condition which may not survive the drought. Declining demand triggers a fall in animal prices. Simultaneously, cereal supply shortages and increased demand lead to a rapid rise in cereal prices, creating a cereals:animal price scissors which cuts deeply into the purchasing power of pastoralists (see Box 3.1).

Box 3.1   Pastoral terms of trade

Subsistence pastoralism is unusual, and most herders achieve food security by exchanging animal products – mainly live animals or milk – for staple cereals. Their exchange entitlement depends on the relative prices of animal products and cereals, and thus on the rate at which animal products can be exchanged for cereals, or 'pastoral terms of trade'. The erosion and eventual collapse of pastoral terms of trade is the key to pastoral famine, and the re-establishment of normal terms of trade determines how fast pastoralists recover afterwards. Figure 3.2 below shows the changing relative values of

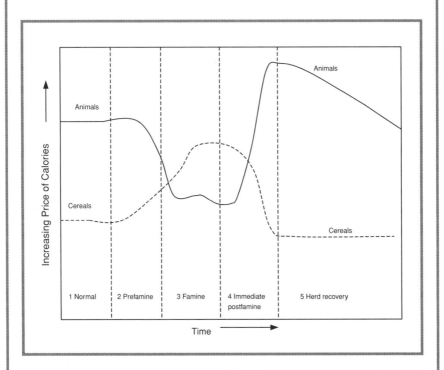

Figure 3.2   Cereals: livestock terms of trade during food crises

live animals and cereals (expressed as the price of calories derived from each) during the full cycle of a pastoral famine.

In a normal situation, the pastoral terms of trade are favourable to herders. Since animal prices per calorie are higher than cereal prices, animals can be exchanged for more cost-effective cereal calories. Early in a drought or other economic disruption, herders face declining milk yields and try to sell more animals to compensate. However, potential animal purchasers have less disposable income, so demand for animals falls. Animal prices are pushed down and cereal prices up, catching herders in a price scissors. This is the pre-famine period, and may reach the stage where calories of cereal origin cost more than calories of meat origin (at which stage it makes sense for herders to eat, not sell, their animals).

In the immediate post-famine period, cereal production and markets are rapidly restored, and cereal prices quickly fall to normal levels. However, animals are in demand – by both herders and others – as a result of post-drought scarcity, and animal prices rapidly rise well above their normal level. During a long recovery period, animal prices fall slowly back towards normal, at the speed of the growth of the overall herd. This is advantageous for herders with animals to sell, but disadvantageous for those who want to reconstitute their herd by buying animals.

Source: Swift 1989b, p. 326

An added difficulty for pastoralists occurs during the recovery phase from a drought. As the rains recover, cereal farmers harvest a new crop, and cereal prices fall. However, the rate at which livestock populations recover, and prices fall, is much slower, since it depends on the reproductive capacity of the small number of heavily stressed survivors. As a result, animal prices stay high for several years after the drought (the number of years depending on the reproduction rate of the species involved, with sheep and goats recovering faster than cattle or camels), and herders who have lost their herds in the drought are unable to buy back animals rapidly to restart their herding economy. Thus acute food insecurity is prolonged for much longer after a drought for pastoralists than farmers. Since many of the animals sold at low prices during a drought are bought by rich farmers or urban people as an investment, they may not come back into the market in response to higher than normal prices, further reducing supply.

Faced by these sorts of food insecurity, pastoralists' own responses are varied. They include:

- mobilizing social networks which provide access to a wide range of people, some of whom may be less affected by the crisis and are thus able to provide food or animals;

- diversification of species herded and greater spatial mobility as ways of exploiting a wider variety of ecological and economic niches;
- wider economic diversification through wage labour and new income earning opportunities.

The most successful examples of project and programme support to pastoral food security in Africa have supported these pastoral strategies, by protecting the tenure and other conditions which favour mobility and flexibility, which encourage livelihood diversification, and which intervene to protect pastoral terms of trade in a crisis.

URBAN FOOD SECURITY

One side effect of the 1980s' concern with 'urban bias' was an assumption that towns were usually better off in terms of food security than their rural hinterlands. As a result, urban food insecurity was widely ignored until the 1990s (Maxwell 1999). Some features of urban food insecurity, and the strategies followed to manage it, are similar to those of rural food insecurity, but there are also key differences. Since urban people spend such a high proportion of their income on food, urban poverty immediately translates into food insecurity. The main feature of urban food insecurity is vulnerability to changes in food prices and wages.

The main sources of food in towns are the market, own production, and public or private transfers (Ruel et al. 1998). Factors affecting the availability and cost of food therefore include household purchasing power, the efficiency of marketing and distribution systems, the extent of urban agriculture, and access to transfers.

Urban households depend even more than rural ones on purchased food: in Accra, Ghana, for example, 90 per cent of urban households depend on the purchase of food, and spend 60–80 per cent of their income doing so (Maxwell et al. 1998). This makes them vulnerable to price changes and declining terms of trade. Inefficiencies in supply and purchasing patterns among poorer households mean that they often pay higher unit costs for their food than other groups. Because they depend on bought food, income is a key variable determining household food security. As a result, the main strategy of urban households for ensuring food security is to secure an income large and consistent enough to feed the household. Food security is sought through wage labour, including by women and children. But underemployment and low wages in the informal economy constrain the ability of poor households to earn enough income to guarantee food security.

Even where they find employment, poor people may earn and spend daily, and so have to buy small quantities of food often, making it impossible to benefit from low prices for bulk purchase. Women who work have less time to prepare food at home, and may shift to processed or prepared foods, including ready-to-eat street foods. Such foods may be cheap on a per nutrient basis, since producers benefit from economies of scale in purchasing and use unpaid family labour, making a shift towards prepared foods rational from the point of view of consumers. But the supply systems of poor urban households may become more vulnerable because of this shift. Urban households may overcome some of the costs of purchasing food by pooling resources and setting up community kitchens, in effect capturing the economies of scale and low labour costs otherwise benefiting street food sellers. But this implies a capacity for community organization which many small groups of poor people may not have.

Food distribution systems are a significant source of vulnerability for urban consumers. Rural–urban and intra-urban food distribution systems are generally informal. In Harare, women small traders buy from wholesale markets and resell in townships at a small profit: 80–90 per cent of the city's population depends on this supply chain (Leybourne and Grant 1999). But the system depends on good transport, since the produce is fresh, and is vulnerable to police clamp-downs on largely informal transport services.

Buying food is not the only option however. Urban households may also grow part of their own food, or benefit from transfers. Urban farming has long

---

Box 3.2   Urban agriculture in Africa

Burkina Faso	36 per cent of families in Ouagadougou are engaged in horticultural cultivation or livestock breeding activities.
Cameroon	In Yaounde 35 per cent of urban residents are farmers.
Gabon	80 per cent of families in Libreville engage in horticulture.
Kenya	67 per cent of urban families farm on urban and peri-urban sites; 29 per cent of these families farm in the urban areas where they live.
Mozambique	37 per cent of households surveyed in Maputo produce food; 29 per cent raise livestock.
Tanzania	68 per cent of families in six Tanzanian cities engage in farming; 39 per cent raise animals.
Uganda	33 per cent of all households within a five-kilometre radius of the centre of Kampala engage in some form of agricultural activity.
Zambia	A survey of low-income households in Lusaka showed that 45 per cent grow horticultural crops or raise livestock in their backyards or gardens on the periphery of the city.

Source: Streiffeler 2000, p. 171

been ignored, but is now being recognized as significant (see Box 3.2). It is now thought that overall perhaps 40 per cent of African urban dwellers farm to some degree, although this is clearly highly variable between towns (Ruel et al. 1998). In Zambia, almost half of urban dwellers cultivate vegetable gardens (and 40 per cent gather wild plant products, although this is declining as the open land area shrinks); these numbers have increased substantially in the last 20 years (Drescher 1999). The cultivated area in Lusaka has expanded considerably, but the phenomenon may be limited as open spaces are built over, and gardening is pushed to the suburbs and surrounding countryside.

As access to land is essential, urban farming tends not to be done by the poorest families or most recent immigrants. Having no access to land, the poorest only grow food on small public spaces during the rainy season. However, farming is a significant, although usually secondary, source of income for other urban poor people. Most urban farmers are women, and farming generally contributes to household consumption, only occasionally to the market. The lack of secure tenure rights to urban gardens may also mean that farmers make little investment in the land, and farming is therefore of low productivity and sustainability. Urban gardening may pose problems of food quality or safety in some circumstances. On the other hand, urban farming offers the opportunity to recycle urban waste.

Several types of transfer contribute to urban food security. Classic food aid programmes often target rural areas, not towns, although formal food security safety nets may be more accessible in towns. Informal interpersonal transfers, including gifts of food from countryside kin or through urban social networks, may be important. There is often a strong seasonality to these, and their contribution to food security is crucial. Transfers from migrants may be in either direction: rural to urban or vice versa. For many urban people, a return to the rural 'home' remains an option of last resort should life in the town become too precarious.

There are significant qualitative differences between urban and rural diets (Ruel et al. 1998). Urban calorie intakes are often lower than rural ones, but urban diets in general are more diverse. The reason may be a combination of the high cost of traditional staples in towns, the greater range of potential substitutes, and the opportunity costs of women's preparation times.

Urban responses to food insecurity are in many respects similar to those of rural people, although there are some differences (Ruel et al. 1998). As with pastoralists, livelihood diversification is an important strategy. Urban households diversify their sources of food and income through increased own production of food or increased labour force participation (including by children), send out wage labour migrants, substitute cheaper foods, borrow or buy on credit, reduce other expenditures, sell assets, send household members to stay with kin elsewhere, reduce their food intake. Formal and informal safety nets may to some extent substitute for each other, so that a strengthening of formal safety nets may lead to a weakening of informal transfers (see Box 3.3).

Box 3.3   Food security strategies in Africa's cities

Recent research in Ghana and Uganda shows that in the context of economic problems and adjustment policies, urban poverty is widespread in both Accra and Kampala, creating deep-rooted problems of urban food insecurity. Food supplies are decreasing in quantity and quality, and people's access to food is declining as formal sector employment becomes increasingly scarce, wages fall and food prices increase. Formal safety nets are absent or inadequate, reflecting a general lack of political attention to the problem of urban nutritional decline. Poor people have therefore developed their own responses to food insecurity, including:

- direct diversification of income-earning activities into self-employment and informal sector employment;
- bartering and trading, including between urban and rural areas;
- reliance on street foods as an alternative to home cooking;
- urban gardening;
- hoarding of essential goods;
- transfers of food or income through informal and kinship networks;
- borrowing and lending food or money;
- a variety of illicit activities such as black market trading, smuggling, embezzlement and theft.

A survey in Accra in 1996–7 found that 53 per cent of urbanites were dependent on informal and self-employment, while 18 per cent were unemployed. Food costs averaged 55 per cent of all household expenditure. Street foods accounted for 40 per cent of total food expenditure amongst the poorest 25 per cent of people. Though more expensive per nutrient than home cooking, they did not require large outlays on ingredients and were available immediately, freeing household members' time for income-generating activities or job-searching. The survey found that 24 per cent of Accra's households are considered food insecure and a further 40 per cent vulnerable. The most vulnerable groups were:

- low-income wage earners, dependent on their incomes to purchase food;
- the indigenous Ga population, whose traditional farming and fishing livelihood had been eroded by the loss of land and fisheries to urban development;
- the 'new urban poor' of unemployed former civil servants, and;
- households headed by single women.

To cope with this the most common household strategies were:

- substituting preferred foods with cheaper foods;
- purchasing street foods;

- mothers limiting their own food intake in favour of their children's;
- borrowing money from friends or relatives.

A similar study in Kampala found many of the same problems, but no widespread malnutrition in spite of a severe collapse in the urban economy. Whilst in Accra land is extremely scarce, in Kampala it is sufficiently available that around 35 per cent of urban households are able to engage in some form of urban farming. Land access is not secure, and is inevitably better in peri-urban than central areas, but in spite of these limitations urban agriculture was found to make a significant contribution to the food security and nutritional status of urban people. The farming is carried out by women, except in households without adult women, and 95 per cent of the food produced is for household consumption.

Source: Maxwell 1998; Maxwell et al. 1998; Maxwell et al. 2000

URBAN/RURAL FOOD SECURITY LINKS

The relative neglect of urban food security reflects the wider problem of the distinction often made between 'urban' and 'rural', in ways which mean that issues are approached, and solutions applied, differently in each setting. This ignores, first the fact that problems such as food security often have similar sets of causes in urban and rural settings; second that the boundaries between urban and rural are far from clear in most cases, making a comparison between settings difficult. This argument, true for urban/rural issues in general, is particularly relevant to food security.

Spatial and sectoral linkages dominate the interlocking livelihoods of urban and rural areas (Tacoli 1998). The ecological interdependence of town and surrounding countryside underlies all these linkages. Sectoral linkages occur when typically rural or urban activities are pursued in the other setting: for example, agriculture in towns, and non-farm or non-rural diversification activities in rural areas. Spatial linkages are created by migration, which rarely involve a once-and-for-all crossing of the rural–urban frontier by individuals and households; rather, migration in both directions tends to create networks of links between urban and rural areas, and even to generate 'multi-spatial' households spread across both areas, in which decisions may be made in a separate location from the activities which follow them. Spatial linkages also depend on the proximity or remoteness of urban areas and their rural hinterlands. Relationships through markets, services, social networks and economic opportunities are all important, and can be detrimental as well as beneficial to food security.

Whatever the relationship, the nature of issues such as food security cannot be understood in either setting in isolation from each other.

An example from a small town in Zimbabwe illustrates some of these linkages (Kamete 1998). In this area, which has a significant population of rural wage labourers, both urban and rural settings provide occasional jobs, markets, and cheap goods, which are more varied and preferred by the poor of the other setting. Livelihoods are derived from interactions between the town and surrounding countryside. For urban people, the countryside offers:

- cheaper food for consumption or resale;
- cheap natural resources: fish, firewood, sand;
- a market for urban goods, with less competition;
- a market for an informal taxi service to town on pay days or weekends;
- casual or specialized employment, including as contractors.

For rural people on the other hand, the town offers:

- provisions and services more available and at better prices than the farm store, or from hawkers;
- a market for rural goods;
- employment in menial underpaid jobs.

The relationships are largely informal, flexible and sporadic, but mutually very significant for livelihoods and well-being. To some extent, rural people (landless labourers without local social support networks) go to town to guarantee subsistence, while town people go to the countryside to earn an income, but this distinction is subtle.

The examples of urban and pastoral food security show how complex the determinants of food security are, and how varied and flexible the best responses are. To achieve food security, households pursue a wide variety of strategies, many of them not directly related to their primary production activity. Such complexity is not well captured by a narrow focus on one or two aspects of household economy or food security. A broader focus is needed.

WIDENING THE ANALYSIS FROM FOOD TO LIVELIHOOD SECURITY

The sustainable livelihoods approach emerged from a critique of earlier attempts to understand crises in household provisioning and food security. The most influential of these was the 'entitlement' approach, proposed by Amartya Sen (1981) as a way to understand famine. This was a radical departure from previous supply side understandings of famine, highlighting instead problems on the demand side. Thus it was able to go some way towards explaining the differential impacts of famine on different population groups, how famine could occur amidst plenty, how the normal functioning of markets (rather than their failure) could also cause famine, and how extraordinary events may not be necessary to trigger famines or food insecurity. It also offered more entry points for policy interventions, and more meaningful early warning indicators to predict famine. Finally, it included production and non-market entitlements, and not just income/exchange entitlements.

The entitlement framework proved to be a powerful tool in understanding food insecurity and directing attention to policies to remedy it. However, the entitlement approach had a number of weaknesses (Swift 1989a; Devereux 1993a). Entitlements are in real life often less clear than the model supposes. In many cases they may be outside the legal framework adopted by Sen, and 'informal' or 'illegal' entitlements are often precisely those that are most important in times of food security crisis. The model adopts a quite passive view of food insecure households and individuals, giving little prominence to the ingenious and sometimes effective strategies that are adopted.

In terms of understanding entitlement failure, the model places too much emphasis on starvation as a cause of death during extreme food insecurity, ignoring epidemic disease which is often the proximate event causing death, and ignoring long-term accumulated weaknesses which make some people more vulnerable than others. Social capital and social networks – often the key safety nets for individuals and households – are not easily assimilated into an entitlement framework, which is more concerned with formal exchange mechanisms. Entitlements assume a 'food first' mentality among the food insecure, which is not observed in empirical studies; in real life, food insecure people make complex choices about trade-offs between acquiring food, selling and keeping assets, and maintaining some aspects of a valued life style (de Waal 1989; Devereux 1993b). In practice, destitution and starvation may be traded off against each other, rather than being experienced as synonymous. In extreme cases, this has been termed 'choosing to starve', when individuals and households deliberately reduce food intake to dangerously low levels in preference to disposing of an asset essential to post-famine recovery.

Another set of critiques focus on issues insufficiently problematized within the entitlement framework. These include a failure to question intra-household distribution issues (although Sen later adapted the model to meet this concern), and the insufficient attention given to cumulative or time-lagged erosion of entitlements, such as how insecurity may accumulate with successive crises leading to increasing polarization between groups, such that apparently unique crises may in fact be part of a longer-term pattern of events. Finally, although later work (Drèze et al. 1995) dealt more explicitly with political economy issues, and the role of political action at the national level, the entitlement framework itself has difficulty in dealing with the way local political forces determine which groups get access to which entitlements.

These critiques raise many points which the sustainable livelihood approach has since attempted to address: food insecurity is a complex arrangement of vulnerabilities, not just vulnerability to the trigger of a particular event; deprivation is progressive and its impacts accumulate so that historical patterns of change are important; vulnerability depends not only on a given set of entitlements but also on the perceived risk that these will collapse or prove inadequate; and vulnerable people have agency – they adopt complex and rational strategies to avoid destitution.

SUSTAINABLE LIVELIHOODS

A working definition of sustainable livelihoods is:

> *A livelihood comprises the capabilities, assets (including both material and social resources) and activities required for a means of living. A livelihood is sustainable when it can cope with and recover from stresses and shocks, maintain or enhance its capabilities and assets, while not undermining the natural resource base (Scoones 1998, p. 5).*

The sustainable livelihood approach is an analytic framework, which seeks to improve our understanding of how people use the resources at their disposal to construct a livelihood. Although it has mainly been developed in a rural context it can also be used to analyse urban livelihoods. The distinctiveness of the sustainable livelihood approach is the attention it gives to contextual and institutional settings which frame livelihood options, its emphasis on the multiple types of capital available as resources out of which people construct livelihoods, and its understanding of livelihood strategies as multiple and dynamic, constructed by the choices of actors in the light of the resources and constraints which they face.

The livelihood approach allows a wide range of influences to be brought into a single frame of analysis. These are illustrated in Figure 3.3.

This figure may be read as follows: situated in particular *settings* (historical, environmental, policy and other), particular assets or forms of *capital* are accessed by households, and used to construct *livelihood strategies*, which result in positive or negative *outcomes*. The role of *institutions and organizations*, which determine in large part the access of households to resources and strategies, is critical.

Sustainability is a key quality of successful livelihoods. Sustainability means both the ability of the livelihood system to deal with and recover from shocks and stresses, by means of coping (short-term, reversible, responses) or by adaptation (a longer-term change in livelihood strategy), and also the ability of the livelihood system and the natural resources on which it depends to maintain or enhance productivity over time.

A sustainable livelihood approach shows that food security is not just an

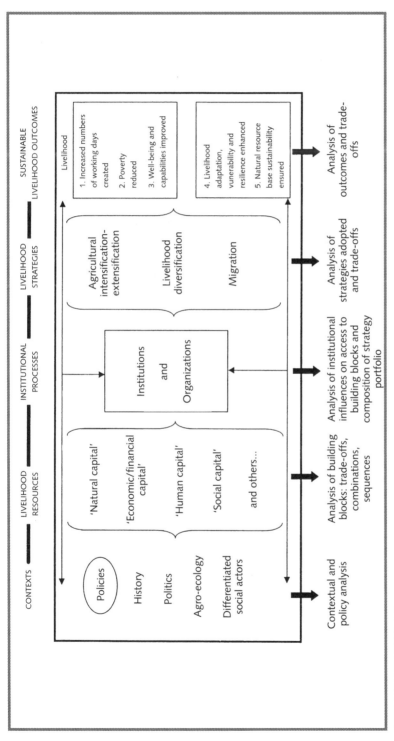

Source: Scoones 1998, p.4

Figure 3.3   The sustainable livelihood approach

issue of productivity, or even the sustainability of production, or of entitlements, but depends on how people, especially poor people, gain access to production and exchange capabilities and to food. This is also true of an entitlement approach, but a sustainable livelihood approach takes a more nuanced view of institutions, how they work and are used by different categories of people, and how they develop over time. Institutions are not seen as given, or as inherently equalizing or exclusive. For example, the precise way in which institutions embody power relations is significant in determining whose food security is guaranteed, and whose is not.

Settings

The settings in which livelihoods are constructed are a crucial part of the analysis (Scoones 1998). Potential important aspects of the context include historical and political factors, current policies, macro-economic conditions, terms of trade, climate, environment, demography and existing patterns of social differentiation. This attention to context arises from a conviction that development and change is path-dependent, that previous events define and limit to some degree the options available for contemporary livelihoods. For example, structural adjustment policies, infrastructural spending changes or administrative decentralization are all likely to alter the range of livelihood options open to different groups. Such influences may widen or narrow the options available; the only general rule is that the specificities and dynamics of the context will inevitably play a role in shaping livelihood choices.

Capitals

Livelihood resources are the various types of capital – the building blocks – available to people and households from which they can fashion a livelihood. They include (Carney 1998):

- *natural capital*, or natural resources including the stocks and flows and environmental services available in particular agroecological settings;
- *financial or economic capital*, including savings and access to credit;
- *physical capital*, including infrastructure and transport;
- *human capital*, including demographic and gender structures, the body of education, skills, knowledge, good health needed to produce effectively;
- *social capital*, including social networks, claims, associations and social relationships more generally, including consensual norms and relationships of legitimate authority.

The capitals become resources for livelihoods as they are put to use, and can sometimes be substituted or traded off against each other, or capitalized on to generate future resources (Johnson 1997). The capital endowments of different groups are thus highly significant in determining the range of livelihood options open to households, and the importance of having capital to generate further capital can often explain much of the observed social differentiation in livelihood strategies.

Institutions

In a livelihood approach, institutional arrangements (understood in the very broad sense of rules and norms which govern individual and group behaviour) and organizational forms play a critical role, since they determine the access of individuals and households to the five types of livelihood resource. Institutions range from customary and local rule systems, determining for example how one group of resource users relates to another in use of pasture or wells on a day-to-day basis, to formal laws and administrative procedures governing the use of forests. Institutions include a range from legal structures to social arrangements backed by moral pressure or sanctions. Such rule systems determine all levels of access to resources, but may be fuzzy: different institutional systems often overlap, creating competing jurisdictions. Individuals and groups manipulate various types of institution and organization to construct their own strategies of resource access. Different institutional arrangements frame access to and use of resources differently for different groups.

Institutions relevant to shaping livelihoods and food security include gender, as institutionalized norms of masculine and feminine behaviour significantly determine the options available to men and women in formulating livelihood strategies. Caste plays a similar role, for instance in restricting access to, and the desirability of, specific production activities for different social groups in an Ethiopian village (Carswell et al. 2000). Various institutions control access to key resources such as land or jobs. Common property arrangements are one type of institutional arrangement regulating the natural capital endowments of individuals and households in particular settings.

Institutions are closely connected to social capital. They may emerge from it, reflect an abundance or a lack of it, or generate particular types of it for particular groups. Institutional functioning often changes over time, in response to contextual changes, or as a result of the adoption of different livelihood strategies which change institutional rules. For example, in Mali and Ethiopia the pursuit of off-farm income, migration, and changed cultivation regimes has led to changed gender norms, family relationships and household structures (Brock and Coulibaly 1999; Carswell et al. 2000).

Institutions are thus not static. Their influence over the distribution of capitals and access to strategies is very significant, not least in how they respond and adapt to changes in the contextual setting, whether dramatic such as drought and a food security crisis, or more measured such as the demographic transition. Institutional sustainability is important. Particular institutional forms, such as community-managed common property regimes, may work successfully under conditions of abundance and equality, but rapidly fail if demand for the resource outstrips supply, or if distribution of power in the community becomes imbalanced (Johnson 1997). The vulnerability of some institutions to such pressures has significant implications for food security, as the breakdown of generally accepted norms and regulations can rapidly exclude the least powerful from what had hitherto been an essential and reliable resource for them. Institutional processes such as these may explain some instances when food security is suddenly threatened, and are an example of where a sustainable livelihood approach has more explanatory or predictive power than others.

Livelihood strategies

In a rural context, households may construct four main categories of livelihood strategy:

- livelihood *intensification*, where the value of output per hectare of land or per animal is increased by the application of more labour, capital or technology;
- livelihood *extensification*, where more land or animals are brought into production at the same levels of labour, capital or technology;
- livelihood *diversification*, where households diversify their economic activities away from reliance on the primary enterprise (livestock or cropping), typically seeking a wider range of on- and off-farm sources of income;
- *migration*, where people move away from their initial source of livelihood, and seek a living in another livelihood system.

Although conceptually it helps to distinguish these strategies from each other, typically households pursue a combination of strategies together or sequentially. Different individuals or social groups may use similar strategies for different reasons. Households may use particular strategies to meet minimum consumption needs in the present, or to achieve ongoing accumulation, corresponding to a distinction between subsistence strategies and livelihood strategies (Davies 1996).

Livelihood strategies are accessible in different ways to different groups of households, using variable combinations of capitals and refracted through the multiplicity of institutions which shape individuals' and households' behaviours. For instance, Brock and Coulibaly (1999) found in two Malian villages that even among similar social groups living in the same agroecological environment, very different strategy combinations were adopted, and different outcomes achieved. Crucial differences hinged on endowments of human capital (gender and age composition of the household), social capital (access to collectively managed resources), and financial capital (level of indebtedness). This differential access has strong associations with class or wealth status, and it is clear that in most cases there are a greater number of strategies open to those with a greater diversity and amount of existing capitals. However livelihood outcomes are not merely a function of capital endowment, even in this broad sense of capital; the range of choices available, and the way they are traded off against one another, depend on very specific local and even personal factors which cannot be generalized.

At the same time, contextual influences far outside the control of individuals or communities, and equally applicable to (although not necessarily having the same impact on) all of them, are also significant determinants of the strategies available. Agroecological setting and climate history are clearly vital. So are national and international influences such as structural adjustment packages and changes in the discourse driving development (for example, new rhetorics about 'gender', 'participation', or 'community management' of natural resources), which alter the resources available and practices which are likely to be supported. Meso-level factors such as the position of a village in relation to communications infrastructure will also influence the decisions households can take and their range of choices.

The level at which livelihood strategies are adopted – individuals, nuclear households, whole extended households, wider economic or social groupings – is also important. In Mali, where study households had 35 people or more, sub-groups within the extended household corresponding to nuclear households co-operated in pursuit of particular livelihood strategies (Brock and Coulibaly 1999), while in Ethiopia, where nuclear households of around six people were the norm, inter-household co-operation was much more common (Carswell et al. 2000). Benefits from particular strategies also accrue at different levels, depending on broad social norms and on internal management within the household.

Livelihood diversification

From the point of view of food security, livelihood diversification is the most important strategy, and is considered in greater detail here.

Livelihood diversification is 'the process by which rural families construct a diverse portfolio of activities and social support capabilities in their struggle for survival and in order to improve their standards of living' (Ellis 1998). The addition of social support capabilities broadens the definition from simple income diversification, although the latter is important.

The diversification pathways open to households or individuals depend on the contextual setting, the capitals required and available, and the ways in which institutional arrangements restrict or encourage certain behaviours. Diversification may be an indication of increased vulnerability, where it is a response to the failure of previous livelihood strategies, or it may be the path to accumulation and investment in the future, leading to a cumulative improvement in livelihood outcomes over time. While diversification is often economically sensible regardless of risk minimization objectives, even the fact that a household might be capable of diversifying its activities is a form of security which might affect actual livelihood strategies pursued (Ellis 1999). What diversification signifies, and whether it leads to more or less sustainable outcomes, can only be discerned from a detailed analysis of particular cases, and even there activities might affect different members of the same family in different ways, benefiting some and disadvantaging others.

Diversification implies a change away from existing patterns of activity, and so diversification is not only the path to a new livelihood outcome, but may also be the agent of social and cultural change. Diversification may alter institutional arrangements, although it may also be channelled through existing institutional arrangements. For example, diversification may be as likely to trap women in customary roles as to change them (Ellis 1999).

It is generally true that the poorest have fewest livelihood options, and that these are least likely to provide sustainable or secure outcomes. Thus livelihood diversification is least available to the poor. This is due to inadequate endowments of all forms of capital, including the forms of human capital (especially education) which would enable them to take up new opportunities, or the social networks which create opportunities. The poor often face greater institutional restrictions, through the lack of self-organization or institutionalized constraints to access to livelihood resources (Swift 1998). Institutional arrangements which cross-cut wealth status may be significant, both in a positive sense where rich members of a social or kin group help poor members of the same group, and negative, when women, elderly or disabled people of any given wealth status may have more restricted choices than others. Human and social capital are particularly important to diversification, as is infrastructure (Ellis 1999). Its differential impact will also depend on factors such as women's asset status, and the availability of poor-friendly credit. Precise capital requirements will depend on the diversification activity pursued, and will be structured by relevant institutions (Carswell et al. 2000).

Livelihood diversification is widespread in Africa. Non-farm income is the source of perhaps 30 to 50 per cent of household income in rural sub-Saharan Africa as a whole, and 80 to 90 per cent in southern Africa (Ellis 1999). Much of this is not only non-farm, but also non-rural. The scale of this has led some observers to argue that diversification is less a means to a sustainable rural livelihood than a process of 'depeasantization', a long-term trend away from agriculture (Bryceson 1999). In this view, livelihood diversification is part of the erosion of an agrarian way of life that combines subsistence and commodity production with an internal social organization based on family labour and village community settlement. If such a change is underway, the sustainability of rural livelihoods is questionable in the longer run. Already the generation gap appearing in many African rural societies suggests that the future is not seen as based around agriculture, whether or not livelihood diversification takes place as a buffer against risk and variability, or as a mechanism of accumulation (see Box 3.4).

Box 3.4   Rural livelihood diversification in Mali

Recent research in two Malian villages reveals the complexity and diversity of rural livelihood strategies in Africa. In both villages the primary source of income is agricultural production for consumption and sale, to which most household labour and capital are dedicated. However, income diversification is almost universally pursued, in order to increase and protect household income and security. The most important diversification strategies are:

● migration for paid employment;
● ownership of plantations in Côte d'Ivoire;
● investment in facilities for processing or trading agricultural products;
● off-farm activities such as spinning and weaving.

Levels of dependency on these activities as a proportion of household income vary widely between households according to the security of their agricultural income. The range of diversified activities pursued also varies between households, depending on access to the resources needed to pursue any one strategy. For example:

● migration of some household members is easiest in large households with sufficient members of appropriate ages, skills and gender for different types of work;
● maintenance of distant plantations is likewise dependent on the household comprising sufficient members to maintain activities at home as well as in the plantations;
● processing and trading require inputs of valuable capital and labour, and are therefore options mainly open to larger, relatively well-off households;
● off-farm activities such as spinning and weaving are carried out by specific age and gender groups and by habitually skilled artisans, and are unlikely to be taken up by individuals outside these groups.

Depending on the structure of the household, the activities pursued, and the levels of need at different times, the benefits of diversified activities accrue variously to individuals or the whole household. The same strategy pursued in different households in some cases increases overall household security, while in others it benefits particular individuals or subgroups within the household, often altering intra-household relationships and changing the household's structure. There is a notable gender dimension to this, with women's diversified production or revenue-earning being more frequently directed to whole-household security.

One exception to this is young women who accrue income specifically to build up their own *trousseau* in preparation for marriage. Marriage itself is seen as a strategy for security, as households' linkages are extended to other households, widening networks of reciprocation and support. This is important because customary law and social linkages were found to be very significant in determining households' access to resources, which are used to pursue their own livelihood security.

The two villages have much in common, including both being subject to Government policies such as decentralization, land tenure regulation and currency valuation. However there are also some key differences: one village had been subject to extensive Government cotton production programmes, while the other had not. In the first village ownership of distant plantations was common, while in the second it was not a feature at all. These factors, along with agro-ecological and social differences, underlie what were found to be quite different patterns of diversification activity and behaviour to ensure livelihood security, in the context of the same macro-level influences.

Source: Brock and Coulibaly 1999

SUSTAINABLE LIVELIHOODS AND FOOD SECURITY

'Food security is a sub-system of needs, neither independent of nor necessarily more important than other aspects of subsistence and survival within poor households' (Davies 1996, p. 18). The reasons some households are food insecure are rooted in the ways entire livelihood systems have changed and adapted, or failed to adapt, to challenges from the ecological and economic environment, including shocks such as drought. Food security is thus usefully seen as one important element of a sustainable livelihood.

A sustainable livelihood approach has many advantages (Farrington et al. 1999). A concern for livelihoods draws on broader notions of poverty. It builds on advances in a wide variety of specific fields of enquiry – intra-household issues, gender, farming systems, governance and others – and provides a framework within which they can be related to one another. It is people-focused, multi-sectoral, and considers multiple actors. It identifies constraints. It links macro- and micro-level factors, showing how they interact. It shows how informal institutions often fit situations better than formal ones and hence are preferred by the main actors. More generally it puts institutions at the centre of livelihoods, and shows how individuals and households are facilitated or constrained in their efforts to construct sustainable livelihoods by institutional arrangements.

Livelihood approaches recognize the significance of assets in determining the food security status of households (Swift 1989a). Assets may be material (such as savings, livestock or jewellery) or immaterial (such as social capital, education or commercial networks), and are not readily assimilated into a conventional food security approach more concerned with production success or terms of trade.

More generally, the sustainable livelihood approach is credited with exposing and unravelling the complexity of rural livelihoods, in the face of development policies which have tended to focus on specific resources or service provision structures, rather than on the people who are to benefit (Carney 1999). In providing a complex picture, it gives a truer impression of rural life and poverty, for instance by showing that strategies such as diversification and migration are rational livelihood strategies, rather than new and desperate phenomena.

These strengths make it a useful framework within which to analyse food security.

A sustainable livelihood approach also has a number of weaknesses, however. Some of its less tangible aspects, such as livelihood security, which is in large part about perceptions but which drives behaviours and practice, are difficult to measure. The approach has so far been good at identifying problems, but less good at finding solutions. A sustainable livelihood approach, like food security itself, is also sometimes difficult to implement in a development context which is still sectorally organized.

The approach has little to say about distributional issues, despite an implicit concern for the poorest. Distributional issues are implicit in the focus on the way institutions frame access to resources, but are not perhaps explicit enough. If, as its proponents claim, the great advantage of a sustainable livelihood approach is that it forces the analyst to ask questions which might otherwise be missed, ways must be found to ensure that issues like distribution necessarily come to the fore in any analysis.

A feature of the sustainable livelihood approach is the way it places current events in their dynamic context, rather than looking at a 'snapshot' of a situation at a single moment in time. This has an impact on the analysis and conclusions at many levels. It brings in the new dynamic understandings of ecology and environment, especially the non-equilibrium processes which create the risks and shocks in the drier areas which most threaten food security. Dynamism is also built into the historicized approach that sustainable livelihoods adopts, seeing current situations as outcomes of past changes. The iterative processes of adaptation and reworking by which households construct their livelihoods are recognized as normal and rational, potentially a sign as much of vitality as of crisis.

However, a focus on dynamism at the local level could lead to wider trends being missed. There is perhaps, as Bryceson (1999) has argued, a danger that the sustainable livelihoods approach's narrow focus on household welfare, and the central place still given to agriculture, means that long-term processes outside this focus are missed: the livelihoods approach ignores a bigger development perspective in which African peasant agriculture is no longer viable, the relevant policy shifts to be made being outside agriculture completely.

CONCLUSION

A livelihood approach situates food needs within a wider set of needs driving people's actions, and within a set of influences, possibilities and constraints which go beyond the 'food first' mentality of much of the food security literature. Food security remains a distinctive concern which it may sometimes be necessary to identify separately from other concerns, and a focus on poor people's access to food should remain central to the analysis. But a wider sustainable livelihood approach can offer a framework within which to understand food security outcomes and behaviour more comprehensively. Within a sustainable livelihood framework, food security is less likely to be treated either as an isolated, or alternatively the only, concern, or to be measured with overly simplistic indicators.

A sustainable livelihood approach may also raise food security as an issue in settings where other approaches would assume that, due to sufficient income or adequate aggregate food production, it was not important. By investigating the complex processes influencing individuals' and households' actions, a livelihood approach is able to identify where populations may be risking their own food security, for example by becoming heavily dependent on vulnerable markets, or where particular groups are unable to maintain food security because of specific asset shortages, institutional restrictions or problems accumulated over time (for example debt, illness, soil exhaustion). A sustainable livelihood approach may reveal hidden vulnerabilities.

CHAPTER FOUR

Food Security and the Environment

Susanna Moorehead and William Wolmer

GONE ARE THE days when food security could be considered independently of the environment. Since the late 1980s, the importance of sustainable agricultural development has been recognized. This shift is in tune with food-insecure people, who do not draw a sharp distinction between feeding their families today and ensuring – to the extent possible – that they will be able to do so in the future. But much of the debate around food security and environment linkages, often tied to concerns about population growth and climate change, has been artificially polarized between two questionable extremes:

- that population growth, climate change and environmental degradation constitute unprecedented challenges to world food security; or
- that population and income growth will drive technological change so as to remove the food production constraints and reach an economically and environmentally sustainable growth path (Norse 1994).

Although the existence of key linkages between food security and the environment is now widely accepted, the nature of this relationship is much contested. There are two opposing factions:

- those who see food security and the environment as being essentially complementary, based on the interdependence between food security and a healthy natural resource base, which promotes mutually reinforcing practices; and
- those who regard them as being in conflict, because the pursuit of food security entails inevitable costs to the environment and environmental protection policies can adversely affect food security (Davies and Leach 1991a, p. 1).

Policy makers have tended to ignore these conflicts and complementarities. A brief history of planning for food security and environmental issues suggests a policy agenda see-sawing between food security and the environment. In colonial times, preservationist environmental policies predominated, epitomized by game parks. After independence, neither production-led nor entitlement-based approaches to food security paid much attention to environmental concerns. In the 1980s, environmental issues returned strongly to the developmental agenda. It is only since the late 1980s, with the ascendance of the idea of sustainable development, that food security and the environment have been considered seriously as two sides of the same coin. Both the World Conservation Strategy (IUCN 1987) and the World Commission on Environment and Development (WCED 1987) argued that if environmental protection was to succeed, it had to take account of those people who depended directly on the environment for their livelihoods. This conceptualization leads directly to the idea of sustainable livelihoods, implicit in which is people's capacity to meet food security needs without compromising that of future generations to do so – that is, without degrading the natural resource base.

But this apparently simple idea belies a number of problematic themes interwoven throughout the relationship between food security and the environment. Some of these are familiar territory for analysts of food security, even though they have rather different implications in the context of the environment. The most important are:

- the meaning of sustainable development;
- levels of analysis and interactions between them;
- analysis of change, especially of shocks and trends; and
- vulnerability and security.

We consider each of these in turn in the next section.

There are also links between the environment and nutrition. People in different environments respond in varied ways to energy stress depending on household structure, ecological setting, stage of development and cultural traditions. Understanding the strategies that people adopt in order to resist and tolerate malnutrition – be they physiological, biochemical, or behavioural – is crucial to understanding the links between people and their environment. The coping mechanisms that enable people to tolerate and adapt to long-term climatic cycles are of necessity different from people's reactions to short-term food security shocks. Longer-term nutritional adaptation can take the form of redeployment of the deposits of muscle and body fat, for example; while short-term shocks, such as seasonal fluctuations in food prices, are met by changing behavioural patterns (for example, by the trading of high protein food to acquire cheaper calories), or by changing consumption patterns.[1]

CONCEPTS AND DEFINITIONS

SUSTAINABLE DEVELOPMENT

Initially, sustainable development focused on environmental sustainability and was concerned with preservation or enhancement of the productive resource base, particularly for future generations (Chambers and Conway

1992, p. 12). It is now recognized that there is little to be gained from singling out environmental sustainability from the web of conflicting and overlapping development challenges. Consequently, sustainable development is increasingly concerned with how trade-offs are made optimally between environmental sustainability and economic and social sustainability, of which food security is an elemental part.

The idea of sustainable development encapsulates the reduction of vulnerability, poverty and welfare issues, social justice, and environmental protection, as well as economic growth and equitable distribution of its gains. In recent years, the more nuanced concept of sustainable livelihoods has been used. This emphasizes the dynamic and constantly changing local-level interactions between how people achieve food security (and other basic needs) and their natural environment (see Chapter 3; Scoones 1998; Carney 1999).

LEVELS OF ANALYSIS

Analyses of food security are conducted at household, national or global levels. Environmental sustainability has been concerned with local and global levels of analysis:

- At the local level:

  the question ... is whether livelihood activities maintain and enhance, or deplete and degrade, the local natural resource base. This is the familiar focus on visible aspects of sustainability. On the negative side, livelihood activities may contribute to desertification, deforestation, soil erosion, declining water tables, salinisation and the like. On the positive side, livelihood activities can improve productivity of renewable resources like air and river water, soil, organic soil fertility, and trees.

- At the global level:

  the question ... is whether, environmentally, livelihood activities make a net positive or negative contribution to the long-term environmental sustainability of other livelihoods. This is the now familiar, but less visible, focus on issues such as pollution, greenhouse gases and global warming, the ozone layer, the irreversible use of the world's store of non-renewable resources, and the use of sinks (such as the sea for carbon dioxide) for pollution emissions.[2]

In this chapter, our main focus is on the local level and the implications for national-level policy, although some of the consequences for food security of global climate change and the biotechnology revolution are considered in Boxes 4.1 and 4.6.[3] Despite recognition of the need to link these levels of analysis, failure to do so remains a characteristic of much food security thinking and practice. The same is true on the environmental side of the debate, although links between micro- and macro-levels have been examined in the context of sustainable agriculture.[4] Even though inextricable connections between food security and the environment at local level are now widely accepted, the two continue to be treated separately in much national and international debate.

Box 4.1   Food security and climate change

Three aspects of projected climate change have the potential to affect agriculture:

- the direct effects of increased concentrations of carbon dioxide;
- the effects of altered weather; and
- secondary effects of climate change on social and economic systems.

Climate change will have the effect of 'shifting' agro-climatic zones. The length of the growing season is likely to change due to a combination of temperature and precipitation changes. In Nairobi, Kenya, for example, a 10 per cent decrease in the length of the growing period would result from either a 1°C increase in temperature or a 10 per cent decrease in precipitation. The spatial shifts entailed by a 10 per cent shorter growing period would mean that the threshold of reliable agriculture ... would move well into the Kenyan highlands. The lowland ranching zone would expand and the tea/dairy zone might disappear as conditions become more amenable to coffee growing. Such an outcome would have drastic consequences for the agricultural economy of Kenya. However, this static analysis does not take account of crop-specific sensitivities to warming and adjustment over time; or of human adjustment. ...

Perhaps the most important question is: *will world food production be able to keep up with both population growth and adverse effects on potential crop yields?* Initial findings suggest that global food production can be maintained at levels that would occur without the effects of climate change, albeit at different prices. Second, the world food system's modelled response does not suggest that the distribution of hunger will change as a result of climate modifications. Adequate food may be produced at the global scale, but significant populations will remain unable to satisfy their nutritional requirements. ... Few studies have asked the more fundamental question: *what is the future of hunger in light of potential climate change?* To a great extent, the ultimate effects of climate change on agriculture and hunger will depend on the effectiveness of adaptive responses on several scales. ... The central questions that remain to be answered are: *what long-term approaches should be developed to maintain adequate adaptive mechanisms and what are the constraints on their adoption?*

Source: Downing 1991

CHANGE: SHOCKS AND TRENDS

Analysing change and its impact on food insecure people and the places in which they live is central to understanding how food security/environment linkages interact and which kind of policy prescriptions will enhance complementarities and reduce conflicts. Like food insecurity, the decline towards environmental insecurity is comprised of short-term shocks (influences of short duration and high intensity) and long-term trends (influences of long duration and low intensity). The sustainability of an agroecosystem has been defined in terms of its ability to maintain productivity in the face of shocks or stress, and the concepts of resilience and sensitivity, now applied to livelihood systems, were originally developed in the context of land degradation (Blaikie and Brookfield 1987; Conway and Barbier 1990). Figure 4.1 illustrates this. The most vulnerable (or hazardous) systems are those which are highly sensitive to shocks and which have low resilience (i.e. find it hard to bounce back). Shocks and trends are useful in analysing food security/environment linkages, especially when applied to particular livelihood systems, the sustainability of which can be assessed according to their sensitivity and resilience to particular shocks and trends.

Shocks and trends occur at different levels and may, but do not necessarily, affect all levels simultaneously. They can change either food security

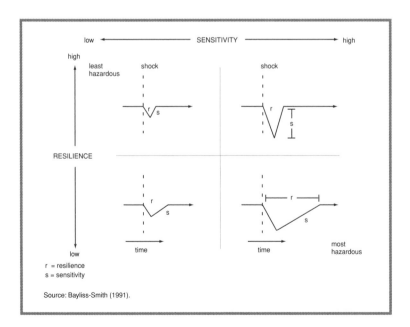

Figure 4.1   Sensitivity of environments and food supply systems

or the environment, or both. If only one is affected, there may be indirect repercussions on the other. Negative trends increase vulnerability to shocks and shocks can intensify trends. Drought is a shock affecting both food security and the environment. A local flood directly affects the environment and food security in the immediate vicinity, but will have only indirect consequences for other levels. A sudden increase in input prices directly affects food security, and will possibly have indirect consequences for the environment if it triggers a change in farming practices. Soil degradation is a trend affecting both food security and the environment, at local and national levels. Increasing pressure on land also affects both, but the extent to which it does so across different levels will depend on overall land/population ratios and tenure arrangements. Declining terms of trade between sold and purchased goods is a trend directly affecting food security at all levels, but has only indirect consequences for the environment (e.g. via eventual changes in crop mixes) (Davies et al. 1991, pp. 27–8).

VULNERABILITY AND SECURITY

Groups particularly vulnerable to shocks, but also least able to cope with adverse long-term trends, have received less attention in the environmental literature than in work on food security. Environmental vulnerability is not automatically so closely correlated with poverty as food vulnerability is, although there is growing recognition of the causalities between the two:

> environmental hazards (such as drought) act on entitlements to reduce the resource base of those who rely on land and water as part of their productive assets, and indirectly for those who rely on the purchase of food at prices which give adequate nutrition on their normal wages or through other exchange entitlements. So environmental changes can also lead to increased vulnerability for some by generating shifts in their entitlements. In this sense, the environment must be seen as integral to food systems, and not as something external and outside them (Cannon 1991, p. 306).[5]

In most cases, vulnerability to short-term shocks is a result of poverty induced by adverse long-term trends. A farmer who has not produced a surplus for many years because of declining soil fertility and who has been unable to invest in drought resistant crops is more vulnerable to drought than a diversified and richer neighbour who has been able to benefit from off-farm income in addition to a production surplus. There is also a synergistic ratchet effect between environmental and food vulnerability: poor land quality leads to lower yields; insufficient food necessitates greater exploitation of land or allows less time to invest in soil-enhancing techniques as income must be earned off-farm; and this further reduces soil quality.

The need to assess the differential impact of environmental change on various social groups is recognized, as is the importance of different social actors in the way natural resources are used and managed (see Box 4.3). Invariably, it is the same people who are food insecure and vulnerable to the effects of environmental degradation. In rural areas they typically include marginal and undiversified resource-poor farmers, female-headed households, landless labourers, pastoralists and displaced people. But the particular manifestation of this double insecurity varies between groups. Pastoralists are vulnerable to declining pasture availability, which reduces milk yields and hence food security. Landless labourers will be affected by the falling demand for casual labour resulting from declining yields. Female-headed households may be especially vulnerable to environmental insecurity if labour constraints prevent them from using anti-erosive farming practices, which will lead to declining food production. It is essential to map out the different impacts of food and environmental vulnerability on different social actors. Failure to do so can lead to policy prescriptions which disproportionately disadvantage these groups.

THEORIES ON THE FOOD SECURITY – ENVIRONMENT RELATIONSHIP

CONFLICTS BETWEEN FOOD SECURITY AND THE ENVIRONMENT

Neo-Malthusianism

Conventional wisdom about the relationship between the environment and food security is that as population pressure increases, people degrade their environment in order to maintain food security. This inexorably leads to a spiral of land degradation, declining productivity and greater food insecurity, culminating in the Malthusian spectre of the world's population literally running out of food (see Chapter 5 and Cohen 1995). Neo-Malthusian debates are infused with a sense of inevitability and catharsis, of the world in general – and the poor in particular – hurtling towards a future in which the world will be unable to feed itself unless drastic measures are taken to prevent people from destroying the natural resources on which they depend. The combination of apparent southern ignorance and northern greed makes for a powerful cocktail.

Some versions of this logic argue that people purposively mismanage their environment for short-term gain, unconcerned with the longer-term effects of their actions and their implications for future generations. Over-intensive or abusive agriculture is the main reason for a range of deleterious impacts on the environment, including land degradation, water scarcity and contamination and pesticide pollution. Other views are more nuanced and emphasize the impossibility of environmentally sound natural resource management under conditions of high population growth, scarce resources and the absence of alternatives to subsistence agriculture. Elsewhere, tenure systems, especially common property regimes, are regarded as inevitably creating the conditions under which resources will be over-used and degraded, elaborated in the 'tragedy of the commons' thesis (Hardin 1968).

Conscious policy decisions to shift to large-scale cultivation to enhance food production can have similar effects. In the case of Sudan, for example, shifting to large-scale mechanized agriculture in the buffer zone between semi-arid lands and savanna to produce food for export has displaced farmers, taken away safety-net lands used in times of drought and disrupted pastoral migration routes, leading to increased degradation in marginal semi-arid lands. Large-scale farmers have benefited at the expense of the poor, but all are living in conditions of increased environmental insecurity (Lado 1993). Even in the much more naturally fertile case of Uganda, it is argued that rising population density and fragmentation of land holdings have led to deforestation and swamp clearance, resulting in erosion, declining soil fertility and falling ground water levels (Mwaka 1991).

Neo-Malthusianism offers the clearest and simplest link between food security and the environment. The data on which such scenarios are based, however, are the subject of heated debate. Few contest that the world's population will continue to rise, although the rate and distribution of that growth is disputed. In general, the world's most poorly nourished populations are growing the fastest (Dyson 1994, Box 4.2). The situation in sub-Saharan Africa is especially alarming, where *per capita* food production has declined by 25 per cent over the past thirty years, compared with developing countries as a whole where it has remained stable (Figure 4.2). There is

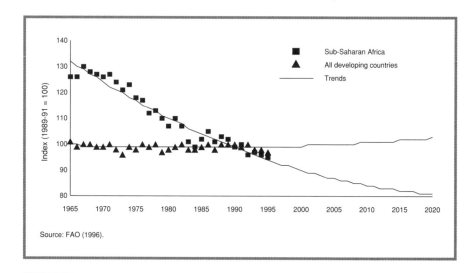

Source: FAO (1996).

Figure 4.2   Food production *per capita* 1965–95

Box 4.2   Population growth and food production: global and regional trends

Few ideas generate more alarm than the prospect that the world may run out of food. Several writers of a neo-Malthusian persuasion have recently expressed serious doubts as to whether in the near future humanity will be able to expand food production to keep up with population growth. ...

Per capita food production during the last decade has increased substantially, and faster than in earlier periods, largely due to progress in Asia. ... Rapid population growth is certainly an important factor behind the contemporary problem of human hunger, but world population growth does not appear to be outpacing food production. ...

Global *per capita* cereal output today is lower than it was around 1984. But if the analysis is conducted below the global level, then the fundamental influence of exceptionally low world cereal prices on production trends in key countries and regions becomes immediately clear. Of the major world regions North America, Oceania and Latin America experienced by far the greatest reductions in *per capita* cereal production during the last decade. Sub-Saharan Africa also experienced a reduction, and there is little doubt that rapid demographic growth has contributed to this region's poor production record. ... In other world regions, containing the large majority of the world's population, levels of *per capita* cereal production were higher in 1987–92 than in 1981–6. ...

But there is no reason for complacency. ... Contemporary world hunger is an immense problem, closely linked to poverty. Several hundred million people do not have reliable access to adequate supplies of food. In the next few decades world food demand will greatly increase, mainly due to population growth. And some poor countries will probably experience mounting difficulties in obtaining sufficient food. But, since the past is still the main base from which to assess the future, it is important to read it with care. In particular, in the last decade world food production has not declined relative to population growth. There has been no abrupt reversal in food production per head, and in this light neo-Malthusian forecasts – for example that global *per capita* food production may fall by 8 per cent during the current decade or that huge famines are both inevitable and imminent – derive little support from recent trends.

Source: Dyson 1994

little consensus on the future of world food supply or on the distribution of supply and demand.

Trade-offs between food security and the environment

A less pejorative view of local communities and their knowledge systems is articulated by those who argue that, although interrelated, strategies to promote either food security or environmental sustainability are often mutually conflicting. Here, the focus is on 'coping strategies' and 'adaptive management' rather than the neo-Malthusian themes of 'irrational' and 'wasteful' land mismanagement in the face of overpopulation. Most common is the contention that poor people are forced to degrade their environment in order to cope with food insecurity.

Conversely, environmental protection can entail food security costs. In Zambia, for example, extending cultivation onto marginal land may increase food production in the short term, but is likely to accelerate land degradation through increased soil loss. Taking marginal land out of production will probably exacerbate short-term food insecurity in areas of high population density. The complementarity of environmental sustainability and food security cannot be taken for granted, and may pose problems for development initiatives that target both as priorities (Drinkwater and McEwan 1994, p. 112) (Box 4.3).

These trade-offs intensify when drought or other shocks hit, and poor farmers must choose between immediate subsistence and longer-term sustainability:

> when the viability of the household as a productive and reproductive unit is threatened by food shortage, farmers often must employ strategies that increase immediate income sources and subsistence levels, but that have detrimental consequences for the natural environment (Frankenberger and Goldstein 1990, p. 21).

Coping strategies which have particularly deleterious effects on the environment include abusive tree-cutting to make charcoal, over-harvesting of wild foods, over-grazing of grasslands and increased planting in marginal areas, all of which degrade soil conditions and augment problems of soil erosion. They may be especially damaging to common property resources, as pressure on them intensifies. People are often aware of the consequences of their actions for the environment and for the future sustainability of their own livelihoods, but have no alternative but to adopt short-term solutions to survive. Poor rural people will seek to maintain their future productive capacity when trying to cope with drought and the threat of famine, but if the choice is between selling remaining livestock or abusive tree-felling, they are likely to hold onto the few remaining private assets they have and cut the trees.

The distinction between food security and environmental degradation is not clear-cut to poor rural people. Common to local people's experiences is

Box 4.3 Trade-offs between food security and the environment: the impact of maize on food security and environmental sustainability in Zambia

Farmers in Zambia grow maize because it significantly increases their entitlement expectations, compared with alternative staple crops. ... This does not mean that maize has had a universally beneficial impact on food security or environmental sustainability in Zambia.

Farmers describe their soils as exhausted or finished, demonstrated by declining yields and deteriorating food security. ... Four principal causes of land degradation were identified: continuous cultivation; soil erosion; monocropping; and fertilizer use. ...

Farmers in the Katete district of Eastern Province employ a range of coping strategies, many of which entail crucial trade-offs between the attainment of short-term, staple-food security and the longer-term sustainability of agricultural production. Short-term strategies include: exchanging labour for food, jeopardizing farmers' own field operations; the sale or barter of bananas, firewood, goats and chickens for mealie meal; reductions in meal frequency affecting labour productivity and children's health; and increasing the cultivated area, thereby decreasing fallow time and increasing conflict over resource use. Nevertheless, farmers employ, or consider, other strategies that may have a positive impact on soil fertility and yields, including: fallowing and rotation; ... growing non-fertilized crops to increase rotation; ... and maintaining traditional crop residue gathering, composting or burning practices which improve soil fertility.

The Zambian Adaptive Research Planning team, part of the Zambian Ministry of Agriculture, Food and Fisheries, has identified a number of food security issues which are now incorporated into the identification of possible technologies to be tested.

● Over-dependence on one staple is a risky food security strategy and contributes to declining soil fertility. The potential to expand production of complementary staples (e.g., cassava, sorghum) needs to be assessed.
● Diversifying the range of crops would benefit people's diets and incomes, as well as soil fertility. Of particular importance is growing more crops, especially those that could fill the gap in vegetable protein between October and February.
● The introduction of an improved fallow system, possibly through the use of agro-forestry species or green manuring techniques, could improve food security and nutrition by providing fuelwood, fodder and additional biomass for composting techniques.
● Dambo cultivation could be expanded, although technologies such as live

> fencing would have to be explored to ensure that households could utilize the dambos without fear of livestock depredations.
>
> This case study highlights two issues: first, the need to sequence interventions to ensure that farmers not only meet short-term food security needs but also consider longer-term measures to improve soil fertility; and second, that national food security goals can have a detrimental effect on household food security, and by extension on the long-term sustainability of national food supplies.

Source: Drinkwater and McEwan 1994, pp. 18–20

that environmental degradation invariably means reduced household production or income, and hence directly affects access to food. There are various reasons why the distinction between food insecurity and the environment does not exist for poor rural people:

- Degradation of the resource base on which food production depends has negative effects on food security. For cultivators this may be soil degradation or worsening climatic conditions; for pastoralists the degradation of grazing lands threatens local livelihoods; while the food security of fishing communities is threatened if pollution, pesticides or over-fishing degrade local fisheries.
- Common property resources are important to food security, particularly in times of stress. Wild leaves, roots, grains, bushmeat and minor forest products provide regular additional flows of food, buffers to seasonal shortages and occasional famine foods, either directly or by yielding items which can be sold. They also provide inputs into income-generating activities such as fuelwood sales. Poor people rely especially heavily on common property resources and their degradation and loss through the encroachment of agriculture into former common property areas disproportionately affects the food security of the poor.
- Rural people's reliance on biomass energy allows for further links between natural resource degradation and access to food. Fuel sufficiency is crucial to food security. Numerous studies from many parts of the world have shown that a shortage of biomass can encourage a shift to foods which require less fuel for cooking but are of a lower nutritional level. Shortages of fuelwood (and of other essential tree products, such as fodder) tend also to be associated with an increase in the time women must spend collecting them. This can compromise food production by removing women's labour from agriculture. Fuelwood shortages can also encourage households to switch to alternative fuels, such as dung and crop residues, which might otherwise have been used to maintain soil fertility (Davies et al. 1991, pp. 19–20).

COMPLEMENTARITIES BETWEEN FOOD SECURITY AND THE ENVIRONMENT

Political ecology

Political ecology refers to a body of literature that combines the conventional concerns of ecology with political economy, seeking to integrate physical and ecological elements with social, economic and political processes. In direct contradiction to neo-Malthusianism, environmental problems in the developing world are viewed as social, economic and political constructs. They are to do with how people use natural resources according to local social relations, with social action and political and economic constraints; and not with mismanagement, ignorance or overpopulation. Consequently:

> a social perspective on the environment, as opposed to one based purely on ecology or technology, shows that the issues of resource degradation and regeneration are intimately linked to questions of power, institutions, livelihood and culture (Ghai 1994, p. 9).[6]

Hunger and famine in marginal lands are best explained not by the limits that the environment sets for human activity, but by changes in economic, political and social systems which affect entitlements to food and other resources (Cannon 1991). This echoes the Boserupian argument that when faced with a land crunch and growing demand for food, farmers adopt intensification techniques which saturate land with more labour, both to make permanent land improvements and to raise output by more frequent cultivation and more careful husbandry.

Few would contest the significant shift in thinking about people/environment linkages that political ecology has brought about:

> collectively this body of work has punched a huge hole in the pressure-of-population-on-resources view, and the market distortion or mismanagement explanation of degradation. In their place it has affirmed the centrality of poverty as a major cause of ecological deterioration (Peet and Watts 1996, p. 7).

Incentive structures, security of tenure, property relations and institutional mechanisms all determine the ways in which people use natural resources to achieve food security. One important dimension is recognition of the gendered nature of environmental issues. Women, as managers of natural resources, have a key influence on the quality of the environment. Rights of access to and control over natural resources tend to be highly gendered, with women invariably having fewer or weaker rights than men. Women and girls are also affected in gender-specific ways by resource degradation: directly because of declining yields in agriculture and livestock; and indirectly through increased workloads in fetching water and fuelwood (Ghai 1994, p. 5). This resonates with similar concerns about the gendered nature of food insecurity.

But political ecology tells only part of the story, given its focus on poor rural societies. In the context of food security, this emphasis is less problematic than in some others. Recently, the call has been made to transform political ecology into a more politically radical and liberation ecology 'the intention is not simply to *add* politics to political ecology, but to raise the emancipatory potential of environmental ideas' (Peet and Watts 1996, p. 37) and to tackle accounts of environment and development from the perspective of the overall contradictory character of relations between societies and natural environments.

Environmental myths   Overturning 'received wisdoms', 'myths', 'orthodoxies' or 'narratives' about environmental degradation and the tendency for poor people to abuse the environment has been the subject of a related area of research. This contends that the threat of desertification has often been over-emphasized, as has that of deforestation and soil erosion.[7] The contemporary agricultural and pastoral landscape has been shaped by a long history of intervention by farmers and herders as well as by the state. There is a tendency to misread environmental history in order to justify neo-Malthusian views and policies (Fairhead and Leach 1996). In fact, rural people may respond to pressure on natural resources in ways which allow for continuing or increased environmental sustainability, even under conditions of increasing population pressure (see Box 4.5; Lindblade et al. 1998). The productivity of the resource base on which people depend for their food security may not have declined as much as some commentators claim, although access to and potential claims over resources have often declined (Murton 1997). This revisionist environmental history articulates with the agenda of the 'new' ecology, which stresses the non-equilibrium nature of agroecological systems, as well as their dynamics and diversity, rather than their finite carrying capacity (Scoones 1995). It is also closely tied to the political climate within which decisions about environment and food security linkages take place. The implication of such challenges for food security is to further strengthen the case against the neo-Malthusians and to redirect attention away from global forecasts and solutions towards more locally relevant responses.

Food and environmental entitlements   Another area of research has taken the idea of entitlements, familiar to food security analysts, to explain links between people and the environment (Leach et al. 1999). Many analyses of people/environment relations conceive of a simple, linear relationship between population and resource availability, affected only by such factors as the level of technology. Little account is taken of social actors and institutions. The concern with community organizations in many approaches to community-based sustainable development serves merely to modify this Malthusian model. A functional community is seen as playing an overall, regulatory role, controlling resource use and technology in such a way as to limit environmental impact in the interests of a collective good. But if environmental issues are framed in terms of 'people in places', rather than simple, static conceptions of natural resource availability, a very different set of issues about people/environment interactions arise, including:

- which social actors see what components of variable and dynamic ecologies as resources at different times;
- how different social actors gain access to and control over such resources; and
- how natural resource use by different social actors transforms different components of the environment.

Analogous to its approach to famine, entitlements analysis is useful in explaining how the consequences of environmental change in general, and access to and control over natural resources in particular, are also socially differentiated. Just as with the food and famine debate, the environmental debate has been dominated by a supply-side focus, often giving rise to Malthusian interpretations of resource issues. But as Sen (1981) observed, absolute lack of resources may be only one of a number of reasons for people not gaining access to the resources they need for sustaining livelihoods. It is important not to polarize this distinction excessively, however, as others have pointed out in the context of famine analysis: resource availability and access are often interconnected. Conflicts over access often intensify when the resources in question become scarce in absolute terms (Box 4.4) (Leach et al. 1999).

Box 4.4   Environmental entitlements: the case of *Marantaceae* leaves in Ghana

The leaves of *Marantaceae* plants are ... collected by women ... and used for wrapping food, kola nuts and other products. ...

The leaves become endowments – people gain rights over them – in different ways depending on whether they lie inside or outside government-reserved forest. Off reserve, the leaves are usually the common property of a village, with an actor's endowment mapping depending on village membership. Where they occur on farmland, collection rights are acquired through membership of, or negotiation with, the appropriate landholding family or farm household. On reserve, endowment mapping depends on the Forest Department's permit system, with women often using established trading relationships as a source of finance for permits. Without such a permit, leaf gathering is illegitimate from the state's perspective, although it may be sanctioned by customary tenure arrangements. ...

The set of entitlements derived from *Marantaceae* leaves may include direct use of the leaves or their sale for cash income. ... Most women involved in gathering leaves prefer to sell them as an important source of seasonal income. ... Women may have to negotiate with their husbands and co-wives ... for labour time to collect the leaves. They find leaf gathering in groups more effective, so collection depends on membership of a regular group or on impromptu arrangements among kin and friends. There is frequently competition between groups for the best sites, as well as competition for leaves among group members. When disputes arise ... a 'queen mother of leaf gatherers' ... helps to mediate them. Marketing effectively depends on establishing a regular relationship with ... traders who will guarantee a reasonable price even at times of year when the market is flooded. ...

The utilities derived from the cash sale of *Marantaceae* leaves contribute to a woman's capability to ensure that she and her children are well fed and to satisfy other cash-dependent basic needs. In particular, the leaves offer a timely source of rainy season income when money is otherwise scarce. But whether a woman can keep control of the income, and how it is used, depends on intra-household bargaining arrangements. ...

Asking which combination of institutions makes the most difference to resource access and control for a set of social actors, or for the dynamics of resource use and management surrounding a particularly valued element of the landscape, may offer innovative, practical insights. These are often overlooked in simplified analyses of people–environment interactions, which tend to concentrate on questions of *per capita* resource availability and ignore issues around different social actors' resource access. Exploring the institutional dimensions of resource use opens up a range of important issues for management and policy which are not addressed as part of conventional analyses based on resource availability alone.

Source: Leach et al. 1997, pp. 22–3

Sustainable livelihoods   The idea of sustainable livelihoods comes closest to merging food security needs with environmental sustainability in mutually reinforcing ways. As Chapter 3 describes, the concept focuses on people's access to adequate stocks and flows of food, cash and other resources to meet basic needs and emphasizes people's ability to act in environmentally sustainable ways. A sustainable livelihood can be defined as one which:

> comprises the capabilities, assets (including both material and social resources) and activities required for a means of living. A livelihood is sustainable when it can cope with and recover from stresses and shocks, maintain or enhance its capabilities and assets, while not undermining the natural resource base (Scoones 1998, drawing on Chambers and Conway 1992, pp. 7–8).

At a practical level, for livelihoods to be sustainable people must have the capacity not only to subsist today, but to do so in such a way as not to compromise both their own and subsequent generations' capacity to survive in the future. To do this, people seek to:

- minimize fluctuations in well-being, consumption and incomes;
- adapt to anticipated risks and sudden shocks in smooth and positive ways;
- be economically viable in the medium to long term;
- manage exploitation of natural resources in ways that will secure their future availability;
- engage in sustainable agricultural or pastoral practices; and
- cement and reproduce reciprocal social ties which insure against failures in productive and exchange entitlements.

Inevitably, the poor are forced to make trade-offs between these often competing objectives. There is growing evidence to show that these trade-offs can be made successfully (Box 4.5; Brock and Coulibaly 1999; Carswell et al. 1999; and see Chapter 3).

Box 4.5   More people, less erosion: the case of Machakos District, Kenya

Over fifty years ago 'the Machakos problem' was understood to be human and animal population increases leading to uncontrolled and unco-ordinated development of large areas of land. This pessimistic neo-Malthusian view of the impossibility of economic development and sustainable environments when coupled with rapid population growth assumes that agroecological zones have a fixed carrying capacity. Sustainability now competes with productivity as the goal of rural development, and semi-arid Machakos is a prime example of an environment in which this competition is played out. A study of the district over sixty years revealed, however, that despite a nearly six-fold increase in the population between 1930 and 1990, the Akamba people succeeded in increasing productivity on both a per hectare and a *per capita* basis, while controlling and even reversing the degradation of natural resources. ...

Over time, the value of agricultural output per head in Machakos District increased four-fold. ... Although a common assumption is that investments and corresponding increases in agricultural productivity are attributable to government and aid institution investments, the case of terracing in Machakos offers a counter-example: here compulsory terracing introduced by the government in the 1940s was gradually replaced by farmer-led innovations in terrace construction. ...

This highlights the theoretical point that high population density may in fact result in greater environmental and economic sustainability through technological advance. The consequences of population increases in this model are:

- increased need for food (more mouths);
- increased labour supply (more hands);
- more generators of ideas (more brains); and
- reduced transaction costs.

Intensification occurred most rapidly in the areas of the district originally most populated, with high-potential land. ... In contrast, areas with relatively low population densities and lower-potential land initially experienced a lower rate of increased productivity, and far fewer technical innovations.

A further advantage of high population density is that transaction costs are lower: for example, roads both cost less to build and are used more. ... The impact on trade and food prices is beneficial, as is the effect of reduced *per capita* costs of social and physical infrastructure such as agricultural extension work, small businesses and community amenities.

The long-term study of Machakos District challenges the view that environmental sustainability is necessarily at risk from population increase, offering a more optimistic alternative version of the interaction of people with their environment, and hence the capacity for secure livelihoods – including food security – in dryland areas.

Sources: Tiffen et al. 1994; Tiffen and Mortimore 1994

POLICY ISSUES

Food security and environmental policies tend to be thought about, planned for and implemented in isolation from each other, which militates against effective integration of food security and environmental issues. In Africa, much energy has been put into the elaboration of both national food security and environmental action plans, but neither has sought in any systematic way to address the other's needs. But even global problems, such as climate change, necessitate a shift from conventional aggregated global policy responses towards ones which link macro-level concerns to micro-level realities. If food security is the point of entry, it is clear that:

> prudent resource management strategies should address two contrasting facets of climate change. They should be informed by the possibility of environmental catastrophe but mindful of the capacity of human societies for adaptive responses to risk. Regional strategies that are adopted in the next decade should be flexible enough to take account of a wide range of possible futures; they should reinforce measures that address existing social, economic, and environmental problems; and they should build in processes that enhance social resilience (Downing 1991, p. 380).

At the international level environmental agendas, in particular, tend to place environmental concerns above people:

since food insecurity is not an issue which directly affects the populations of the north, except in extreme circumstances of war or natural disasters, environmentalists' concerns do not need to take account of people's food security (Davies and Leach 1991b, p. 43).

Paradoxically, though, there is greater pressure from northern governments on poor farmers in developing countries to pursue sustainable agriculture than there is on northern farmers to do so. An important exception to this line of reasoning is the recent 'doubly green revolution' thesis (see Box 4.8). There have, however, been some important changes and reappraisal within development agencies. Links between environment and poverty more generally are now explicit; and few environmental organizations now fail to mention the impact of their prescriptions on local people, reflecting a growing concern in recent years with the impact of preservationist policies on them.[8]

Neo-Malthusianism has been highly influential in policy circles and northern popular opinion and has been an important justification for aid flows to Africa.[9] The policy solutions for neo-Malthusians are drastic curtailing of population growth rates and substantial increases in food supply, often through intensification of large-scale agriculture. At a local level, neo-Malthusian logic is used to support destocking programmes to prevent over-grazing and measures to prevent soil erosion. To help balance supply and demand, some argue that the inefficient conversion of cereals into animal protein should also cease.

The main policy implication from the trade-offs school is that the nature of the trade-offs is key. Nowhere is this more apparent than in current debates about genetically modified crops and their potential to enhance or damage food security (Box 4.6).

Famine mitigation policies are another example of the need for judicious trade-offs to maximize policy effectiveness: if implemented in a timely and effective manner, they can alleviate the conditions which force poor people to degrade their environment. One specific policy suggestion is that public works during periods of food shortage can be designed to improve local natural resource management (e.g. soil conservation, water harvesting and re-establishment of forest reserves). In Namibia, in the 1992–93 drought, the government drilled hundreds of boreholes and provided fodder to protect herders' assets (livestock). Environmentalists were critical, however, on the grounds that this artificially preserved large herds, causing accelerated degradation especially around water points (Devereux et al. 1993, p. 53). Whereas the Malthusian implication of this would be to regulate herd size, recent analyses of dynamic eco-systems and livelihoods would imply a much more complex (and effective) series of trade-offs. A related argument is that famine mitigation programmes need to incorporate rehabilitation, in order to help people restore the sustainability of their livelihoods after a shock. Implicit in much of the logic of linking relief and development is the need to optimize trade-offs

---

Box 4.6 Food security and environment trade-offs:
genetically modified crops

The biotechnology revolution is the subject of much heated debate and has polarized opinion. Depending on one's viewpoint, the move to genetically modified (GM) crops has the potential to provide global food security once and for all or constitutes a major environmental, political and economic hazard.

The potential productive gains from GM crops to poor farmers in the developing world could derive from the engineering of plants and animals with specific resistances to pathogens and pests or tolerance to drought, salinity or soil nutrient depletion. GM crops could also potentially require less fertilizer and pesticides than the currently available improved varieties – inputs which are too expensive for the poorest of the poor. Research is being conducted on using biotechnology to increase the content of iron or Vitamin A in foods to address widespread micro-nutrient deficiencies. Reduced pesticide use would also bring environmental gains and the more intensive production of GM crops could relieve pressure to convert forests, watersheds, rangelands and hillsides to agricultural production.

On the other hand, GM crops also carry significant risks to food security and the environment. A major concern is that GM seeds tend to be developed and commercialized by large profit-motivated life-science corporations. The resultant emphasis on high value agribusiness crops and patenting of new varieties means that food insecure farmers may find seeds unavailable for the crops they grow, or too expensive. The development of 'terminator' technologies designed to prevent farmers from saving and resowing their own seed has engendered particularly strong opposition. Widespread adoption of GM crops could also promote monocultures at the expense of traditional varieties (and hence erode biodiversity). There are also worries about the food safety risks associated with GM crops and about 'genetic pollution' via the outcrossing of undesirable traits to the wild relatives of GM crops.

Source: Paarlberg 1999

between immediate and longer-term food security needs.[10] Box 4.7 provides some practical steps from a Zambian case study of how farming systems research projects can do this by integrating food and environmental security objectives.

Research on political ecology and environmental entitlements also leads to particular policy implications. These arise from the belief that programmes and projects concerned with conservation and sustainable development will succeed only if they address social factors influencing the way people interact with the environment. Such factors include:

Box 4.7 Practical steps to integrate food security and environmental
sustainability: farming systems research

Evidence from Zambia suggests that, at the level of local implementation,
farming systems research projects need to remember six things if they are
successfully to support the mutual goals of food security and environmental
sustainability:

1 Both analytical and on-farm research activities need to take account of
   how people attempt to develop sustainable livelihoods from their initial
   endowments base; the relative vulnerability of these livelihoods and how
   people try to cope with shocks and stresses; and how different 'patches'
   within the landscape can be utilized in diverse and well-integrated ways.
2 There is a need to identify a *sequenced* set of short- and long-term
   research interventions that will aim initially at improving food security,
   but subsequently will address the issue of ensuring that such measures
   are environmentally sustainable (e.g. new crop and variety introductions
   can be followed by and incorporated into soil fertility improvement measures such as inter-cropping, green manuring and productive fallowing).
3 The time taken by farming systems research teams before they are satis-
   fied with on-farm research results needs to be reduced. If control over the
   management and evaluation of on-farm variety trials is handed over to
   farmer research groups, it is quite feasible for them to produce a consensus on their conclusions in one or two seasons. Farmers are then likely to
   turn attention to the rather more important question of how the new
   varieties, and other technologies, can be made more widely available.
4 Attention needs to be paid to the impact of new technologies on social
   differentiation and relations of production. The possible conflicts need to
   be identified within and between households regarding the choice of
   options for combining the components of their endowment basis, and
   who selects and benefits from the entitlement options. If no attempt is
   made to ascertain how a crop or new technology is incorporated into a
   household's production activities and how this affects social relations, it
   cannot be guaranteed that the long-run impact on food security, equity
   or the environment will be positive.
5 Agricultural production is rarely the only element in people's livelihoods,
   and indeed may not even be the key element. A greater awareness of the
   range of means by which people obtain entitlements will raise questions
   about the interactions between on- and off-farm activities, and how they
   compete with or complement each other with respect to land, labour and
   capital resource demands.
6 The net effect of the adoption of a livelihoods approach is to commit

farming systems researchers to seeing their role in the large rather than in the small. The question of actual impact on people's lives can no longer be ignored; as attention is turned to the double requirement of working more closely and in more detail with small-scale farms, it becomes ever more clear that to play an advocacy role, farming systems researchers need to build collaborative relations with others from the field up.

Source: Drinkwater and McEwan 1994, pp. 23–5

- access to employment and resources such as land, credit and food;
- tenure systems for management of land, water, trees and marine resources;
- gender relations; and
- empowerment or the level of control people exert over resources and decision-making processes which affect natural resource management (Ghai 1994, p. 1).

Questioning the ways in which policy narratives conventionally link the community and the environment focuses attention on social differences and ecological variability and dynamics in people/environment relations. If they are to be effective, community-based interventions, whether to improve food security or environmental sustainability or both, need to take account of informal and formal institutional arrangements, and of people who are excluded from them. This view necessitates explicit recognition that outcomes need to be negotiated through processes which may be conflictual. Although the main emphasis of this analysis is on the local level, links between local settings and the wider macro picture are also vitally important.

Exploding environmental myths has in part been in response to neo-Malthusian conviction that, in Africa in particular, there are too many people and too much livestock, and that both are leading to environmental degradation. Much contemporary development practice, in both governments and donor agencies, perpetuates such conventional wisdom, even though it is increasingly challenged from both a food security and an environmental point of view. Policies based on such misapprehensions, it is argued, can be harmful to the livelihoods of poor people and ecologically ineffective as well. In the context of the Ethiopian highlands, for example:

if degradation is the product largely of political and economic conditions unfavourable to soil conservation, then appropriate solutions are more likely to lie in the realm of institutional and tenurial reform, rather than in attempting to educate and force farmers to adapt erosion control techniques of which they may already be aware (Leach and Mearns 1996b, p. 29).

The most obvious point of convergence between food security and environmental policy concerns is food production, including management of land, water, forests and fisheries, often in increasingly marginal and ecologically fragile areas. The new emphasis on sustainable livelihoods is vital in this respect, as a means of tackling food security and environmental concerns in tandem. Conceptual shifts are not always followed through with changes in the ways governments and donors plan. There are, however, some important recent policy changes in this respect, including the adoption of a sustainable livelihoods framework by the UK's Department for International Development. At a policy level, this approach seeks to analyse food and environmental concerns as part of a whole. It attempts to reduce constraints which prevent people from taking the longer-term view required to conserve the resource base on which they depend now and in the future. This has implications for immediate food security needs (e.g. leaving land fallow; changing cropping patterns to enhance soil fertility; undertaking anti-erosion measures; restricting tree-cutting; gathering common property resources selectively), but longer-term needs will be more easily achieved because of the use of more sustainable production strategies. One of the clearest expositions of the ways in which such an approach can be operationalized in the context of food production is the Doubly Green Revolution thesis (Box 4.8).

CONCLUSION

For poor rural people, the distinction between food security and the environment is false, but they are forced to juggle immediate needs against longer-term ones. Analyses of linkages between food security and the environment have tended to be conceptualized as either inherently conflictual or, less often, complementary. It is now acknowledged that food security and environment cannot be separated into distinct boxes, but rather are mutually implicated in the concept of sustainability. Food security is sustainable only when the natural resource base is not undermined. Environmental protection rarely succeeds without taking account of those people who depend on the environment for their livelihoods, including for immediate food needs. Although most national environmental strategies stress the importance of conservation for sustainable development and food plans speak of the need for 'environmental friendliness', the details of how this will be achieved are rarely spelled out and are often contested, as the GM crops debate reveals. An understanding of the trade-offs and strategies by which poor people attempt to develop sustainable livelihoods would provide policy makers with a better platform from which to tackle food security and environmental concerns in mutually reinforcing ways.

Box 4.8 The Doubly Green Revolution

A second Green Revolution (and hence increased public investment in agricultural research) is urgently needed, yet a revolution that does not simply mirror the approach of the first. The technologies of the first Green Revolution were developed on experiment stations that were favoured with fertile soils, well-controlled water sources, and other factors suitable for high production. There was little perception of the complexity and diversity of farmers' physical environments, let alone the diversity of the economic and social environment. ... The new Green Revolution must not only benefit the poor more directly, but must be applicable under highly diverse conditions and be environmentally sustainable. By implication, it must make greater use of indigenous resources, complemented by a far more judicious use of external inputs.

In effect, we require a Doubly Green Revolution, a revolution that is even more productive than the first Green Revolution and even more 'green' in terms of conserving natural resources and the environment.

Over the next three decades it must aim to:

- repeat the successes of the Green Revolution
- on a global scale
- in many diverse localities

and be:

- equitable
- sustainable
- and environmentally friendly.

While the first Green Revolution took as its starting point the biological challenge inherent in producing new high-yielding food crops and then looked to determine how the benefits could reach the poor, this new revolution has to reverse the chain of logic, starting with the socio-economic demands of poor households and then seeking to identify the appropriate research priorities. Its goal is the creation of food security and sustainable livelihoods for the poor.

Success will not be achieved either by applying modern science and technology on the one hand, or by implementing economic and social reform on the other, but through a combination of effort that is innovative and imaginative. It will require a concerted effort on the part of the world community, in both the industrialized and developing countries, the application of new scientific and technological discoveries in a manner that is environmentally sensitive and, above all, the creation of new partnerships between scientists and farmers which will respond to the needs of the poor.

Source: Conway, 1997, pp. 9–10

CHAPTER FIVE

Famine in Africa

Stephen Devereux

DURING THE TWENTIETH century famine was systematically eradicated from its traditional homes, one after the other: first Russia, then China, then India and Bangladesh. The only region that has not succeeded in ridding itself of famine is sub-Saharan Africa. Since the mid-1970s, the label 'land of famine' has resided exclusively in Ethiopia and Sudan, and the Horn of Africa remains the last corner of the world where a famine seems destined to occur at least once every few years. For this reason, and because a famine is the most extreme manifestation of food insecurity, it remains necessary to include a chapter on famine in any study of food security issues in contemporary Africa.

Famines have afflicted Africa for millennia. The Horn of Africa and the Sahel have suffered countless famines since before records began, mostly triggered by natural disasters such as drought, locusts or livestock disease, but often precipitated or exacerbated by raiding, conflict and war. A drought-triggered famine occurred in Ethiopia as long ago as 253BC, and more than 40 mass mortality famines have been recorded during the past thousand years (Webb and von Braun 1994, p. 21). In the West African Sahel, famines occurred every 7–10 years during the seventeenth century and every five years during the eighteenth century (Watts 1983, p. 100). The worst food crisis in Africa's history was the 'Great Famine' of 1888–92, which killed one-third of the Ethiopian population and inflicted almost equivalent suffering on neighbouring Somalia and Sudan and on Tanzania. The Great Famine was particularly severe because three natural triggers acted simultaneously across large geographical areas: a severe drought, a rinderpest epidemic that destroyed 90 per cent of Ethiopia's national cattle herd, and infestations of locusts and army worms.

During the twentieth century drought continued to be a trigger for many African famines, but conflict was a contributory factor as early as the 1905–7 Maji Maji rebellion in Tanzania. The Biafran war of the 1960s heralded the ascendance of conflict as the major direct or indirect cause of food crises in postcolonial Africa, often in countries of southern, central and west Africa – Angola and Mozambique, Uganda and Zaire, Liberia and Sierra Leone – that had not historically been famine-prone. Deng (1999) records over 20 localized famines in southern Sudan between 1945 and 1998. Until the 1970s 'natural' triggers – drought, floods, locusts – dominated,

but since the 1980s most famines in this region are attributed to a combination of political and natural triggers – insecurity or war *plus* drought.
Clearly, contemporary famines in Africa are characterized by much greater
causal complexity than in the past.

Table 5.1 lists 21 twentieth century African famines, together with their
causal triggers and mortality estimates. Famine mortality statistics are
notoriously unreliable, and where famines are associated with conflict it is
often impossible to separate the two causes of death from each other.
Several 'war famines' are omitted from Table 5.1 for precisely this reason,
including: Angola 1974–6 and 1993–4, Zaire 1977–8, Liberia 1992–3 and
Sierra Leone 1995–8 (see von Braun, Teklu and Webb 1998).

This chapter is structured as follows. The next section briefly examines
'outsider' and 'insider' understandings of what a famine actually is. The
main body of the chapter focuses on famine causation. Alternative

Table 5.1   Selected twentieth century African famines

Years	Location	Causal triggers	Estimated mortality
1902–8	Nigeria (Hausaland)	Drought	5 000
1906–7	Tanzania (south)	Conflict	37 500
1913–14	West Africa (Sahel)	Drought	125 000
1917–19	Tanzania (central)	Conflict & drought	30 000
1922	Zimbabwe	Drought	47
1929	Tanzania	Drought	500
1943–4	Rwanda	Conflict & drought	300 000
1949	Malawi (Nyasaland)	Drought	200
1957–8	Ethiopia (Tigray)	Drought & locusts	250 000
1966	Ethiopia (Wollo)	Drought	50 000
1968–70	Nigeria (Biafra)	Conflict	1 000 000
1969–74	West Africa (Sahel)	Drought	101 000
1972–5	Ethiopia (Wollo & Tigray)	Drought	350 000
1974–5	Somalia	Drought	20 000
1980–1	Uganda (Karamoja)	Conflict & drought	30 000
1982–5	Mozambique	Conflict & drought	100 000
1983–5	Ethiopia	Drought	800 000
1984–5	Sudan (Darfur, Kordofan)	Drought	250 000
1988	Sudan (south)	Conflict	250 000
1991–3	Somalia	Conflict & drought	400 000
1998	Sudan (Bahr el Ghazal)	Conflict & drought	70 000

Notes:
This table is compiled from the following sources: Africa Watch 1991; Ahmed and Green 1999; Bryceson
1990; Caldwell and Caldwell 1992; Deng 1999; Devereux 1993a; de Waal 1997; Iliffe 1979, 1987, 1990;
Seaman 1993; Vaughan 1987; von Braun, Teklu and Webb 1998; Watts 1983; Wolde Mariam 1986. A
discussion of the reliability of individual mortality estimates is provided in Devereux 2000.

approaches to explaining and analysing African famines are discussed – demographic, climatic, economic (market failure, the entitlement approach) and political theories (including war). This is followed by a brief discussion of the evolution of famines in Africa, from the precolonial past to the postcolonial present. Finally, famine 'coping strategies' are discussed, and the Conclusion draws implications for policy.

WHAT IS FAMINE?

Dictionary definitions of famine reflect the observations of outsiders rather than the experience of those who suffer famine directly. Western definitions tend to be variations on 'virulent manifestations of intense starvation causing substantial loss of life' (Kumar 1990, p. 173). This definition contains three widely accepted elements – food shortage, starvation, and excess mortality – but it embodies an implicit theory which is not always accurate. Famines have occurred:

1 *with no food shortage at all.* Writing about the Wollo famine of 1973, Sen notes that 'a modest increase in agricultural output for Ethiopia as a whole is recorded by the National Bank of Ethiopia (1976) for the famine year' (Sen 1981, p. 92);

2 *where excess mortality was caused by disease, not starvation.* Epidemiological surveys during the Somalia famine of 1991–3 found that: 'As in other famine-related disasters, preventable infectious diseases such as measles and diarrhoea were the primary causes of death' (Moore et al. 1993, p. 935);

3 *with no excess mortality at all.* In Tanzania and Sudan, villagers talk about 'famine that kills' (Iliffe 1979; de Waal 1989), as distinct from famines that cause hunger and destitution but do not result in death.

'Insider' perceptions of famine differ from outsiders' in two crucial respects. Firstly they see famine as a problem of destitution, not (necessarily) starvation, and secondly, they perceive famine as an intensification of 'normal' processes, not as an extraordinary event – for instance, a drought-induced famine is comparable to a severe episode of agricultural seasonality. These distinctions are important because they have implications for policy responses. In particular, if insider perspectives are to be incorporated, humanitarian interventions should aim to preserve livelihoods as well as lives, and relief should be linked to rehabilitation and development programmes (Buchanan-Smith and Maxwell 1994). Moreover, the recognition that famines are health crises as much as food crises implies radically adjusting response priorities in terms of the mobilization and delivery of emergency supplies. Of course, these observations apply more to famines triggered by natural disasters or economic crises than those associated with hostile political circumstances such as civil war.

Perhaps the best 'outsider' definition is the following by Walker (1989, p. 6), which is one of the few that recognizes the key features of 'insider' definitions:

> Famine is a socio-economic process which causes the accelerated destitution of the most vulnerable, marginal and least powerful groups in the community, to a point where they can no longer, as a group, maintain a sustainable livelihood.

WHY DO FAMINES HAPPEN?

Like thinking on food security, thinking on famine causation has gone through several phases, though consensus has never been achieved and the debate remains unresolved. At first famine was seen as an 'act of God': droughts, floods and locusts destroyed crops and, where people depended on simple production systems and undiversified livelihoods, crop failure led inevitably to hunger and starvation. In the late eighteenth century, Malthus and others blamed the 'laws of nature' behind inexorable population growth: at both national and global levels, growing populations must eventually exceed the capacity to feed everyone. More recently, as economies and societies have become more sophisticated, famines are increasingly seen as 'acts of man': either markets and transport infrastructure are not sufficiently developed to redistribute food from surplus to deficit areas, or food is – deliberately or inadvertently – prevented from moving into areas that need it because of government policies or war.

This disagreement over whether famine should be conceptualized as a 'natural disaster', an economic crisis or a 'complex political emergency' still polarizes the famine literature. A useful resolution might be to examine each famine independently and apply the appropriate analytical tools to each case, rather than selecting one approach and dismissing all alternatives. Similar observations apply to other dimensions of disagreement in the literature. For instance, it is striking how approaches to understanding famine tend to reflect the disciplinary backgrounds of the writers who advocate them.

There is also an unresolved tension between explanations that focus on famine as an *event* and those that analyse famine as a *process*.[1] Academics who see famine as a discrete event include *climatologists* who analyse the effects of drought or flood, *economists* who describe market failure and 'entitlement collapse', and *political scientists* who examine the relationship between government policies or civil war and famine. Conversely, analysts who focus on slow onset processes include *demographers* who calculate ratios between people or livestock and natural resources such as arable land, *environmentalists* who argue that famine in semi-arid areas is related to desertification and might in future be caused by global warming, and *economists* who see famine as a manifestation of low levels of infrastructure development and high levels of household poverty (Table 5.2).

Table 5.2 reveals why it is difficult to accept any one theory as the single 'correct' explanation for all famines. Famines are too complex to be explained entirely by demographic pressures, bad weather, economic models or political regimes alone. Clearly, no famine can be attributed solely to a 'shock' such as a drought: underlying factors – political, demographic and socio-economic processes – make people vulnerable to natural disasters or economic and political crises. As will be seen, a 'food availability decline' (supply failure) at the national level only leads to famine for specific groups of people who face declining access to food (effective demand failure). It is the combination of several sets of adverse factors that create particular famine events: trigger shocks *plus* underlying processes, supply *plus* demand failure, or drought *plus* poverty. It is these complex interactions that have made the analysis of famine so controversial and the eradication of famine so difficult to achieve.

The complexity and multiplicity of famine determinants has led some writers to propose that a 'systems' approach to famine analysis might be more appropriate than a disciplinary-biased set of theories each competing for paradigm dominance. These writers (Cannon 1991; von Braun et al. 1998) consider the entire 'food system' of a country or a 'vulnerable group' and examine empirically how shocks to individual components – food production, food distribution and food consumption – contribute to specific famines. Perhaps only war, with its multiple effects on every stage of the food chain from production and storage through to trade and aid flows, can be viewed as a comprehensive explanation of (a certain type of) famine. All other explanations tend to focus on the collapse of one element in the food system, and therefore do not explain the inherent vulnerability of that system to shocks. In practice, livelihood shocks such as 'natural disasters' – but not 'political disasters' such as war – are relatively easily addressed

Table 5.2 Famine theories and disciplinary biases

Discipline	Underlying factors or processes	Precipitating factors or events
Demography	Malthusianism (population pressure)	Epidemics
Climatology	Desertification; global warming	Drought or flood
Economics	Weak infrastructure; poverty	Entitlements failure; market failure
Politics	Colonialism; government policies	War ('complex emergencies'); international response failure

nowadays; it is vulnerability and political will that remain as the real stumbling blocks in addressing and eradicating famine.

Next, this chapter reviews and critiques the main theoretical approaches to understanding famine, starting with demographic theories, then climatic and environmental theories (including the 'entitlement approach') and finally politics and war.

DEMOGRAPHIC THEORIES

In 1798 the Reverend Thomas Malthus wrote his 'Essay on the Principle of Population', which was to provide the dominant theory of famine for almost two hundred years. The basic Malthusian argument can be expressed in a sequence of apparently logical steps.

1   Population and the demand for food increase at a parallel rate over time.
2   Natural resources, especially arable land, are limited in supply.
3   Rising demand for food can be met either by more extensive or more intensive cultivation of land.
4   Land is not only scarce, it is also of variable quality: as population pressure causes more land to be cultivated, increasingly marginal soils will be brought into cultivation, leading to falling productivity.
5   Once the 'extensive margin' of cultivation has been reached (when no more arable land is available) it will become necessary to intensify production (to increase yields per unit of land). But this too will eventually lead to falling productivity, as returns to labour and other inputs diminish.
6   Diminishing returns mean that food production will eventually grow slower than population.
7   Given fixed natural resources, population must stabilize at the maximum possible level of food production.
8   Therefore, starvation acts as a natural check on population growth, with famine maintaining an equilibrium between the need for food and food supplies.

There are several criticisms of the standard Malthusian argument (see Chapter 4). For one thing, famines do not in fact check or control population growth. There is evidence of post-famine 'baby booms' from many twentieth century famines, partly because famine mortality tends to be concentrated on vulnerable groups within the population, such as the elderly and the very young, while reproductive adults are most likely to survive. Following the 'Great Leap Forward' famine in China of 1958–63, during which an estimated 30 million people died – making it the worst famine in mortality terms in history – the lost population was entirely recovered within 15 years, and there has been no famine in China since (see Figure 5.1). The last famine in Bangladesh, in 1974, led to an estimated

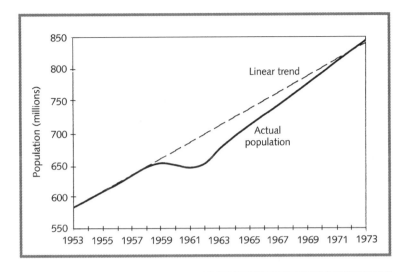

Figure 5.1 Demographic impact of China's 'Great Leap Forward' famine

Source: Derived from Field 1993, p.17

1½ million excess deaths, which amounted to 2 per cent of the national population at that time. However, with a population growth rate of 3 per cent *per annum*, the entire loss of lives to famine in 1974 was made up in a single year (Field 1993).

Moreover, Malthus simply failed to foresee the immense revolutions in agriculture, transport and communications that would accompany the industrial revolution of the nineteenth century. Technological improvements in agriculture, especially in Western Europe and North America, have dramatically raised agricultural productivity. Most people in the West no longer live on the land, yet despite (or perhaps because of) this transition to urban-based livelihoods, they are much less vulnerable to famine than they were two hundred years ago. Western Europe is the most densely populated continent in the world, only 7 per cent of Europeans live in rural areas and make a living out of farming, and yet the European Community continues to produce large food surpluses every year.

Equally significant has been the revolution in transport and communications infrastructure during the twentieth century, which has facilitated massive and rapid flows of food from surplus to deficit countries. Malthus wrote his 'Essay' as an Englishman living on an island, with the implicit assumption that self-sufficiency was imperative for food security (an assumption which remains the basis of many governments' food security strategies even today, as seen in earlier chapters). But the transport and communications revolutions have made international transfers of food not only possible but economically rational: many countries choose to special-ize in non-agricultural production and use their export earnings to import the food that they need, rather than maintain a policy preoccupation with self-sufficiency which might be economically irrational. Japan provides a case in point. The densely populated islands of Japan cannot and should not strive for food production self-sufficiency, yet as one of the wealthiest countries in the world, Japan can hardly be categorized as food insecure or vulnerable to famine, even though a high proportion of its food consump-tion needs is imported.

Finally, it is a curious paradox that this most famous theory of famine (at least until Sen's entitlement theory of the early 1980s – see below) has never been used to explain any particular famine event. Although many African countries, such as Malawi and Rwanda, currently carry the label 'Malthusian crisis', the fact that population growth is a 'slow onset' process means that theories of famine based on Malthusian demographics have little explana-tory power in 'rapid onset' food crises. It requires a sudden shock to a vulnerable food system to precipitate a famine, rather than a steady decline in productivity of land leading eventually to a shortfall in food availability. Perhaps the most useful application of Malthusian theory, therefore, is to see demographic pressure as a background or underlying factor that increases vulnerability to precipitating events or triggers such as a drought. On its own Malthusian theory is insufficient.

Since the 1970s several other demographic factors contributing to famine have been proposed, which might be characterized as 'neo-Malthusiasm'. Neo-Malthusians argue that while there are surplus produc-ing areas such as North America and Western Europe at present, the world itself is an 'island' with a limited carrying capacity, so the global capacity to produce food will eventually reach a plateau, just as Malthus predicted would happen for Britain two centuries ago. Recently a number of studies have projected food demand and food supplies into the twenty-first century. Some of these conclude that within a few decades the world will in fact face severe constraints on its ability to feed all its populations. Notable factors in this analysis include the increasing rapid urbanization of China, which will soon make it the world's largest importer of food (Brown 1995). This predicted diversion of food surpluses to meet China's consumption requirements has potentially serious implications for world food prices and for the availability of food aid to low-income food deficit countries in Africa.

A second neo-Malthusian argument can be crudely characterized as 'death control outstripping birth control' in low-income countries. Successful immunization campaigns and basic health programmes have reduced infant mortality rates and raised life expectancies in sub-Saharan Africa, but fertility rates have remained high for a combination of economic and sociocultural reasons. Moreover, a recent 'Africa Poverty Status Report' (White 1999) con-cluded that there is a large unmet demand for contraception in Africa.

Addressing this demand could reduce fertility rates, household poverty levels and population pressure on Africa's fragile ecosystems.

There is also cross-country evidence that fertility preferences are a function of urbanization and income levels, with wealthier urban families throughout the world choosing to have fewer children than the rural poor. Throughout rural Africa, children become involved in farming and domestic chores at an early age – boys herd livestock and girls assist their mothers with food preparation and water and firewood collection. West African children are estimated to be net contributors to the household by the age of ten. In urban areas, by contrast, children have lower economic value and are more expensive to raise. Urbanization, immuniszation and primary health programmes are causing even poor families to adjust their fertility decisions as the survival chances of their children improve, so family sizes have already started falling in some parts of Africa. In many high income Western countries a 'demographic transition' to zero net population growth has already occurred, and it is very likely that this demographic transition will occur worldwide once economic conditions in poor countries improve. Far from population increasing exponentially and indefinitely, as Malthus predicted, demographic modellers now project global population stabilizing at around nine billion in the mid-twenty-first century – well within the 20 billion that some agronomists see as the limit to global food production potential.

Other neo-Malthusian arguments focus not on population totals *per se*, but on the impacts of population growth, firstly on livelihood opportunities and secondly on dependency ratios. The first argument is that measures of demographic pressure should relate population figures to economic opportunities. For example, the number of people/km^2 of irrigated farmland might be a more critical statistic than the total population of a region. Where people depend on the land for their livelihoods a very low population density can be associated with higher vulnerability to food insecurity and famine than a wealthy urban area where densities could be as high as 200 people/km^2. The second argument is that high population growth rates (3–4 per cent in many African countries) lead to high dependency ratios – the number of 'consumers' or dependants divided by the number of 'producers' or workers in a household. This creates particular stresses in poor households and, in farming communities, can lead to partition of land to unviably small fragments over time. These are valid concerns. However, it remains true that it is the value and variability of available economic opportunities that is the key determinant of vulnerability, not population numbers or population density in itself.

In drought-prone West Africa and the Horn the 'contra-Malthusian' argument seems more relevant than conventional Malthusianism. Boserup (1983) argued that population concentration leads to economies of scale in the provision of rural infrastructure such as transport, irrigation and also trade, making these areas easier to reach with trade and aid flows, so that sparsely populated areas such as the Ethiopian Highlands are more vulnerable to famine than densely settled areas such as towns, even though people in towns are alienated from producing the food that they consume. Contradicting Malthusian predictions, Africa arguably suffers from excessively *low* population density (no 'Boserup effect') plus high population growth rates (which perpetuates poverty), leading to persistent vulnerability to famine.

The policy prescriptions proposed by Malthusians and neo-Malthusians focus on restricting population growth. In its more benign form this suggests spreading access to birth control or family planning methods more widely; in its more extreme form it can imply compulsory sterilization programmes or China's 'one child family' policy. In Bangladesh during a drought in the early 1970s some women were provided with food aid only on condition that they were sterilized. Another policy implication of Malthusianism is 'triage' or 'lifeboat ethics', which argues that maintaining the global Malthusian equilibrium requires allowing people to starve if they are unfortunate enough to live in countries where food production is unviable and population growth is 'too high'. These policy prescriptions result from a misdiagnosis of the problem. In the West a demographic transition to low fertility regimes occurred only *after* living standards rose. Sustainable solutions to the 'population crisis' require addressing the problem rather than the symptom: policies should aim to reduce poverty rather than strive to keep the numbers of people at low levels.

CLIMATIC AND ENVIRONMENTAL THEORIES

Theories of famine based on climatic variability or environmental degradation can be divided into two groups: theories based on long-term processes ('climatic/environmental determinism') and those based on climate-triggered livelihood shocks ('bad weather events'). 'Climatic determinists' make alarmist projections based on observations of deteriorating meteorological or environmental indicators. 'Bad weather' analysts examine the impact of drought or flood on livelihoods, food supplies and access to food.

Climatic and environmental processes

Examples of adverse environmental and climatic processes include desertification and global warming. Concern about desertification, especially in the West African Sahel and the Horn of Africa, peaked in the 1980s but have since receded from the discourse on famine. According to the desertification hypothesis, a combination of arable land being lost to population pressure, deforestation and overgrazing, together with the possibility (though this remains disputed) of a long-term decline in rainfall in dryland farming areas of Africa and Asia, will cause declines in crop production and exacerbate food insecurity in already marginal areas, leading eventually to famine. This theory (as argued by Susanna Moorhead in this volume on 'Food Security and the Environment') is controversial, mainly because the evidence on the scale and impact of 'desert creep' is inconclusive.

Like desertification, the discovery during the 1980s of the phenomenon of global warming prompted apocalyptic predictions about the implications for global food security in the twenty-first century. According to global warming theorists, if current rates of temperature change continue in the coming decades, sea levels will rise in densely populated low-lying areas like Egypt (the Nile) and Bangladesh (the Ganges), displacing millions of people and creating land shortage and food scarcities. Also as global temperatures rise, rainfall will decline in already dry areas such as the arid and semi-arid Sahel. Africa is thus particularly vulnerable to global warming, because of its heavy dependence on rainfed agriculture. Global warming will reduce water availability for agriculture, affecting both crop yields and the carrying capacity of land in respect of livestock.

However, desertification, global warming and other 'climatic determinism' hypotheses suffer from a weakness that is shared by all 'process' theories of famine, namely, a tendency to view the poor and vulnerable as passive victims who will take no action in response to long-term threats to their livelihoods. As with Malthusianism, it is difficult to reconcile slow-onset processes like 'desert creep' or gradually rising sea levels with rapid-onset food crises.

Bad weather events

In the 1960s it was often argued that the world was girdled by two 'famine belts': a cold belt running across northern Europe and north Asia, characterized by short growing seasons where crop failure was caused by extreme cold; and a hot dry belt running across Sahelian Africa through South Asia to China, where famines were precipitated by drought-induced crop failure in rainfed agricultural systems. It is true that Russia experienced over one hundred famines in one thousand years and that most of these were triggered by extreme cold (Dando 1980, p. 147), while most famines in Africa and India were historically triggered by agricultural droughts. For poor farmers whose survival depends heavily on growing their own food, the threat of crop failure remains the major source of vulnerability they face in non-conflict contexts.

The mechanism whereby drought can lead to famine is straightforward but multi-dimensional. First, a drought reduces crop production (so it undermines direct access to food by producers). Second, drought reduces the value of assets that people can sell to buy food (livestock become thin and die, and there is an oversupply of livestock and other assets on the market as people sell or barter their possessions for food). Third, drought raises food prices because large numbers of people shift from being self-provisioning food producers to being market-dependent consumers (so drought threatens access to food through the market). Fourth, drought reduces employment opportunities because of its contractionary effect on local economies (so earned income for purchasing food is also reduced). Finally, drought reduces informal support systems because of 'covariate risk' – if everybody in the area is equally affected, the ability of richer community members to help their poorer neighbours is impaired (so drought threatens access to food through local 'moral economy' transfers).

On the other hand, the assertion that 'drought = famine' is too simplistic. Firstly, it assumes a totally closed economy: a localized drought leads to a decline in food and livestock production, leading to starvation among the affected (local) population. However, we need to explain why food does not come in from outside the drought-affected area, in the form of either trade or aid, to compensate for reduced food availability in the drought zone. Drought disrupts production, not distribution. Secondly, climatic theories imply that everyone is equally affected: but we know that even in the worst famines, the rich rarely starve. So a robust theory needs to explain why some people have better access to food than others, even when food is scarce. Thirdly, especially in drought-prone areas people have developed resilient livelihood systems to protect them against seasonality and drought. In most cases where drought has led to famine, several years of sequential droughts have preceded the food crisis. The Ethiopian and Sahelian famines of the early 1970s, for example, were preceded by six or seven years of low rainfall. In other words, it is only once household or community coping strategies have been exhausted that a sequence of droughts will produce a famine.

This leads to the final critique, namely that drought does not always result in famine. Many parts of the world, from the United States of America to the Middle East, have suffered severe droughts, but these have not produced the food crises that occur in Africa. Why not? Because, as suggested above, drought does not cause famine, but vulnerability to drought does. Drought does not lead to famine where food distribution systems are better developed and more responsive to localized food crises, and where people affected by drought are wealthier (and are therefore able to draw on the market for food when their sources of food through production or assets fail), or else are better protected against drought, either through having more effective coping strategies of their own or through government and donor support.

To sum up, critiques of climatic theories can be reduced to a single argument. 'Drought causes famine' is not a theory of famine causation, it merely identifies the trigger for certain famines. Inability to cope with drought – at the individual, household, community or national level – is the underlying cause of drought-triggered famines. Drought causes crop failure, but vulnerability to drought causes famine.

ECONOMIC THEORIES

Economists have explained famines mainly in terms of the role of markets. 'Market failure' explanations – including speculation, hoarding and market fragmentation – are assessed below. This is followed by a discussion of Sen's 'entitlement approach', which blames 'demand failure' rather than a failure of supply – people afflicted by famine being unable to command food from the market even if supplies are adequate.

Market failure

Markets respond not to needs, but to purchasing power. If people starve because they cannot afford to buy food from well-functioning markets, this is not a market failure, but 'entitlement failure' due to poverty (see the next section, 'The entitlement approach'). Market failure occurs when traders fail to respond to signals of effective demand, or when prices rise excessively due to market fragmentation, speculation or hoarding. Food markets can fail in the allocation of food either over time (due to hoarding) or across space (because of fragmented markets). As a generalization, hoarding is more of a feature in South Asian famines (where markets are fairly well integrated), whereas fragmented markets are more prevalent in African famines (where the population is dispersed and economic infrastructure, including markets, is weak). These are now considered in turn.

During food crises people might store food for either precautionary or speculative reasons. Economists interpret this behaviour in two ways. The first views hoarding as economically rational behaviour that smoothes food supplies over time and ensures that prices do not rise excessively but accurately reflect food availability. Similarly, if people hoard in anticipation of shortages and then release limited quantities of food on to the market as prices rise, this spreads the impact of the food shortage more evenly over time, and is therefore a sign of a well functioning market. A second interpretation does see speculation and hoarding as market failure. Hoarding for speculative purposes removes food from the market and drives prices up excessively, at which point traders will release food and enjoy excess profits, while the poor who cannot afford to buy food at such inflated prices might simply starve. In economists' jargon, the demand for food is price inelastic: people will pay whatever they can afford in order to get enough food to survive, even to the point of destituting themselves, and this makes it possible for traders to drive prices up to unreasonably high levels. In this interpretation of the role of markets during food crises, rationing of scarce food through the price mechanism occurs not over time, but between rich and poor consumers, and traders have often been blamed for causing or exacerbating famines by exploiting this dependence on marketed food supplies. Similarly, many famine analysts have observed that food crises act as stratifying mechanisms – transferring assets from those who have food to those who need it.

Which interpretation is accurate? One key to answering this question is information. If market agents (both traders and consumers) have good information about future food availability, then their decisions will be rational and prices will be accurate. If information is limited or inaccurate, however, excessive storage (whether for panic or profit) will exacerbate scarcities and turn a minor food problem into a major food crisis. A classic example is the Bangladesh famine of 1974, when a minor shortfall in rice production caused by floods was magnified by excessive withdrawal of rice from the market, following overly pessimistic predictions of the flood's impact on harvests. Prices spiralled out of control and excluded thousands of people from buying food, who died as a direct consequence (Ravallion 1987). It is the dual role of food as both a subsistence necessity and a marketed commodity that creates these problems. Assume that, on average, 80 per cent of cereals production is consumed on the farm by the farming household, and 20 per cent is sold in a normal year. Now a 10 per cent drop in production will cause a 50 per cent drop in market release – and a corresponding hike in food prices. The smaller the marketed surplus in a given locality, the more sensitive the market will be to fluctuations in production. This sensitivity will be reflected in variable food prices – and it is the poor who are most vulnerable to food price variability.

This leads to the second explanation in the 'market failure' category – fragmented markets. According to neoclassical economic theory, when markets are well integrated, efficient and competitive, traders will respond immediately to signals of demand. If food production falls in one region, prices will rise, triggering inflows of food from surplus regions elsewhere until prices return to equilibrium. Price differentials between surplus and deficit areas should reflect only transactions costs such as transport and storage, plus a reasonable profit margin for traders. Integrated markets reduce the risks associated with market dependence, by smoothing food flows and prices over space and time (see Bob Baulch in this volume on 'Markets and Food Security'). In reality, many famine-prone areas are characterized by fragmented rather than integrated markets, either because of weak economic infrastructure (poor communications networks, bad roads, high transport costs, limited availability of trucks and storage facilities) or because of the disruptive effects of conflict and war. In rural Africa, high transactions costs discourage traders from responding to food shortages in isolated communities – traders have little incentive to supply small, poor villages far from main roads with limited volumes of food for a limited period of time (Devereux 1988).

The fragmented nature of markets in rural Africa is evidenced by the phenomenon of 'price ripples' during food crises. When food production collapses an immediate consequence is that formerly self-provisioning farmers become market dependent consumers. They sell assets such as livestock, even at very low 'distress' prices, in order to buy food in local markets, which drives food prices up. Now if these markets were well integrated with markets in neighbouring districts and beyond, traders would react by bringing in food from elsewhere, meeting local demand and pushing prices down again. Instead, market fragmentation means that food supplies dwindle in local markets despite escalating prices. This forces people to migrate out to neighbouring markets where food is available at lower prices – at least until this influx of famine migrants reduces food supplies and pushes prices up there, forcing them to move on in a constant search for markets where food is available at affordable prices. Thus prices rise in 'ripples' spreading outwards from the epicentre of a famine zone, and this explains why famine-afflicted rural people often migrate to cities where markets are large and food prices are stable.

The existence of 'price ripples', which were first recorded during the Bangladesh and Ethiopian famines of 1974 (Seaman and Holt 1980), has implications for both famine theory and policy. Price ripples provide support for 'food availability decline' theories: people can face starvation simply because of a lack of food in famine zones, in the absence of trade and aid inflows. It follows that – notwithstanding the suspicion and hostility which traders often face – the development of markets and strengthening of trading activities can provide effective 'famine-proofing' and help prevent localized food shortages becoming localized famines. Famines are more likely to occur where traders are absent and markets are weak than where competitive and efficient markets for food and other commodities exist.

The entitlement approach

Amartya Sen's influential book *Poverty and Famines* (1981) decisively shifted the focus of famine analysis from the supply side to the demand side. The entitlement approach emphasizes access to food, or peoples' relationship to food, rather than the availability of food. Sen shows that famines have occurred even with plenty of food in the afflicted country, because people have differential access to that food, which is determined by their individual 'entitlements'.

Strictly speaking, the entitlement approach is not a theory of famine causation. It seeks to analyse *how* famines happen; it does not claim to explain *why* they happen. Sen points out that there are many ways of (legally) acquiring food, which he groups into four categories of 'entitlement': production, trade, own-labour, and inheritance and transfers (Table 5.3). Individuals are food secure if the sum of their entitlements generates enough food to keep them well nourished. Conversely, during a famine people are 'plunged into starvation' (Sen 1981, p. 47) because their entitlements to food collapse, leaving them unable to feed themselves. For example, if maize fields are destroyed by locusts, this reduces farmers' production-based entitlement to food; if the price of a cash crop falls, this reduces their trade-based (or exchange) entitlement; if a labourer loses his

Table 5.3	Entitlement categories		
Category	**What it is**	**In other words . . .**	**Types of people**
Production-based entitlement	The right to own what one produces with one's own (or hired) resources	What one grows	Food crop farmers
Trade-based entitlement	The right to own what one acquires through exchange of commodities	What one buys	Grain merchants Cattle dealers Moneylenders
Own-labour entitlement	The right to self-employment or to sell one's labour power	What one earns	Salary earners Landless labourers
Inheritance and transfer entitlement	The right to own what is willingly given by others	What one is given	Remittance receivers Food aid recipients

or her job, this reduces his or her own-labour entitlement; and so on. Unless alternative entitlements are found to compensate for this entitlement collapse – for example, emergency food aid, which represents an increase in 'transfer entitlement' – death is inevitable.

Sen also introduced an important distinction between 'endowments' – what one owns – and 'entitlements' – what can be acquired by exchanging endowments for other commodities. Most people own a range of assets – livestock, radios, jewellery and so on – that can be sold for food. The set of commodities that can be acquired through exchange (barter or sale) is defined by the 'exchange entitlement mapping'. An individual's entitlement can fall below subsistence needs in one of two ways: either because of a fall in endowment (livestock death), which is a direct entitlement collapse; or through a fall in 'exchange entitlement mapping' (food price inflation, falling livestock prices, falling real wages), which amounts to declining terms of trade between assets or income and food prices.

During drought-triggered famines in Africa, the two problems often occur together. Firstly, harvests fail, so farmers resort to the market, financing food purchases through distress sales of livestock and assets, then food prices rise because of reduced supply and increased demand, and livestock prices fall because of reduced demand or excess supply (leading to exchange entitlement collapse). This pattern is so common in African droughts that early warning systems often monitor livestock/grain price ratios as an indicator of distress (see Chapter 8).

Another important concept introduced by Sen (1981) is 'derived destitution'. It is not only farmers who are vulnerable to production shocks, but also those whose livelihoods are derived from farmers' incomes, such as agricultural labourers and providers of rural services. When farmers lose their crops during a drought and are forced to sell their assets to buy food, they also spend less on non-essential services such as haircuts, which reduces the income of rural barbers and makes them as vulnerable to famine as the farmers themselves.

Among the many positive features of the entitlement approach are the following:

- *It emphasizes demand, not supply.* The 'food balance sheet' approach to estimating food aid requirements simply calculates the total amount of food available and divides this by population size to determine the 'food gap' in metric tonnes or kilocalories per person. The entitlement approach highlights the inadequacy of this crude method. Since effective demand (or wealth) is unevenly distributed in every society, access to food will also be distributed unequally: rich people can acquire more food than the poor, and can afford to pay higher prices. The entitlement approach can explain famines that occur with no decline in food production or availability at either local or national level. Sen (1986, p. 3) also cautions against 'Malthusian optimism' – just because there is enough food in a country does not mean that everyone is food secure. For example, the Great Bengal famine of 1943 occurred with no food shortage in Bengal – it was in fact caused by wartime hoarding and price inflation which drove rice prices up beyond the reach of poorly paid agricultural labourers, as a result of which three million people died.

- *It allows vulnerable groups to be identified.* The entitlement approach disaggregates food availability and access to the level of specific groups of people, who might be defined geographically, demographically or occupationally. For example, a famine might afflict pastoralists if disease destroys livestock herds, thereby undermining their endowments so that a famine occurs even if food production is unaffected. By analysing the sources of entitlement to food of various groups of people, it is possible to develop a vulnerability profile for each livelihood system, and therefore to predict both the potential causes of famines and the likely impact of livelihood shocks. Even when a national food security threat arises, the entitlement approach emphasizes that each population subgroup faces distinct sets of food security risks. During a drought, for instance, farmers risk losing their crops, pastoralists lose their livestock, and agricultural labourers suffer falling real incomes as prices rise and demand for their labour declines. These events force these groups of people towards famine along quite distinct causal pathways, irrespective of whether the country overall is in food deficit or not.

- *It suggests more appropriate policy interventions.* The conventional response to famine is to move food aid into affected areas or refugee camps and distribute it as free rations to the affected population. This intervention follows logically from a diagnosis of the problem as 'too many people, too little food'. But if the food problem is due to an exchange entitlement decline or a market failure, a more appropriate and sustainable intervention might involve restoring entitlements in other ways. For example, cash handouts might attract traders to a remote area, building marketing networks that will survive beyond the immediate crisis, and could bring food prices down. (Of course, it could also be inflationary, if there is a bottleneck in food supplies.) Similarly, cash- or food-for-work – provided people are relatively fit, and only in conjunction with other support to vulnerable groups who are not able to work – can be used both to target aid on the truly needy and to build infrastructure such as feeder roads that will improve transport, communications and marketing systems (see Chapter 10).

Despite its innovative and important insights, the entitlement approach has been criticized. At first Sen was seen as denying the importance of food shortages in explaining famines, mainly because he concentrated in *Poverty and Famines* on trying to demonstrate that several famines had occurred with no food shortage. But Sen replied that this was merely a matter of emphasis, and that entitlements had relevance not only for explaining how famines can occur because of adverse shifts in the distribution of access to food (with no decline in overall availability of food), but also for predicting how the impact of a food availability decline would be disaggregated among various groups of people. Nonetheless, although Sen intended the entitlement approach to provide a holistic framework capable of being applied to the analysis of any and every famine, his critics have argued that in practice it explains South Asian famines better than famines in Africa – especially recent African famines which are associated more with conflict than with drought. Sen himself listed several additional limitations of the framework.

1   Some entitlements are ambiguously defined, such as common property resources like land, water and trees. The entitlement approach is predicated on individual ownership of commodities, but in African communities resources are often managed communally rather than individually, and complex rights are held over these resources by various groups and institutions. For example, in much of rural Africa land is owned by the state, controlled by community leaders (chiefs or headmen), and utilized by farmers or pastoralists who have only usufruct rights to this land. This ambiguity in property rights makes it difficult to aggregate an individual's or household's entitlement to food.

2   Similarly, Sen recognizes that entitlements applies only to legal rights over assets and food. 'Extra-legal' transfers such as looting during a war are excluded from this framework. Yet cattle raiding and requisitioning of food stocks are typical of conflict-induced famines, so the entitlement approach has little to say for situations where individual

ownership rights are violated. The word 'entitlement' itself is rather misleading in that it suggests a moral as well as legal right to food. In reality, contemporary famines often involve gross violations of the right to food.

3 Sen also concedes that the approach excludes the possibility of 'voluntary starvation'. The entitlement approach assumes that people facing food shortage will simply convert their entitlements into food (e.g. by selling their assets) to survive. However, several studies conducted during the 1980s revealed that food rationing is a universal and immediate response to shortage, since rationing consumption protects livelihoods and the viability of the household in the longer term (see the discussion of 'coping strategies' below). Famine-affected people choose hunger to preserve their assets and avoid destitution. In extreme circumstances, the household might survive the famine as a unit by protecting its key productive assets (including economically active adults) while some of its members (typically young children and the elderly) actually die. The entitlement approach cannot explain this apparent paradox.

POLITICS AND WAR

The causes of contemporary famines are never purely technical – crop failure, food price rises, and so on. All famines are explained by a combination of 'technical' and 'political' factors, where political factors include bad government policies, failure of the international community to provide relief, and war. African famines in particular have evolved from being triggered mainly by drought to being triggered mainly by civil war, and even when drought is the trigger, national governments and the international community are increasingly held accountable for failing (or refusing) to prevent the drought from developing into famine.

Virtually every country that has suffered famine in the past twenty years has suffered a war at the same time. Von Braun et al. (1998, p. 3) lists eight famines in Africa during the 1990s, seven of which were associated more directly with civil war than with drought or dubious agricultural policies – in Angola, Ethiopia, Liberia, Sierra Leone, Somalia, Sudan, and Zaire. In every case, famine was an instrument or a by-product of war. This is a fundamental shift in the character of famine. Drought-triggered food emergencies no longer need to become famines because the logistical capacity exists (where local coping mechanisms are inadequate) to intervene. Conversely, where governments are neglecting or persecuting their drought-affected populations, or where the international community is not moved to intervene, a drought can still develop into a famine that is almost always preventable.

'Political famines' or 'war famines' do not operate according to the economic logic of food demand exceeding food supply that all other theories of famine share: a different analytical framework is required. In political famines – those precipitated either by government policies or by conflict and civil insecurity – the rich are as vulnerable as the poor, sometimes more so. Keen's (1994) analysis of the 'winners' and 'losers' in the Sudan famines of the 1980s, for example, established that the *wealth* of Dinka pastoralists made them acutely vulnerable to cattle raiding by government militia and others, until their livelihoods were so weakened that they succumbed repeatedly to famine.[2] The emergence and perpetuation of this 'asset trans-fer economy' (Duffield 1993) in south Sudan was facilitated and legitimized by the indifference or hostility of the Sudanese government towards the Dinka people (see Box 5.1).

For those who view famine as an 'economic disaster' (Sen 1981, p. 162) it is logical to assign causality to the victims' poverty – people starve because they lack the means to acquire food. For others who view famine as a 'polit-ical disaster', its victims are defined not by economic but by political powerlessness. 'The real roots of famine may lie less in a lack of purchasing power within the market (although this will be one of the mechanisms of famine) than in a lack of lobbying power within national (and inter-national) institutions' (Keen 1994, p. 213).

According to de Waal (1997), the underlying cause of famine in contem-porary Africa is a failure of political accountability, both by national govern-ments and by international relief organizations. A 'political contract' imposes enforceable obligations on rulers to provide for certain needs and rights of their citizens, specifically, the need for food and the right to free-dom from famine. 'In the most effective anti-famine contracts, famine is a political scandal. Famine is *deterred*. The contract is enforced by throwing out a government that allows it to happen or otherwise punishing those in power' (de Waal 1997, p. 5). Sen argued that the conquest of famine in India is fundamentally due to 'respect for liberal civil and political rights – a free press, competitive elections and the other institutions of a liberal democ-racy' (de Waal 1997, p. 7). By contrast, famine persists in Africa where these institutions are absent or are too weak to allow an enforceable anti-famine political contract to be agreed and enforced. It is significant that famines in Africa are generally confined to rural areas: 'urban bias' means that govern-ments draw up implicit 'political contracts' with their urban constituents, but rural citizens are often not protected in this way.

Not only domestic governments but international donors might also have an interest in ignoring or promoting famine. There are suspicions that the Reagan administration's deliberately delayed response to the Ethiopian famine of 1984 was prompted by the knowledge that famine had toppled Emperor Haile Selassie ten years earlier, so that withholding food aid might similarly undermine the Marxist Dergue regime (Shepherd 1993).

Famine can be either a by-product or an instrument of war. War impacts negatively on food systems in a variety of ways. These are described below with examples from recent African 'war-famines'.

- *Food production is disrupted.* During a war, the ratio of food producers to food consumers falls. Farmers are conscripted, displaced, interned in camps, disabled or killed. Soldiers and militias 'requisition' food, livestock and assets from the civilian population ('Soldiers eat, peasants provide' – Teodros, a nineteenth century Ethiopian emperor). As elements of 'scorched earth' tactics, military groups on either side of a conflict cut down trees, poison wells, and burn granaries and fields of crops. In 1980, for instance, the Ethiopian government burnt, bombed and mined 140 000 hectares of land in Tigray. In neighbouring Eritrea 10 per cent of agricultural land was taken out of production by 1987 because of land mines. To prevent guerillas hiding in millet fields during a war in Chad, crops were burnt. In all these cases, civil war led directly to famine.

- *Trade and aid flows are disrupted.* War makes transport routes inaccessible: roads are mined, roadblocks are set up, bridges are damaged or destroyed, trucks and fuel are diverted to military uses. Civil insecurity or food blockades make the movement of food into war zones impossible. During 'Operation Red Star' in 1982, the Ethiopian army isolated Eritrea from surplus-producing areas within Tigray, blocked flows of food from Sudan and bombed local markets. Attacks on grain mills and granaries further undermined the grain trade in and around Eritrea. Governments that are prosecuting civil war against elements of their own population (e.g. secessionist movements) often ban relief agencies from intervening in conflict zones, or try to seize control of food aid. In 1984 Mengistu refused food aid into Eritrea and Tigray; as a consequence 400 000 Tigrayans fled to Sudan. In 1988 the government of Sudan refused donors access to war-affected Kordofan: 7 per cent of the displaced population died every week. The town of Juba in south Sudan was under siege for much of the 1980s and early 1990s. There were blockades on food and population movements and strict control of trade. Relief convoys were attacked and planes were shot at. In Somalia in 1986, more than 80 per cent of food aid was taken by the army or militias. Sometimes military and commercial interests coincide. Examples include profiteering within garrison towns in Sudan, Eritrea and Somalia by traders and military personnel; and attacks on relief supplies in South Sudan in 1988 by military personnel, to maintain high prices. Civilians in garrison towns including Monrovia (Liberia), Asmara (Eritrea) and Hargeisa (Somalia) had their property and food looted.

- *Local economies are disrupted.* Household entitlements to food (incomes and assets) collapse during a war: food and cash crop production are reduced, petty trading activities contract, and local markets for goods and services are undermined. Government and donor social and economic programmes (immunization, clinics, education, income-generating projects) are halted. Pastoralists in

Somalia had their livelihoods undermined when government troops attacked livestock herders at water points, poisoned wells, and destroyed water tankers. In Southern Sudan large numbers of livestock were confiscated and killed, causing destitution.

- *Coping strategies are undermined.* Communities are divided by war, shattering informal social support networks. It might become impossible for relatives to send remittances. In Southern Sudan, mines and roadblocks restricted access to wild foods around besieged garrison towns. Important sources of wild foods (forests and shrubs) were cleared to deny cover to opposing forces.
- *Refugees are created.* People are displaced from the land, from their homes, from their normal livelihoods and social support systems. Having lost their assets, incomes and access to food, they are extremely vulnerable and need assistance, but they are susceptible to communicable diseases due to overcrowding and poor sanitation in refugee camps.

Many of these factors contributed to the creation of famine conditions and excess mortality in the recurrent recent famines in south Sudan, as outlined in Box 5.1.

Box 5.1 Case study: The 1998 famine in Bahr el Ghazal, southern Sudan

In mid-1998 southern Sudan suffered its fourth major famine in ten years, resulting in an estimated 70 000–100 000 deaths and prompting observers to describe south Sudan as gripped by a permanent humanitarian crisis. As von Braun et al. (1998, p. 2) emphasize, 'famines in Africa must be explained in a long-term context', and nowhere is this more true than in south Sudan. Since the civil war restarted in 1983 an estimated 1.3 million people have been killed, 800 000 have fled from the south to the north and 400 000 have become refugees in neighbouring countries.

But the roots of contemporary political instability and livelihood insecurity in south Sudan go far back into Sudanese history. According to Keen (1994, p. 211) famine in Sudan reflects a long history of politically powerful groups exploiting 'their superior access to political power (including the direct use of force) in order to extract economic benefits from politically weaker groups'. Keen documents an almost unbroken sequence of livestock raiding, grain looting and enslavement of the population of south Sudan dating back to the 1820s, either initiated or tolerated by successive colonial (Turko-Egyptian and British) and post-independence administrations. The British decision to annex south Sudan to north Sudan in 1947 is seen by many as the source of Sudan's ongoing political turmoil, and as such is an underlying cause of recent famines. Southern resistance against Khartoum started soon after independence in 1956, prompted *inter alia* by the government's apparent indifference to a famine in Bahr el Ghazal in 1959.

Recent famines in Sudan exemplify the lethal relationship between drought and conflict, which often interact so closely that they are inextricable as causal mechanisms. For example, the drought in western Sudan in 1984–5 prompted hundreds of those who lost livestock because of failed pastures to 'restock' their herds by mounting violent cattle raids into northern Bahr el Ghazal, thereby exporting famine conditions to a region which was not directly affected by the drought. During the 1990s, counter-insurgency activities in northern Bahr el Ghazal have resulted in the displacement of over 600 000 people, the loss of almost 60 per cent of all livestock, and the abduction of possibly 10 000 women and children into forced labour and slavery. As a result of this systematic undermining of local livelihood systems over many years, mortality rates during the 1998 Bahr el Ghazal famine – which were comparable among the settled resident population to those recorded in Wollo, Ethiopia in 1973 or in Darfur in 1985 – were twice as high again among groups who had been internally displaced by conflict and physical insecurity.

The 1998 famine followed a year of 'insecurity incidents' in Bahr el Ghazal – aerial bombing, counter-insurgency and conventional warfare between Government of Sudan troops and the Sudan People's Liberation Army (SPLA), which intensified during the crucial farming months of April to July 1997. The distribution of rainfall during the 1997 agricultural season was also abnormal – above average at first, then below average – which reduced crop harvests and created severe food deficits throughout the region. Livestock died, were sold at 'distress' prices, or slaughtered for consumption. People were killed in fights over water. Food prices rose sharply, especially in counties where insecurity disrupted trade routes. People migrated out from the epicentre of the famine in search of lower food prices, higher livestock prices and work opportunities.

Despite their egalitarian ethic and established risk-pooling and reciprocity arrangements, many afflicted Dinka communities were unable to cope with the crisis by drawing on their own resources and their networks of social support. Consequently, informal community support systems contracted, as reflected in one local name for the famine – *cok dakruai*, which means 'famine of breaking relationships'. Late and inadequate deliveries of food aid, due to a failure of donors' information systems to predict the crisis, contributed to escalating excess mortality rates.

Source: Summarized from Deng 1999

Each of the theories discussed above adopts a particular perspective on the complex crises that are labelled 'famines'. In Africa, the analytical contributions of climatologists, demographers, economists, sociologists and political scientists all have relevance and offer useful insights, but no single theory adequately explains all famines at all times. The following section briefly examines general trends in the determinants of vulnerability to famine in Africa over time. This overview is necessarily schematic and simplified: detailed and more rigorous histories can be found elsewhere (see for instance Iliffe (1987), Watts (1983) on northern Nigeria, Pankhurst (1989) on Ethiopia and Keen (1994) on southern Sudan).

THE EVOLUTION OF FAMINE IN AFRICA

Most famines in precolonial Africa were triggered by natural disasters – drought or locusts which devastated crops, cattle disease which devastated livestock herds. These natural triggers operated in contexts where local economies were weak (subsistence oriented, not integrated with wider markets) and the logistical capacity to intervene in food crises was lacking. Some writers have argued that 'moral economy' redistributive mechanisms in precapitalist communities buffered weaker members against livelihood threats, but it is now recognized that these informal social insurance mechanisms provided limited resilience against covariate shocks, given the narrow economic base of these communities. Moreover, even in precolonial times conflict, slavery, cattle raiding and other forms of civil insecurity were significant factors in explaining food crises, contradicting benign views of egalitarian village life in precolonial Africa.

In the colonial period natural triggers persisted, but macroeconomic and political vulnerability to famine decreased in much of Africa,[3] due to the (uneven) development of communications and transport infrastructure, together with the initiation of early warning systems and relief intervention mechanisms by colonial administrations which recognized the need to alleviate food crises in order to achieve and retain political legitimacy. As a result of this combination of 'effective government, good transport, wider markets and some increase in average wealth' (Iliffe 1987, p. 158), the colonial era was associated with a decline in the number of mass mortality famines, and with a reduction in the scale of mortality following natural disasters.

Microeconomic vulnerability due to household-level poverty and fragmented markets persisted, however, with a shift in famine causation being attributed to a shift from what later came to be labelled as 'food availability decline' to 'exchange entitlement decline'. One Nigerian farmer contrasted the drought famine of 1913–14 with the (less severe) food crisis of 1927, which was also triggered by drought but exacerbated by grain hoarding, by stating: 'In 1914 we had money but no grain, in 1927 we had grain but no

money' (quoted in Watts 1983, p. 308). In the 1970s Marxist writers identified the penetration of capitalism into subsistence-oriented economies
during the colonial period – the commodification of food, the expansion of
cash cropping – as heightening peasants' vulnerability to natural disasters
or economic shocks,[4] but with hindsight these vulnerabilities now appear
to have been transitional, and the benefits of incorporation into national
and global markets have generally outweighed the risks, at least in terms of
reducing vulnerability to mass mortality famine. Hunger and malnutrition
have not been eradicated from formerly famine-prone countries like
Tanzania and Nigeria, even if famines have been.

After independence historically famine-prone African countries took one
of two routes. Some, like Tanzania, continued to make progress in reducing
vulnerability to famine (see Box 5.2). In stark contrast, in many other
countries independence was associated with increased political instability
and the emergence of famines where militarization, repression, counter-
insurgency and civil war played major roles. These countries saw a rise in
political vulnerability and a radical shift in the nature of famine. The
modern era of 'political famines' began with Biafra – a region of Nigeria
which had not previously been vulnerable to famine, and has not been
since – in the late 1960s. Since Biafra a number of African countries which
were not historically famine-prone have suffered conflict-triggered food
crises (Angola, Mozambique, Liberia, Sierra Leone, Zaire), while others
which had been susceptible to famines triggered by natural disasters experienced 'complex emergencies' in which the respective roles of drought and
civil instability were difficult to disentangle (Ethiopia, Sudan). The overlay
of natural and political triggers ('war + drought') in economically vulnerable contexts remains responsible for the recurrent famines that persist in
the Horn of Africa today.

Box 5.2   Case study: famines in Tanzania

Famines, mainly triggered by unreliable rains, were frequent events in precolonial Tanzania. A major famine occurred in 1888–92 which was causally
related to the 'Great Famine' that killed one-third of the Ethiopian population at the same time. Following a severe drought in 1888–9, Ethiopia's
rinderpest epidemic entered northern Tanzania in 1891, destroyed 90 per
cent of cattle herds and resulted in the death by starvation or hunger-related
disease of between two-fifths and three-quarters of the pastoralist Maasai
(Iliffe 1979, p. 124). Also during the 1890s Tanzanian farmers suffered
repeated plagues of locusts which devastated crops and, together with
drought in 1898, resulted in 'appalling losses' of human life: 'One observer
guessed that more than 750 000 people died of hunger in the whole
country between 1894 and 1899' (Iliffe 1979, p. 125).

During the colonial period famines in Tanzania became politicized. The Maji Maji rebellion of 1905–7 was brutally put down by the German Governor, Graf von Götzen, using famine as an explicit strategy. According to Iliffe (1979, p. 193), von Götzen 'decided to create a famine throughout the rebel area', which was achieved by German troops seizing food and destroying crops, following the view expressed by one of von Götzen's colonels, that 'only hunger and want can bring about a final submission'. Total deaths during the Maji Maji rebellion are estimated at 250 000– 300 000, though this includes deaths during the conflict as well as deaths from famine. During World War I a combination of food and livestock requisitioning by German and British troops plus a drought in 1917–18 created a famine during which 30 000 people died in Dodoma district alone, about 20 per cent of the district's population.

After World War I, Tanzania enjoyed 'a growing freedom from famine due to improved communications, the government's growing capacity to inter-vene, the spread of drought-resistant crops, and wider participation in the commercial economy which provided a certain protection against bad years' (Iliffe 1979, p. 315). Although episodes of food shortage continued to recur, most did not result in excess mortality because of a combination of effective local coping strategies (such as migration to find work) and effective relief interventions. An exception to this positive record was in 1929, when administrative incompetence in one district resulted in late delivery of food aid and an estimated 500 deaths (Bryceson 1990, p. 69). Thereafter, droughts caused acute food shortages in 1943, 1948–50, 1952–5 and 1960–1, 'which in the past would have killed enormous numbers' (Iliffe 1979, p. 471), but timely interventions restricted actual deaths to a few people in 1943 and 1949. After independence, potential famines were averted in 1974–5 and again in 1980–1, through government imports of food in the former case, and effective early warning information plus a rapid donor response in the latter (Bryceson 1990, pp. 207–9).

Similar narratives could be reconstructed for many other countries in sub-Saharan Africa. Many countries that are not conventionally perceived as 'famine-prone' have also experienced food crises that can be described as minor famines or 'near famines'. This is particularly true of countries bordering the drought-prone Sahelian countries (e.g. the northern savan-nah districts of coastal West African countries such as Ghana and Nigeria) and the drought- and conflict-prone Horn of Africa (e.g. Kenya and Tanzania). These countries tend to experience the climatic and political problems of their neighbours but to a milder extent – localized drought, say, or an influx of refugees. In northern Nigeria (Hausaland), for instance, famines triggered by drought occurred in 1913–14 – resulting in 'great human mortality' (Mortimore 1989, p. 38) – and again in 1972–4, both periods being associated with devastating famines throughout the West African Sahel.

Southern Africa has also suffered from periodic droughts which are generally, but not always, adequately ameliorated through a combination of indigenous 'coping strategies', additional food imports and distribution of food aid. Vaughan (1987, p. 1) found oral evidence of famines in colonial southern Malawi in 1903, 1922, and 1949–50, though the first two resulted in dearth rather than death and the scale of mortality in the last was very limited. The official death toll for the 1949–50 drought-triggered famine was 100–200, which Vaughan (1987, p. 162) dismisses as 'a gross under-estimation', though without venturing an alternative figure.

Finally, it is worth briefly considering cases of successful famine preven-tion in post-colonial Africa, as these experiences can offer lessons for the management and eventual eradication of food crises elsewhere in the future. Examples of recent 'averted famines' in Africa include Kenya and Botswana in the mid-1980s, and Zimbabwe and Southern Africa (as a region) in the early 1990s. Perhaps the key common factor linking all these cases is *political will*, on the part of both the national governments con-cerned and the international (donor) community. When information systems predicted an impending food crisis, governments mobilized their resources to import food and at the same time appealed for aid, and in every case the donors responded adequately and promptly. By contrast, most food crises in the Horn of Africa during the 1980s and 1990s were characterized by government hostility to the afflicted population, or by bad relationships between the national government and the international com-munity. In such contexts, early warning information is either suppressed, ignored, or disbelieved (see Chapter 8), governments either fail to respond or actively obstruct relief efforts, and the international community is either slow to react or must violate national sovereignty to channel food and other supplies to famine zones.

Even in the worst famines which provoke an international humanitarian response, it should be noted that food aid covers a relatively small proportion of food consumption needs. People facing food crises survive largely on their own resources, The final section of this chapter explores these responses, which have been labelled, rather misleadingly, 'coping strategies'.

FAMINE 'COPING STRATEGIES'[5]

The literature on famine 'coping strategies' emerged out of a concern to understand how rural people survive during drought-triggered food crises. Although the term itself is problematic (as Seaman (1993, p. 27) puts it: 'In current development jargon, Africans do not starve, they "cope"'), the fact remains that people facing a food shortage make strategic decisions about how to bridge their consumption deficit. During the 1980s, a number of case studies from Africa and South Asia suggested a common pattern in the nature and sequence of strategies adopted by rural people facing food crises. Corbett (1988) synthesized these studies and generalized a pattern of three discrete stages, reflecting increasing desperation: insurance mechanisms (e.g. savings), disposal of productive assets, and destitution behaviour (distress migration). The sequence of adoption is determined not only by the *effectiveness* of each strategy in terms of bridging the food gap, but also by the *cost* and *reversibility* of each action (Watts 1983). Strategies which have little long-run cost are adopted first (such as drawing down savings and calling on remittances). Strategies with higher long run costs that are difficult to reverse are adopted later (e.g. selling the household's plough). Finally, survival strategies (e.g. migrating off the land) reflect economic destitution and a *failure* to cope.

The early literature on coping strategies suffered from a failure to recognize consumption rationing as a routine austerity measure, reflecting instead an assumption that the first concern of hungry people is to raise or protect their food consumption. De Waal (1989) observed people 'choosing hunger' rather than selling key productive assets during a famine in Western Sudan, and even in non-famine contexts, smaller portions and cheaper diets are routinely adopted by the poor as a relatively costless way of making limited resources go further. The contemporary literature on coping behaviour recognizes that households facing food shortages are forced to trade off short-term consumption needs against longer-term economic viability. These trade-offs can be illustrated as a decision tree (see Figure 5.2) where the split between 'protecting' or 'modifying' food consumption reflects a harsh choice – whether to dispose of key productive assets and buy food, or hold on to these assets and go hungry in order to protect future livelihood. These difficult choices have profound implications for the household's immediate survival and future viability.

Davies (1996, p. 19) distinguishes between a 'food first' definition of coping strategies, these behaviours being 'designed to maximize immediate consumption' in situations of food scarcity, and a 'sustainable livelihood' definition, which sees coping strategies as 'designed to preserve livelihoods', which might incorporate food consumption rationing to protect future livelihoods. Another way of looking at this distinction is as a choice between 'erosive' and 'non-erosive' behaviour (de Waal 1989): strategies that draw on *additional* sources of food and income and so do not undermine livelihoods are 'non-erosive', while strategies that *deplete* the household's asset base and thereby undermine its future viability are 'erosive'. Seen in this light a decision to ration consumption rather than sell assets to buy food is entirely rational.

This distinction is illustrated in Figure 5.3, which also reflects the existence of sequences *within* as well as *between* discrete strategies (Devereux 1993b). The point at which any particular strategy is pursued to the extent

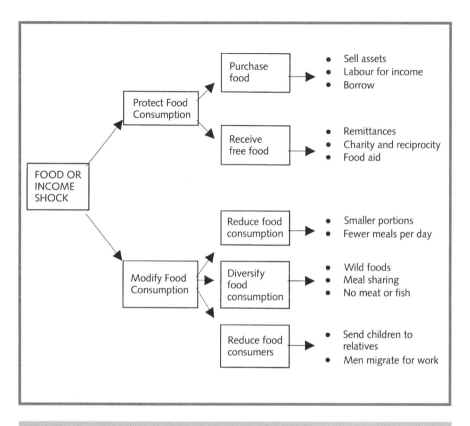

Figure 5.2 A categorization of coping strategies

Source: Adapted from Devereux 1993b, p. 53

that it becomes 'erosive' is difficult to assess, but is related to the long-term cost and irreversibility of any action that is taken.

'Informal safety nets' are a subset of coping strategies, referring to those strategies that involve drawing on support from other households. There is a strand in development studies, going back at least to Scott's influential book *The Moral Economy of the Peasant* (Scott 1976), which depicts subsistence-oriented agrarian societies as bound together by affection and mutual self-interest in a complex web of support networks that serve to spread risk and to protect vulnerable members. Swift (1989) defines the 'moral economy' as the range of non-market redistributive mechanisms that are found within communities and occur mainly within extended families and kinship groups.

There is some blurring over the boundaries of the moral economy – it clearly includes transfers between friends and neighbours (such as interest-free loans) but not exploitative transfers (such as high-interest moneylender loans), but the line between assistance and exploitation is

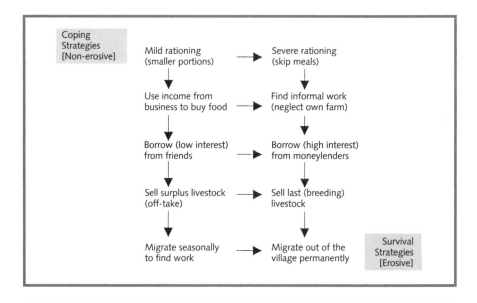

Figure 5.3   Coping versus survival strategies

often difficult to draw. Moreover, as Davies (1996, p. 37) points out, the 'moral economy' is not necessarily very 'moral'. 'There is nothing intrinsically 'welfarist' about the moral economy: indeed, it often engenders relations of subservience and dependence'. Informal safety nets can take one of two forms: *vertical transfers* (from richer to poorer households) and *horizontal transfers* (between equally poor households) (Swift 1993, p. 5). In general, vertical transfers are made for reasons of affection, duty, or patronage, and reciprocity is not expected, whereas horizontal transfers are often made to spread risk or smooth consumption over time, with the expectation that 'help' given now will be reciprocated when required in the future.

Adams (1993) found through monitoring of food disposal behaviour in Malian villages that poor farmers gave away as much as 20 per cent of their cereal harvests to others, about half as *zakkat* (obligatory religious contributions to Muslim clerics and destitutes) and half as voluntary gifts to relatives, friends and visitors. Adams also recorded daily transfers of commodities between friends and neighbours – mostly women – as well as many cases of giving or sharing meals. During the hungry season, as many as 25 per cent of production deficit days in these households were covered by non-market transfers of food, with most families giving as well as receiving assistance. In difficult years, the extent of this redistribution increased in response to need, but in crisis years (mainly severe droughts) it contracted because generalized production failures left no surplus for redistribution. This reveals the limitations of informal safety nets during crises such as famine. If entire social networks are subjected to generic shocks or covariate risks (such as a drought that affects all members of a community equivalently), then informal safety nets are likely to be least effective precisely when they are most needed.

Like most coping strategies, calling on friends and relatives for assistance is usually an intensification of existing activities rather than a completely new and unusual behaviour. In the neat linear sequence posited by Corbett (1988) and others, 'begging' comes near the end of the line, presumably because of its high social costs, but 'borrow grain from kin' comes very early. Devereux (1993b) suggests that a more nuanced gradation characterizes each cluster of coping strategies (such as informal safety nets, sale of assets, dietary change, or alternative income sources). Coping strategies are adopted in multiple, iterative layers; several strategies are adopted in parallel and each strategy is pursued with increasing intensity at increasing cost or irreversibility as conditions deteriorate, until ameliorated by a countervailing event such as a good harvest or the delivery of food aid.

To sum up, in the coping strategies literature, drawing on social networks is seen as an effective mechanism of dealing with minor shocks and idiosyncratic risks (such as seasonality or illness), but not with severe shocks or covariate risks (such as a major drought). Except for households with strong connections to wealthy relatives or generous patrons, this strategy offers limited relief and is rapidly exhausted. Moreover, as Swift (1993) points out, 'collective' coping mechanisms such as reciprocity and other informal redistribution arrangements in African communities are being steadily undermined by processes of economic change ('extension of the market'), political change ('extension of state power') and demographic pressure ('growth of population').

CONCLUSION

Although famines do still occur occasionally in other continents, sub-Saharan Africa remains the last region where a famine can be expected to occur at least every few years. Famines are the most visible and extreme manifestation of *acute* food insecurity. Africans also suffer, as other contributions to this book reveal, the severest consequences of *chronic* food insecurity, as measured by nutritional status and related indicators. However, the two sets of problems are causally quite distinct, and require different remedial interventions.

Although nutritional risk in rural sub-Saharan Africa is closely correlated with local food production and seasonal food price fluctuations, this chapter has emphasized that vulnerability to famine is explained at least as much by political factors as by climatic or economic shocks. Recent African famines have been triggered by civil war more often than by drought, and in several cases donors' reluctance or inability to intervene has compounded the crisis.

While the problems facing African agriculture might be regarded as 'economic' in origin and amenable to 'economic' solutions (such as investment in research and extension services), the problem of famine is political in origin and requires explicitly political solutions. The potential to eradicate famine is greater than at any time in Africa's history, but achieving that urgent goal requires the application of political will – by both national governments and the international community – to a degree that has been tragically lacking to date. Until an effective 'anti-famine contract' is established between every government and its citizens – and enforced if necessary by international humanitarian intervention – Africans will continue to die in famines that, in most cases, can and should be prevented.

CHAPTER SIX

Food Marketing

Bob Baulch

MARKETING ISSUES are frequently neglected in food security analysis. Yet, as the nexus that connects food producers with food consumers, marketing represents one of the most critical linkages in the food system. With increasing migration to the cities and specialization within the rural sector, effective marketing systems will become ever more important in ensuring food security in Africa.

The central problem of food marketing in developing countries may be summed up by the statement that 'food prices are too high, crop prices are too low' (Timmer et al. 1983). This statement, which is known as 'the food price dilemma', focuses our attention on the dual role that food prices play in most developing countries. For consumers, especially poor consumers, who spend a large proportion of their incomes on starchy staples, prices are a key determinant of food consumption levels. For the very poor, survival itself may hinge on low food prices. For producers, crop prices are a major factor governing incomes and cropping decisions. Over the long term, the incentives provided by crop prices are thus a critical (though by no means the only) determinant of the adequacy of food supplies. The inverse impact that food and crop prices have on consumers and producers focuses policy makers' attention on the level of marketing margins and costs, and creates a significant dilemma for them in both the short and long terms.

This chapter aims to introduce the main concepts and issues that arise in the analysis of food marketing in developing countries. It begins by describing the functions of markets and marketing, and the different types of agricultural marketing enterprises that may perform these functions. Next, some of the approaches that are used in assessing food marketing systems are identified, followed by an analysis of the different roles that the public sector may play in food marketing. The chapter concludes with a case study, which applies many of the concepts introduced to maize market liberalization in Tanzania.

FUNCTIONS OF MARKETS AND MARKETING

Agricultural marketing transforms products over time, space and form through storage, transportation and processing. Through markets, the ownership of goods and services are exchanged and prices are discovered (or formed). These functions of markets and marketing are summarized in Figure 6.1.

In order to understand the three marketing transformations (storage, transportation and processing) it is necessary to understand two key concepts: arbitrage and transfer costs.

Arbitrage refers to the process in which traders decide to engage in transportation, storage or processing by comparing prices in different locations, in different months, or for different product forms. *Transfer costs* are the fixed and variable costs, which traders incur in their arbitrage activities. In addition to the physical costs, which people usually associate with the three marketing transformations – storage costs (warehousing), freight or processing costs – there are a number of other important elements of transfer costs, which are often as important as these physical cost elements.[1] Some of these categories are outlined in Table 6.1. It is also important to realize that while two of the marketing transformations are non-reversible

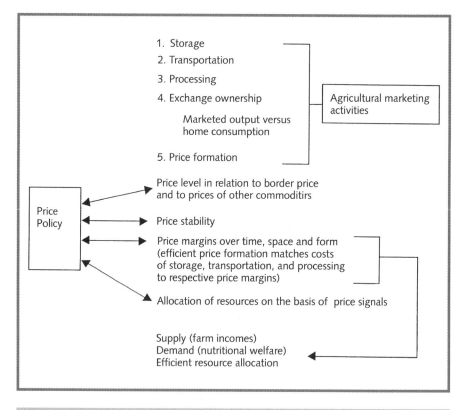

Figure 6.1   Functions of markets and marketing

Source: Timmer 1989

Table 6.1 The three marketing transformations

Transformation	Arbitrage over	Transfer costs	Is the transformation reversible?
Storage	Time	Physical (warehousing) Financial (opportunity cost) Product losses	No
Transportation	Space	Freight Loading and unloading Trade taxes	Yes
Processing	Product form (including quality)	Processing costs Recovery ratios Quality differential	No (except for a few odd exceptions)

(since negative storage is impossible and – in most cases – so is reverse processing); it is usually possible to reverse transportation. It should not, however, be assumed that the freight and other transfer costs associated with transportation are symmetric (indeed, it often costs more to ship grain from a supplying area to a consuming area than it does to send grain in the reverse direction).

In practice, the three marketing transformations become intertwined as transportation takes time (and therefore involves an element of storage), storage is often preceded by drying and grading (and therefore involves low-level processing), and the quality of food crops in different locations or seasons vary. Nonetheless, price analysts find it useful to distinguish between each of these three transformations in evaluating whether food markets are competitive, whether traders' marketing costs are reasonable, and deciding on what interventions or policies are needed to improve food marketing in a given situation.

Two useful techniques for identifying and assessing the efficiency of the three marketing transformations are marketing chain diagrams and marketing margin calculations (Timmer et al. 1983). Marketing chain diagrams are flow charts that portray the links between the production and consumption of a crop. Figure 6.2 shows an example of a marketing chain diagram for rice in northern Ghana. Marketing margins calculations may be either gross or net. Gross marketing margins are simply the difference, or 'spread', between the prices for a commodity at two different stages of the marketing chain, e.g. the difference between the retail price of rice in urban areas and the price at which traders will purchase paddy from farmers in rural areas. Net marketing margins are gross marketing margins minus the costs traders incur in their marketing activities. High gross marketing margins are often assumed to indicate that food traders are making excessive profits, but usually may be explained in terms of the high marketing costs traders incur. Table 6.2 shows the average marketing margins associated with the Ghanaian rice marketing chain in Figure 6.2.

AGRICULTURAL MARKETING ENTERPRISES

A range of different enterprises can undertake the marketing transformation listed in Table 6.1, and it is important to realize that different types of enterprises may be preferable for different commodities and/or in different situations. Abbott, the former head of FAO's Marketing and Credit service,

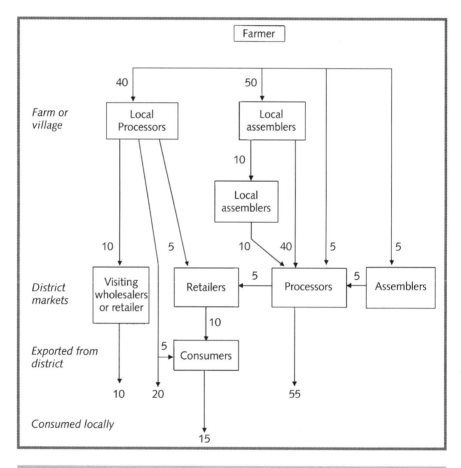

Figure 6.2   Marketing chain for rice, Atebubu District, Ghana

Note: Numbers indicate the percentage through a particular channel.
Source: Southworth 1981 and Timmer et al. 1983

Table 6.2 Average marketing margins for rice produced in Atebubu District and retailed in Kumasi, Ghana, January through July 1977

Item	Cedis per tonne[a]	Percentage of retail price
Atebubu market wholesale price[b]	2216.93	83.0
Producer price[c]	<u>1894.38</u>	<u>70.9</u>
Assemblers' gross margin	322.55	12.1
Commissions	(20.06)	(0.8)
Transport	(90.28)	(3.4)
Handling and storage	(8.00)	(0.3)
District tax	<u>(30.10)</u>	<u>(1.1)</u>
Assemblers' net margin	174.11	6.5
Kumasi wholesale price[b]	2525.00	94.5
Atebubu market wholesale price	2216.93	83.0
Processors' gross margin	308.07	11.5
Transport	(50.06)	(1.9)
Parboiling	(40.13)	(1.5)
Milling	(60.19)	(2.2)
Handling	(16.03)	(0.6)
Commissions	<u>(20.00)</u>	<u>(0.7)</u>
Processors' net margin	121.66	4.6
Kumasi retail price[b]	2671.80	100.00
Kumasi wholesale price	<u>2525.00</u>	<u>94.5</u>
Retailers' gross margin	146.80	5.5
Handling	(6.50)	(0.2)
Stall rental	<u>(7.00)</u>	<u>(0.3)</u>
Retailers' net margin	133.30	5.0

Notes:
(a) Paddy prices at the producer and Atebubu market wholesale level were converted to their milled equivalent at a 0.62 milling ratio. One cedi = 0.87 US dollars in 1997.
(b) Market prices are the average of monthly price figures collected by the Ministry of Agriculture from January through July 1977.
(c) The producer prices are the average of prices recorded in the farm survey for producers in the Kwame Danso area.
Source: Southworth 1981 and Timmer et al. 1983

has devised the following useful classification of agricultural marketing enterprises:[2]

1 *Indigenous private enterprises* are small firms, often based around a family run business, where capital is owned by one of the managers of the enterprise. As capital is often scarce, they tend to have very low

cost structures, making full use of family labour and only making out-lays on equipment and other capital that is indispensable to their operations. Since decision making is highly concentrated in such firms, they are able to take advantage of unexpected market condi-tions, and tend to work best for products where attention needs to be paid to quality (e.g. fresh fruit and vegetables, livestock). Concentra-tion of decision making also makes indigenous private enterprise highly innovative, although their ability to respond to changing mar-ket conditions is often tempered by unavailability of working capital. Sometimes family ties and kinship groups are used to extend traders' geographical areas of operation and access to working capital.

Indigenous private enterprises are undoubtedly the most common form of agricultural marketing enterprise in developing countries, but are often viewed with suspicion by policy makers if they are associ-ated with particular ethnic groupings (e.g. Asians in East Africa, or the Chinese in Southeast Asia). In grain markets, large indigenous private enterprises are also frequently accused of 'hoarding', 'profiteering' and other forms of price manipulation.

2 *Transnational Corporations* (TNCs) are enterprises which buy or sell goods in a number of different countries, and which enjoy easy access to both export and international capital markets. Examples of TNCs engaged in agricultural marketing include: Booker-Tate, Cargill, Del Monte, Geest, Harrison & Crosfields and Unilever. TNCs utilize their access to international markets to obtain capital at preferential rates, to hire skilled workers internationally (in particular management and engineers) and to obtain plant and other processing equipment from overseas. Because of their close connections with buyers in export markets and access to capital and technology, they are well equipped to compete in export markets, and often have brand names associ-ated with their organizations. They are also well placed to take advan-tage of economies of scale and scope in marketing, and are well placed to extend high-yielding seeds and improved crop varieties to the farmers who supply their buying stations/processing plants. Although the senior management of TNCs are usually expatriates, TNCs often train and promote nationals to take over the running and management of local factories, plantations and outgrower schemes to reduce their high cost structures.

TNCs are often viewed with suspicion by developing country governments because of their size, connection with international capital markets and reliance on expatriate management. Abbott (1987) argues that these disadvantages need to be set against the con-tribution they can make to agricultural development, technology transfers, and the development of processing and export industries. Careful advance negotiations between the host government and TNCs can often ensure that a high proportion of the benefits and foreign exchange their activities generate are retained in country. Conditions can also be specified for the training and transfer of management to nationally recruited staff.

3 *Cooperatives* are marketing enterprises that are owned by, and operated on behalf, of those who use its services. Cooperatives allow their members to attain economies of scale and scope in input procurement and output marketing, usually by spreading fixed costs over a wide base. They may also be able to raise prices by increasing the bargaining power of their individual members *vis á vis* traders and consumers. Cooperatives are rarely able to match the cost efficiency of indigenous private enterprise, but are well suited to the assembly and sale of standardized, relatively non-perishable products (such as coffee, cocoa and cotton) in pre-established markets. Cooperatives also tend to be active in the field of input supply (especially fertilizer) in many countries. Cooperatives tend to perform best in situations where their members are well educated and 'homogenous' (i.e., they all belong to the same ethnic or religious group).

Developing country governments tend to favour cooperatives because of their distrust of indigenous private enterprise, and their desire to see that farmers receive 'fair' prices. Some African countries have even established export monopolies for their cooperative enterprises (e.g. the West Cameroon Cooperative Union monopoly over coffee). These government established cooperatives often tend to 'backfire', as their protected status allows costs to rise, and management becomes unable to maintain control over an ever increasing scale of operations. Smaller, 'bottom-up' cooperative organizations established by farmers or traders themselves tend to be more successful.

4 *Parastatals* (which include marketing boards and state trading companies) are enterprises that are set up under government direction with government capital. While they may be autonomous in their day-to-day operations, major operating decisions are usually subject to the approval of government. They have been found to be useful instruments to implement government pricing policies, to impose marketing monopolies, and to raise bargaining power in domestic or international markets. Food grain parastatals are often charged with food price stabilization activities via the operation of buffer stocks and control over imports and exports of food (e.g. Kenya's National Cereals Produce Marketing Board, the National Milling Corporation in Tanzania, or Zimbabwe's Grain Marketing Board). Some export marketing parastatals attempt to control enough of the total or seasonal volume of a commodity to be able to influence international prices (e.g. the Costa Rican Coffee Institute (ICAFE) and the Cyprus Potato Marketing Board). Parastatals may be assigned monopolies in domestic markets in order to concentrate sales of produce through a

particular processing plant, and to facilitate the collection of credit repayment and other dues from small farmers.[3]

Parastatals tend to be most useful for regulating the marketing of priority standardized commodities such as cereals, coffee, cocoa and cotton. Since they usually have substantially higher cost structures than indigenous private marketing enterprises, or are required to perform uneconomic activities, they usually require subsidies from the government. The level of such subsidies can represent a significant share of the government budget, and is best controlled by linking subsidies to specific parastatal activities, and ensuring that the parastatal does not compete with private sector trade. The management of parastatals must also be strong enough to take hard-headed business decisions and resist the multiple, and often unrealistic, demands placed upon them by politicians.

THE ROLE OF THE PUBLIC SECTOR IN FOOD MARKETING

The role of the public sector in agricultural and food market development is a highly controversial question. Some neo-classical economists argue that the state should confine its activities to the provision of infrastructure and public goods that facilitate food marketing. Other economists, of a structuralist persuasion, argue that the strategic and political importance of food means that its marketing should be controlled by the State. A third group (amongst which I would place myself) argues that selective interventions in food markets can be justified in situations where there are market failures and imperfections, and/or for distributional and equity reasons. In this regard, three main roles can be identified for the public sector in food marketing: state trading, price stabilization, and market development/regulation.

STATE TRADING

This was the model adopted by many of the parastatal marketing boards set up in East and West Africa during the colonial era or shortly after independence. The advantages of such marketing boards are, in principle, that they allow the State to control both producer and retail prices, thereby ensuring that pricing is 'fair' and protecting both farmers and consumers against 'exploitation' by private sector traders. Through the imposition of pan-territorial and pan-seasonal prices, state trading also allows government to pursue food price stability and 'spatial egalitarianism' (Bryceson 1993).[4]

The operational problems associated with state trading are well known (Bates 1981; Timmer 1989). The food price dilemma leads governments to try simultaneously to raise producers crop prices while reducing the price consumers pay for food. The only way they can do this is by squeezing marketing margins, and subsidizing the costs of the food marketing parastatal. Furthermore, since the operating costs of parastatals tend to be higher, usually, than those of private traders, 'rent seeking' behaviour by their employees is common. These costs tend to escalate over time so the efficiency of the parastatal deteriorates. Due to financial constraints and inefficiency, parastatals are often unable to pay farmers for their produce on time and payment delays may take several months (or in the worst cases, years!). Where parastatals are unable to procure or to meet consumer demand, unofficial, 'parallel' markets in food tend to develop.

Under both internal and external pressure to liberalize their economic systems, most African governments have abandoned attempts to operate monopoly state trading systems for food. However, many food marketing parastatals retain a significant share of domestic markets for some grains and export crops.

PRICE STABILIZATION

Unstable crop prices hurt producers, especially small farmers who may be risk averse, and who are discouraged from producing more than they need for their own consumption needs by uncertainty about changes in crop prices between planting and harvest. Unstable food prices hurt consumers, especially the urban and landless poor, who rely on frequent purchases of cheap, starchy staples to meet their calorie needs. Governments in many developing countries have consequently attempted to stabilize the prices of the principal cereals consumed.

Most governments that attempt to stabilize food prices do so using a combination of public storage and trade policy (Timmer 1989; Monke et al. 1997). Public storage usually involves the procurement of grain by a parastatal marketing agency in years when there has been a good harvest and prices are low, and releasing grain for sale to the consumer in years when there has been a poor harvest and prices are high. Figure 6.3 shows how such a classic buffer-stock scheme works in the absence of international trade. D represents the demand curve for maize and P^{target} represents the price at which the government wishes to stabilize the price of maize in (say) the capital city of the country. In years when there is a poor harvest (represented by supply curve S^p) the grain marketing parastatal needs to release quantity AB of grain from storage in order to prevent maize prices from rising above P^{target}. Conversely, in years when there is a good maize harvest (represented by supply curve S^g) the parastatal needs to buy quantity BC of maize in order to prevent prices falling below P^{target}.

A number of problems with this strategy for stabilizing maize prices should be apparent. First, we do not know whether good harvests in some years will automatically offset poor harvests in other years. In particular,

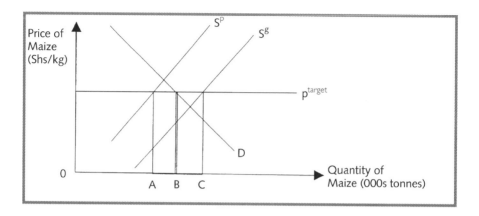

Figure 6.3   Price stabilization using a buffer stock scheme

there can be no guarantee that there will always be enough maize in the marketing parastatal's storage silos to stabilize prices at P^{target}. If the domestic supplies of grain run out (this is known as a 'stock-out') food prices will have to rise unless the government can obtain extra grain supplies from abroad. Second, it is well known that the cost of storing grain in public sector facilities is often quite high when compared with the costs of private grain storage or importing grain from abroad. Indeed, if the country's own maize harvests are not too closely correlated with world production, it could be cheaper for the government to export its maize surplus in good harvest years, store the foreign currency it earns in the bank, and then import maize with this hard currency in years of poor harvest. This method of stabilizing food prices is known as a 'buffer-fund' and requires the government to grant the food marketing parastatal a monopoly in the importation and exportation of grains.[5] Third, for political reasons, few governments will want to rely on international trade for their additional grain requirements. So, in reality, the choice facing policy makers is not whether to use buffer-stocks or buffer-funds to stabilize food prices, but what should be the relative importance of these two means of price stabilization.

Finally, it is important to note that, in practice, price stabilization does not require food marketing parastatals to set pan-seasonal or pan-territorial prices. Many countries stabilize their food prices by setting a price floor below which producer prices should not fall, and a price ceiling above which retail prices should not rise. Crop and food prices are free to vary according to supply and demand within the band between the floor and ceiling price. This makes the graphical analysis of the operation of a buffer-fund[6] a little more complicated than in Figure 6.3, but the same general principles apply. Furthermore, it is not necessary that the floor price at which the food marketing parastatal buys produce from producers, or the ceiling price at which it sells to consumers, are pan-territorial. For example, the food marketing parastatal in Indonesia, Badan Urusan Logistik (BULOG) adjusts the prices it pays to farmers according to the costs of storage and transportation in different locations. The two principal advantages of the use of price bands to stabilize food prices are that:

- the food marketing parastatal does not need to buy and sell more than a proportion of national grain production; and
- the prices at which the parastatal buys and sells grain can be adjusted to take account of transportation, storage and other transfer costs.

As such, price bands reduce the fiscal costs of price stabilization and permit lower cost, private sector traders to play a significant role in internal grain marketing.

MARKET DEVELOPMENT AND REGULATION

Many agricultural economists argue that the public sector's principal role in agricultural marketing should be to provide the infrastructure, information and regulatory systems that allow private markets to develop and function efficiently.[7] The underlying rationale is that the existence of public goods and market failures create externalities which can best be overcome by government interventions. Private sector traders may be prepared to invest in processing plants, storage facilities and trucks for their exclusive use. However, investment in roads, ports, and – in most cases – telecommunications that confer wider benefits to all market users will require some government involvement. It is vital for efficient marketing that farmers, traders and consumers have good information on prices. However, such information is unlikely to be provided by private agents because external benefits cannot be captured. Where private agents possess good information they are likely to withhold it in order to gain market power. Hence, it is argued, the state should be responsible for providing public goods, such as transportation and communications infrastructure plus a market intelligence system.

In order for food markets to develop and thrive it is also important that there should be a regulatory framework. This includes the establishment of grades and quality standards, weights and measures, food safety standards, and rules and legal codes concerning contracts. The existence of such a regulatory framework, although sometimes resisted by traders in the short term, usually pays large dividends in terms of reducing transfer and transaction costs and stimulating the development of markets over the long term.

CASE STUDY: MAIZE LIBERALIZATION IN TANZANIA

During the 1980s, Tanzania carried out a market liberalization programme that completely transformed maize trading. The market share of the

National Milling Corporation (NMC), the food marketing parastatal, has collapsed, and the private grain trade has grown rapidly in its place. This experience is in contrast to other Eastern and Southern African countries, such as Kenya and Malawi, where liberalization has been less comprehensive, and the private sector response has been more limited (Beynon et al. 1992; Jones 1994). The first two parts of the case study discuss the particular conditions that led to the collapse of state marketing in Tanzania. The performance of the emerging private sector in maize marketing is then discussed, and the final section identifies areas of policy intervention where the Tanzanian government could do more to support private trade.

FOOD MARKETING UNDER STATE CONTROL

Between independence in 1961 and liberalization in 1984 the state exerted control over maize marketing in three main areas:

- *Imposition of a single marketing channel.* Between 1973 and 1984, the NMC was the only legal channel for marketing and milling maize. The NMC arranged its purchases through the *Ujamaa* collectivized villages. The NMC was also the sole legal agent allowed to trade grain with other countries.
- *Imposition of price controls.* The state purchased grain from farmers at pan-territorial and pan-seasonal producer prices. After 1974 pan-territorial consumer prices were also introduced. The government suppressed real producer prices, and consumer maize flour prices were heavily subsidized.
- *Restrictions on grain movements.* Restrictions on domestic grain movements were most severe immediately prior to liberalization when individuals were only allowed to transport up to 30 kg of grain between districts.

The Tanzanian government's motives for intervention stemmed from a profound distrust of private trade, which it believed to be inherently exploitative. There was also a desire to eliminate the market dominance of Asian traders, who were seen as hostile to the project of 'nation building' (Gordon 1994). The government justified state trading on equity and food security grounds. Pan-territorial pricing was seen as an important instrument to equalize access to the market for consumers together with rewards for producers across all regions (Bryceson 1993). The government believed that it could do a better job at stabilizing prices and moving grain from surplus to deficit areas than private traders could.

State control has provided numerous opportunities for rent seeking by government and NMC officials, who enjoyed privileged access to subsidized and rationed credit, foreign exchange and food. State control over consumer prices was also an important instrument to gain vital political support from urban consumers.

However, the performance of state marketing in Tanzania was poor. Producers were commonly paid late, or were sometimes unable to sell their grain to the NMC after the main cropping season, when it became unable to cope with the desired volume of post-harvest sales. The NMC also became incapable of satisfying urban demand for subsidized flour. The provisioning capacity of the NMC declined markedly in 1979 because of the transport shortages triggered by war with Uganda. The NMC proved incapable of coordinating purchasing, distribution, processing and sales across the country, and became increasingly reliant on importing maize to supply to consumers in the capital, Dar es Salaam (Bryceson 1993). There were few incentives to improve management and performance, and it is likely that many staff diverted their effort into rent seeking rather than productive activities. The government seemed willing to cover any level of marketing loss, a factor that perpetuated weak management and poor performance.

Producer and consumer prices were set according to political objectives, and their impact on the financial position of the NMC was rarely considered. Consumer prices were particularly subject to political interference, and were drastically reduced during the late 1970s and early 1980s because of concerns about the urban cost of living and falling real wages (Bryceson 1993). The government's policy of pan-territorial producer prices imposed large costs on the NMC because it encouraged production in areas where there were large costs in transporting maize to major markets. This policy was responsible for the enormous growth of maize production in the Southern Highlands, which are over 1000 km southwest of Dar es Salaam.

State trading generated enormous losses because of inefficiency and pricing policy. In 1980 the combined losses and subsidies of the NMC were equivalent to 3 per cent of GDP or 8.5 per cent of government spending (Gordon 1994). The NMC's losses were also covered by commercial bank borrowing, so that agricultural marketing debts absorbed half of all commercial bank credit by the late 1980s (Jones 1994). These losses impacted on Tanzania's macroeconomic stability, because they widened the fiscal deficit, expanded domestic credit and accelerated the rate of inflation.

Because of the failings of the NMC, many farmers and consumers came to rely on the parallel market for grain. Although there is little data on the volume of private trade during the period of state control, it is likely that such trade was very significant. Gordon (1994) estimates that private trade supplied 8–15 per cent of the Dar es Salaam market during the early 1980s. This figure was probably much greater elsewhere because NMC activities were highly concentrated on Dar es Salaam.

LIBERALIZATION AND THE GROWTH OF THE PRIVATE SECTOR

In response to the enormous fiscal strain imposed by the NMC's losses and mounting donor pressure, the Government of Tanzania began a programme of food market liberalization in 1984. The sequencing of the

Table 6.3   Maize marketing reforms in Tanzania since 1984

Year	Reforms
1984	Movement restrictions raised from 30 kg to 500 kg.
	Maize flour subsidy removed.
	Differentiation of producer pricing between premium and non-premium areas.
1985	Roadblocks to intercept illegal grain movements removed.
	Primary Cooperatives reinstated with purchasing monopoly.
1987	All quantitative restrictions on grain movements removed.
	Strategic Grain Reserve created.
1988	Traders allowed to purchase from Primary Cooperatives.
1990	All national level restrictions on private trade lifted.
	Some regional and district level restrictions remain.

Sources: Coulter and Golob 1992, Bryceson 1993, Gordon 1994

maize market reforms is summarized in Table 6.3. By 1990 virtually all restrictions on the private trade in grains had been removed. As a consequence, the private trade in grain grew rapidly in response to liberalization. In 1985 private trade supplied 50 per cent of the Dar es Salaam market; by 1992 this figure had increased to 80–90 per cent (Coulter and Golob 1992). State marketing is now largely restricted to procurement in the Southern Highlands for a 150 000 tonne capacity Strategic Grain Reserve (SGR) created in 1987. This section explains the rapid growth of the private sector through an analysis of prices and marketing margins.

Figure 6.4 shows changes in the real official (NMC) producer and consumer prices. The graph shows that official consumer prices declined sharply during the late 1970s and early 1980s, and that the margin between the consumer and producer price narrowed. NMC losses and subsidies were large during this period because the official marketing margin was insufficient to cover the NMC's operation costs. Following liberalization in 1984, the consumer price rose because subsidies were removed. The graph shows that NMC sales fell sharply during this period because of the removal of subsidies and the growth of private trade.

In order to understand the collapse of NMC sales and the growth of private trade, it is necessary to compare official and open market prices and margins. Figure 6.5 compares real official producer and consumer prices with open market prices offered to producers in the Southern Highlands and consumers on the Northern Coast (Dar es Salaam).[8] During 1983 and 1984 open market prices were well above official prices. This was because of poor harvests and the heavy subsidization of official consumer prices. Open market prices fell sharply between late 1984 and 1986 as food availability increased. The removal of official consumer price subsidies further narrowed the gap between open market and official prices. Since 1987 open

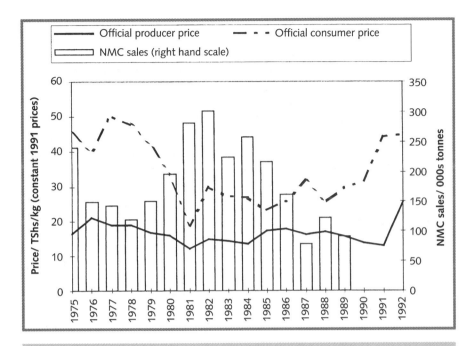

Figure 6.4 Official marketing margins and NMC sales

Source: Gordon 1994

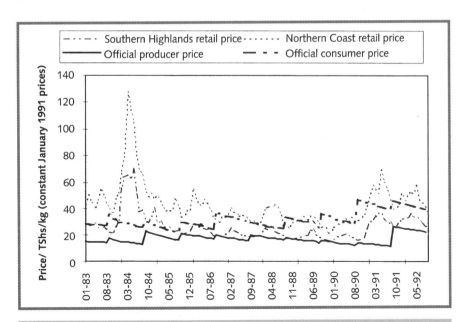

Figure 6.5 Open market and official producer and consumer prices

market prices have generally been within the official producer price and consumer price band. This has allowed private traders to co-exist with the NMC, and to capture a large market share.

Figure 6.6 compares the official and open market marketing margins calculated from the price data shown in Figure 6.5. It shows that official margins tended to increase over the reform period as subsidies were removed while open market margins tended to decline. Indeed, since 1987, open market margins have generally been lower than the official market margin. Under these conditions it is impossible for the NMC to compete with private traders, except in the remotest areas where official pan-territorial producer prices remain above open market producer prices.

THE PERFORMANCE OF EMERGING PRIVATE SECTOR MARKETING

There is considerable evidence that maize marketing in Tanzania has become more efficient since liberalization. Private sector margins have declined as traders' transfer costs have fallen. Trucking costs have declined because of greater import availability and improved infrastructure (Bevan et al. 1993). The abolition of restrictions on grain movement means that private traders no longer incur the substantial costs of evading state restrictions. Private sector trade appears to be highly competitive with the number of traders increasing greatly since liberalization. There seem to be few

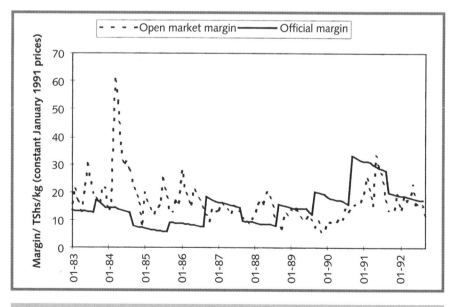

Figure 6.6 Comparison of official and open market margins

Source: Drawn from price data in IBRD 1994

barriers to entry, and there is even some evidence that maize markets have become more spatially integrated (Gordon 1994). Empirical studies find no evidence that traders earn excess profits, and their margins reflect marketing costs and risk premiums (Santorum and Tibaijuka 1992; Gordon 1994).

Despite these signs of improved performance, there are several obvious weaknesses in private sector trade. Private traders still operate on a very small scale and have not been able to integrate their operations vertically. Most new traders come from farming backgrounds and rely on agricultural earnings to raise their start-up capital (Santorum and Tibaijuka 1992). Few traders own vehicles, and hiring vehicle space is difficult in remote areas. Private sector costs would probably be much lower if traders operated at a larger scale and were better capitalized. These constraints have slowed the growth of the private sector grain trade after the initial, enormous, growth in the number of traders after liberalization. The private sector trade appears to be restricted to spot transactions and longer term relationships, such as forward transactions, and quality premiums have not emerged (Beynon et al. 1992). Private traders rarely engage in storage despite seasonal price increases of 30–40 per cent. Most 'within crop year' storage is carried out by farmers, and the SGR provides the only significant storage across crop years.

AREAS FOR POLICY INTERVENTION IN LIBERALIZED MARKETS

Government policy should aim to further the process of liberalization, which has brought obvious benefits. It should also attempt to support private sector development by tackling market failures and providing public goods.

Continued state engagement in marketing should be limited to a few clear objectives. In Tanzania, state marketing activities are now largely restricted to the SGR and the Primary Cooperatives, which procure for the SGR at pan-territorial prices. These agencies are advantaged by their access to credit and guaranteed market. However, the continuation of these subsidies to the SGR and cooperatives must be justified according to a full analysis of the costs and benefits of price stabilization. It is possible that the Government's price stabilization objectives could be achieved more cheaply by further liberalization measures. These measures include holding public auctions for SGR grain purchases, contracting the private sector to carry out storage, and/or liberalizing the cross-border trade in maize. One likely, adverse, consequence of the reduction in state trading is the decline of maize production in the Southern Highlands, whose producers have relied on price support from the NMC.

Increased state intervention could be justified in certain areas to further private sector market development. The growth of the private sector grain trade has clearly been impeded by the failure of credit markets. The Tanzanian government could work with the financial sector in attempting to find new ways of increasing access to credit amongst traders. The use of inventory credit where produce is offered as collateral offers some potential in this regard. The Government also has a role to play in providing public goods that facilitate more efficient food marketing. These include the provision of infrastructure, such as roads and market buildings by the Ministry of Civil Supply, the Market Development Bureau's dissemination of price bulletins and crop forecasts, and the enforcement of regulations (such as standard measures and quality grades) that assist food marketing by the private sector.

CONCLUSION

If Africa is to attain greater food security, it is essential that more attention is paid to food marketing. Yet, as with so many areas of economic analysis, there are no magic solutions or blueprint plans for improving the efficiency and equity of African food marketing systems. With the implementation of liberalization and structural adjustment programmes in recent years, the policy debate has moved away from a simplistic debate on 'state versus market' towards an appreciation of the strengths and weaknesses of different types of agricultural marketing enterprises. There is now greater recognition of the problems inherent in the types of state trading and price stabilization schemes that were popular in the 1960s and 1970s. By the same token, there is also a growing understanding of what the indigenous private sector can (and cannot) achieve given the climatic variability, poor infrastructure and pervasive market failures that characterize many countries in sub-Saharan Africa. As a consequence, selective interventions in food markets are likely to be needed for some years to come. By applying the techniques for analysing food markets outlined in this chapter, it is hoped that readers will gain a greater understanding of the operation and efficiency of African food markets on case by case basis. The key policy challenge is then to discover innovative ways to blend different marketing functions and enterprises together, so that they will complement and reinforce each other.

CHAPTER SEVEN

Food Aid and Trade

Christopher Stevens and Jane Kennan

WHAT IS IT ALL ABOUT?

OVER THE PAST quarter century an increasing number of countries in sub-Saharan Africa (SSA) have come to rely upon imports for a growing share of their food supply. Yet most have substantial agricultural resources and many are important exporters of agricultural goods. Does it make sense to export some agricultural items, such as coffee and cocoa, and to import others, such as wheat? Would it be more prudent to shift agricultural production away from exports towards satisfying domestic demand? Is food self-sufficiency a desirable goal, or even an attainable one?

These are the questions addressed in this chapter. The answers need to take account not only of the basic reasons why all countries trade and the opportunities – and pitfalls – that they experience, but also of the startlingly large changes that have occurred in *world* agricultural production and trade in recent decades.

The changes experienced in SSA have their counterpart elsewhere: to an extent, they have been fostered by trends in the international market. There has been a major shift in the structure of world agricultural trade over the past thirty years. This reflects, in turn, policies pursued in major producing regions. It has been associated, in particular, with the emergence of the European Union (EU) as a substantial producer of commodities which historically it imported. If such policies change – as they are likely to in the next decade – so will the advantages and disadvantages of SSA's current pattern of production and trade. It is vital that those concerned with food security understand the implications for their work of these changes which they cannot control and to which they must adjust.

The world market changes have been especially marked for cereals, which represent the commodity group of most interest to Africa. The continent has been absorbing a growing share of world exports at a time when the total volume of trade has also risen rapidly.

Although some of Africa's imports have been supplied as food aid, most have been in the form of commercial imports. This has been viable, despite the fall in world prices for most SSA exports, because the world price of imported cereals has fallen even more. This situation may be about to change. Future world supply and demand may well be influenced by the outcome of several policy changes currently on the agenda.

The three major forthcoming changes in the trade environment with implications for African food security are:

- the extension of agreed World Trade Organization (WTO) rules to temperate agriculture and related reforms to Europe's Common Agricultural Policy (CAP);
- the phasing down of special and differential treatment for developing countries;
- the erosion of trade preferences for SSA's exports.

CONCEPTS AND DEFINITIONS

It is self-evident that food is in a different category from many goods: without food people will die; without shoes or radios or iron sheeting they may be (severely) inconvenienced, but the stakes are not so high. This leads many to argue that food supply is too important to be left entirely to the market, and that it is dangerous for a state to become reliant for its supplies on world trade. There is much good sense in such arguments. But just as there are dangers in being over-reliant on international trade in agriculture so there are also costs (potentially catastrophic ones) in failing to take advantage of the opportunities provided by trade.

The key is to understand the dynamics of the world market, the ways in which it can contribute to food security and also the dangers that are lurking for the unwary. This section introduces some of the concepts and ideas needed to appreciate the analysis of recent trends.

WHY TRADE?

There are many reasons why in practice the current pattern of trade is the way it is, but underlying these are two fundamental ones that apply equally to agricultural and non-agricultural goods. They are to take advantage of: economies of scale, and differences in resource endowments. The day-to-day effect of government policies and private attempts to influence markets only modifies the effect of these fundamental forces which, between them, exert a major influence on the goods and services that any given country can export successfully and those that it needs to import.

Economies of scale simply mean that most goods are more expensive to produce in small amounts, and get cheaper to produce as the scale of production increases. This happens because, with larger-scale production, it becomes possible and economical to use specialized machinery and equipment, and to split the work up among many different people who become expert in an aspect of production.

The international trade of small countries – like many of those in SSA – is very strongly influenced by the fact that most goods are cheaper to produce on a large scale. The range of goods in which small countries can achieve an efficient scale of production is more limited than for large countries. This is why small countries are usually more open to trade than large countries (as measured, for example, by their ratio of exports to gross national product (GNP)). For small countries to try to produce all goods at home would be hopelessly inefficient.

Differences in resource endowments

The existence of scale economies helps to explain why countries trade, but what determines the products they export and import? The answer is that countries have different resource endowments. Where a particular resource is relatively abundant it will tend to be relatively cheap, as will the goods whose production uses a lot of that resource. The country concerned will thus tend to export these goods, and to import goods whose production uses a lot of resources that are more abundant in other countries.

What exactly is a resource? In the context of trade, this term refers to any input to production that cannot move among countries. For example, inputs that are freely traded on world markets, such as ginned cotton, are not resources in this sense, because any country can buy as much of them as it can afford. However, land suitable for growing cotton is a resource. There are many specific sorts of resources, but they can be grouped conveniently into three categories: natural resources, human resources and infrastructure.

Natural resources are the most obvious category – and so is their effect on international trade. Countries with soil and climate suitable for growing coffee tend to export coffee, while those with large oil reserves tend to export oil. More generally, countries with relatively abundant natural resources tend to export mainly primary or processed primary commodities.

Some countries that export mainly primary products are rich, because their natural resources are abundant in an absolute sense, too – Saudi Arabia, for example. But some are poor: their meagre natural resources are *relatively* abundant simply because they have so few other resources – Chad, for instance.

A country's *people* are its most important resource. Only a small fraction of the world's population is internationally mobile, so the scope for one country to buy skilled labour from other countries is limited (although not entirely absent). Moreover, educated, disciplined labour is the key input to production in the two biggest and fastest-growing sectors of world trade: manufacturing and the provision of services.

The more skilled a country's labour force, the more likely is that country to be an exporter of manufactures. In particular the more likely it is to export the sorts of manufactures that command good prices on world markets, such as high-technology or skill-intensive goods.

A country's *infrastructure* – transport and communications, and the supply of electricity and other utilities – plays a double role in trade:

- poor infrastructure is clearly a barrier to trade – if a country's roads are poor and there are no cold storage facilities at the airport, it cannot export fresh vegetables;
- good infrastructure is a resource – there are many activities, both in manufacturing and in services, which require a reliable supply of electricity or excellent telecommunications.

Most forms of capital other than infrastructure cannot be regarded as a resource nowadays. Machinery and equipment are freely traded, and buildings can be constructed anywhere in a year or two. The finance for this can come from direct foreign investment or by borrowing on the global financial market. The pattern of trade does not usually depend fundamentally on the presence or absence of money, machines and factories. Many capital-intensive activities, for example, are also skill-intensive, and hence even if a country builds factories it will not be able to export competitively if skilled labour is scarce.

By contrast, if a country's other resources – for example its climate and soils, or its educated labour force – make it a potentially competitive exporter of some product on world markets, then it will usually be able to obtain the financial and physical capital needed to realize that potential. This is true even if the production process is highly capital-intensive.

The purpose of this review of the *fundamental* factors determining the scale and composition of a country's trade is not to divert attention from the many other factors that influence trade patterns in practice. These range from tastes, which vary widely, both among countries and among people, to the existence of restrictive patents. The firm owning a patent may either refuse to license its product or process to firms in other countries, or do so only under the condition that the output is not exported. This gives its own country a virtual monopoly of that product on world markets. Protectionist policies in some countries may make it impossible for other countries to trade profitably in the goods in which they are richly endowed. The reasons for the emphasis on fundamental determinants of trade is that for most SSA states they point to the central role of agriculture.

COMPARATIVE ADVANTAGE

In other words, many SSA states have a comparative advantage in agriculture, but what does this mean in practice? What does someone concerned with food security need to know about comparative advantage?

Comparative advantage means that countries specialize in those goods which they can produce *relatively* cheaply – and export these in order to import other goods which it would be *relatively* more costly to produce at home. The term 'relative' has a double meaning in this context: it refers to one good as compared with other goods, and to one country as compared with other countries.

One important question is whether comparative advantage is unchanging. Does the concept lock countries into particular lines of production and do its proponents argue, for example, that SSA must forever export unprocessed primaries to grace the tables of rich Northern households? Or can countries acquire (or lose) a comparative advantage in the production of a particular good or service, and can government policies affect this process?

The answer is that comparative advantage does change, and there are ways in which this process may be speeded up (or hindered). But usually it does so slowly, over time and within limits, most notably those imposed by resource endowments. Hastening the evolution of comparative advantage may mean adopting policies that help to develop the resources that are needed to sustain a different level of competitive production, such as investment in human capital.

Another important question is how the lessons derived from theory should be adapted to cope with the fact that most states ignore comparative advantage to some extent in their policies. The EU's CAP, for example, represents a major attempt to 'interfere with comparative advantage', that is to allow Europe to produce and export goods which could more efficiently be produced abroad. The cost of this interference is borne by European citizens (through higher prices and lower economic growth) as well as by third parties (such as Argentina or Philippines) whose exports are disrupted. These distortions may make less competitive the production of some goods in which SSA has a comparative advantage (such as some staple cereals). They may also, in circumstances explained in the next section, make it possible for SSA to export competitively items in which it might not have a comparative advantage.

The answer is that SSA policy must take account of such restrictions, and opportunities, but that they only modify, and do not alter fundamentally, the goods in which each state has a comparative advantage. The EU's policies may, for example, make it financially attractive for Swaziland and Zimbabwe to devote part of their agricultural resources to producing sugar for export and to use the revenue to pay for imported cereals, but they will not allow them to develop a competitive heavy industry or sophisticated manufacturing sector for which the endowments of resources are lacking. Direct and indirect subsidies to promote such sectors will only result in a wasteful misallocation, leaving other sectors (including agriculture) less prosperous and productive than they could have been.

Moreover, policy makers must always bear in mind that the distortions of other states (and the problems and opportunities that they create) may be transitory. If the EU changes its policies, sugar production in Swaziland and

Zimbabwe could become less attractive relative to cereal production. Since it takes time and resources to shift agricultural production from one crop to another, those concerned with food security policy should always keep an eye on the medium term. This chapter identifies some of the main changes likely to be important over this time horizon.

MARKETED OR NON-MARKETED CROPS

The distinction between agricultural production destined for exports and that consumed on the local market is often described as a conflict between *cash* crops and *food* crops. This is not very helpful terminology, and it is not used in this chapter. It is unhelpful both because the terms are imprecise and – more importantly – because it diverts attention away from the really important distinction.

What are cash crops? If the term is used to describe agricultural items that are sold in a market, then it covers not only exports but also production traded on a country's domestic markets. And many cash crops are also food crops, e.g. groundnuts, beans and beverages.

The most useful distinction for this chapter is between products that a farming household grows primarily for its own consumption, selling any surplus in an informal way to neighbours, and crops that have to be sold in some form of market transaction. This is because marketing involves the producer in a transaction in which s/he may be a weak partner and in which prices may be volatile (so that the farmer faces a double vulnerability: to the weather and to the market). Exporting *may* put the farmer in a weaker bargaining position than domestic sale, but this is not certain.

From the viewpoint of trade, agricultural activities may best be divided into three categories relating to the level and type of market transaction:

- subsistence agriculture (informal sale only), which does not involve a market transaction;
- domestically oriented, import-substituting agriculture, which involves a transaction on a market that the government may try to regulate (for good or ill, effectively or ineffectively);
- export-oriented agriculture, which involves two market transactions (on the domestic market and, additionally, on an international market that cannot be influenced effectively by small exporting states).

This categorization directs our attention to the way in which the distribution of gains will be influenced by the market power (or lack of it) of each actor. Even if a country as a whole may be better off exporting agricultural products, and using the proceeds to import food, it does not follow that all farmers will gain. The moderately poor may lose (and the very poor may not have the opportunity to participate even if they wish to do so) if domestic or international markets are uncompetitive.

TERMS OF TRADE

Economists use the words *terms of trade* to describe the ratio between the prices of a country's exports and of its imports. There are several types of terms of trade, which measure different ratios. The most commonly used is the *net barter terms of trade*. This is the ratio between one unit of a country's exports and one unit of its imports. For example, the net barter terms of trade show how many tonnes of coffee Kenya must export to import one tonne of petroleum.

The terms of trade are normally used to describe changes in the ratio of export and import prices over time. In other words, what is of interest to Kenya is not how many tonnes of coffee it has to export in order to import one tonne of petroleum, but whether as time passes it is having to export more or less coffee for that tonne of petroleum. If the price of coffee rises relative to that of petroleum, so that one tonne of coffee will now buy more petroleum, there is said to be a *favourable movement* in the terms of trade. If the opposite occurs, there is an *unfavourable movement* in the terms of trade.

The terms of trade that are most usually calculated for Africa, and other developing country regions, are between primary product exports and manufactured imports. This is because Africa exports mainly primary products and imports mainly manufactures. What we need to know is whether the volume of manufactures that Africa can import with its export revenue is increasing or decreasing. The answer is that, for most parts of Africa for much of the last two decades, it has been decreasing.

Another use of the terms of trade, however, is to examine the relative price of agricultural imports and exports. In 2000, will one tonne of Kenya's coffee exports buy more or less wheat imports than it could in 1985? It is these *intra-sectoral terms of trade* that are of importance when identifying which types of agriculture are the most profitable. The next section explains how SSA's recent agricultural trade pattern can be related to movements in the intra-sectoral terms of trade.

PRODUCER AND CONSUMER SUBSIDIES

What is an agricultural subsidy? It is any transfer of income to farmers which comes about as a result of government actions and would not occur if trade (domestic and international) were unrestricted.

Some subsidies are obvious. When the EU uses European taxes to buy and store surplus European dairy products, it is a subsidy. Similarly, when the EU pays exporters to sell beef to Côte d'Ivoire or South Africa at below the cost of production (knocking out Burkinabe and Namibian exports in the process), this is also a subsidy. Such subsidies are conventionally called *producer* subsidies.

But there are other, less obvious, subsidies. If government regulations artificially restrict supply on to the domestic market (for example through heavy protectionism), price levels rise and consumers have to pay more for their food than they otherwise would. Such transfers from consumers to producers are known as *consumer* subsidies.

Most developed countries have used both producer and consumer subsidies to support their farmers. SSA states have often used consumer subsidies (in the form of import tariffs and quotas) to protect some domestic agriculture. But producer subsidies have been limited by the budgetary stringency that has afflicted most SSA states over the past decade.

RECENT TRENDS

THE CHANGING PATTERN OF IMPORTS

The regions which have seen the most rapid increase in imports over the past 30 years are the former Soviet Union (FSU), followed by the Near East and Africa. Since the mid-1970s, Africa (sub-Saharan and North) has seen a steady increase in its share of world cereal imports (Figure 7.1), the absolute volume of which has also been rising. Whereas in 1975 Africa absorbed 8 per cent of world imports, by 1998 this had increased to 16 per cent. The continent's share of world rice imports shot up after the mid-1970s (reaching a peak of one-quarter or more for the decade from 1982) before stabilizing. Wheat and flour imports, by contrast, have seen a less spectacular but steadier increase. Wheat (and wheat flour) is a particularly significant African import. Africa absorbs just under one-quarter of world

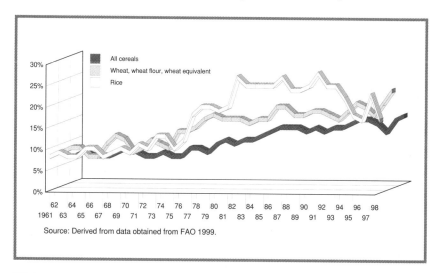

Figure 7.1   African imports of cereals, wheat and rice as a percentage of world imports, 1961–98

imports, compared with one-eighth in 1975. Since it is the cereal that has been most influenced by policy changes in the EU, Africa should take special note of the danger that future food supplies could be affected by European policy changes.

These increasing shares have been of a rapidly growing cake. In 1961, the total volume of world cereals imports stood at 80 million tonnes (Table 7.1). By 1998 it was over three times this level, at almost 250 million tonnes. Hence, the absolute increases in Africa's imports have been more substantial than the rates of share change might suggest. In 1998, Africa's cereal imports were over eight times greater than they had been in 1961, and over six times greater than in 1970; wheat accounted for two-thirds of the total.

A significant part of these imports goes to North Africa. Imports of cereals into North Africa are far higher on a *per capita* basis than into SSA (Figure 7.2). Indeed, on a *per capita* basis SSA absorbed, in 1998, a smaller volume of cereal imports than North Africa, Asia or Latin America and the Caribbean. Imports of around 27 kilos per head in SSA compare with almost 80 kilos into Latin America and over 140 kilos into North Africa.

In addition to cereals, imports of sugar (and especially refined sugar) are important. Africa absorbs over one-quarter (27 per cent) of world refined

Table 7.1 World and African imports of cereals, 1961–98 (million metric tonnes)

Year	World			Africa			African imports as share of world imports		
	Cereals	*Wheat*	*Rice*	*Cereals*	*Wheat*	*Rice*	*Cereals*	*Wheat*	*Rice*
1961	79.8	46.1	6.6	5.0	3.6	0.5	6%	8%	8%
1971	117.4	57.0	8.6	8.6	6.5	1.0	7%	11%	11%
1981	232.3	102.7	13.8	23.3	16.0	2.8	10%	16%	20%
1989	237.9	110.0	14.4	29.5	20.2	3.4	12%	18%	24%
1990	223.1	105.3	12.2	28.4	19.0	3.1	13%	18%	25%
1991	229.3	117.4	12.9	29.1	20.0	3.7	13%	17%	28%
1992	254.9	130.1	14.8	36.6	20.3	3.7	14%	16%	25%
1993	231.7	116.4	15.9	35.1	21.0	3.9	15%	18%	25%
1994	226.5	111.0	17.7	35.0	22.2	3.9	15%	20%	22%
1995	245.9	114.3	21.4	34.9	22.2	3.9	14%	19%	18%
1996	239.2	113.3	20.4	29.7	19.1	3.6	12%	17%	17%
1997	242.2	119.6	18.8	37.1	23.5	4.3	15%	20%	23%
1998	249.6	120.2	27.0	40.9	27.3	4.7	16%	23%	17%
Avg. annual change	3.1%	2.6%	3.9%	5.8%	5.6%	6.1%	2.6%	2.9%	2.1%

Source: FAO 1999

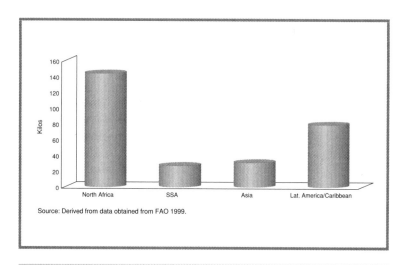

Source: Derived from data obtained from FAO 1999.

Figure 7.2   Total cereal imports *per capita*, 1998

sugar imports, although this share has not shown any marked upward secular trend over the past 35 years. Much of this comes from the EU, which has increased its share of the world sugar market, largely at the expense of tropical sugar cane producers such as Zimbabwe. Other notable increases in food imports are in various vegetable oils and in milk products, most notably dried milk and butter, both of which increased by large percentage amounts on sizeable absolute volumes.

THE REASONS FOR AFRICA'S IMPORT GROWTH

Why have food imports into Africa grown? Among the explanations put forward are:

- the easy availability of food aid has depressed domestic agricultural production, either through market forces (by driving prices too low) or because it has allowed governments to neglect their farmers;
- artificially low world prices resulting from the subsidies paid by Northern governments to their farmers have made commercially imported food cheap, especially in countries with overvalued exchange rates;
- there have been changes in tastes among African consumers, particularly those living in urban areas, in favour of products such as wheat that cannot be grown in many countries;
- domestic agricultural production has not grown fast enough to keep pace with population growth, and imports have simply filled the gap.

Several of these explanations are considered at other points in the book.

This chapter examines three of them: the relationship between food aid and total imports; the relative price of commercial imports; and the relationship between import and production growth.

THE ROLE OF FOOD AID

Is food aid the culprit? Has its easy availability pushed down prices on African markets, encouraged new consumer tastes, and allowed governments to neglect farmers? It is true that a significant part of SSA's increase in cereal imports has been supplied as food aid. But, despite this rapid increase, food aid does not account for the bulk of the region's imports.

The share of food aid in SSA's total cereals imports has varied from year to year (reaching 40–50 per cent for much of the second half of the 1980s and the early 1990s), but has since fallen (Figure 7.3). Its average share in 1995–8 was lower than in 1975–8 (17 per cent and 25 per cent respectively). In 1970 SSA received three-quarters of a million tonnes of cereals food aid; by 1998 this had increased to 2.2 million tonnes (an annual average rate of increase of 3.8 per cent), representing about one-seventh of the region's total cereal imports. The most rapid growth occurred in the period up to 1984, when cereal food aid imports peaked at 6.1 million tonnes, with another, slightly lower, peak in 1992 (5.9 million tonnes). SSA is now the second most important world destination of food aid after Asia (Figure 7.4). The surge in the share of food aid going to the category 'other' in Figure 7.4 is associated with the break-up of the Soviet bloc.

Except in a couple of years, food aid has always represented less than

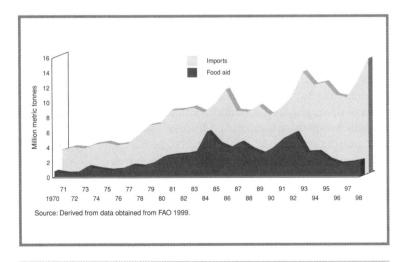

Source: Derived from data obtained from FAO 1999.

Figure 7.3   SSA cereals imports and food aid, 1970–98

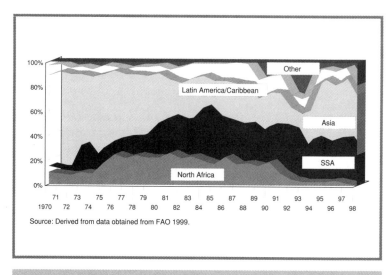

Figure 7.4 Regional shares in total world cereals food aid shipments, 1970–98

half of SSA's cereals imports. In other words, commercial imports have had the greater *quantitative* impact on importing states. Food aid's *qualitative* role will only have been different (for good or ill) if governments and donors have chosen to use it in a different way from commercially imported food.

Nonetheless, food aid is an important part of supply, and the redirection of food aid towards SSA is especially evident when the analysis is under-taken on *per capita* terms. In 1998, cereals food aid *per capita* into SSA was over 18 times as large as into North Africa, nearly three times as large as into Latin America/Caribbean, and over three times as great as into Asia (Figure 7.5). This reflects the relatively small population of SSA (particularly in comparison with Asia), the serious balance of payments problems of many countries of the region (which have made it a prime target for donors), and the incidence of drought and emergencies in the area.

This dependence on food aid is a source of danger. Food aid availability increased in the 1980s, reaching levels that were well in excess of the mini-mum level guaranteed under the Food Aid Conventions of 7.6 million tonnes. But cereals food aid shipments have since fallen sharply: from 15.1 million tonnes in 1992/3 to just 8.8 million tonnes in 1998/9 (FAO 1999) and the guaranteed floor provided by the Food Aid Convention has also been lowered – to 4.9 million tonnes in 1999. The fall in shipments to low-income food-deficit countries in SSA was even greater: from 5.9 million tonnes to 2.2 million tonnes, a decline of 63 per cent (compared with a drop of 42 per cent for all countries).

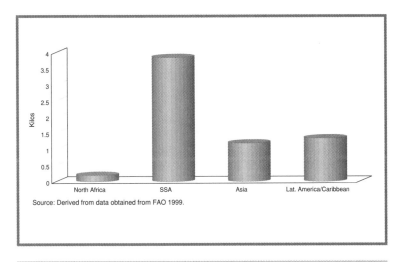

Source: Derived from data obtained from FAO 1999.

Figure 7.5 Cereals food aid *per capita*, 1998

THE ROLE OF CHANGING TERMS OF TRADE

The greater part of Africa's imports of cereals has been made on a commercial basis rather than as food aid. This means that the cereals have had to be paid for largely out of earnings from exports, both agricultural and non-agricultural. Yet the prices of these exports tended to fall during the 1980s. Africa's traditional agricultural exports have faced volatile markets which for the last 15 years, in most cases, have been extremely weak.

Does it make *financial* sense to export agricultural goods with falling prices and to import other agricultural goods? Would increased food self-sufficiency be *financially* attractive? Put in more technical language, what have been the intra-sectoral terms of trade between agricultural exports and cereal imports?

There are many factors – social, economic and political – to take into account when assessing the appropriate balance between export-oriented and import-substituting agriculture. It is also important to anticipate potential future changes. But a foundation for this analysis is knowledge of whether African states have gained or lost in commercial terms by using some agricultural resources for exports instead of domestically oriented production.

The intra-sectoral terms of trade describe the relative price of Africa's imported and exported agricultural products. Farmers can choose whether to produce for the domestic or the export market, and government policy can influence the decision. Although often stated as a choice between *food crops* and *export crops*, this is an unhelpful description (see above). But, however the alternative activities are described, an essential piece of knowledge on which they should be based is the relative price of exports and imports.

A majority of African states have seen either stability or a favourable movement in their intra-sectoral terms of trade for food over the past three decades taken together, but a comparison with the most recent decade suggests that this is no longer the case (Figure 7.6). If the horizontal bar is to the right of the vertical axis in Figure 7.6, it shows that the country concerned has experienced a favourable movement in its intra-sectoral terms of trade; and the longer the bar, the more favourable the terms of trade shift. If the bar is on the left of the vertical axis, it shows that there has been an unfavourable movement in the terms of trade.

Although there has been a fall in the world price of the food items that SSA exports, there has been an even greater fall over the past three decades as a whole in the price of the food items it imports. In this respect, SSA states have tended to fare better than South Asia and South America. The greatest gains, both absolutely and relative to the performance of other regions, seem to have occurred during the 1960s and 1970s. Fewer African states saw a favourable movement or stability during the 1980s. The

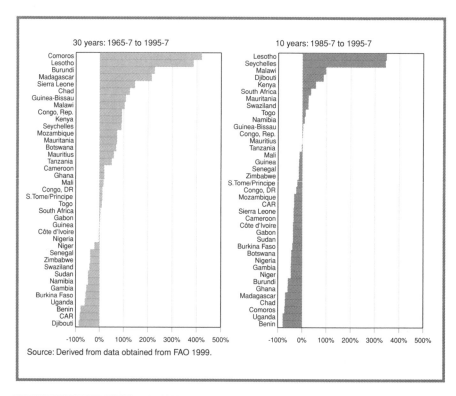

Figure 7.6   Change in net barter terms of trade for food

mid-1990s, the end-point for the figure, were a period in which world cereal prices were unusually high (as a result of drought in several major producing regions).

This trend over three decades may provide a part of the explanation for Africa's increasing share of world imports. It has become financially more attractive to devote agricultural resources to export-oriented crops and to import some basic foodstuffs. Whether or not it is sensible to do this from a broader economic or a social perspective is more questionable, and is dealt with in other parts of this book.

By the same token, if in future the trend in world food prices changes (as the right-hand side of Figure 7.6 suggests is already happening), the dependence of Africa on imported food could become much less attractive. Governments might be faced with a difficult choice between spending increasing amounts of scarce foreign exchange on imported food or letting the population (especially the urban population) go hungry.

Which exports have done best?

Which of Africa's agricultural exports have done best in relation to their terms of trade with cereal imports? This section looks at two groups of SSA's exports:

- the eight most important traditional agricultural exports – groundnut oil, palm oil, coconut oil, coffee, tea, cocoa beans, cotton lint and sisal,
- five 'high-value' agricultural exports that owe their high prices to EU trade and agricultural policy.

The net barter terms of trade between the eight traditional agricultural export crops and imports are plotted in Figure 7.7. The figure shows five-year moving average figures to smooth the considerable year-to-year fluctuations that have occurred.

The dominant picture presented by these line graphs is that medium-term variations have been more substantial than long-term trends. Between 1970 and the mid-to-late-1980s there were two large cycles of unfavourable followed by favourable movements.

The scale of these cycles is sufficiently large to represent a serious management problem for governments. The ratio between the price indices for coffee and cereals more than doubled, for example, between 1981 and 1987; but by 1990 it had fallen to below its 1981 level, and it continued down until 1993. Although in broad terms half of Africa's agricultural exports have purchased an increasing amount of food imports over the period since 1970, Africa's planners do not know from one year to the next how much wheat they will be able to obtain for their tea, coffee or sisal exports. Prudent planning should take full account of this uncertainty.

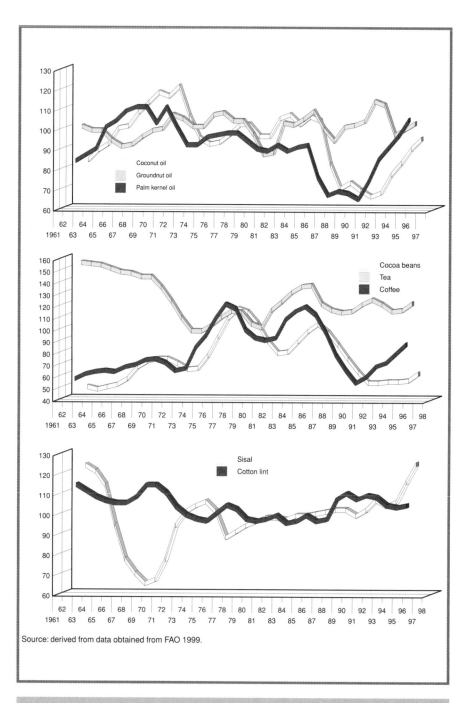

Figure 7.7   Net barter terms of trade: most important traditional SSA exports and cereals imports (1979–81 = 100, five-year moving averages)

A number of African countries have begun to export non-traditional agricultural products which, like traditional items such as sugar and beef, enjoy special preferences in the EU market. There has been growth, especially, in exports of horticultural and floricultural products.

The net barter terms of trade between these non-traditional SSA agricultural exports and cereal imports are plotted in Figure 7.8. The products covered are sugar, pineapples, green beans, grapefruit and cut flowers. In all cases the terms of trade moved strongly in favour of the exports during the period covered.

There are two reasons for the success of some African states in promoting high-value exports. One is that the countries have become very efficient in producing *and transporting* the products (a particularly important factor in the case of the non-traditional items). The second is that SSA has benefited under the Lomé (now succeeded by the Cotonou Convention) Conventions from preferential access to the European market. Because of the CAP, prices in the European market are artificially high. This means that, because of CAP protectionism, African countries cannot export as much to Europe as they might like, but the prices they receive for the agricultural items they are allowed to sell are much higher than would be the case if the CAP were abolished.

Because the more favourable movement for these products is due to the CAP and preferences, the gains are, in principle, particularly vulnerable. Any reforms to the CAP that tend to reduce the level of protection accorded to European farmers and favour third party suppliers could result in a fall

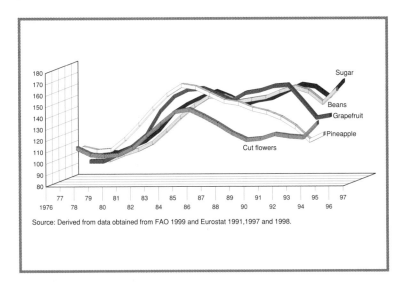

Source: Derived from data obtained from FAO 1999 and Eurostat 1991,1997 and 1998.

Figure 7.8   Net barter terms of trade: most important SSA exports and cereals imports (1979–81 = 100, five-year moving averages)

in the prices received by African exporters and an increase in competition from other suppliers. A similar effect would result from the erosion of Lomé/Cotonou preferences.

It appears, therefore, that the growing cereal imports of SSA have been made more sustainable than they otherwise would have been by favourable terms of trade movements, especially for non-traditional and traditional 'preferential' items. These terms of trade could move in an unfavourable direction either as a result of increased cereal prices or as a result of a relative decline in the price of African exports. As explained in the next section, the combination of the Uruguay Round and the EU's extension of deep trade preferences to countries in Latin American, Eastern Europe and, perhaps, South Africa, will tend to erode African preference margins in the EU market. Hence, it is entirely possible that the intra-sectoral terms of trade will be adversely affected on both sides. A small increase in world cereal prices, when combined with a relative fall in Africa's export prices, could have a more negative effect on food availability in the continent than would be expected by looking at either side of the equation in isolation from the other.

HOW MAY THE WORLD POLICY ENVIRONMENT CHANGE?

FORECASTS OF WORLD SUPPLY AND DEMAND

Various attempts have been made to forecast the evolution of world cereals supply and demand. All are subject to many constraints, most notably:

- on the demand side, the assumptions made about the extent to which China shifts to a meat-based diet reliant upon imported feed grains;
- on the supply side, assumptions made about future yield increases.

The nature of these two issues is such that the term 'assumption' is really a polite way of saying 'guess'.

A review of four such forecasts shows that the main debates concern not whether the world can supply growing demand, but whether it can supply it in a sustainable manner and at an affordable price (FSG 1996). Although the models all suggest that the rise in demand will be substantial, they also suggest that meeting demand should be feasible on a global basis provided that appropriate policies are in place and public investments are undertaken.

Despite this general optimism (see Table 7.2), there are major areas of uncertainty and conjecture. The models provide a framework for discussing the prospects for world cereal markets in the long term and for identifying priority areas for policy and institutional reform and for public investment. But they are not definitive statements of the most likely outcome.

The 'attention focusing' role of the forecasts is important since the outlook for SSA, even in the most optimistic projections, is bleak (Table 7.2). *Per capita* consumption increases projected by the models will be minimal,

Table 7.2   Consumption and import demand projections: total cereals, all uses

Results	1990[a]	FAO – 2010	IBRD – 2010	IFPRI – 2020
World consumption:				
Million tonnes	1734.00	2334.00	2289.00	2679.00
Growth rate[b] (%)	1.70	1.57	1.39	1.50
Per capita in kg/year:				
World	331.00	325.00	325.00	336.00
SSA	124.00	140.00	124.80	139.00
South Asia	184.00	181.00	186.70	220.00
• India	185.00	—	188.30	223.00
FSU and Eastern Europe	829.00	693.00	685.60	705.00
East Asia	279.00	319.00	334.30	306.00
• China	298.00	—	370.90	358.00
Latin America and Caribbean	240.00	296.00	281.00	286.00
Near East/North Africa	349.00	386.00	370.40	382.00
North America	879.00	590.00	855.80	913.00
Western Europe	415.00	590.00	459.60	550.00
Others	459.00	590.00	505.10	481.00
Trade:[c]				
Level of imports to LDCs (million tonnes)	87.00	162.00	210.00	188.00
Growth rate (% p.a.)	3.70	3.01	4.41	2.41
Import demand (million tonnes):				
SSA	9.00	19.00	14.00	26.00
South Asia	2.00	10.00	31.00	22.00
• India	−1.00		14.00	−2.00
FSU and Eastern Europe	27.00	−5.00	−16.00	−15.00
East Asia	23.00	35.00	59.00	28.00
• China	4.00		22.00	22.00
Latin America and Caribbean	11.00	26.00	29.00	15.00
Near East/North Africa	39.00	72.00	73.00	68.00

Notes:

(a) Actual values in 1990: Mitchell and Ingco, *World Food Outlook*, 1993.

(b) Growth rates for 1990 are for the period 1980–90.

(c) Trade measures the projected level of net food deficit in developing countries – as such it does not account for the net trade position of the ex-CPEs, which is subsumed under the 'developed' region.

Source: FSG 1996

resulting in an increase in the number of malnourished.[1] This is due primarily to faltering development. Neither income nor agricultural production *per capita* are expected to rise. Agricultural failure plays a central role in this outcome since the sector is both a source of income for low-income groups and a means of replacing imports which become unaffordable on commercial terms for most countries. The majority of low-income food deficit countries are in SSA, and this region is expected to be the least able to counter increasing world food prices and declining food aid.

THE URUGUAY ROUND

The Uruguay Round of multilateral trade negotiations (so called because it was launched in Punta del Este in Uruguay in September 1986) involved 117 states, almost three-quarters of them developing countries. The eighth in a series dating from 1947, it was launched to assert some multilateral influence over the increasing diversity of trade-related policies by including new areas (such as temperate agriculture and services), by reinforcing the institutional framework for trade monitoring and adjudication, and by continuing the process of lowering tariff and non-tariff barriers to trade. Although a follow-up to the Uruguay Round negotiations on agriculture began in March 2000, it will take some years to complete and so the Uruguay Round remains the foundation of current trade rules in agriculture.

There are two main sets of products from the negotiations. The first is a collection of documents covering general principles and agreed rules for trade. These were signed in Marrakech in April 1994. The second comprises the changes to trade policy that each contracting party agreed during the Round to make. A large part of these consist of lengthy tariff schedules listing the alterations to tariffs that will be introduced over the next six years.

These run into thousands, probably hundreds of thousands, of pages. And, since the devil is in the detail, the precise changes that will occur to world trade are as likely to be found in the second set of documents as in the first.

Seven years of, often tough, negotiations smoothed many of the hard edges of the original proposals. Nonetheless, a number of notable innovations resulted from the Round. These included:

- the creation of a World Trade Organization (WTO) to replace the General Agreement on Tariffs and Trade (GATT) Secretariat;
- the application over time to temperate agriculture of rules more akin to those that have applied to manufactures for decades;
- the phasing out over the period to 2005 of the Multifibre Arrangement;
- the erosion of differential treatment between developed and developing countries (apart from the least developed);
- the extension of an agreed framework of the rules for trade-related intellectual property rights and services.

This section provides an overview of the principal features of the Uruguay Round agreement on agriculture relevant to the present discussion and indicates why change may be less than was anticipated in the many models that have attempted to simulate the impact of liberalization. The changes can be grouped under two headings: those concerned with reducing consumer subsidies to agriculture (primarily through an erosion of import barriers that restrict supply); and those concerned with a cutting of taxpayer subsidies (notably through controls on direct subsidy payments to farmers).

Reducing import barriers

Under the Uruguay Round Agreement agricultural protectionism (especially in developed countries) is being reduced through two instruments:

- the conversion of all import restrictions to tariffs (a process known as 'tariffication'); and
- guarantees of minimum market access.

Most of these changes are being applied in different ways to three groups of countries: industrial, developing and least developed. SSA states fall into all three groups (see Table 7.3). For example, Kenya is classified as a developing country but not as least developed. It will have to reduce its tariffs on imports of agricultural products by 24 per cent over the ten years to 2005. This is less than the reduction that the USA, the EU and other industrial countries (which include South Africa) will make (36 per cent over six years). But it is more than Tanzania – a least developed country – which does not have to cut its tariffs at all.

Since SSA will be particularly affected by changes to EU policy, for reasons explained in the preceding section, special attention is given to the changes that Europe is making. In addition, illustrative examples are provided on African policy changes.

Tariffication

Developed countries took advantage of temperate agriculture's exclusion from normal GATT disciplines to develop a complex array of measures to keep out imports. These often provided very high levels of protection to domestic producers. The EU's system of variable import levies for cereals and livestock products, for example, made it impossible for imports to undercut domestic producers.

As a first step in applying to temperate agriculture the same sorts of disciplines as have long applied to industrial products most, but not all, of these different ways of restricting imports have been converted into tariffs. (Exceptions include, for example, the EU's entry price system for horticulture).

Table 7.3   WTO status of SSA countries

Country	Year of accession	Development status
Angola	1994	Developing
Benin	1963	Least developed
Botswana	1987	Least developed
Burkina Faso	1963	Least developed
Burundi	1965	Least developed
Cameroon	1963	Developing
Central Africa	1963	Least developed
Chad	1963	Least developed
Congo	1963	Developing
Congo, DR	1971	Least developed
Côte d'Ivoire	1963	Developing
Djibouti	1994	Least developed
Gabon	1963	Developing
Gambia	1965	Least developed
Ghana	1957	Developing
Guinea	1994	Least developed
Guinea Bissau	1994	Least developed
Kenya	1964	Developing
Lesotho	1988	Least developed
Madagascar	1963	Least developed
Malawi	1964	Least developed
Mali	1993	Least developed
Mauritania	1963	Least developed
Mauritius	1970	Developing
Mozambique	1992	Least developed
Namibia	1992	Developing
Niger	1963	Least developed
Nigeria	1960	Developing
Rwanda	1966	Least developed
Senegal	1963	Developing
Seychelles [a]		Developing
Sierra Leone	1961	Least developed
South Africa	1948	Industrial
Sudan [a]		Least developed
Swaziland	1993	Developing
Tanzania	1961	Least developed
Togo	1964	Least developed
Uganda	1962	Least developed
Zambia	1982	Least developed
Zimbabwe	1948	Developing

Note:

(a) observer governments

But tariffication will not necessarily result in any major liberalization. The contracting parties have considerable latitude in setting the level of these tariffs. The EU and most African states, for example, have set them at very high levels.

Under the Uruguay Round Agreement, the maximum tariff rates for these products are described as 'bound tariffs'. Each contracting party has established a bound (or maximum) tariff for every item and also agreed the date by which tariffs will be brought down from pre-Uruguay Round levels (known as 'base rates') to this new maximum.

The position on cereals for all the countries of Southern Africa is summarized in Table 7.4. In most cases, the countries of Southern Africa have

Table 7.4 Southern African bound tariffs for cereals

Country	Bound tariff for all agricultural goods [a]	Exceptions for cereals (HS Chapter 10)			
		Code	Description	Bound tariff	Base tariff
Angola	55% ceiling [b]	1001	Wheat/meslin	15%	
Kenya	100% ceiling	None			
Malawi	125% [c] ceiling	1002	Rye	50% + 20%	Free
		1003	Barley	50% + 20%	Free
		1004	Oats	50% + 20%	Free
Mozambique	100% ceiling	None			
Tanzania	120% ceiling	None			
Uganda	80% ceiling	1002.00	Rye	50% + 10%	
		1004.00	Oats	50% + 10%	
		1008.10	Buckwheat	70% + 10%	
		1008.30	Canary seed	50% + 10%	
Zambia	125% ceiling	1001	Wheat/meslin	45%	
		1002	Rye	45%	
		1003	Barley	45%	
		1004	Oats	45%	
Zimbabwe	150% [d] ceiling	1006.30	Rice; semi/wholly milled	25%	30%

Notes:

(a) Unless otherwise stated.

(b) Plus import tax of 0.1 per cent of declared value.

(c) Without prejudice to existing concessions which are under Article XXVIII renegotiations.

(d) Without prejudice to concessions of Schedule LIV of Zimbabwe.

Source: WTO 1996

simply established a single maximum tariff rate that will apply to all, or almost all, temperate agricultural products. The Uruguay Round Agreement identifies both this general rate and the exceptions: the products which will not be subject to this standard rate, and the specific levels of tariffs that will apply in each case. Hence, for example, Kenya has established a bound tariff for all agricultural products of 100 per cent, but Uganda has an 80 per cent tariff for most items but somewhat lower rates for rye, oats and canary seed (60 per cent).

It can be seen that, in all cases, the bound tariffs are very high, but the picture is not quite as it may appear. Because contracting parties to the WTO may not, under normal circumstances, impose tariff rates that are higher than the bound rate, many African countries have taken the opportunity provided by the agreement to set these maximums at levels that are considerably above the ones currently applied. In other words, the actual tariffs applied to imports of cereals will often be lower (possibly much lower) than those indicated in the table. This means that the country concerned will be able to increase tariffs, should the need arise, without breaching the bound level and, hence, their WTO commitments.

Tariff cutting

The second step of liberalization is to start cutting these new tariffs. Tariffs are being reduced by *an average* of 36 per cent over six years by developed countries. Middle-income developing countries (such as Zimbabwe) also have to cut their tariffs, but by less and over a longer period: by 24 per cent over ten years. Least developed countries (such as Uganda, Zambia and Malawi) do not have to reduce their tariffs at all.

This does not mean that all import tariffs are falling necessarily by over one-third (for developed countries) or one-quarter (for developing countries), only that the *average* cut will be of this magnitude. Moreover, these average reductions are not trade weighted. This has left scope for countries to maintain higher-than-average levels of protection on some items. Hence, for example, if the tariff on an unimportant product imported negligibly is reduced by 45 per cent, the tariff on a major product need be cut by only 21 per cent to achieve an *average* reduction for the two products of one-third. The only constraint on such averaging is that there must be a minimum reduction of 15 per cent in every tariff line.

The EU has not taken advantage of this opportunity to make less than average cuts on the most important cereals. For no CAP product is the tariff cut being set at the minimum level of 15 per cent, although for some 'sensitive' items tariffs are being cut by only 20 per cent and, for a very limited number of less sensitive ones, cuts of 50 per cent and 100 per cent are being made (Swinbank 1996).

Where the EU has taken advantage of the latitude provided by the Uruguay Round is in setting the initial tariffs and establishing a method for day-to-day implementation. The Uruguay Round Agreement gave contracting parties scope to decide on the 'appropriate' average world market price for the base period when determining the tariff. Because the base period selected, 1986–8, was one of low world market prices, the conversion of the EU's variable import levies into tariff equivalents could have had the perverse effect of increasing the level of protection. To avoid this, the USA insisted during the Uruguay Round negotiations that the EU accept an additional constraint with respect to wheat, rye, barley, maize and sorghum. It undertook to ensure that the tariff was set at a level, and applied in such a way, that the imported price for cereals would not be more than 55 per cent higher than the domestic intervention price. In order to give effect to this commitment the EU has had to reinvent something like the old variable import levy system but within the parameters set by the tariff. The import charge is determined on a fortnightly basis for six categories of cereals with the aim of ensuring that the final price, including customs duties, will approximate 155 per cent of the effective intervention price.

The broad distribution of tariff reductions in a representative group of developed countries for a range of cereals is indicated in Table 7.5. In the case of all three cereals covered in Table 7.5, the EU's base tariffs are higher

Table 7.5 Comparison of estimated *ad valorem* tariff equivalent, 1986–8, and tariffs declared in country schedules (%)[a]

Industrial country	Rice			Wheat			Coarse grains		
	Estimate 1986–8	UR base	Diff.	Estimate 1986–8	UR base	Diff.	Estimate 1986–8	UR base	Diff.
Australia	13.5	0.0	−13.5	0.7	0.0	−0.7	0.0	0.4	0.4
Canada	na	0.9	na	30.0	57.7	27.7	39.0	34.7	−4.3
United States	1.0	5.0	4.0	20.0	6.0	−14.0	4.0	8.0	4.0
European Union	153.0	360.5	207.5	103.0	155.6	52.6	133.0	134.4	1.4
Japan	500.0	na[b]	na	651.0	239.6	−411.4	679.0	233.1	−445.9
New Zealand	0.0	0.0	0.0	0.0	0.0	0.0	0.0	7.2	7.2
Austria	0.0	0.0	0.0	188.0	400.0	212.0	108.0	241.0	133.0
Finland	na	10.0	na	239.0	352.0	113.0	342.0	204.0	−138.0

Notes:
(a) Selected commodities where tariffication was applied and are subject to safeguards.
(b) Delayed tariffication.
Source: World Bank 1995, p. 12

than the estimated 1986–8 level of tariff equivalent. In both rice and wheat, the increase between the 1986–8 average and the Uruguay Round base level is greater than the cuts that have been made during the Uruguay Round implementation period.

In other words, import protection is still higher at the end of the implementation period than it was in the base period of 1986–8. For the other countries listed in the table, the picture is more mixed. In half of them, the Uruguay Round base tariff for wheat is higher than the 1986–8 average tariff equivalent, and only in the case of Japan is it substantially lower.

Even a cut of one-third from a very high level is still a substantial import barrier. The EU retains tariffs of around 100 per cent for some of its cereals. Future negotiations *may* agree more substantial cuts, but it is reasonable to expect Europe's 'heartland' agricultural products to remain heavily protected well into the twenty-first century.

Special safeguards

It is clear that these changes do not amount to 'substantial liberalization'. This conclusion is reinforced by the consideration that further protection is provided by a variable element called a 'special safeguard clause', which is added automatically to the tariff when the actual import price falls more than 10 per cent below the average 1986–8 import price. Protection against exchange rate changes is given by the fact that import prices will be calculated in national currencies.

Minimum access

The capacity of developed countries to use these provisions to continue to restrict imports on their most vulnerable commodities is limited only by the establishment of minimum levels of imports for every product. As with tariff cutting, different rules have been agreed for developed and developing states. The minimum level of imports agreed for developed countries is an initial 3 per cent of 1986–8 domestic consumption. This will be expanded to 5 per cent over ten years. For developing countries, access must rise from 1 per cent to 4 per cent over the same period. This requirement does not apply to the predominant staples in the traditional diet of a developing country, which are exempt from any minimum access requirement.

The GATT Secretariat has calculated that such minimum access will create market opportunities for, among other products, 1.8 million tonnes of coarse grains, 1.1 million tonnes of rice, 807 000 tonnes of wheat and 729 000 tonnes of dairy products (GATT 1994, p. 6). But even this opening has been tempered by 'anti-surge' devices.

The EU has managed to offset the impact of these minimum access requirements by setting against them existing preferential imports such as those of sugar from the African, Caribbean and Pacific (ACP) states, sheep meat from New Zealand and elsewhere, New Zealand butter and manioc from Thailand (Swinbank 1996). New tariff quotas to reach the minimum access thresholds have been opened up for only a limited range of products, notably 'high quality' beef, pig meat, poultry meat, eggs, butter, specified cheeses and two cereals. The cereals are 300 000 tonnes of 'quality' wheat and 500 000 tonnes of maize into Portugal (Swinbank 1996). These, together with the tariff quotas already agreed for agricultural products under the Europe Agreements with the Central and Eastern Europe states will, the EU believes, fulfil its commitments under the Uruguay Round.

Reducing subsidies

Import controls are not the only ways in which governments have distorted agricultural trade. Most developed countries have provided substantial subsidies to their farming sector. As explained above, such support is conventionally divided into consumer subsidies (resulting from artificially inflated prices created by supply restrictions) and producer subsidies (direct and indirect transfers to agriculture funded by the tax system). Export subsidies, which developed countries often use to ensure that their products can compete on price with those from other states, are just one vehicle for providing this support.

The Uruguay Round has agreed cuts in subsidies. The reduction in import tariffs described above implies some cut in consumer subsidies. In addition, there are reductions in producer subsidies of various kinds.

Domestic subsidies

Aggregate producer subsidies are being cut under the Uruguay Round. The extent of the cut varies between developed, developing and least developed states. For developed countries, producer subsidies are being cut by 20 per cent over six years. Developing countries must cut them by 13.3 per cent over ten years. The least developed states do not have to make any cuts.

These cuts are with respect to the levels applying in 1986–8. They are expressed in terms of an Aggregate Measurement of Support (AMS) which applies globally to all supported commodities, with credit allowed for actions already taken since 1986.

Some government support schemes have been put into the so-called 'green box'. These are exempt from any reduction. Such supports are defined as those 'having no, or at most minimal, trade distortion effects' and include:

- publicly financed R&D;
- early retirement schemes for farmers;
- payments for long-term land retirement.

There is a strong view that despite the GATT's intentions some of the green box supports being proposed by developed countries are actually linked to production, which will not fall, therefore, by as much as expected. The EU position on the reduction of domestic subsidies has to be seen in the light of the MacSharry reforms of May 1992, which have a crucial role to play in enabling the EU to reduce its AMS by the requisite amount. The reforms combine a substantial reduction in support prices (especially for cereals) with direct aid, linked to set-aside in the case of large farmers, to offset the resulting loss in revenue. It was agreed at Blair House in November 1992, that the area and headage payments would be deemed to be decoupled from production and, hence, exempt from reduction under the AMS cuts. 'For common wheat alone, this reduced the AMS of the "new" CAP compared to the AMS of the base period by 3.8bn ecu at a stroke' (Swinbank 1996). An assessment of the subsidy reductions of the EU and other major producers by the World Bank suggests that by the end of the implementation period subsidies will indeed be lower than they were in 1986–90, but not by enormous amounts (World Bank 1995, p. 17).

Export subsidies

The Uruguay Round agreed reductions in export subsidies. This may assist developing country exporters in the third markets, but it may also increase the cost of supplies to food-importing developing countries.

Developed countries have agreed to reduce by 36 per cent the *value* of direct export subsidies from their 1986–90 base level (often higher than current levels) and to cut the *quantity* of subsidized exports by 21 per cent over six years. For developing countries, the reductions are two-thirds of those applying to developed countries and the implementation is extended to ten years. No reductions need to be made by the least developed countries.

While significant, these cuts will still leave very substantial export subsidies in place. GATT has estimated the total level of export subsidies by developed countries in the base period as US$19 billion. Cereals, dairy products and meat receive the largest subsidies. Moreover, food aid and unsubsidized exports are not covered by these commitments.

The ability of the EU to comply with the Uruguay Round Agreement on export subsidies depends crucially on the volume of production and world prices. The fillip to world prices in the mid-1990s undoubtedly eased the problem, but there is a widespread view that this is a cyclical movement that cannot be expected to continue. If, despite the reduction in general subsidies to agriculture, the level of production continues to outstrip domestic consumption then the EU will face increasing difficulty in meeting its targets for the volume of subsidized exports. In such circumstances, it might be necessary to tighten further the production limiting measures, such as set-aside, already introduced under MacSharry. But the effect on the cereals sub-sector may be muted if the MacSharry curbs are widened (in the sense of being applied to more commodities) rather than deepened (in the sense of being tougher on products like cereals that are already subject to them). One plausible view is that:

> within the six-year implementation period of the Agreement, the EU is unlikely to face serious export constraints. ... The problems become more acute the further forward one looks. ... The situation threatens to become unsustainable if by the early 2000s the EU has embarked upon another enlargement to embrace states of Central and Eastern Europe (Swinbank 1996).

Effects on price stability

If the Uruguay Round Agreement is unlikely to have a substantial effect on world prices in the short to medium term, will it alter price stability? There is some reason to suppose that, perversely, it may exacerbate instability even though it represents a step along a path that ought, eventually, to reduce instability. This is because it will fail fundamentally to alter the pressures on producers and consumers in protected markets to adjust to world supply shocks while, at the same time, leading to a rundown in carryover stocks.

One reason why the world market for cereals has been volatile is that it is a residual market, although not to the same extent as, for example, sugar. A large section of the world's producers do not necessarily adjust output as world prices rise or fall, because there is no direct feed through to the revenues they receive. Similarly, a substantial proportion of the world's consumers are also insulated from changes in world market prices and do not adjust. The burden of adjustment, therefore, is borne by producers and consumers in the less regulated national markets who, consequently, have to alter their production/consumption levels by more than would otherwise be required.

As is clear from the foregoing analysis, this situation will not change fundamentally as a result of the Uruguay Round Agreement. Europe's farmers will still receive revenues that are largely decoupled from world price levels, and Europe's consumers will fail to reap the benefits of lower priced imports.

On the other hand, one area in which the Uruguay Round Agreement is likely to have an effect concerns stocks for which public authorities have responsibility. Although the changes will not necessarily reduce 'surplus production' in the true economic sense of the term by any substantial amount (i.e. production in excess of the level that would be sustainable under unrestricted trade) it will tend to reduce 'surpluses' in the sense of cereal mountains and the like. These large surpluses have been made available (with greater or lesser effectiveness) to ease the adjustment problems of food importing states during times of cyclical shortage. This buffer is likely not to be available on anything like the past scale for the foreseeable future. As substantial recipients of food aid, North and sub-Saharan Africa may be particularly adversely affected by this change.

CHANGING PREFERENCES

The EU hierarchy

As explained above, one reason for the favourable movement in the terms of trade between some SSA agricultural exports and cereal imports is the artificially low prices of the latter (which may be affected by the Uruguay Round), while another is the artificially high prices of the former (which may be affected by CAP reform and the erosion of preferences). The EU preference system has grown up over time and is particularly complex (see Figure 7.9). It provides different degrees of preference to various groups of developing countries. As indicated by the boxes (which lists the two countries with the highest and lowest *per capita* GDP in the band), the depth and breadth of these preferences are not necessarily related to the level of development of the recipient country.

The Lomé/Cotonou Convention (to which all SSA states except South Africa belong) earns its place at the apex of the trade hierarchy in at least three ways:

- it provides the most extensive set of trade preferences, covering *all industrial products* that meet the rules of origin as well as most tropical and mineral products;
- the tariff reductions and relief from non-tariff barriers tend to be particularly deep, e.g. duty-free access for all industrial products and full relief from the Multifibre Arrangement, which does not apply to Lomé states;
- concessions on CAP products which, whilst limited, are more substantial than those on offer to most of the ACP's competitors.

The next layer in the EU's hierarchy is formed by the bilateral agreements that it has signed with almost all of its geographical neighbours to the south and east. Each of these agreements is different, but in general they provide substantial preferences but on a more limited number of products than those covered by the Lomé Convention. The first bilateral agreements were signed during the 1960s and were non-reciprocal. In recent years there has been a trend to frame new agreements, and convert old ones, within the context of the creation eventually of a free trade area.

The bottom tiers of the hierarchy are formed by the standard generalized system of preferences (GSP) and, below that, the standard most-favoured nation (MFN) terms that the EU is obliged to offer all other WTO members. The GSP is currently available to most developing countries. In general terms, the product coverage of the GSP tends to be more limited than under

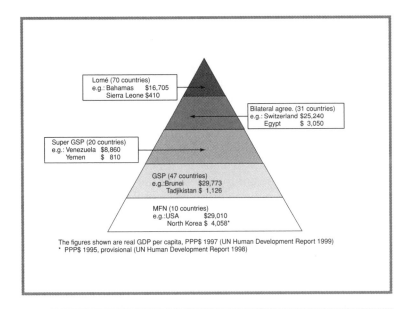

The figures shown are real GDP per capita, PPP$ 1997 (UN Human Development Report 1999)
* PPP$ 1995, provisional (UN Human Development Report 1998)

Figure 7.9 The hierarchy of preferences

the other agreements, and often the cuts in MFN tariffs or relief from non-tariff barriers are less generous.

One band of the hierarchy remains to be explained: the Super GSP. It is a superior tranche of the GSP that provides more favourable treatment than the standard. During the mid-1980s, the EU began to accord to countries on the UN's list of least developed states an improved GSP which, on many commodities, provided access terms that were as favourable as those under the Lomé Convention.

Then, in 1990, the Community agreed to extend, initially on a temporary basis, this Super GSP to four countries of the Andean Community – Bolivia, Colombia, Ecuador and Peru – partly as a result of US pressure to join in an anti-narcotics drive and partly because of Spanish desires to improve policies towards Latin America. In 1991, the EU accorded to the countries of Central America, again on a temporary basis, Super GSP treatment for their agricultural, but not their industrial, exports. These extra preferences were continued in the new GSP, and were extended to Venezuela.

The EU's policy evolution

When the first Lomé Convention was negotiated, Community-level development co-operation was still in its infancy. There were few clear principles to establish the objectives of its efforts and how these differed from the larger, longer-established programmes of the member states. The Lomé

Convention stood apart from the Community's other trade relations in terms of the breadth and boldness of its vision.

The situation today is very different. Now Lomé/Cotonou is just one of the EU's trade agreements that provide some states with access to the European market that is more liberal than that available under MFN treatment. All have evolved over the years and in an international environment that differs markedly from today's.

The completion of the Single European Market has removed the last vestiges of formal member state 'national' trade policy, and the Lomé/Cotonou trade regime (as with all of the Union's other country- and region-specific accords) must be compatible with the global framework of Union trade and trade-related policy. The Maastricht Treaty has given a clear set of objectives for European development policy and has set in train a discussion of the distinctive roles of Union- and national-level action with the statement that the two are to be 'complementary'. Moreover, the Union has acquired a more muscular set of instruments for implementing development policy outside the Lomé/Cotonou confines.

The changing position of the European Development Fund (EDF) within the array of Union-level avenues for aid illustrates a wider set of changes. The mechanism of the EDF for providing aid pre-dates Lomé and has its origin in a period of European history that has long passed. It now appears increasingly to be an anomaly. This state of affairs has come about with the increasing size of European aid funded directly from the EU budget, the evolution of the practice of providing multi-annual commitments despite the budget's annual time frame and, with the Maastricht Treaty, the formalization of the objectives and modalities of the development co-operation at an EU level.

During 1995 the costs of this anomaly became clear when the EU member states had to balance their commitments (entered into during the Edinburgh Council of December 1994) to increase external spending from the budget against the need to provide adequate funding for Lomé IVbis at a time of public expenditure compression in most of them. The result was that the ACP received almost no increase in their aid, whilst most other regions saw substantial increases.

One feature of this evolution is that exceptions from MFN treatment are now viewed in a more sceptical light in the international arena than in times past. In the opinion of the EU, the preferential access provided to ACP exports was justified under Article XXIV of the GATT read in the light of Part IV and, in particular, Article XXXVI Para 8 under which developed countries 'do not expect reciprocity' for preferences given in trade negotiations to less developed countries.

This position was challenged in 1993 by the GATT Panel established to investigate Latin American complaints concerning the banana regime. Whatever the merits of this particular expression of view, the immediate questions about the validity of the Lomé Convention under the EU's GATT obligations were quickly removed when, in 1994, the Union sought and obtained a waiver from the MFN Rule under Article XXV. However, the incident highlighted the less tolerant attitude of the international community towards trade regimes that can be portrayed as being discriminatory, and the issue of 'GATT compatibility' was to the fore in the EU's policy making over an appropriate trade regime with the new South Africa.

The provisions of GATT, and now the WTO, relating to trade preferences are complex and controversial. Essentially, the problem is that because it is non-reciprocal, the Convention is difficult to defend under Article XXIV and, because it does not cover all developing countries, it is suspect under Part IV. Although the GATT waiver provided some respite, the problem has not gone away. With both the Lomé Convention and the waiver expiring in February 2000, the EU and ACP have the task of finding a secure successor regime that will be WTO-compatible.

IMPLICATIONS FOR FOOD SECURITY

Although the immediate effects of the Uruguay Round and CAP reform for world cereal availability and prices may be limited, a plausible case can be made that it would be prudent for Africa to start planning now for a future that may be more food insecure. This is because:

- the heavy import dependence of many African states is already a source of great vulnerability to changes elsewhere (as the high world prices of 1996 illustrated);
- further change to Organization for Economic Cooperation and Development (OECD) agriculture is on the cards for early this century (although it would be rash to forecast either the speed or extent of such change given the laboured progress of the Uruguay Round);
- there may be more profound short-term changes affecting the intra-sectoral terms of trade for African agriculture that need to be taken into account.

The thread of the argument is that: the principal achievement of the Uruguay Round has been to start the process of applying normal GATT disciplines to agriculture but at the cost of limited change in the short term; the changes that will be made may have disproportionate effects on Africa (especially North Africa) because of its particular dependence on wheat imports and the EU as a supplier; the impact of liberalization affecting Africa's imports may be reinforced by the effects of liberalization on its exports; and that the potential adverse effects of a rundown in publicly managed stocks in OECD states may be greater for Africa than other regions, both because of its dependence on food aid and because its fragile balance of payments position makes it ill-placed to cope with world price instability.

In other words, those concerned with Africa's poor agricultural development should not be lured into a false sense of security by the modest degree of change likely to result *directly* from the Uruguay Round and CAP reform. This conclusion is reinforced if attention moves beyond the Uruguay Round to other potential shocks to the system. As the current high world prices for cereals illustrate, the Uruguay Round and CAP reform are not the only changes that will affect world food supply.

The changes most likely to be of particular interest to Eastern and Southern Africa concern the EU regime for sugar, beef, tobacco, horticulture and floriculture. Changes that reduce European prices and/or increase competition from other third parties will tend to make these products relatively less financially attractive. The question which then arises is whether the increase in world cereal prices (when translated into changes in the relative attractions of imports, which are largely of wheat, and domestic production, which includes the preferred cereal, white maize) is sufficiently large to provoke a change in the balance of production within the region.

CHAPTER EIGHT

Food Security Information Systems

Stephen Devereux

THE NEED FOR adequate information on food security at the global, national and sub-national levels received fresh impetus with the adoption of international targets for the eradication of hunger and malnutrition at the World Food Conference in 1974,[1] and the less ambitious World Food Summit goal in 1996 of 'reducing the number of undernourished people to half their present level no later than 2015' (WFS 1996, p. 1). According to the Sixth World Food Survey, more than 840 million people worldwide were undernourished in 1993 (FAO 1996). The World Food Conference prompted the establishment of the Global Information and Early Warning System (GIEWS), while the World Food Summit Plan of Action included a commitment to establish national 'food insecurity and vulnerability information and mapping systems' (FIVIMS).[2] The FIVIMS Technical Guidelines argued that baseline information is often lacking on

> ... who the food insecure are, how many they are, what their characteristics are (location, livelihood systems, access to resources, age, gender, etc.), the nature of their food insecurity (structural, transitory, or both), and the depth of their undernutrition (FAO 1997, p. 11).

Given this current interest, this chapter focuses on *information needs* and *institutions* to reduce food insecurity in Africa. The following sections will discuss early warning systems, food security information systems at national and sub-national levels, and agricultural market information systems.

EARLY WARNING SYSTEMS

As discussed in Chapter 5, the threat of famine has not yet been eliminated from Africa. Famines occur because they are not prevented. Four sets of factors prevent adequate and timely responses to food crises – lack of *information*, weak *institutions*, problematic *politics* and *logistical* constraints. Although physical obstacles – the inaccessibility of affected communities, poor roads, lack of trucks or fuel – do inhibit relief operations, logistical constraints are often exaggerated as a cause of famine mortality. Given the global proliferation of modern transport infrastructure and communications technology, logistical constraints merely 'exacerbate the adverse consequences of late decisions' (Buchanan-Smith and Davies 1995, p. 24). The key variables in famine prevention are failures of institutions and politics, not logistics and perhaps not even information.

INFORMATION

An early warning system is 'a system of data collection to monitor people's access to food, in order to provide timely notice when a food crisis threatens and thus to elicit appropriate response' (Buchanan-Smith and Davies 1995, p. 4). First generation early warning systems were supply focused, based on 'food balance sheet' indicators of aggregate food availability: food production and import forecasts. The Food and Agricultural Organization (FAO)'s GIEWS was established in 1975 with two main aims:

> (a) to monitor continuously the world food supply/demand conditions so as to assist governments in taking timely and appropriate measures in the light of quickly changing conditions; (b) to identify countries or regions where serious food shortages and worsening nutritional conditions are imminent, and to assess emergency food requirements (FAO 1985, p. 1).

Following the failure of early warning systems to prevent the African famines of the mid-1980s, national and international attention focused on the importance of obtaining more accurate and timely early warning information. It was argued that better *prediction* would improve the capacity for timely *response*. Between 1985 and 1990 eight new early warning systems were set up in the Sahel and Horn of Africa alone, adopting expensive, high-technology methodologies, such as remote sensing and electronic dissemination of bulletins.

Second generation systems moved towards multi-indicator approaches. Demand-side 'access' variables were added – notably socio-economic indicators such as market price data and household food stocks, and behavioural responses such as livestock sales and migration patterns. A 1989 review of GIEWS reported that:

> Over the past two years, special emphasis has been placed on the monitoring of changes in local market prices of basic foodstuffs ... prices are one of the few such indicators for which a continuous and disaggregated database is available (FAO 1989, p. 3).

The late 1980s also saw a move towards *local-level* systems – small-scale, often run by non-governmental organizations (NGOs), bypassing or complementing central government systems. The model for localized early warning is the system in Turkana District, northern Kenya (see Buchanan-Smith and Davies 1995). This is a sub-national, decentralized system which focuses on pastoralists rather than crop farmers. It monitors the sequential deterioration of a range of environmental, economic and human welfare indicators, with information being explicitly linked to interventions. In 1990/1, the system predicted and helped to trigger a timely response to a food crisis provoked by a combination of drought and livestock raiding. Although the Turkana experience has many positive lessons to offer other countries, it is expensive to run and the feasibility of expanding the system to larger geographical areas is doubtful.

A trend in the opposite direction during the 1990s was towards integrated or coordinated *regional* early warning systems. For example, the Southern Africa Development Community (SADC)'s Regional Early Warning Unit has the objective of linking early warning systems throughout Southern Africa and publishes a 'Food Security Quarterly Bulletin' from Harare which includes both a 'SADC Regional Assessment' and eleven 'Country Chapters' (SADC 1997). The *Comité permanent Inter-états pour la Lutte contre la Sécheresse dans le Sahel* (CILSS) monitors drought in the Sahel, and a less well developed Intergovernmental Authority on Development (IGAD) initiative connects national early warning systems in East Africa and the Horn.

The boom in African early warning systems since the 1980s, together with rapid developments in electronic communications technology, has virtually eliminated information bottlenecks as a contributing cause of famine. However, early warning systems do have limitations. Most national systems remain over-centralized, production centred and drought focused – chronic and localized food insecurity are not adequately monitored. Despite the rhetoric about disaggregated, decentralized early warning systems that incorporate locally specific conditions and household coping strategies, for most governments and donors early warning is still about aggregate food supplies – harvest forecasts, food balance sheets and food aid requirements.

Early warning systems reflect the dominant concern of the international community – to prevent mass starvation. Success is measured in terms of saving *lives*, not *livelihoods*. The danger is that this preoccupation with extreme events results in a neglect of less severe or less visible forms of food insecurity, such as hunger-related diseases, seasonal hunger, and chronic undernutrition. Excess mortality in India from 'regular deprivation' has been estimated at 3.9 million every year – more than the 3 million casualties of the Bengal famine of 1943. This 'silent famine' is virtually ignored by the international community and even by the local media. As Drèze and Sen (1989, p. 214) point out: 'Starvation deaths and extreme deprivation are newsworthy in a way the quiet persistence of regular hunger and non-extreme deprivation are not'. Clearly, the purpose of any information system, from a local newspaper to a global early warning system, conditions the type of information it collects – and omits to collect.

Table 8.1 below lists the main categories of information and indicators collected by early warning systems, the sources of this information, and some problems or gaps associated with each.

Table 8.1   Information collected by early warning systems

Category	Indicators	Collection	Problems or gaps
Food Production (*Supply-side indicators*)			
Meteorology	Rainfall	Satellite/rain gauges (climatologists)	Unreliability of forecasts (e.g., false El Niño prediction in 1997/8) Localized rainfall variability
Agriculture	Crop production	Crop assessments (agronomists)	Underestimates non-cereal crops Ignores pastoralists and livestock
Socio-Economic (*Demand-side indicators*)			
Economic	Market prices	Market monitoring (economists)	Do rising prices reflect normal seasonality or food crisis? Ignores entitlements collapse
Social	Coping strategies	Household surveys (social scientists)	Difficult to 'scale up' to national level Difficult to interpret – 'normal' behaviour or intensification?
Health and Nutrition (*Outcome indicators*)			
Nutrition	Anthropometry	Growth monitoring (nutritionists)	Late indicator, not a predictor Parents may ration before children, but only children are monitored
Health	Morbidity	Clinic records (health personnel)	Not necessarily food related Needs medicine, not food aid

As Table 8.1 suggests, information needs are limitless but time and financial resources are limited, so choices need to be made and priorities need to be set. Instead of asking what information is needed, we should ask: 'What are the costs associated with inadequate information?' In another context, Chambers (1993) talks about 'optimal ignorance' and 'acceptable error'. In food crises, however, the costs of ignorance and error are counted in human lives. Errors in key statistics can create major discrepancies in estimated food aid requirements. Probably the most dramatic example in history is China's 'Great Leap Forward' famine of 1958–62, when inadequate information about food shortages in rural areas contributed to up to 30 million deaths.

FOOD BALANCE SHEETS

Despite the proliferation of various categories of data, as discussed above, the tendency to see food security purely in terms of aggregate food availability remains. This approach is exemplified by the FAO's 'food balance sheet' framework. National food availability (production + stocks − postharvest losses + commercial imports − exports) is compared with consumption needs (national population × subsistence requirements[3]) to determine the size of the surplus or deficit ('food gap'). Completing the circuit provides a useful policy rule of thumb for intervention by government or donors: food aid requirement = consumption needs − food availability.[4]

Despite its popularity as a policy tool, the food balance sheet approach has several significant deficiencies, including the following:

- The *measurement* of both food availability and consumption requirements is highly problematic. A 10 per cent underestimation of either food supply or food needs would result in a shortfall of 800 000 tonnes of staple cereals in a chronically food insecure country like Ethiopia, which needs an average of 8 million tonnes *per annum*.
- The balance sheet implies an equal *distribution* of food among all members of the population. The more unequal the access to food, the greater the danger of 'Malthusian optimism' (Sen, 1981) – 'There is enough food to go around, so there is no food problem'. This happened in the Bangladesh famine of 1974: more food was available than in the previous 2–3 years, but hoarders withdrew rice from the market, creating an artificial food deficit.
- The balance sheet also focuses too heavily on staple cereals, often neglecting *non-cereals*. But in tropical countries, plantain, cassava and other non-cereal crops are important – sometimes the dominant – sources of nutrition (85 per cent of food production and consumption in Uganda is plantain). In pastoral societies, livestock products (meat, milk, blood) are as significant as cereals.
- The emphasis on *food production* does not allow for the consideration of *food systems*. Rural households are regarded as subsistence units whose dominant activity is food production, with few alternative sources to on-farm production. Income from sales of livestock and cash crops is ignored, as are off-farm incomes (petty trading, beer brewing, fishing, remittances) and a variety of 'coping strategies' that contribute to poor peoples' livelihoods and food security.

In low-income food deficit countries – as the majority of countries in Sub-Saharan Africa are – the estimation of national food production is especially crucial for the calculation of the annual food gap, and the national food balance sheet is highly sensitive to errors in this estimate. Two predominant sources of quantitative crop production data are agro-meteorological crop yield models (remote sensing, Normalized Difference Vegetation Index (NDVI)) and pre-harvest crop assessment missions (where production = area planted × yield). All methods of crop production estimation are problematic, for several reasons.

1 The use of *agricultural inputs* such as chemical fertilizers and high-yielding varieties can double or treble yields, but some farmers have access to these inputs while others do not.

2 *Intercropping* of cereals and legumes (e.g. maize and beans) is very common but rarely recorded, but yields on pure stands differ significantly from yields on intercropped plots.

3 *Secondary food crops* (especially roots and tubers such as cassava and yam) are invariably underestimated in crop assessment surveys, despite their importance as food security crops.

4 Similarly, *minor food crops* (vegetable gardens, fruit trees, wild plants) are excluded from most agricultural surveys.

5 Farmers often adjust their *cropping patterns* from one year to the next, but models and assumptions about farmer behaviour are slower to adjust.

6 On-farm *storage* levels are variable and difficult to assess, and farmers are often secretive about the contents of their granaries.

7 Quantifying *post-harvest losses* is controversial – 'guesstimates' range from 15 to 40 per cent – and more studies are needed before this variable can be measured with confidence.

The case study in Box 8.1, which summarizes alternative assessments of Zambia's food balance sheet for 1998, reflects many of the difficulties described above.

Box 8.1   Case study: Zambia 1998 – food surplus or food crisis?

In May 1998 an FAO/World Food Programme (WFP) Crop and Food Supply Assessment mission presented its findings to the Government of Zambia. The key conclusion was that El Niño-induced weather anomalies had severely affected crop production in 1997/8 – in particular, production of maize, traditionally Zambia's staple food, was 43 per cent lower than in 1996/7. The mission concluded that Zambia required 660 000 tonnes of cereal imports to meet the population's consumption needs, of which only 360 000 could be provided commercially (due to limited import capacity and low foreign exchange reserves), leaving an uncovered deficit of 300 000 which could be met only through food aid (concessionary imports plus targeted emergency relief). But these figures, and the underlying methodology from which they derived, were questioned by other donors. In June 1998 a consultative donor meeting in Lusaka tasked a Food Security Assessment Mission to review the methodology used in the compilation of the 1998/9 food balance sheet to reassess the crop forecast statistics and the estimated food aid requirement.

FAO/WFP's computation of Zambia's food balance sheet draws heavily on the Central Statistical Office (CSO)'s annual Crop Forecast Survey. Several fundamental problems were identified with this methodology. First, the sample is too small – 10 100 farmers out of 720 000 are surveyed (1.4

per cent), stratified into small-, medium- and large-scale farmers. Second, the survey design is unreliable, since it concentrates on staple cereals and does not adequately monitor root crops, tubers and secondary cereals.[5] Third, the forecast underestimates income from produce sales, yet since agricultural liberalization in 1994 there has been a boom in production of food and non-food cash crops such as cotton, tobacco and paprika. These crops performed well in 1998 (despite a poor maize harvest because of flooding), generating income for food purchases for approximately 200 000 outgrower farmers. Finally, various sources of survey and sampling error undermine the credibility of data generated by the Crop Forecast Survey. These include outdated crop zones, limited technical capacity of CSO enumerators, and inadequate logistical support (e.g. lack of transport to the field).

The Food Security Assessment Mission drew on a survey of root and tuber crops to recalculate the national food balance sheet. This reassessment revealed that the widespread belief that white maize is Zambia's staple food may no longer be valid. The recalculated food balance sheet estimated that cassava alone would contribute 36 per cent of total kilocalorie contribution from domestic production in 1998/9, ahead of maize (33 per cent) and sweet potato (20 per cent). The two main root and tuber crops thus contributed more than half (56 per cent) of Zambia's total kilocalorie production, while the four major cereals – maize, millet, sorghum and rice – contributed just over one third (37 per cent) between them (Wood et al. 1998).

INSTITUTIONS

Information is only the first part of any early warning system. Equally important are the institutions that gather, analyse and respond to information. Better *information* makes famine easier to *predict*, but better *institutions* are needed before famines become easier to *prevent*. Data that do not become information and knowledge do not lead to action. Buchanan-Smith and Davies (1995) identified institutions as the 'missing link' between famine early warning systems and effective rapid response mechanisms, and they advocated more effective partnerships between stakeholders (especially national governments and international donors) as central to the success of any early warning system.

Despite dramatic improvements in prediction of (mainly) drought-induced food crises in the last 15–20 years, these have not been matched by equivalent improvements in responsiveness. Fatal delays still occur, most often due to institutional and political (not information) bottlenecks, both within the government structures where early warning systems are located and in terms of their broader political context. As Buchanan-Smith and Davies (1995, p. 2) argue:

> *it is not the severity of the crisis, but relations between international donors and national governments which tends to be the single most important determinant of the timing and scale of the international response.*

It is in negotiating the complex web of relationships within and between government departments, and between national governments, donors and NGOs, that critical time lags can develop, with potentially fatal results. Yet these relationships are characterized by mutual dependence: governments and donors depend on NGOs for information, governments depend on donors for food aid and technical resources, donors cannot (or will not) intervene in a food crisis until the government requests assistance. When these critical relationships become politicized, the tenuous chain that runs from information to action is broken (see Figure 8.1). This explains why one of the key recommendations of the book by Buchanan-Smith and Davies is that famine early warning systems should be jointly owned by government and donors, to maximize the transparency, credibility and effective utilization of early warning information.

Famines were averted during the 1980s in Botswana, Cape Verde, Kenya and Zimbabwe, but what role (if any) did early warning systems play? A free press and democratic pluralism might be the best early warning system a country can have. Much depends also on the relationship between governments and donors. Kenya and Botswana, both 'friends of the West' during the 1980s, received generous amounts of food aid quickly when needed, and the international response to the 1991–2 drought in southern Africa was equally prompt and adequate. Ethiopia and Sudan, with their Marxist and Islamic fundamentalist governments respectively, were not so lucky. During the 1980s famine in Ethiopia, when President Reagan diverted aid from Africa in order to support the Contra rebels in Nicaragua, the Speaker of the House accused the US government of 'being willing to starve Ethiopians so that it can kill Nicaraguans'. In 1991, the American government blocked its food aid shipments to Sudan for several critical months, on the spurious grounds that Sudan had refused to declare a famine. Many observers believe this was a punishment for Sudan's support for Iraq during the Gulf War. In all of these cases, information about the crisis was available in good time.

Institutional problems that limit the effectiveness of early warning systems include the following:

- *Poor integration into government structures.* Typically, early warning data collection and reporting functions are separated among several Ministries (Agriculture, Health, Planning).
- *Separation of data collection activities from policy-making processes.* People who collect and report early warning data typically have no independent decision-taking responsibility.
- *Problematic relationships between donors and governments.* Donors

provide technical support and funding for national early warning systems, but governments have their own priorities.

- *Lack of institutional memory.* Systems are rarely institutionalized, due to high staff turnover in government, donors and NGOs, combined with a 'project' approach to early warning.
- *Emergency response dominates long-term planning.* Political enthusiasm and donor support for early warning systems tends to be high in the aftermath of a famine but then steadily evaporates year by year.

All these issues combine to undermine the effectiveness of many early warning systems. A review of Sahelian systems in 1994 found that 'there is no real system of integration between the information collected, the decision made by the national government or donors, and the subsequent action taken' (Club du Sahel 1994, p. 10). Donor-funded systems are rarely integrated into existing structures and institutions from their inception, which is why 'handing over' is often impossible. Donors tend to support information systems as projects with limited time frames, 'the institutional consequence of this is that nothing is left when a project comes to an end'. Donors respond to this criticism by arguing that 'the issue of withdrawal was more a question of the national structures taking over the projects, rather than the withdrawal of foreign assistance' (Club du Sahel 1994, p. 10). To which national governments point out that donors generally invest little time or effort in capacity building and institutionalization of early warning or food security information systems.

Figure 8.1 shows the many stages and two-way flows of information and decision making that characterize an early warning system, illustrating the points at which the process can break down.

THE FUTURE OF EARLY WARNING

Despite their problems, as discussed above, early warning systems have been fairly successful in their own terms. Where food crises are not contained, this is invariably because emergency aid, not information, is 'too little, too late' – for reasons related almost entirely to bureaucratic inertia and political posturing. Nonetheless, the future for national early warning systems in Africa is uncertain. These systems were set up essentially to monitor drought and crop failure, but they might already be outdated, for various reasons related to the changing nature of both information technology and food crises.

A remarkable feature of the 1990s was the 'information revolution', specifically the rapid expansion of the World Wide Web and of computer networking, which makes it possible for information to be transmitted instantaneously from almost anywhere on earth to anywhere else, and has revolutionized disaster management (Stephenson and Anderson 1997). Remote areas are no longer remote in this age of e-mail, the Internet,

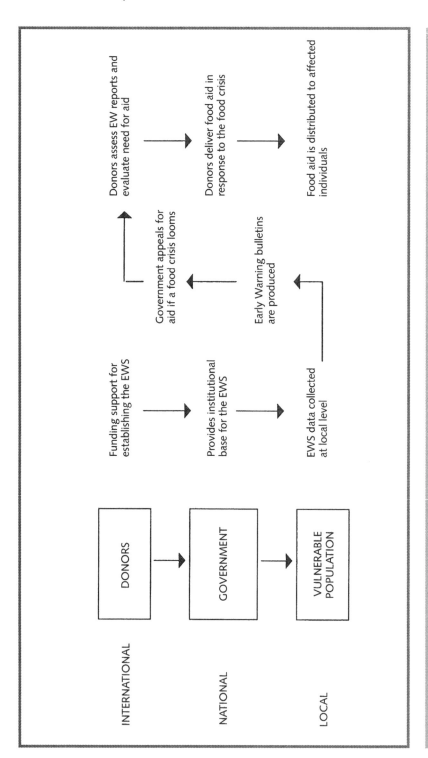

Figure 8.1   The process of famine early warning and response

jet-setting journalists and a 'globalizing' culture of greater openness and interdependence. Bulletins produced by early warning systems such as United States Agency for International Development (USAID)'s Famine Early Warning System (FEWS) and FAO's GIEWS are now accessible on the Internet. Soon every district agricultural extension officer in Africa will be able to send regular reports on crop, livestock and water conditions to the capital city – or direct to the international donor community when a crisis is looming – electronically. The major role for remote sensing and Geographical Information Systems (GIS)-based early warning systems will probably be restricted to forecasts – and if the impact of the 1997 *El Niño* on Africa is representative, high-tech forecasting will continue to get it wrong as often as it gets it right.

A confounding factor is the changing nature of food crises. Conventional early warning systems have become expert at predicting droughts, analysing their impacts and calculating appropriate food aid responses, and interventions to alleviate drought-induced food crises (as in the 1991 southern African drought) have become adequate and timely. But food crises in Africa are increasingly related to civil conflict, which is more difficult either to predict or to prevent. Unlike drought, which is a slow onset disaster giving governments and donors several months to respond, 'complex emergencies'[6] can erupt in a matter of days and can leave an affected population cut off from food markets and aid channels. Despite efforts in the mid-1990s to develop 'political early warning systems', predicting conflict-related emergencies remains elusive and the returns on doing so remain uncertain, given the obvious difficulties (including physical danger and the need often to violate national sovereignty) of delivering food and medical supplies to conflict zones.

In conclusion, the following suggestions are made for improving early warning systems to address some of their limitations as described above.

- Early warning systems should move beyond their narrow focus on *extreme events* and on *food supplies*. They should become integrated with 'livelihood monitoring systems' that regularly assess *non-famine processes* (such as chronic food insecurity and seasonal under-nutrition) and incorporate indicators of *access to food* as well as food availability.
- On the *supply* side of the food security equation, early warning systems should improve their data collection with respect to non-cereal food crops, especially roots and tubers. On the *access* side, early warning systems should improve their analysis of market-based access to food, by estimating income from cash crops, livestock sales and off-farm economic activities.
- In terms of methodological approaches, early warning systems should become more flexible and should draw on qualitative information (e.g. the 'food economy' approach scores availability of wild

foods from 0 to 5) and participatory food security assessments that go beyond 'crop assessment missions'.

- Greater use will inevitably be made of e-mail and the Internet for data gathering and information dissemination. Major investments will be needed, not just in computer hardware and software but also in providing training in information technology to relevant staff, from the capital city to district level.
- Prediction of humanitarian crises other than slow-onset famines needs to be improved, as does response capacity. This may require pre-positioning of strategic food reserves near potential flashpoints such as south Sudan and the Great Lakes region. It will certainly require a strengthening of the legal framework to enable the United Nations and donor agencies to override national sovereignty during complex emergencies involving violations of the right to food.
- Regional early warning units should be linked more closely to regional response mechanisms. Either solutions need to be found within the region itself (within SADC 'triangular transactions' could source food surpluses from, say, Zimbabwe to meet a deficit in Malawi), or co-ordinated food aid appeals should be launched at the regional level (as happened in SADC in 1991–2).
- Finally, Buchanan-Smith and Davies' argument for joint ownership of early warning systems should be acted on by all stakeholders. Donors need to give more commitment to early warning systems than a time-limited project allows. Governments need to support early warning systems with personnel and other resources instead of relying on donors to provide the bulk of technical and financial assistance. Since loss of institutional memory is a major problem, documentation must be comprehensive and continuously maintained.

FOOD SECURITY INFORMATION SYSTEMS

In some countries, early warning systems are being complemented or superseded by broader-based food security and nutrition information systems. Food security is determined by four sets of factors: food *availability*, *access* to food, food *consumption*, and *nutritional status*. The framework in Figure 8.2 illustrates the relationship between these variables and suggests indicators of each that can be used for food security assessment and monitoring.

This complex causality makes it impossible to identify just one or two food security indicators for assessment and monitoring purposes. Nutritionists might argue that nutritional status is a sufficient indicator of food insecurity from the national level (headcounts of undernourished citizens) down to the individual (anthropometry). But nutritional status is only an *outcome* of food insecurity; it has no *explanatory* power. Nutritional status is determined not only by food intake, but also by health care, water quality, sanitation and child care. These are key determinants of individual well-being, but they are additional to food security indicators such as the quantity and quality of diet.

Alternatively, agriculturalists might claim that food production is the key determinant of whether a country, region or household is food secure in a given year. Yet food availability at national or local level is determined not only by domestic food production, but also by imports and stocks. National food availability might be greater than production if additional food is imported, or less than production if some of the harvest is exported. Even at the household level, food *availability* tells us nothing about who has *access* to that food. [7]

Figure 8.2 might suggest that a direct link exists from food availability to food access to consumption and to nutritional status, but this would be simplistic. Nonetheless, policy makers often assume that interventions at any point in this chain will achieve a direct impact in terms of reducing undernutrition or food insecurity. Policies to increase food *availability* by promoting food production, initiatives to improve *access* to food by providing income through cash-for-work projects, or efforts to increase food

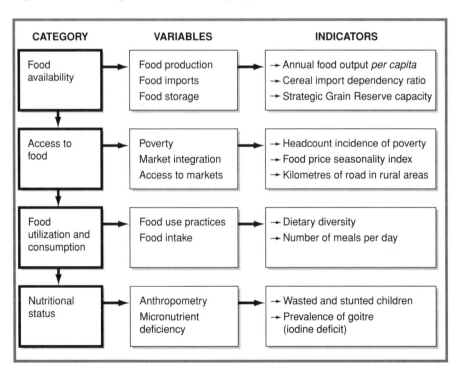

Figure 8.2 A conceptual framework for monitoring food insecurity

consumption by school feeding schemes all have improved *nutritional status* of the food insecure as their ultimate objective. Yet all of these interventions might fail because the linkages are more complex than they appear. School feeding schemes might have little impact on child nutritional status if parents simply reallocate household resources away from providing food for that child. Cash income provided to male household heads might impact less on child consumption than food aid provided to mothers.

Studies have found that the extent to which increased income at the household level improves child nutritional status depends as much on the source, regularity and control (especially by gender) of income as on the amount of income itself. This cannot be understood without a gender analysis of intra-household relations in the local community, yet few (if any) food security information systems take these 'sociological' variables into account. Also, it is often the case that certain groups of people are marginalized within their communities (an example is the San, or Bushmen, of Botswana), and that these groups display symptoms of poverty and undernutrition reflecting chronic food insecurity. A food security information system that does not incorporate these socio-cultural indicators will neglect an important element of causality.

All attempts to monitor food security are measuring (or estimating) proxy or indirect indicators at best, so great caution must be exercised in interpreting these statistics. Most countries do collect food security information at several levels – as the case of Zambia illustrates (see Box 8.2) – but these sources of information are rarely coordinated at either the national or sub-national level.

Apart from specific famine early warning and food security information systems, most countries collect information on agriculture, demography, health and nutritional status which has relevance for food security assessment and monitoring. This includes: national population censuses, agriculture surveys, agro-ecological zoning, market monitoring, health centre records, Demographic and Health Surveys (DHS), food consumption surveys, household income and expenditure surveys, poverty assessments and participatory poverty assessments (PPAs), household food economy assessments, livelihood monitoring, and vulnerability mapping. Not all of these data sources are fully exploited for their usefulness in food security monitoring terms. An important task facing any food policy analyst or policy maker is to examine systematically all existing sources of data such as these, to assess their relevance and comprehensiveness, identify data gaps, and avoid costly duplication of effort. Information is expensive, and compiling data is always more cost-effective than collecting it again. Unfortunately, data collection and reporting tend to be as territorially divided between government ministries at national level as they are among the international donors, and coordination of databases and information bulletins is rarely achieved.

Box 8.2   Food security information systems in Zambia

A large number of institutions are involved in food security monitoring in Zambia, which operate at various levels.

1 *Global and regional early warning systems*, including FAO's GIEWS, USAID's FEWS, and SADC's Regional Early Warning System.
2 *National early warning and food security information systems*, notably the National Early Warning Unit, which incorporates the Agricultural Marketing Information System and Health Information System data provided by the Ministries of Agriculture and Health respectively.
3 *Community-level and district-level food and livelihood monitoring systems*, which are dominated by networks of national and international NGOs such as the Programme Against Malnutrition (PAM) and CARE International's Food Security Project in Southern Province.
4 *Household food and livelihood information systems*, most prominent among these being the Food Security, Health and Nutrition Information System (FHANIS) under the Central Statistical Office (CSO).
5 *Area-specific food information systems*, such as the CSO's agricultural censuses and surveys, which cluster households into Standard Enumeration Areas to produce an annual Crop Forecast Survey, Area Measurement and Crop-Cutting Survey, and Post Harvest Survey.

NATIONAL FOOD SECURITY INDICES

The 1990s saw a rise in the popularity of welfare indices such as UNDP's 'Human Development Index' (HDI), and indices of the incidence, depth and severity of poverty (P_0, P_1 and P_2). Food security has its own indices, though they are less well established. Typically, food security indices incorporate both food availability and food access indicators, making them more comprehensive than the supply-driven food balance sheet.

The FAO's 'Aggregate Household Food Security Index' (AHFSI) is based on three variables: *per capita* dietary energy supply (DES), derived from FAO's national food balance sheets; *per capita* gross national product (GNP) in purchasing power parity units; and the coefficient of variation in income distribution, as a proxy for the distribution of calories. *Per capita* DES is compared with a cut-off point for minimum energy requirement, and the annual instability of the DES is taken as a proxy for risk or vulnerability. This approach allows three indicators to be derived: the *prevalence* of food inadequacy (an estimate of the numbers of undernourished people);

the *intensity* of food inadequacy (which estimates the depth of undernutrition in terms of the 'food gap' between calorie availability and calorie needs); and the *risk* of food insecurity (or the likelihood of national food availability being inadequate in any year). The index itself is ordinal ($0 \leq$ AHFSI ≤ 100), and is therefore most useful in monitoring trends over time at the national level or comparing relative food insecurity across countries (FAO 1997).

As with all information systems, the AHFSI is only as good as the data it draws on. The FAO used a similar methodology in estimating global food inadequacy for the Sixth World Food Survey (FAO 1996). The proportion of the population consuming less than the minimum calorie requirement is derived parametrically (the assumption being that total calories are distributed log-normally around the mean DES level, and that this distribution is invariant over time) rather than being based on actual household data. FAO argues that these 'admittedly unsatisfactory' (FAO 1997, p. 3) assumptions were necessary due to unavailability of household-level data-sets on the distribution of energy intake (or reliable proxies). This methodology generated the estimate for 1992 of 841 million chronically undernourished people in developing countries, a figure which provided the baseline against which progress towards the World Food Summit goal of halving the number of undernourished people in the world by the year 2015 is to be measured. In a strong critique of the FAO methodology, Smith (1998) argues that data limitations and a methodological bias towards the level of national food availability[8] and against the distribution of food consumption within countries means that this measure should not be used for making cross-country comparisons or for tracking trends in food insecurity, 'including making policy judgments about the success or failure of efforts to improve food security' (Smith 1998, p. 437).

USAID's Food Security Index is a composite index with two components built on five indicators. The 'national food self-reliance' index combines indicators of *food production* (domestic food production *per capita*) and *food import capacity* (gross foreign exchange earnings). The 'household food access' index uses proxies for three determinants of household ability to demand food: *income levels* (measured by GNP *per capita*), *income distribution* (proxied by child mortality – the under five mortality rate) and *food prices* (proxied by daily calorie supply). This index reflects the model shown in Figure 8.3 (compiled from Manarolla 1991).

A number of questions arise about the usefulness and credibility of food security indices.

1 *What does the index tell us that we didn't already know?* By definition, an index is a relative measure. Perhaps its main use is as a mechanism for ranking countries in relation to each other – as the HDI does. It adds little to the understanding or analysis of food insecurity within each country. The USAID Food Security Index combines five variables

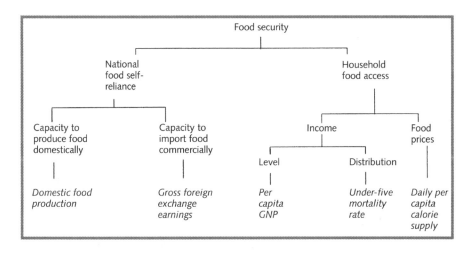

Figure 8.3   USAID's Food Security Index

that proxy national food availability and household access to food, and generates a listing in which the following five countries were found to be the most food insecure in the world in 1990: Mozambique, Somalia, Ethiopia, Sierra Leone, Chad. Yet any informed observer could have come up with the first three or four of these countries without needing to construct composite indices. The index is tautologous: countries are food insecure if they do not produce enough food and are too poor to import it; households are food insecure if their incomes are low, food availability is limited and children are dying.

2   *What doesn't the index tell us?* The USAID index listed Sudan as only the 18th most food insecure country in the world in 1990 (Guinea Bissau, Haiti and Yemen are among the 17 more food insecure countries). Yet Sudan in 1990 was just one year away from a major famine. Why did the index not predict this? Because any index which tries to capture such a complex concept as food security in a single statistic is only as good as the variables which are included in its compilation. The USAID index does not include political vulnerability factors such as civil conflict or lack of political will. The Sudanese government actually *exported* sorghum to Europe during the 1991 famine – but the Food Security Index cannot capture this perverse outcome. Also, a composite index risks obscuring significant shifts or contributions by one of its component elements. If food availability rises by 20 per cent but inequality deteriorates by 20 per cent at the same time, then an index that gives equal weight to these two elements would not change at all. So it might be more sensible to rank countries by levels of the individual indicators.

3 *How can a food security index be used?* If famine prediction is not an appropriate application of a food security index, perhaps its usefulness lies in identifying which variables are likely to influence food security, or to analyse the causes of a deterioration or improvement in food security status retrospectively. For example, if the index improves, decomposing it will reveal whether this was due to a rise in food production, import capacity, average incomes or income distribution, or a fall in food prices. Even in this case, however, interpretation is difficult. It is quite possible for one variable – say, *per capita* GNP – to improve with no improvement in food security as proxied by an outcome indicator – say, the under-five mortality rate. In southern Tanzania, for instance, the commercialization of maize during the 1980s prompted a substantial increase in marketed output, but child nutritional status actually deteriorated, as maize was diverted from feeding children to being sold for cash (Geier 1995). A mechanistic application of the index would wrongly have concluded that there was an improvement in food security in Tanzania during the 1980s.

SUB-NATIONAL FOOD SECURITY

As long ago as 1985, a review of GIEWS recommended 'strengthening the monitoring of indicators which reveal the food situation of specific affected groups more clearly' (FAO 1985, p. 6). Two basic approaches exist. The first divides the country *geographically* (by area), the second divides the country *functionally* (by population sub-groups). While the second approach is clearly preferable, the first dominates, for practical reasons. Countries are governed by administrative units – provinces, districts – and data collection activities are usually organized around these area-based units. The second approach is known as 'functional classification' and requires collecting information on categories of people – livelihood systems (farmers, pastoralists, landless labourers), demographic cohorts (children under five, lactating mothers, the elderly), or 'vulnerable groups' (female-headed households, the disabled, refugees). An intermediate approach with relevance for food security monitoring is food-related disaggregations (agroecological or 'food economy' zones).

For the food security analyst or food policy decision maker, area-based disaggregations have several significant limitations.

1 *Data reporting areas are not socio-economically homogeneous.* Within a single district or agroecological zone there might be foodcrop farmers, cash crop farmers, agro-pastoralists, traders, and others. Given this reality, the best option might be to identify the *dominant livelihood system* in each sub-national area and to use this as the basis for data collection and reporting.

2 *Individual and household livelihoods are diversified.* The importance of *diversification* as a livelihood strategy among poor and food insecure groups is increasingly recognized – e.g. small farmers are also petty traders who sell goats and migrate to remit income. How can this complexity of household-level livelihood systems be captured in an area-based information system?

3 *Livelihood systems are dynamic – they evolve over time and adapt rapidly in times of stress.* Livelihoods derived mainly from farming switch to alternative sources of food and income during a drought. A comprehensive vulnerability assessment should include variables that provide an indication of *alternative livelihood opportunities* in a given locality.

WFP's 'Vulnerability Assessment and Mapping' (VAM) reports (e.g. for Zambia (WFP 1996) and Senegal (WFP 1997) reflect the methodological difficulties associated with disaggregating food security information by administrative units. The analysis of vulnerability by district disguises not just inequality within districts but differences across diverse groups of people. Many alternative classifications are possible, but data limitations preclude analysis by livelihood systems or geographic zoning. An agricultural survey in Western Province, Zambia, for example, identifies nine 'agroeconomic zones' (Maimbo et al. 1996), which bear no relation to the boundaries of the six administrative districts but lead to very different conclusions about the causes, extent and distribution of food insecurity within the Province. Clearly, district-level food security data cannot reflect the complex diversity of multiple livelihood systems in rural Africa.

An increasingly important geographical distinction for food security analysis and policy is rural *versus* urban, though this dichotomy is not always clear-cut and many families in developing countries spread their livelihood risk by dividing their members between a rural farming and an urban cash-earning household. Urban food insecurity is less well documented and understood than rural food insecurity, but as urbanization and urban poverty rise so urban food insecurity is increasing rapidly throughout the world. In 1960 only 19 per cent of the population of sub-Saharan Africa was urbanized, but this figure reached 45 per cent by the year 2000. Being net purchasers of food, these households are food insecure because of poverty rather than low agricultural productivity. Urban poverty will almost certainly become the dominant source of food insecurity in the twenty-first century. It follows that new or adapted methodologies for conceptualizing and monitoring urban food insecurity are urgently needed (see Chapter 3).

The identification and mapping of food insecure people is a *descriptive* exercise, but for policy purposes it is necessary to *analyse causality*. Several analytical frameworks have emerged in recent years for assessing food insecurity at national and sub-national levels. Prominent among these are WFP's VAM, SCF-UK's Food Economy approach with its associated

RiskMap software, USAID's FEWS (an indicator-based, aggregated system), and CARE's Rapid Food Security Assessment (participatory, bottom-up, community level). VAM is linked directly to organizational policy objectives – specifically, estimating food aid needs and targeting food aid.

Box 8.3 describes the 'food economy' approach, which is gaining credibility among some donors and governments. Three types of output are generated by the approach: *baseline assessments, applications* and *derivations.* Baseline food economy assessments have been undertaken (and in some cases, updated) in several African countries, including Ethiopia, Sudan, Ghana, Angola, Tanzania and Zimbabwe. 'Applications' include using the approach for food needs assessment in refugee camps, and an impact simulation of an *El Niño* event in Zimbabwe, drawing on the baseline database (Boudreau 1998). An example of a 'derivation' is work in Mozambique, which follows food economy principles but adapts the methodology for health-related purposes.

The conceptual framework of the food economy approach – based on disaggregating household livelihoods according to sources of food and income – is rarely challenged, but the participatory methodology (see Box 8.3) is controversial. Typical criticisms concerning the credibility and use of data include:

Box 8.3 The food economy approach

The 'food economy' approach and its associated 'RiskMap' computer software are methodologies for vulnerability analysis that were developed to account for a reality which is not accommodated by the food balance sheet and similar aggregated approaches – namely, that a production, market or income shock is differentially distributed among the affected population, and that it is essential to separate out the impact on various groups if an analysis is to be accurate and useful.

The conceptual basis is Sen's 'entitlement approach', which identifies four sources of household food security – production, employment income, trade (exchange of assets for food) and transfers (gifts, including food aid). This composite understanding of livelihoods offers a major advance on conventional food needs assessment methodologies, which in effect regard rural smallholders as entirely dependent on subsistence *production* – employment income, trade and informal transfers are ignored – so that any shock to the harvest requires an equivalent flow of compensatory food aid to offset the household's deficit. A 'food economy' analysis points out that the impact of a shock to any food source varies across households according to their specific dependence on that source. For example, a self-provisioning household will lose half of its food supply following a drought that causes a 50 per cent decline in food production, but a household which derives half its food from production and half from trading will lose only 25 per cent of its food supply in the same drought.

The methodological starting point for a food economy analysis is the sub-division of a country into a number of 'food economy zones', each charac-terized by a dominant livelihood system, which are generally not related to administrative boundaries but may display some overlaps with agro-ecological zones. Various secondary sources and primary data collection techniques – especially community-level PRA with focus groups of 'rich', 'modal' and 'poor' men and women – are used to describe the population in terms of the following determinants of food security and vulnerability: (1) population size; (2) 'normal' sources of food and cash income; (3) surplus food production and cash earnings; (4) food stocks, livestock ownership and cash savings; (5) distribution of employment between local, in-country, neighbouring and distant countries; (6) markets used by local people for sale of labour, livestock and informal employment, ranked by relative importance; (7) availability of wild foods in times of scarcity (Seaman 1996, pp. A3/1–7). Data on sources of food and income are expressed as a per-centage in relation to 'normal food supply' (e.g. livestock off-take might provide 25 per cent of 'rich' households' income in a 'normal' year), or as an index (e.g. wild food availability is scored from 0 to 5).

Once the baseline assessment has been completed and the livelihood systems of the three categories of households are known for each food econ-omy zone in the country, these data can be entered into a computer database and the RiskMap software programme can simulate the impact of perturba-tions or shocks to the livelihood systems. The analysis of vulnerability is done in two stages (Seaman 1996, pp. A3/1–9): first, the initial impact of the shock is derived for each category of household, in terms of the likely reduction in 'normal' food supply; second, the ability of households to compensate for the deficit without external assistance (e.g. by drawing down food stocks, selling livestock to purchase food, or increasing wild food consumption) is estimated. The difference between the estimated food deficit and the population's ability to compensate for this shock can then be used to derive the minimum food aid requirement for the affected population.

In fact, the approach has been put to this use, though only in refugee camps to date. However, donors are sceptical about the accuracy of baseline data collected only once using rather crude qualitative techniques – this is not a monitoring system – and then scaled up for quantitative policy pur-poses. Also, the originators of the food economy approach believe that households should not be forced to adopt 'erosive' coping strategies (such as selling all their livestock) before assistance is provided, as this would leave them more vulnerable to future shocks. The approach argues for saving livelihoods, not just lives, and because it collects information on the full range of food options available in any given livelihood system, it provides informa-tion to donors and policy makers that should allow for early intervention.

- the presentation of data in ranges (e.g. 40–50 per cent of income derives from agricultural labouring) rather than 'precise' figures is seen as a weakness in the methodology rather than a reflection of the diversity of reality;
- the methodological emphasis on key informants and stratified focus groups is regarded as casually talking to a few community members who may or may not be 'representative';
- the use of PRA methods such as proportional piling is not amenable to quantification because it is relativistic and because of 'scaling up' problems from community to higher levels;
- the categorization of communities into 'poor', 'modal' and 'rich' households is predetermined and simplistic, and cannot portray accurately the distribution of wealth within communities.

Notwithstanding these critiques, a strength of the food economy approach is that it identifies the multiple impacts of a shock such as drought on household livelihoods, which should facilitate a more discerning set of recommendations than a request for X thousand tonnes of food aid. Also, the food economy approach has a range of powerful applications in policy areas which are unrelated to food needs assessment. By illustrating graphically and simply (a) how poor and vulnerable people make a living; and (b) how their livelihoods will be affected by specific shocks; it becomes possible to demonstrate to policy makers (c) what are the most appropriate interventions to support and promote the livelihoods of poor and vulnerable people, not only in emergencies but in relief, development or rehabilitation contexts that are independent of food emergencies.

The preceding discussion suggests a number of areas in which food security information systems could be improved, including the following.

- Most countries now have a number of information systems related to food security, but these are divided among government ministries, donors and NGOs. These systems urgently need to be *coordinated* and *rationalized*. One possible mechanism for doing so is FIVIMS, which was initiated after the World Food Summit in November 1996, partly to monitor global progress towards the Summit goal of halving the number of undernourished people by 2015, but mainly to establish an umbrella or framework at national level for food security monitoring systems.
- Food security data within countries should be collected by *population category* (e.g. by adopting a 'functional classification' of the population, or by identifying discrete 'vulnerable groups'), instead of by *geographic subdivisions* of the country (administrative units such as provinces and districts), as is currently the case in most information systems.
- High priority should be given to improved understanding of *urban food insecurity*, including the links between urban poverty and under-

nutrition, and the effectiveness of 'split households' as a strategy for diversifying livelihoods and spreading risk between rural and urban sources of food and income. New indicators need to be devised for monitoring urban food insecurity, and new or adapted methodologies might also be required.

• Assuming that PRA techniques will become increasingly popular in the coming years, food security analysts and policy makers should receive training and practical experience in applying these methods – and interpreting the findings – in both urban and rural communities in their own countries.

MARKET INFORMATION SYSTEMS

An agricultural market information system is a 'service, usually operated by the public sector, which involves the collection, on a regular basis, of information on prices and, in some cases, quantities of widely traded agricultural products from rural markets, as appropriate, and dissemination of this information on a regular basis through various media to farmers, traders, government officials, policy makers and others, including consumers' (Shepherd 1997, p. 2).

Agricultural liberalization has created new needs for food security information systems. When governments withdraw from agricultural markets, consumers and producers are exposed to price variability from which policies such as price subsidies and pan-territorial pricing had previously protected them. Detailed information on the nature and extent of market imperfections can inform government decisions about retaining residual food security roles for its agriculture parastatal, such as setting floor prices for producers and ceiling prices for food purchasers, or maintaining a strategic grain reserve in case of food shortages (Wyeth 1992).[9]

It is especially important to monitor market prices, because the abolition of fixed prices, together with the dismantling or contraction of marketing parastatals, have exposed the rural poor to new forms of food insecurity associated with weak markets – food price seasonality and possible exploitation (low producer prices, high consumer prices) by grain traders. There are many reasons why isolated rural areas are likely to be ignored by private traders or face high food prices, not all of which indicate exploitative practices by traders. Many of these reasons relate to high transactions costs – inaccessibility and poverty of small communities, traders' lack of storage and transport capacity, and limited information about effective demand. Unlike grain parastatals, private traders do not have a food security mandate, nor can they cross-subsidize losses in poor, remote areas with profits from wealthier urban markets.

Food price monitoring is a particularly sensitive and early indicator of adverse shifts in food security status. In subsistence-oriented agricultural communities, small changes in production can cause large swings in marketed food supply: 'if 10 per cent of a crop is sold as surplus, a 5 per cent fall in yield would cause a 50 per cent fall in surplus sold, after subsistence needs are met' (Seaman and Holt 1980, p. 289). Food prices can be expected to rise rapidly when production falls and self-provisioning producers become market-dependent consumers.

Apart from collecting and providing market information to policy makers as part of a *monitoring* system, the *dissemination* of market information to traders, smallholder producers and consumers has gained importance as the role of markets in promoting food security has expanded during the 1990s. Efficient markets require efficient flows of information. 'In general, the major aim of providing market information is to increase the levels of integration of markets through enhanced market transparency' (Helder and Nijhoff 1995, p. 3). In order to stimulate private competition, market development and the movement of produce from surplus to deficit areas, traders need accurate and timely information, especially on prices. Similarly, farmers should have access to the same information, to assist them in selling their produce for the highest prices, or at least to ensure that they receive fair prices, while consumers should be aware of where they can buy food at the lowest prices locally.

Several African countries now have agricultural marketing information systems. They are no longer confined to the crisis-prone Sahel and Horn, though their early warning systems were the first to incorporate market-related information. The Somaliland *Market Prices and Trade Bulletin*, for example, includes trend data on the Somaliland shilling/US dollar exchange rate, goat prices in local markets and rice/goat terms of trade, as well as retail prices of rice and sorghum, the staple food crops (Government of Somaliland 1995). Elsewhere, information systems have been an integral component of the agricultural liberalization process. Zimbabwe established an Agricultural Policy Management and Marketing Information System following the introduction of its Economic Structural Adjustment Programme in 1991. Tanzania, Zambia and many other countries collect and disseminate information on wholesale and retail prices and supplies of major food crops, export crops, livestock and inputs (seeds and fertilizers). Dissemination takes place through local radio and newspapers, and is intended to inform farmers, traders, consumers and government itself about, in particular, food availability and affordability in local markets. For food security purposes, this is useful for monitoring both potential food crises (i.e. as a component of an early warning system) and the evolving process of food market integration.

The multiple uses of market information are well expressed in the stated objectives of Ethiopia's market information system (Government of Ethiopia 1997, p. 1):

The main objective of the monthly Market Information Bulletin is to assist policy makers, analysts, donors and other partners *involved in the development of the Ethiopian economy through provision of information on cereal prices, grain flows and market trends with the aim to improve their decision making, monitor monthly market developments, assess operational efficiency of markets and marketing policy in the country. The monthly bulletin is supplemented by a related* weekly market information update *(a weekly market information flash and radio broadcast). The weekly updates are designed to benefit all grain marketing participants* (producers, wholesalers, retailers, transporters, and consumers*)*.

Table 8.2 summarizes typical user groups, information needs and outputs, and dissemination channels for contemporary market information systems in Africa.

Market information can be useful not only in identifying a food problem, but also for suggesting appropriate policy interventions. For example, during the 1991–2 drought in southern Africa the government of Namibia considered introducing food vouchers and cash-for-work (rather than food aid and food-for-work) to provide access to food through the market for rural people who had lost their crops and livestock. This advice was based on evidence that the private sector marketing system, both formal (large

Table 8.2 Market information systems: user groups and dissemination channels

User groups	Information need	Information output	Dissemination channel
Traders and farmers	Wholesale commodity and farm input prices at urban markets	• Wholesale price reports • Market commentary	• Radio broadcast • Newspapers • Price Boards
Small farmers and consumers	Retail prices at nearby local markets	• Retail price reporting	• Local radio • Price Boards
Government and donors	• Retail prices • Supply and demand conditions • Volumes traded • Sources	• Month/quarterly price series • Periodic price analysis • Quantities and sources	• Monthly/Quarterly Price Bulletin • Early Warning Bulletin • Formal and informal government/donor briefings
All	Market prices and market developments	• Annual crop analysis • Market and marketing issues	• Television broadcast • Annual crop reviews

Source: Adapted from Helder and Nijohoff 1995, p. 5

commercial importers and millers) and informal, is relatively efficient. Namibia is never self-sufficient – typically, 40 per cent of cereal consumption needs to be imported – and in 1992–3 commercial food imports increased by more than 80 per cent over non-drought years. Despite suffering a 70 per cent decline in cereals production, Namibia did not experience a food shortage during the drought, and a potential tragedy was averted through a combination of public and private responses, with the private sector contributing two-thirds (68 per cent) of national food supply (Devereux and Næraa 1996). Fears that food shortages would cause price inflation on restricted market supplies proved to be unfounded. Market monitoring conducted for the Early Warning and Food Information Unit's monthly Household Food Security Bulletin found little evidence of excessive food price rises, even in isolated communities (NISER 1993).

On the other hand, as with other single indicators, market information systems tell only part of the food security story in a given locality at a specific time. They reveal very little about the situation of the people who use those markets, especially the vulnerable. Food prices and supplies might be of limited relevance to the marginalized poor who survive largely outside the market economy and whose vulnerability and food insecurity derive from different sources. It makes little sense to monitor price levels and trends as a potential indicator of distress, except in contexts where vulnerable people depend primarily on markets for their food – which is the case not only in urban areas, but also for rural groups such as landless labourers and, to a larger extent than is commonly supposed, pastoralists.

Policy makers also need to have some idea of the strength and flexibility of food markets in times of stress. Will grain traders deliver food to deficit areas following a production shock? If an 'entitlement collapse' is the problem, then the answer is probably not, since people who have lost crops and livestock will have little income to exert pressure on markets that will drive prices up and attract traders. On the contrary, food is often exported from famine zones to lucrative markets elsewhere (see Chapter 5). In this case the failure of food prices to rise should not be taken as evidence that markets are functioning smoothly to meet subsistence needs. Interpreting food price movements is complicated and should be supplemented by information about the food insecure people that the system is designed to protect. Food insecure or vulnerable groups themselves should be a primary source of information about their economic circumstances, access to markets, and related issues.

Despite their popularity, most market information systems are motivated and funded by donors on a project basis, and many face an uncertain future whenever the current phase of project funding expires. Namibia's Household Food Security Monitoring System offers a case in point. The author was involved in setting up this system, and compiled the Household Food Security Bulletins for eighteen months during 1992–3. Unfortunately, plans to hand over the system to the government in 1994 fell through when the Ministry of Agriculture failed to designate a member of staff to take responsibility for the system, following a public expenditure review which froze all public sector posts.

The difficulties of institutionalizing these information systems are comparable to those faced by early warning systems. As noted earlier, systems that are set up with financial and technical support from donors are typically intended to be handed over to local staff, but often the government has no real commitment to the system and instead sees donor involvement as an opportunity to reallocate its scarce resources to other priorities, while the donors often put too little effort into integrating local staff and training them towards ultimately handing over the system.

Box 8.4 describes agricultural market information systems in the Sahelian countries, which have achieved notable successes but are also subject to uncertainty over their long-term sustainability.

Box 8.4   Market information systems in the Sahel

An assessment of market information systems in seven Sahelian countries (Club du Sahel 1994) found that all countries surveyed had some form of data collection and reporting on food prices, but that the systems were at different stages. At minimum, prices of a range of basic food items were collected periodically, often every week, and reported in a published bulletin and/or on national radio. Burkina Faso's market information system, for instance, reported weekly on consumer and producer prices for staple foods (millet, maize, sorghum and rice) from 37 markets. Mali's Cereals Market Information System collected staple food prices from 75 rural and urban markets, assessed cereals stocks and quantities traded, and published weekly, monthly and quarterly bulletins, while its Livestock Market Information System provided information on the cash incomes of pastoralists and agro-pastoralists.

Criticisms of the *information* side of the systems were few. Most countries used appropriate data collection methodologies and techniques for data processing and statistical analysis. In Senegal a concern was expressed that the number of markets monitored was rather limited. On the *dissemination* side, reported results were generally considered to be reliable and accurate. However, in some countries there were lengthy time lags between data collection and reporting. In Niger prices were broadcast on the radio every ten days, but monthly reports analysing price data were published too late to be useful.

An important question considered by the assessment was: *'What real use is made of this information and by whom?'* Different countries revealed different experiences. In Chad, 'the cereals and vegetables prices for four major markets are broadcast over the radio. The producers view this information in a favourable light as it enables them to negotiate better prices for the purchase of their products. However, the traders complain about a loss of earnings' (Club du Sahel 1994, p. 65). By contrast, 'the information in Mali is reportedly useful to the traders, but not to the producers. In Burkina Faso, it is useful to the NGOs and the traders, but not to the consumers' (Club du Sahel 1994, p. 16). One possible explanation for the findings from Mali and Burkina Faso is that traders tend to be more mobile than producers, hence are better able to move stocks around in response to price signals. This is also beneficial for food security if it promotes price equalization (excluding transport and transactions costs) across markets. Market information systems can be seen as fulfilling a market integration function which is vital in a time of agricultural liberalization.

A question about market information systems throughout the Sahel concerned their sustainability. Prices were not disseminated in Mauritania and Chad during 1994, and the future of the Burkina Faso and Mali systems was extremely uncertain after 1996, due to financing constraints: 'the running cost is deemed too high for the national authorities to take over in the long term' (Club du Sahel 1994, p. 16).

CONCLUSION

A high proportion of information on food security in developing countries is collected by or on behalf of bilateral and multilateral donor agencies, international NGOs, and Northern-based researchers and development professionals. The hierarchical relationship between information collectors and users is paralleled in the hierarchical components of information systems (Davies 1994): *data* are raw (unanalysed) facts and figures, which are often collected by Southerners for Northerners; *information* is analysed data, this transformation invariably occurring outside the community and often outside the country where the data were collected; *knowledge* refers to the understanding of disseminated information; and *use of information* refers to acting on information received. The separation of data collection from data analysis often extends to a separation of information production from information users (policy makers). The limited involvement of Southern governments, organizations and professionals in the process gives obvious cause for concern. Is the extraction of food security data from Southern countries and communities really in their best interests (and if so, how?) or does this process primarily serve the interests of outsiders?

One by-product of the information revolution of the 1990s was a proliferation of global databases on issues directly or indirectly related to food security and nutrition – FAO's *Agrostat*, the World Bank's *World Development Indicators*, and the World Health Organization's *Global Health For All*. This information explosion creates both opportunities and dangers. On the positive side, more information is better than less, and in terms of famine prevention, prediction and response capacity are certainly enhanced by the rapidly increasing volume and speed of information flows. On the other hand, there are concerns about the extent to which information is concentrated under the control of those who collect and analyse it – especially the 'international community', which has its own agendas and priorities – as opposed to those who are ultimately supposed to benefit from the information use – food insecure countries and vulnerable communities. As remote sensing, computerized mapping and electronic databases become ever more sophisticated, are national information systems being marginalized? As the gap between national and global information systems rapidly widens, what are the implications for national involvement, commitment and capacity building?

Buchanan-Smith and Davies (1995) saw the 'missing link' between famine early warning and response precisely in terms of this gap between *national suppliers* and *international users* of data, and argued for a more integrated approach and a stronger institutionalization of this relationship, which would include national and expatriate technical staff working closely together in jointly owned information systems. Instead, technological advances plus donor exasperation at the perceived deficiencies of local data gathering and reporting systems have contributed to a political economy of food security information analogous to the economic stratification that often accompanies market liberalization – the 'information rich' get richer and the 'information poor' get poorer. The reasons for this are broadly 'political' – the international community claims to react more immediately to humanitarian crises than many national governments are willing and/or able to do – and 'technical' – international agencies have the resources and the technology to invest in sophisticated information gathering, analysis and reporting. Both these arguments justify by-passing or extracting data from national information systems, rather than building their capacity. Although staff from the Ministries of Health or Agriculture may be involved in the data collection process, rarely are the data processed and analysed in-country, nor are local statisticians trained in reporting (including digitization and mapping) of the information that subsequently appears in, for instance, monthly FEWS Bulletins on the Web.

Policy makers and technicians in Africa must not allow themselves to become marginalized by the ongoing information revolution. Technological sophistication creates access barriers for those who lack the necessary equipment or expertise, and entrenches power inequalities between those who control finances and information and those who do not. Governments must insist on the development and maintenance of integrated food security information systems that meet national needs and involve national staff fully. Donors should commit themselves to this partnership not just by providing funding, software and technical assistance, but by making an explicit long-term commitment to the development and *institutionalization* of information systems, including providing training in information technology and the new methodologies for monitoring food insecurity.

CHAPTER NINE

Nutrition and Intervention Strategies

Helen Young

MALNUTRITION IN ITS various forms contributes to about one-third of all deaths of young children in developing countries. Protein energy malnutrition, nutritional anaemia, iodine deficiency disorders and vitamin A deficiency are the four major clinical forms of malnutrition in the developing world. According to estimates by the ACC/SCN (United Nations Administrative Committee on Co-ordination – Sub-Committee on Nutrition), about 150 million children under five are underweight[1] (27 per cent) and 182 million children (33 per cent) are stunted[2] (ACC/SCN 2000). Approximately 40 million children suffer from vitamin A deficiency and some 200 to 300 million people are afflicted with iodine deficiency. Roughly 350 million women suffer from nutritional anaemia (ACC/SCN 1993).

Nutritional trends in sub-Saharan Africa (SSA) appear to have worsened in the early 1990s, following a period of little change between 1985 and 1990. This bucks the general trend in other parts of the world, where the nutritional situation either showed marked improvements or remained similar to previous years (ACC/SCN 1994). The most recent *Report on the World Nutrition Situation* calculated for six regions in the world the numbers of children under five years who were stunted during 1980 and 2000. The number of children in the 25 SSA countries for which data were available increased from 35 to 47 million, an increase of 74.5 per cent (ACC/SCN 2000). Both the prevalence of stunting and the population of children under five years old increased. In the other regions, population size increased while the prevalence of stunting decreased, resulting in either a decrease or no change in the number of stunted children. Two countries – Nigeria and Ethiopia – accounted for about half (52 per cent) of the stunted children in Africa in 1995. The report concluded that trends defined two broad groups of countries in SSA, those that improved over time and those that worsened. Countries achieving the highest rate of decline included Nigeria and Zimbabwe; those where the prevalence increased included Ethiopia and Madagascar.

The most serious and extreme nutritional problems in the world today, particularly in Africa, are found in emergencies. Civil unrest and also drought have adversely affected food production and access to food in much of Africa, large parts of which currently face emergencies. Nutritional crises result from the emergency itself, as people's entitlements fail and they do not have enough food to eat, but they also occur because of failures in the international relief system to meet those needs.

The most food insecure groups are undoubtedly refugees and the internally displaced who are dependent on an international relief system. In mid-1997 there were 12 million refugees and internally displaced people in SSA. Most of these had been affected by nine national and regional emergency situations, the two largest being the Great Lakes region (Burundi/Rwanda/Tanzania) and Liberia/Sierra Leone, which together accounted for over half of the total (ACC/SCN 1997). Because a common characteristic among these situations is that the displacement of people is associated with civil wars, these conflicts have often rendered the affected people inaccessible to humanitarian aid. Relief provision is therefore often on an *ad hoc* basis as security permits.

The prognosis for the nutritional well-being of people affected by emergencies is grim. Protein energy malnutrition and micronutrient deficiency diseases occur on a proportionately greater scale than in a stable non-emergency context. Some of the micronutrient deficiency diseases found among refugee populations, such as scurvy, pellagra and beri beri, have not been seen in stable situations for more than 30 years. A range of strategies is now in place to prevent or address these deficiencies (see section on Action – Nutrition Strategies), although the problem has not been eradicated.

The two greatest constraints to providing adequate relief, particularly food assistance, are restricted access to the affected population and limited resources. Throughout Africa, from Angola to the Great Lakes Region, to Sudan and Somalia, the distribution of relief has been severely hampered by problems of access, principally as a result of insecurity but also because of poor transport networks, particularly in remote landlocked areas. This problem is beyond the control of people working on the ground, but given its overriding importance in determining the success of a relief programme it must be recognized as an overriding constraint.

WHAT IS MALNUTRITION, AND WHO IS AFFECTED?

The term malnutrition covers a broad range of clinical conditions in children and adults that result from deficiencies in one or a number of nutrients. Undernutrition, on the other hand, usually refers to an insufficient consumption or intake of energy, protein or micronutrients, which in turn leads to nutritional deficiency. This assumes that there is a recommended level of food intake below which the probability of nutritional deficiency is greatly increased.

Pacey and Payne (1985) define malnutrition as:

> *a state in which the physical function of an individual is impaired to the point where she or he can no longer maintain adequate performance in such*

processes as growth, pregnancy, lactation, physical work, resisting and recovering from disease.

Malnutrition has greatest impact on rapidly growing infants and young children and can seriously harm their physical and mental development. With the exception of pregnant and lactating women, adults are usually least vulnerable to malnutrition as for them physiological growth has stopped. Severe malnutrition in adults is usually associated with debilitating disease, such as HIV/AIDS, or with acute starvation in famine conditions.

Women in developing countries in their twenties and thirties are pregnant on average for five years and lactating for ten years. This raises their nutritional requirements significantly, and represents a tremendous physiological burden. Many women have been undernourished since early childhood, which means they are short in stature. This makes them more likely to give birth to a baby of low birthweight (less than 2.5 kg). Nutritional anaemia and iodine deficiency among women are associated with high rates of foetal loss and perinatal mortality. There are also high risks of maternal death.

Protein energy malnutrition, which is the most common form of malnutrition occurring among infants and pre-school children, covers a range of clinical disorders that are the result of an inadequate intake of energy and protein, as well as other nutrients. Marasmus and kwashiorkor are the two clinical forms of protein energy malnutrition. Both conditions are associated with growth failure but may be distinguished by their own particular clinical characteristics. The main distinguishing characteristic of kwashiorkor is oedema, while marasmus is represented by a severe loss of body weight or wasting, although many malnourished children present features of both marasmus and kwashiorkor (Waterlow 1992).

Apart from growth failure and the characteristic physiological changes, malnutrition is also associated with lowered resistance to disease, increased risk of mortality, learning difficulties, poor mental development and reduced physical activity. Malnourished children characteristically suffer anorexia, and therefore often refuse food when offered.

An insufficient intake of particular minerals or vitamins in the diet may lead to specific deficiency disorders, for example, vitamin A deficiency (xerophthalmia), iodine deficiency disorders (goitre and cretinism), nutritional anaemias (iron and folate), niacin deficiency (pellagra), thiamine deficiency (beri beri), and vitamin C deficiency (scurvy). These conditions are not restricted to young children, but are found in all age groups. Iron deficiency anaemia in infants and children is associated with impaired physical and cognitive development.

Thus a wide range of clinical conditions result from an insufficient intake of either a specific nutrient or a combination of nutrients.

WHAT CAUSES MALNUTRITION AND HOW HAS THIS INFLUENCED RESPONSE?

Perspectives on the causes of malnutrition have evolved during the past four decades, which in turn has shaped responses to the problem of malnutrition. There has been a radical shift from identifying single factors such as protein deficiency as the principal cause of malnutrition, to increasing awareness of the complex relationships between multiple causes.

Malnutrition was initially considered as a medical problem: kwashiorkor was widely reported and was cured by high protein foods. Protein deficiency and hence the 'protein gap' was seen as the most extensive nutritional problem of the 1940s and 1950s. In preventing hunger and famine, global food supply and overall food availability was considered the main concern.

By the early 1960s the interaction between protein and energy in the aetiology of protein energy malnutrition was better understood by nutritionists, which led to the later belief that overall energy supply was the key issue to be addressed. Malnutrition was no longer only a medical problem to be treated, as it was gradually accepted that malnutrition could be marked by growth failure without specific clinical symptoms. Attention began to shift towards the undernourished and to prevention, which raised social and economic issues of access to food by the poor, as well as questions of overall food availability and supply.

The complexity of the nutrition problem was recognized during and after the World Food Conference in 1974, which resulted in a multi-sectoral nutrition planning approach. An effort was made to develop a detailed model, including all determinants of nutrition and their relationships. The difficulties (or impossibility) of designing a detailed general model of malnutrition, combined with political naivety about governments' real commitment to reallocate resources for solving the nutrition problem, soon resulted in this approach being abandoned. Despite this, most nutritionists agreed on the multi-sectoral character of the nutrition problem.

Poverty was recognized as the overriding factor causing malnutrition.[3] The various aspects of poverty, in terms of access to food and health, comprised the multiple causes of malnutrition (see Table 9.1). Attempts to quantify the poor were based largely on estimates of people whose food intake was considered inadequate, which led to some confusion as undernutrition became synonymous with poverty (Cutler 1984). It is now recognized that the undernourished are not confined to an underclass. Lipton (1983) suggested combining both income and food intake in estimates of absolute poverty: 'ultra-poverty normally prevails wherever household outlay, with about 80 per cent spent on food meets below 80 per cent of caloric requirements.'

During the 1980s the public health significance of vitamin A deficiency, iron deficiency anaemia and iodine deficiency became widely recognized.[4]

Table 9.1 Reported micronutrient deficiencies among African refugees dependent on food rations

Iron deficiency anaemia	Somali refugees in Ogaden, Ethiopia 1986/87
Xerophthalmia (vitamin A deficiency)	Eastern Sudan 1984–85
Beri beri (thiamine deficiency)	Liberian refugee camps in Sierra Leone
Scurvy (vitamin C deficiency)	Eastern Sudan 1984 North west Somalia 1985 Hartisheik, Ethiopia, 1989 Kassala, Sudan 1991 Kenya 1994
Pellagra (niacin deficiency)	Mozambican refugees in Malawi 1989, 1990 & 1991

Source: Center for Disease Control, 1992

Towards the end of the decade there were serious concerns about the sporadic outbreaks of specific micronutrient deficiencies occurring among refugees and displaced people dependent on international food aid.[5] Although occurring on a much lesser scale, these outbreaks were scandalous given that many of these deficiencies had been thought to have been virtually eradicated, and also given the role of the international community in providing suitable food assistance.

The 1990s saw the advent of strategic planning, as operational programmes sought to develop nutritional strategies that focus on the underlying causes of malnutrition, not this time with the multi-sectoral approach of the 1970s, but instead with a community-based approach based on the project cycle: assessment, analysis and action. United Nations Children's Fund (UNICEF) was the driving force behind this initiative, and based on successful experience in Iringa, Tanzania, the Fund has reformulated its entire nutrition strategy based on the Triple A Approach (UNICEF 1990) (Box 9.1). The strength of this approach is the use of a simple conceptual framework of the underlying causes of malnutrition (see Figure 9.1) as the basis of assessment, analysis, monitoring and evaluation, combined with a community-based approach including people's participation and social mobilization. Implicit in this are the concepts of:

- *Self-reliance:* awareness of the nutrition situation, social mobilization and real participation. Thus the 'programme' gradually becomes a 'movement'. Training is necessary at all levels.
- *Sustainability:* true community participation should mean that people feel they own the programme and have a vested interest in its success.
- *Scale:* community-based programmes.

Box 9.1 The UNICEF Triple A Approach –
Iringa, Tanzania as a case example

The Iringa programme was one of the first experiments with the Triple A
Approach supported by UNICEF and World Health Organization (WHO).
Community participation (also referred to as social mobilization by UNICEF)
was generated by *a vigorous campaign approach*, which involved contact-
ing every village and showing motivational films, a verbal introduction to the
programme and its objectives, *training, and the weighing and vaccination*
of all children in the village. Every quarter, each of 168 villages in Iringa, sub-
mits a report on the nutritional status of its children and on deaths occurring
in that quarter (JNSP 1989).

This monitoring was coupled with a series of programme activities, which
resulted in a decrease of severely underweight (less than 60 per cent weight-
for-age (WFA) of the Harvard standard) from 6.3 per cent in 1982 to 1.8 per
cent in 1988. There was also a marked decrease in the prevalence of children underweight (less than 80 per cent WFA) from around 48 per cent to
around 37 per cent.

The reduction occurred gradually, with the most dramatic changes occurring early in the programme. Although the data are highly aggregated the
improvements in nutritional status appear to be spread uniformly throughout the region (JNSP 1989).

Many aspects of this approach have now been endorsed and adopted by
other international organizations and national governments.

International initiatives in the 1990s resulted in 'a call to arms' in 'meeting the nutrition challenge'. In 1992, on the occasion of the International
Conference on Nutrition (ICN) and with the participation of UN organizations and other agencies, the governments of 159 states adopted the World
Declaration and Plan of Action for Nutrition, thereby declaring their deter-
mination to eliminate hunger and reduce all forms of malnutrition. At the
ICN governments agreed to develop national plans of action, with technical
expertise from UN agencies. They also reiterated their commitment to the
nutrition goals of other UN conferences, including in particular the 1990
World Summit for Children. Since the ICN many countries in Africa have
developed national plans of action, and a range of projects has been
implemented (see section on nutrition strategies). At the World Food Summit in 1996, governments and UN agencies declared that it was intolerable
that more than 800 million people do not have sufficient food to meet
their needs, and reaffirmed the right of all to adequate nutrition and food
security.

A CONCEPTUAL FRAMEWORK OF THE UNDERLYING CAUSES OF MALNUTRITION

A conceptual framework is a practical tool which presents a set of coherent and comprehensive ideas that jointly explain a particular phenomenon, in this case the process leading to malnutrition. An understanding of the underlying causes of malnutrition is vital for informed decision making. The UNICEF conceptual framework (Figure 9.1) presents the causes of malnutrition and shows how they relate to one another. Change in these factors will affect nutritional well-being, so if the process of change is to be

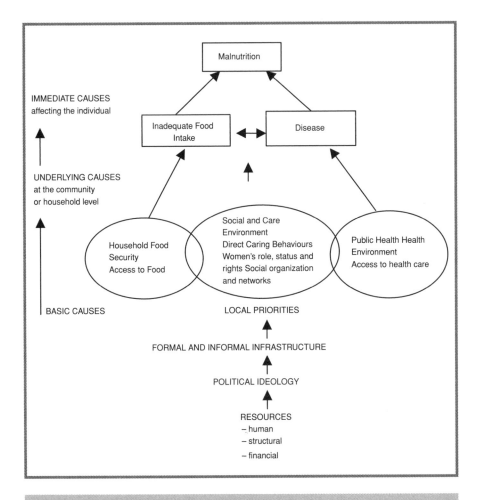

Figure 9.1 A conceptual model of the causes of malnutrition

Source: Adapted from the UNICEF Framework of Underlying Causes of Malnutrition and Mortality (UNICEF 1990)

modified in any way, the first step is to understand how and why it comes about, hence the need for conceptual understanding of the causes of malnutrition.

Several causative models illustrating the aetiology of malnutrition have been developed (Pacey and Payne 1985; UNICEF 1990). The common feature of all these models is that malnutrition serves as the starting point from which the model is extended backwards to explain causes or the process leading to malnutrition. Consequently nutritional status and malnutrition are often seen in terms of the outcome of other factors. This is also seen in conceptual models of famine, such as Sen's entitlement theory (Sen 1981), where malnutrition and excess mortality are considered the outcome of famine.

The framework proposed by UNICEF includes three levels of causes of malnutrition: immediate, underlying and basic. The two immediate factors are food intake and disease, which in turn are affected by the underlying causes usually operating at the household or community level. These include household food security, basic health services and health environment, and maternal and child care. The basic causes operating at higher administrative levels are influenced by potential resources, economic structure and political and ideological superstructure. The framework distinguishes between causes which operate at different levels of society starting with the household and working backwards to include the community district or region. This is particularly important, as causes or problems must be addressed at the level at which they operate.

IMMEDIATE CAUSES

The two immediate causes of malnutrition that affect the individual directly, are inadequate food intake and disease. A healthy diet includes amounts of all types of nutrients. When the intake and balance of these nutrients is insufficient the bodies responds by either producing a characteristic nutritional deficiency (type I response) or by a failure to grow, leading to malnutrition (type II response).

Health and nutrition are closely linked, as disease contributes to malnutrition, while malnutrition makes an individual more susceptible to disease. The relationship is therefore cyclical: the one exacerbates the other as shown in Figure 9.2.

Disease may lead to malnutrition through: loss of appetite, malabsorption of nutrients, diarrhoea and associated loss of nutrients, altered metabolism, which increases the body's need for nutrients. In turn severe malnutrition increases the incidence, duration, and severity of infectious disease. The relationship between moderate malnutrition and disease is less clear although it does appear to affect the duration of disease. Malnutrition is associated with a lowering in immunity, and changes to the structure and function of the intestinal mucosal surfaces, which affects absorption of nutrients.

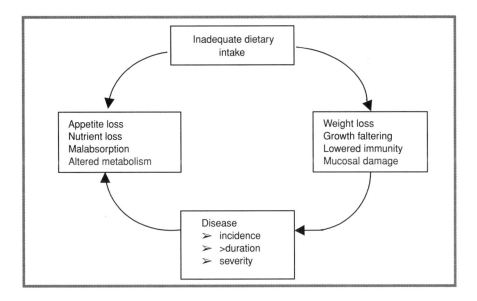

Figure 9.2 The malnutrition infection cycle

Source: Tomkins and Watson 1989

UNDERLYING CAUSES

Household food security

Definitions and explanations about household food security abound in other chapters of this book, so rather than repeat material from elsewhere, a brief overview will be given. In the simplest terms, food security is about people's access to food and has been defined as 'access by all people at all times to the food needed for an active and healthy life'. For a household this means how able they are to secure adequate food, either through their own food production or food purchases, for meeting the dietary needs of all its members. The ability of a household to produce food depends on a wide range of factors, depending on whether production is agricultural, livestock, or horticulture, and other factors, such as access to available fertile land, the availability of labour and appropriate seeds and tools, and the climatic conditions. Food purchases are influenced on the one hand by the household's income, and on the other by the availability and prices of foods in local markets.

Seasonality In many rural communities nutritional status fluctuates according to season. In rural Africa, for example, many people suffer a regular 'hungry' season prior to the harvest which often coincides with an increase in malnutrition, due to less food available, higher food prices, and seasonal increases in disease, such as diarrhoea or malaria due to the rains.

Following the harvest most children experience 'catch-up' growth. Because of the importance of normal seasonal changes any situation must be considered in the context of 'what is normal for the time of year'.

Coping strategies In an emergency, whatever the cause and situation, people's access to food may be affected, forcing them to alter their normal practices. People facing regular episodes of drought and famine have usually developed complex strategies for coping with these events. The main aim of these strategies is to preserve productive assets which are needed to sustain a living or the family in the future.

An early response to food insecurity is often making changes to the diet, such as reducing the family's consumption or switching to cheaper but less desirable or nutritious foods. As a result of these dietary changes, in context malnutrition can be an early indicator of famine. An important question is who within the household is eating less, or eating inferior food? It may or may not be the children.

Impact of war on coping strategies Food insecurity during peacetime is rarely as severe as the famines created as a result of war and conflict. War and violence prevent people from following the strategies that would otherwise allow them to cope, for example by restricting people's movements, controlling trade or via social disintegration. War coping strategies even though restricted appear to follow closely those of households affected by peacetime famine (Curtis 1995).

Public health – basic health services and the health environment

The health environment includes all those aspects of the environment that influence exposure to infectious disease. Public health problems are very often concentrated where population density is high and infrastructure, including provision of basic services, is weak, for example in poor urban areas or in a newly formed relief camp, where there may be overcrowding, inadequate housing, poor water supply and limited sanitation. All of these factors will contribute to an increased exposure to and therefore incidence of disease. This in turn will contribute to malnutrition, which in turn will affect the outcome of disease in terms of its incidence, duration and severity.

The provision of local health services, and access to those health services, influence treatment of infection. Inadequate or late treatment places a child at increased nutritional risk by prolonging the disease. In an emergency the health services may be seriously disrupted, thereby increasing the health risks.

The social and care environment

Malnutrition can occur even when a household has access to adequate amounts and types of food as well as access to appropriate sanitation, water, and health services. The social environment within the household and local community directly affects the ability of a family, and individual household members to care for themselves and ensure good nutrition.

Childcare and sound feeding practices are essential elements of good nutrition and health. The care of the child is affected by a wide range of behaviours that in turn affect child nutrition. There is the direct care of the child by members of the family, in particular the mother. But of additional importance are the support given by the family or community to the adult members of the family, and the behaviours that influence how the household food supply is shared among its members, or attitudes to modern health services, water supplies and sanitation (Engle 1992).

The care of children is closely linked with the cultural, social and economic situation of the household and the situation of women (Longhurst and Tomkins 1995). Resources for improving care exist at the household level: income, food, time, attitudes, relationships and knowledge. If the status of women is low they may have little control over the resources within the family; so although they may have major responsibilities for child-rearing they do not have the resources to carry it out. The values of the society also obviously strongly influence the priority given to the care of physiologically vulnerable members of the household, including children, women and the elderly.

Among resource poor households there are likely to be severe constraints on caring behaviours, such as the poor health and psychological state of the mother, the absence of key family members, or the break-up of the family. Some of the constraints on care might be self-imposed. For example, people may decide to reduce their family's food intake in order to preserve what little food they have, alternatively they may switch to cheaper but less nutritious food.

Because of the many roles and responsibilities women have, they need to receive care in order to offer the optimal care needed to ensure healthy children. Some caring activities require physical effort while others require attention, emotional support, and verbal interaction. If mothers or alternative caregivers are ill, tired or depressed, this will limit their care-giving ability. It may also limit their access to resources needed for care giving.

Displacement or forced migration is likely to cause severe social disruption and upheaval. This may break links with extended family and wider social networks who would normally support the family in the care of their children. Alternatively, new social networks or groups may have evolved, such as local non-governmental organizations (NGOs) or church relief groups.

Importance of all three groups of underlying causes

These three groups of underlying causes are *three necessary conditions* for adequate dietary intake and health, and so for good nutrition. A failure in any will contribute to malnutrition. Thus even in the most severe famine, household access to food is necessary but not sufficient to ensure adequate nutrition.

The three groups of underlying causes are usually closely related and inter-linked; food security and use of health services are heavily influenced by the social environment and the care givers' behaviour and use of resources. For example, if a mother is having to spend long hours queuing for food assistance she will have less time available for selecting and preparing nutritious meals and for responding to the emotional needs of her children.

Within the three clusters of underlying causes are the necessary conditions to ensure adequate nutrition; each is necessary but not sufficient for nutritional well-being. Where there are several causes of malnutrition operating simultaneously the outcome is considerably worse than the sum of the combined individual effects. In other words the relationship between the underlying causes is synergistic (multiplicative rather than additive).

Basic causes

Just as the three groups of underlying causes are closely inter-related, they are themselves the result of the unequal distribution of resources in society. Such basic or structural causes also need to be analysed and acted upon.

In their development of the concept of resources as a basic cause of malnutrition and mortality, UNICEF make a useful distinction between human, economic and organizational resources, and stress the importance of analysing who controls these resources.

The wider social situation and conditions, including power structures, property and other resource relations and division of labour, obviously wield a considerable influence over food security, the social and care environment and public health.

Basic services are provided to people through formal and non-formal institutions, so their relative efficiency and strength are bound to affect the three groups of underlying causes.

In situations of civil war, violence, insecurity and oppression may lead to complete social collapse and the breakdown in civil society. New networks may develop based on political alliances, in place of traditional links based on economic and social interdependence. New leaders emerge, who may be less accountable than traditional leaders, as their power comes from external factors such as wealth or arms rather than from the support of the population they claim to represent. A constantly changing social and political arena is increasingly the context of current emergencies.

It is necessary to understand how these wider social and political factors affect household food security and also caring behaviours within the community and within the household, and subsequently are a basic cause of malnutrition and mortality, as they impact on all underlying causes of malnutrition.

STRATEGIES TO ADDRESS MALNUTRITION

The second half of this chapter is concerned with nutrition intervention strategies. These should be considered and planned within the context of the programme cycle (Figure 9.3). This provides a useful breakdown for nutrition related activities, between assessment, analysis and a range of direct nutrition interventions or actions.

ASSESSMENT

Nutrition assessments at the population level encompass a wide range of approaches and procedures, which vary according to the aims and objectives of the assessment, the local context – including the administrative level at which the assessment is initiated – and the organizations involved. To gain a more complete understanding of the nutritional situation, nutrition assessments may take a range of perspectives of the problem, for example:

1 The nature, extent, severity and distribution of malnutrition (the outcome of inadequate nutrition).
2 The main causes of malnutrition (analysis of the process whereby an individual or population became malnourished in the first place).
3 Who in the population is affected and why (important to know for targeting purposes).
4 The views and opinions of local people, particularly women (important in relation to community participation and programme success).

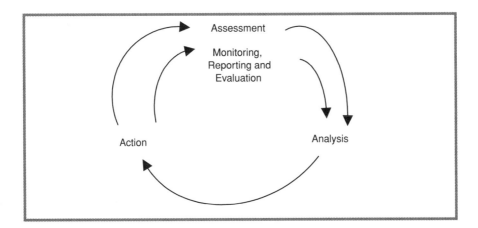

Figure 9.3 The project cycle

There are three distinct types of nutritional assessment:

1 Assessment as part of the programme cycle in the process of development, for example, the community based assessment in Iringa,
  Tanzania (Box 9.1). This would include initial assessment, and ongoing surveillance as part of the monitoring and evaluation process.
2 Nutritional surveillance as part of a Famine Early Warning System, for
  the purposes of emergency preparedness, for example, the nutritional
  surveillance activities of Save the Children UK, which contributes to
  famine early warning in Ethiopia.
3 Emergency needs assessment, which includes both rapid initial
  assessment, and more detailed follow-up assessment once the situation has stabilized.

There are some types of vulnerability assessment which might loosely be
considered as a nutritional assessment. Vulnerability assessments seek to
identify areas and populations that might be threatened by food insecurity.
In Africa, this is an important tool in famine early warning and relief
planning.

For public health purposes protein energy malnutrition among infants
and young children is assessed by means of anthropometric measurements
of growth failure in infants and young children, rather than by clinical
examination (however, during anthropometric assessments the presence
of nutritional oedema is also noted).

For assessing the underlying and basic causes of malnutrition a range of
quantitative and qualitative methods are used, including household surveys, review of secondary information, rapid appraisal and participatory
rapid appraisal techniques. These are reviewed in Young and Jaspars (1995).

Measuring malnutrition for growth monitoring, surveys and surveillance

There are two categories of anthropometric assessment:

1 Assessment of individual nutritional status, for the purposes of:
   a) growth monitoring or,
   b) nutritional screening.

2 Assessment at the population level:
   a) as part of the project cycle in development programmes, for
      example, the integrated nutrition programme in Iringa, Tanzania,
      and nutrition surveillance activities in South Africa (Box 9.5).
   b) as part of emergency preparedness activities, for example nutri-
      tional surveillance for famine early warning systems.
   c) as a 'one-off' assessment of the current nutritional situation, for
      example, as part of an emergency needs assessment (many
      examples are given in the Reports on the Nutrition Situation of
      Refugees and Displaced Persons (RNIS)).

All involve assessment of the anthropometric status of individual children.[6]

The recommended measurements for assessing nutritional status for the purposes of nutritional surveillance or screening are weight and height. If a child is either too young or too sick to stand, length rather than height is measured. Mid-upper-arm circumference (MUAC) is sometimes used. Comparisons of weight or height measurements are meaningless unless differences in age and sex are taken into account. This is why the measurements must be transformed into nutritional indices, such as weight-for-height (WFH), height-for-age (HFA) and weight-for-age (WFA). A nutritional index is derived by comparing a child's measurement with that expected of a child of the same age from a reference population. The index may also be derived by relating to a reference child of the same height, rather than the same age. This is useful when age is unknown.

By calculating nutritional status in relation to a set of reference values, the nutritional status of children of different ages or heights may be compared. The WHO recommends the use of a single reference standard[7] based on data from the US National Center for Health Statistics (NCHS) (WHO Working Group, 1986). This allows comparisons between countries. See Box 9.2 for a summary of nutritional status and indices.

The reference standards are available in various forms; complete tables, laminated cards, charts and computer software programmes. Some countries, for example India, have produced their own internal reference values.

Arm circumference is usually considered to be independent of age as it changes little between one and five years in a normal child. It therefore gives a simple anthropometric measure of wasting, without having to refer to a reference population. However, mean MUAC values across ages do show a definite age dependent increase of about 2 cm between the ages of 6 and 59 months, thus younger children are more likely to have low MUACs. This explains why the MUAC predicts childhood mortality better than height- and weight-age adjusted indicators in community based studies (de Onis and Habicht 1996). For this reason it is particularly useful as a screening tool to select those children most at risk. MUAC-for-age reference data and also MUAC-for-height have now been developed which allow a better comparison of arm circumference across age groups (de Onis et al. 1997).

Low birth weight The birth weight of a baby is an important anthropometric indicator, which reflects both the duration of gestation and the rate of foetal growth. It may be considered as a prospective indicator of the child's future health and nutritional status as well as a retrospective indicator of the mother's nutritional and health status. As such it is a pivotal indicator in programmes aimed at pregnant and lactating women and young children. Children born with weights below 2.5 kg are defined as low birth weight. Reliable birth weight data are often scarce. Those data collected at hospitals may be skewed towards better-nourished mothers who are more likely to give birth in such institutions. Nevertheless, attempts need to be made in community-based programmes to track birth weights.

Low birth weight is less prevalent in SSA than in South Asia. However, it increases when food is short and the demands for agricultural labour are high and therefore the seasonal effects in SSA are important.

Box 9.2   Nutritional status and nutritional indices

Two types of growth failure associated with malnutrition:
Wasting: the result of recent rapid weight loss or a failure to gain weight caused by a reduction of body stores of fat and muscle. Wasting is readily reversible once conditions improve. Wasting is evidence of acute protein energy malnutrition.
Stunting: develops as a result of inadequate nutrition over a long period. Stunted children have relatively normal body proportions but may look younger than their actual age. Unlike wasting, the development of stunting is a slow cumulative process and it may not be evident for some years, at which time the child's nutrition may have improved. By two years of age height deficits may be irreversible.

The three main nutritional indices are:
Weight-for-Height reflects recent weight loss or gain and so is the best indicator of wasting. It is also useful when age is unknown.
Height-for-Age reflects skeletal growth, and so is the best indicator of stunting.
Weight-for-Age is a composite index as it reflects wasting or stunting or a combination of both.

The two main methods for converting body measurements into indices:
Z scores (or SD scores): a measure of the distance between the child's value and the expected value of the reference population. It is expressed in multiples of the reference standard deviation value corresponding to the same mean (or expected mean). In the reference population 95 per cent have Z scores between -2 and $+2$, which is the normal range.
Percent of the median: the child's value is expressed as a percentage of the expected value for the reference population.

Cut-off points:
Children are classified as malnourished if their nutritional status falls below an agreed cut-off point, such as 80 per cent of the reference median. The choice of cut-off point is somewhat arbitrary and may vary. For example, if resources are very limited the cut-off point used to select children for supplementary feeding programmes may have to be reduced to limit the numbers of children admitted.

Measuring malnutrition in adults Increasing attention is being paid to assessing malnutrition in older children, adults and the elderly. Women, especially during pregnancy and lactation, have long been considered a nutritionally vulnerable group while in some emergencies, high rates of malnutrition among adults and the elderly have been noted.

The most useful measure of malnutrition in adults is body mass index (BMI), defined as weight (in Kg) divided by the square of height (in metres). The same index is used to define grades of obesity. Thus for adults there is no need for reference data. The cut-off points for classifying BMI among adults are shown in Table 9.2. Average BMI in most adult groups falls in the range from 19 to 21. Two groups who are known to have BMI below average are the Kenyan Samburu (17.6) and the Dinka from South Sudan (17.6). Both groups are unusually tall.

Adolescence, which occurs from around 10 to 18 years of age, is a period of rapid growth and the anthropometric indices to assess wasting, which are used for children, are not applicable. WHO recommends that adolescent wasting is assessed by calculating body mass index for age (weight/height^2 for age). BMI for age scores are compared with reference data for American children and a cut-off point below 5th percentile indicates malnutrition. Height-for-age is used to assess stunting in the same way as for younger children and the same cut-off points apply.

Assessment of the nutritional status of children and adults allows conclusions to be drawn about whether there is generalized undernutrition in a community, or whether other factors such as childhood infections or feeding practices are more important (Bailey and Ferro-Luzzi 1995). Generalized undernutrition is likely to be a result of household food insecurity, although care must be taken before making such assumptions.

Less data is available on the nutritional status of adults, compared with children. Data from Congo, Ghana, Mali, Morocco and Tanzania, gave a range of between 0.3 and 2.8 per cent of adults falling below the cut-off of 16 BMI (Bailey and Ferro-Luzzi 1995). These data-sets were from stable non-emergency populations. In an emergency context much higher proportions of malnourished adults are to be expected. In Somalia in 1992–3,

Table 9.2 Classification of malnutrition in adults by body mass index (BMI)

BMI	Nutrition Status
>20	Normal
18.5–20	Marginal
17–18.5	Mild malnutrition
16–17	Moderate malnutrition
<16	Severe malnutrition

Source: Bailey and Ferro-Luzzi 1995

the relief agency Concern found that most adults had a BMI of less than 16 and consequently used a cut-off of 13.5 as one of the admission criteria to their adult therapeutic feeding programmes (Collins 1995).

ANALYSIS

Analysis is the essential link between assessment and response, and deserves to be considered separately from assessment as it includes not only analysis of the information generated by the assessment process, but also analysis of the available resources, practical constraints and other factors that will determine programme design. In broad terms, the process of analysis may include:

- analysis of the type and extent of malnutrition;
- analysis of the relative importance of the underlying causes of malnutrition and their inter-relationships;
- analysis of who (which households) are most seriously affected and why (vulnerability analysis);
- understanding of local perceptions and priorities, including coping strategies;
- analysis of available resources, including technical, financial and infrastructure;
- consideration of practical constraints, including access to resources and the timeframe for response.

These types of analyses are pre-requisites for informed decision making, in particular, the prioritization of programme interventions, the choice of specific programme design characteristics, and the development of proposals for effective nutrition intervention strategies.

The ACC/SCN of the United Nations publishes Reports on the Nutrition Situation of Refugees and Displaced People every three months, which provide updates on rapidly changing situations. The information is obtained from a wide range of collaborating agencies, both UN and NGO. The information is mainly about nutrition, health, and survival in refugee and displaced populations (home-based emergency affected populations are not included). Definitions and benchmarks are given for a number of indicators, as shown in Table 9.3.

ACTION – NUTRITION STRATEGIES

Malnutrition is complex, and different types of policies and programmes are needed to effectively alleviate poverty and malnutrition (see Box 9.3), including a combination of macro-economic policies and more targeted interventions.

A broad range of interventions impact on nutrition, in the areas of health, food security, and child and maternal care. For example, if the three

Table 9.3 Indicators, definitions and benchmarks

Indicator	Definition	Benchmark for guidance in interpretation
Wasting	Less than −2 SDs, or sometimes 80% wt/ht NCHS standards, usually in children 6–59 months.	5–10% usual in African populations in non-drought periods >20% 'undoubtedly high and indicating a serious situation' >40% 'a severe crisis'
Oedema	Clinical sign of kwashiorkor	'any prevalence detected is cause for concern'
Crude mortality rate		1/10 000/day 'serious situation'
Under five mortality rate		>2/10 000/day 'emergency out of control'

clusters of underlying causes are considered, interventions that have a beneficial impact on nutrition include: provision of health services (essential drugs, Expanded Programme of Immunization (EPI), Mother and Child Health (MCH) services, Control of Diarrhoeal Diseases (CDD) etc.); education and literacy programmes; housing; environmental sanitation, and water supply; and food security initiatives (promoting access to food through income transfers, food subsidies, employment programmes).

Those actions that are broadly considered free-standing nutrition projects or components include:
- nutrition and health education including promotion of appropriate infant feeding and use of complementary foods, and the promotion, protection and support of breastfeeding;
- growth monitoring as part of wider MCH services;
- micronutrient supplementation programmes (for example, vitamin A, iron and folate);
- food processing, particularly local production of appropriate weaning foods (blended food) and food fortification programmes (iodine, vitamin A, pre-mixes of micronutrients);
- nutrition rehabilitation – therapeutic feeding and treatment of micronutrient deficiencies;
- supplementary feeding;
- food distribution programmes;
- food related income transfer programmes (food-for-work, cash-for-work, food stamps or vouchers).

The last three categories of nutrition intervention relate most directly to food security. The last three programmes are concerned with transfer of

---

Box 9.3   The World Bank and nutrition programmes in Africa

Up to 1991, most nutrition programmes supported by the World Bank were through the health sector. Two of the more successful World Bank supported projects were in Senegal (Senegal Community Nutrition Project) and in Madagascar (Projet Sécurité Alimentaire et de Nutrition). Both projects included targeted supplementary feeding, growth monitoring, micronutrients and IEC. They achieved an improvement in nutritional status of the target population, high levels of community involvement, and the focus on nutrition allowed for good technical input and monitoring.

Many World Bank projects have involved NGOs in different sectors. Typical interventions by NGOs include nutrition education, surveillance, growth monitoring, micronutrient deficiencies, income generation, food supplements and community initiatives. Often NGOs have greater experience at field level, and some may have a primary focus on nutrition. In addition their greater flexibility in hiring staff and adding components as compared with line ministries is beneficial. However, their activities are often poorly coordinated, and the technical and managerial quality may vary. In addition their coverage is limited, which limits opportunities for scaling up.

Source: Kennedy 1991

resources to target households, thereby raising the households' real income (Rogers 1995), as well as directly addressing their nutritional needs.

Although for the purposes of this review these interventions can be broken down into related activities, they are likely to differ quite considerably within each category according to the combination of activities they form a part of, and their specific objectives. For example, supplementary feeding in a stable context is intended as a preventive measure as all children are provided with additional food, or it may be a means of providing support to socially vulnerable groups. In contrast in an emergency setting supplementary feeding may be a lifesaving measure as the supplementary food is the only source of food available to a vulnerable household. The point to note is that it is not the type of intervention that is critical, rather it is the objectives of the intervention. The objectives should relate directly to the underlying causes of malnutrition in a given context, which reinforces the centrality and importance of developing a locally specific model of the causes of malnutrition.

For a given problem, it is usually necessary to combine a range of activities tailored for a specific purpose. For example, inappropriate feeding practices and caring behaviours may require nutrition and health education, but also improved food security to promote access to more and better quality foods, and also to free up time for caring activities.

Strategies to prevent micronutrient deficiencies have often been heralded as 'magic bullets', for example vitamin A supplementation of populations, but it is important to realize that in any context a single strategy is rarely as effective as a combination of strategies. For example, in response to the micronutrient deficiencies found in emergency affected populations, the World Food Programme (WFP) recommends a range of strategies. These include in order of priority:

- Promoting access to fresh fruit and vegetables through local production, for example, home or kitchen gardens, community gardens, access to local markets, beer brewing, or even through exchange of ration food items for other locally available commodities.
- Provision of fresh vegetables or fruit in the food basket.
- Including in the food basket a food rich in a particular vitamin or mineral, for example, groundnuts in the rations of Mozambican refugees in Malawi in 1989, which are a rich source of niacin. (This population suffered *pellagra*, caused by niacin deficiency.)
- Providing fortified food, such as oil fortified with vitamin A, iodized salt, fortified or enriched cereal based foods or blended food. WFP now routinely includes fortified food aid commodities in emergency rations.
- Distributing nutrient supplements, for example, ascorbic acid tablets (vitamin C) to Somali refugees in Eastern Ethiopia in 1987.

Nutrition and health education

Dietary and other behaviours that affect food intake are influenced by a wide range of factors, and in most cases education cannot expect to change behaviour without a concurrent improvement in economic circumstances. Increased income is usually associated with an improved intake of iron, vitamin A and protein for example (see Box 9.4).

Changes in food consumption patterns require shifts in deeply ingrained family habits and cultural norms. Long-term shifts require several years of consistent effort and monitoring of impact.

Women's education and literacy is perhaps the key aspect of education that will directly affect almost all aspects of their coping or caring capacity, thereby improving the nutrition within their household. In the long run, improved education will contribute to lowered fertility, and better employment opportunities; and these in turn will enhance household food security, health and caring capacity (Gillespie and Mason 1991).

While adult education/literacy classes should be a priority, carefully tailored education on child feeding/child care will help to impact directly on behaviours. Specific negative behaviours must first be identified together with potential beneficiaries, and then ways of addressing these problems must be designed.

Box 9.4   The Nutrition Communication Project (NCP), Niger: a food based approach to dietary change

In Niger, a pilot nutrition education project, with a focus on vitamin A, began in January 1991, implemented by the Ministry of Public Health, Nutrition Division, with support from USAID. The project's aim was to test ways of improving vitamin A status of vulnerable groups by influencing the purchase and consumption of vitamin A-rich foods as well as their commercial production.

Selection of the 'right' foods to promote calls for careful research into seasonal availability, vitamin A content, cost, consumer acceptance, ease of preparation and time required, current consumption levels, and the possibility of increasing it. In Niger the messages were developed upon the realities of existing gender roles related to food provision, and small changes were encouraged.

In Niger, food availability is seasonal, so different foods were promoted for each season. In the post-harvest months, most families still have some disposable income after they have paid their debts. So during this season the more costly animal sources of vitamin A (liver) had to be promoted. Since liver is an animal source of vitamin A, it contains a pre-formed and readily available form of the vitamin which is stored in the human body. In the hot season months (March–May), mangoes are plentiful, providing an abundant source of vitamin A. In the cool dry season (November to February) focus was put on increasing production of greens in dry season commercial gardens (adequate water was available for this, and commercial dry season vegetable production existed). The foods promoted were already eaten, were inexpensive and diverse, appealing to both taste and seasonal availability.

The channel chosen for disseminating information was village drama, built upon a traditional medium but incorporating changes that would allow for local management/supervision and a systematic means of conveying project messages. The drama was put on by village drama teams. A second phase of the project expanded the project area, refined project messages, and tested a more extensive range of communication channels (interpersonal education, flipchart-size counselling cards, postcard size counselling cards, radio dramas and radio spots). Subsequent evaluations found that knowledge of the importance of vitamin A rich foods increased significantly, and showed important increases in both purchasing and consumption behaviour.

Source: Parlato and Gottert 1996

Growth monitoring

Growth monitoring is a principal activity in MCH programmes throughout the developing and developed world. Growth monitoring involves following changes in a child's physical development by taking regular measurements of weight and sometimes length, ideally every month or at least every three months.

This information is plotted on the child's growth chart. The chart is on a 'road to health card' usually kept by the mother, which also records appointments at the MCH clinic, the child's and parents' names, date of birth, address, siblings and immunization status.

Target growth rates are based on the WHO/NCHS reference values, by comparing the child's growth with two reference curves on the chart; an upper curve which is the median growth curve for boys, and a lower reference curve which is the third centile for girls. Concern is not with whether a child is on a given centile at one point in time, but whether the child's pattern of growth falls along the same centile band as age increases. It is more important that a child's growth moves in parallel with the reference growth curves than the child's weight at any particular time. Growth faltering is defined as no change or an actual decrease between successive measurements. This is useful for the early detection of health and nutrition problems and can be used as a basis to stimulate discussion between health workers and mothers about child health, nutrition and the possible causes of the current failure (see Box 9.5).

In practice, there are often problems of poor attendance or difficulties understanding growth charts on the part of both health workers and mothers. Interpretation of changes in weight vary considerably. As

---

Box 9.5 Nutrition surveillance and intervention, South Africa

There is now a move towards community based programmes and nutrition surveillance. The Department of Health has developed an integrated nutrition programme with a health-based component and a community based aspect. Although it is still early, a number of lessons have been drawn, in particular that growth monitoring can be used to promote community based surveillance, and to provide information upon which the communities can act. Emphasis has also been placed on training, supervision and information dissemination; and on building on existing infrastructure and capabilities.

Source: Fincham 1997

Levinson (1991) succinctly put it, ' . . . the effectiveness of growth monitoring is, most basically, a function of the effectiveness of interventions which it can trigger'.

Production of local blended foods

Blended foods are a mixture of cereals and other ingredients, including, for example, pulses, dried skimmed milk, and possibly sugar and or some kind of vegetable oil. There are a number of processes for the commercial production of blended foods including for example, dry blending of milled ingredients; toasting or roasting; extrusion cooking. The final product is usually milled into powder form and fortified with a vitamin mineral premix. Extruded and roasted blended foods are 'pre-cooked' and therefore require minimal cooking, which preserves levels of micronutrients. Some pre-cooking is essential to ensure micro-organisms present in the cooking water are killed.

Blended foods tend to provide significantly higher levels and better quality protein than cereals. The Codex Alimentarius Commission of the Food and Agricultural Organization (FAO) recommend in the order of 15 g protein per 100 g blended food, together with increased levels of micronutrients and sometimes additional fat (FAO Codex Alimentarius Commision 1991). Blended foods were originally designed to provide protein supplements for weaning infants and younger children or for low cost weaning foods in developing countries, for example, *Faffa* in Ethiopia, *Likuni Phala* in Malawi, *Musalac* in Burundi. Some of these products are now used in the general ration for adults and children as a means of providing an additional source of micronutrients. Studies among refugees in Ethiopia, Tanzania and Nepal, have shown that blended foods are acceptable and eaten by everybody (Mears and Young 1998). Even though the blended food that was distributed was not itself familiar, it was easily recognizable as porridge and could be prepared easily into an already familiar dish.

Blended foods have also been designed for use in nutritional rehabilitation programmes. These products are more expensive than regular blended foods, partly because of their higher quality ingredients and higher specification packaging. They also contain a wider range of micronutrients suitable for the needs of malnourished children.

Previously, most blended foods for emergency use originated in the USA. Corn soy blend (CSB) and wheat soy blend (WSB) are provided to the WFP, by the USA. With the inclusion of blended foods in the general food rations for emergency relief programmes, WFP are increasingly using locally produced blended foods and in some countries, particularly Kenya (Box 9.6), local production of blended foods has increased to cope with this demand. Local purchase of food aid commodities where readily available, is preferable to importing food aid from distant countries, for reasons of cost, efficiency and the support given to local African economies.

Box 9.6 Production of pre-cooked fortified blended food in Kenya

Up to 1992 only a small quantity of raw blended foods had been produced in Kenya. During 1992 the demand for blended foods outstripped supply, as large numbers of Somali refugees flowed into Kenya and Ethiopia (350 000 in total). At the same time Kenya was experiencing one of its worst droughts in recent history.

In the face of such need, UNICEF supported a Kenyan company, The House of Mange, to produce a pre-cooked fortified blended food product (UNIMIX) (Hertz 1997). The company previously had experience in the production of biscuits, pastas and other food items. UNICEF financed the purchase of the first four 'extruders' and the company repaid UNICEF over the next four years. The most popular composition of ingredients is 75 per cent maize and 25 per cent soya flour, although wheat and millet have occasionally been used. Initially UNIMIX was used mostly for supplementary feeding programmes for children below five years old and lactating mothers. More recently it has become the policy of UNHCR and the WFP to include small amounts of blended food in the general rations of emergency affected populations in order to provide an additional source of micronutrients.

Between 1992 and 1997 over 30 000 tonnes have been produced for UN organizations, ICRC, NGOs and individual donors. Most has been used in the East Africa Region, although consignments have been sent to Angola and North Korea. The maintenance of a high standard of quality and hygiene has been a challenge, and there have been some complaints about product quality among refugees in Tanzania.

Source: Mears and Young 1998

According to Djikhuizen (1997) the capacity for local blended food production in Africa is several times the demand. Major companies exist in Kenya, Ethiopia, Malawi, Botswana and South Africa, with smaller ones in Uganda, Sudan, Eritrea and Burundi. The total capacity of these factories together is close to 100 000 tonnes per year. The total market for locally produced blended food for emergency and development activities by UN agencies, bilateral donors and NGOs is around 75 000 tonnes per year worldwide, with about half in Africa.

However, the market for low cost weaning foods for the lower economic sector consisting largely of urban wage earners is relatively unexplored. Given the high rates of malnutrition there is certainly a need. Such products need to be promoted through MCH systems, educational radio programmes and other information channels, while the private sector could market the product through its retail outlets and markets. This would require that different private manufacturers act together and produce a product under a common name, in cooperation with the government. Such a social marketing system had, until the recent civil unrest, been very successful in Burundi (Dijkuisen 1997).

Food fortification

The fortification of foods with essential micronutrients, particularly iron, iodine and vitamin A, has been practised for many years and is responsible for better nutrition throughout the developed and developing world. Fortification is usually a long-term option as it takes time to set up and establish, and requires the commitment of governments. A food may be fortified to increase the level of specific nutrient(s) within it, or to restore nutrients lost during processing by enriching it with the depleted nutrient (fortification of cereal flour and dried skimmed milk powder). Foods may be fortified with single nutrients (salt with iodine, vegetable oil with vitamin A), or with several vitamins and minerals combined in a pre-mix (this ensures that the correct concentration is present in the pre-mix). Levels of fortification are set so that consumption of the food in the expected amounts contributes significantly to nutritional requirements while still remaining within the safe upper limit. In addition the fortificant must not alter the taste, smell, look, texture, physical structure or shelf-life of the food vehicle.

One of the possible drawbacks of fortification is that it only benefits those who consume the fortified food, and so the positive impact of fortification very much depends on who eats the fortified food and how regularly.

Fortification of salt with iodine is being successfully adopted in a number of developing countries, but requires sustained support and trouble shooting technical problems. Initially it requires legislation, a centralized salt supply, and the necessary equipment, funding and distribution systems. The main effect of dietary deficiency is on the developing brain. The prevalence of the most severe form of brain damage, i.e. endemic cretinism, can be as high as 1 to 2 per cent of the total population. This was seen in the past in parts of the Democratic Republic of Congo and Cameroon before the introduction of control programmes.

In Cameroon the increase in availability and consumption of adequately iodized salt at the household level was accompanied by an almost complete normalization of urinary iodine levels and a dramatic reduction in the prevalence of goitre (ICCIDD 1996).

Processed foods, such as margarine, white flour and dried skimmed milk, have had some of their micronutrient content removed during processing. These foods are therefore frequently fortified to compensate for this loss. For example, all dried skimmed milk available as food aid is fortified with vitamin A. In industrialized countries, white flour is routinely fortified.

Micronutrient supplementation

Vulnerable individuals can be temporarily protected by the administration of supplements. However, the success of such programmes on the scale needed depends on a number of factors, many in common with other aspects of health. Constraints are common in supply and logistics, access to health posts or other distribution points, training of staff and communicating to recipients, adherence to the daily regime, to name but a few. Despite these constraints, the supplements are usually cheap and potentially highly cost-effective.

The major focus of supplementation programmes are:

- Iodine: iodized oil, administered by injection or orally. A single injection of iodized oil can prevent deficiency for up to five years, and by mouth for around 12 months.
- Iron: distribution of daily iron (and possibly folate) supplements, particularly to pregnant and lactating women.
- Vitamin A: periodic distribution (usually every four to six months) of vitamin A for children in areas of vitamin A deficiency (100 000 IU dose for children from 6 to 12 months, and 200 000 IU dose for children aged 12 months and over). Coverage has been increased in recent years by providing supplements during National Immunization Days (NIDs) or other mass campaigns such as periodic anti-helminth campaigns.

Worldwide, of the 78 countries where vitamin A deficiency is known to be a public health problem,[8] 61 have policies supporting vitamin A supplementation in children. Unfortunately, Africa lags behind (but see Box 9.7).

Box 9.7   The National Micronutrient Malnutrition Control Programme, Tanzania

In Tanzania, separate programmes for prevention and control of iodine deficiency disorders (IDD), vitamin A deficiency (VAD) and iron deficiency anaemia (IDA) have been formulated. The IDD control programme consists of targeted distribution of iodized oil capsules, with universal salt iodization as the long-term goal. The VAD control programme consists of vitamin A capsule distribution and stimulation of demand for foods rich in vitamin A. The programme on IDA is mainly targeted at pregnant women and promotes the production and consumption of iron and folic acid rich foods.

Source: Extract from Lorri 1997

Nutrition rehabilitation – therapeutic feeding

The broad aim of therapeutic feeding is to treat severely malnourished children and thereby to reduce the level of mortality among children under five years of age. Severe malnutrition is an extremely serious medical and social disorder. Without treatment there is a very high probability these children would die, as severe malnutrition is strongly associated with an increased incidence, severity and duration of disease. Unlike supplementary feeding, the overall aims and objectives of therapeutic feeding programmes are more specific, and less controversial.

In stable situations the therapeutic feeding of severely malnourished children is usually undertaken within a hospital as the numbers are quite small relative to the child population (less than 1 per cent) or alternatively children may be treated at home (Ashworth and Khanum 1997). In contrast in times of acute food insecurity or famine, there is often the need to start up therapeutic feeding centres specifically to treat the increased numbers of severely malnourished.

There are three phases of therapeutic feeding:
- *Phase One – initial treatment for one to three days.* Life-threatening problems are identified and treated, specific deficiencies are corrected, metabolic abnormalities are reversed and feeding is begun.
- *Phase Two – rehabilitation for four to six weeks.* Intensive feeding is given to recover most of the lost weight; emotional and physical stimulation is increased, the mother is trained to continue care at home, and preparations are made for the discharge of the child.
- *Phase Three – follow-up.* After discharge the child and family are followed to prevent relapse.

The dietary treatment of severely malnourished children has radically improved during the past few years, a result of the availability of more detailed guidelines on the treatment of severe malnutrition (WHO 1995). Unfortunately these guidelines are not generally available beyond a small circle of nutritional experts and informed NGOs as they remain in draft form. However, other papers have broadly described the principles of the overall approach (Briend and Golden 1993; Golden 1996; Ashworth et al. 1996). The manufacturers of therapeutic food products have put the guidelines into action by producing pre-packed ready-to-mix therapeutic foods which have been shown to produce superior results in treating malnourished children.[9]

Dehydration on admission to therapeutic feeding programmes is treated with a modified version of the WHO oral rehydration salts (ORS). If the ordinary ORS is given the child is likely to suffer heart failure. There are two milk formulas, F75 therapeutic milk which is intended for children during the initial phase of treatment, and F100 therapeutic milk which is used during the rehabilitation phase. These are similar to high energy milk (HEM) which is commonly found in therapeutic feeding centres, except they have additional minerals and vitamins, including potassium and magnesium.

Despite the improvements in feeding protocols and the availability of appropriate therapeutic foods, there remain the practical constraints of lack of staff motivation and supervision which remain a major determinant of overall programme performance. Schofield and Ashworth (1996) reviewed the performance of 79 treatment centres worldwide and found that case fatality rates had remained unchanged since the 1950s and are typically 20–30 per cent, and sometimes as high as 50–60 per cent. This was attributed to 'faulty case management', particularly inappropriate diets high in protein, energy and sodium and low in micronutrients; prescribing diuretics for oedema; and outmoded teaching manuals. Fifty six per cent of expert practitioners reported that kwashiorkor was a 'protein deficiency' and this was why high protein diets were prescribed, which illustrates how 'out-of-date' they were.

Supplementary feeding

There are several categories of supplementary feeding depending on the context and objectives. All supplementary feeding programmes provide a food ration to a target individual within a household, with the explicit intention of reducing or eliminating the nutrient gap between the person's actual food consumption and presumed nutritional needs.

The distinguishing programme characteristics include:
- the target groups;
- whether the ration is consumed on-site (wet feeding) or is taken home (dry feeding);
- whether the programme is principally preventative or intended to rehabilitate moderately malnourished groups.

The target group in stable situations is usually children under three or five years,[10] moderately malnourished children, and occasionally pregnant and lactating women. In emergencies, supplementary feeding may also target the elderly, sick or convalescent, malnourished adults, and socially vulnerable groups, including orphans. In an emergency affected population, the vulnerable groups qualifying for supplementary feeding can sometimes total as much as 50 per cent of the population (Curdy 1994).

Wet feeding requires the target groups to attend daily to eat their cooked rations. Infants and young children are usually accompanied by their mother or another carer. Dry feeding on the other hand requires only intermittent attendance to register and collect the weekly or fortnightly rations. The foods given vary but often consist of a fortified blend of cereals and pulses. Alternatively, when given to all children under three, it may take the form of complementary foods, intended to supplement breastmilk during the weaning period.

In emergency situations, the primary objective of supplementary feeding is 'to treat children who are moderately malnourished and to prevent severe malnutrition developing' (Mears and Chowdhury 1994). Clearly, the curative goals of feeding outweigh the preventative goals in this context. Apart from the immediate objectives of increasing the food intake of the target groups, there are wider goals of supplementary feeding, including providing:

- health and nutrition education;
- micronutrient supplementation;
- a safe environment for promoting breastfeeding, and other positive caring behaviours;
- a focus for women's activities, such as literacy classes, income generation and social organization.

There is considerable debate around the need for supplementary feeding; in stable situations there is widespread evidence that supplementary feeding fails to produce the expected weight gains (Beaton 1993). The reasons for this are many, including poor attendance, limited coverage of the programme, or a sharing of the ration with others thereby reducing the amount consumed by the targeted individual. An alternative view is that the failure to record the expected weight gains were because the additional energy was consumed by more energetic activity than usual (play) and metabolic adaptation, particularly greater resistance to infections. The conclusion from this was that supplementary feeding programmes were fulfilling two purposes; acting as both a nutritional supplement, and secondly as an income transfer to the family as a whole.

In emergencies, the arguments against supplementary feeding are that it is frequently a supplement to nothing given the failure in the general ration, or alternatively it acts as a substitute for the normal diet.[11] It is also criticized for distracting attention away from the major issues of providing an adequate general ration for all affected by the emergency. Where the target groups comprise a large proportion of the affected population there is in effect a two-tier system of distribution, one through the general ration and a second through supplementary feeding.

Emergency food distribution programmes

The distribution of free food aid to emergency affected populations is becoming increasingly common as the scale and severity of emergencies increases. Between 1989 and 1993, worldwide emergency food needs increased from US$1.1 billion to US$2.5 billion per year (Van Nieuwenhuyse 1995), which has meant a reversal in the relative importance of food aid for emergencies compared with food aid for development. The vast majority of emergency food aid and food aid for protracted refugee and displaced persons operations is distributed in SSA and Southern Europe (FAO 1993). In 1997 FAO/WFP approved 13 Emergency

Box 9.8   Operation Hunger: food support as a safety net in South Africa?

Operation Hunger was founded in 1980 in response to a crippling drought in the former homeland Kwa-Ndebele, and provided food aid to food insecure families. By 1993, Operation Hunger had expanded its operations and was providing support to hundreds of thousands of vulnerable households throughout the country. Limited targeting reduced the amount of time field staff had to spend in any particular village and contributed to Operations Hunger's ability to serve hundreds of communities. Operation Hunger initiated development projects that were designed to strengthen the capacity of vulnerable households to feed themselves. However, in 1994, Operation Hunger reviewed its activities and found that the provision of food aid had not improved the nutritional status of recipients. Anthropometric data from villages showed that significant percentages of children remained stunted and underweight. Food aid was not, by itself or linked to standardized development projects, addressing these nutritional problems. Operation Hunger had neglected critical issues affecting nutritional well-being like water supply, environmental sanitation, diets, weaning practices, micronutrient supplementation and health care.

It was thought that food support could have a greater impact on nutritional vulnerability if it was more meaningfully linked to local capacity-building efforts, health education and awareness campaigns, and development interventions like water supply and environmental sanitation programmes. Operation Hunger initiated the Integrated Development Pilot Programme in 1995 to see whether food support could be used as a development as opposed to a relief intervention. It was concluded that food support programmes can contribute to child growth if they are well targeted, development oriented, monitored for impact, and short term. Operation Hunger now uses growth monitoring programmes to target households experiencing periods of stress. Households whose child is shown to have faltering growth receive an immediate visit from Operation Hunger field staff and community nutrition workers (CNWs). Initial interventions range from nutrition education to short-term feeding or even hospitalization. Another possible intervention is linking household members with emergency employment opportunities in the area.

An evaluation concluded that this approach has yielded positive results, including a positive effect on weight gain of children. However, local residents in project sites still see growth monitoring primarily as a tool for making decisions about food allocations. Furthermore, retaining CNWs is becoming problematic.

Source: Breslin et al. 1997

Operations valued at US$422 million for 16 million beneficiaries (*Food Outlook* of the FAO GIEWS 1997). In Africa, these include Democratic Republic of Congo, Rwanda, Burundi, Ethiopia, Tanzania, Uganda, Somalia, Liberia, Sierra Leone, and continued food assistance in Angola and Mozambique.

Emergency food distribution is reviewed in depth by Jaspars and Young (1995a). A range of activities are combined in the process of food distribution, including:

1 Resourcing food assistance programmes
2 Food procurement, including local purchase
3 Needs assessment
4 Targeting strategies
5 Planning/determining rations
6 Logistics (shipping, delivery and local transportation and storage)
7 Implementation of the distribution to beneficiaries
8 Monitoring and evaluation
9 Phasing out or stopping the distribution

Nutritional considerations are paramount in needs assessment, targeting, planning rations, the process of actual distribution, monitoring, evaluation and phase out.

The broad aim of emergency food distribution is to save lives, by alleviating hunger and starvation, and thereby preventing malnutrition and mortality. Even though nutritional goals are uppermost it is widely acknowledged that food aid has an economic and social role which is fundamental to the recovery of an emergency affected population. For example, among refugees who are almost totally dependent on relief, food rations represent possibly their only economic resource. They must barter or sell rations to acquire additional foods and other necessities.

Evaluations of the use of food aid have shown that even the most destitute beneficiaries use a proportion of their food allocation for purposes other than immediate consumption. In Turkana, North West Kenya, for example, severely drought affected Turkana pastoralists used a part of the food aid they received to share with relatives, meet social obligations, trade or barter, to pay for school fees or medical expenses (Oxfam 1997).

Emergency food aid is political; in situations of strife and civil conflict it becomes bound up in the dynamics of the conflict, and in extreme cases is used to sustain combat without resolving it (Macrae and Zwi 1994). How this happens varies, but it is principally linked with the way in which parties to the conflict control access to food, either by withholding food assistance from areas or groups sympathizing with the opposition or alternatively, by directly benefiting from international material assistance.

The need for emergency food distribution is determined by an assessment, which should also assess how much food is needed and of what type, and who needs food assistance (targeting) and how they can be most easily reached. In protracted emergencies, the food needs of refugees for example, are determined during the Food Assessment Mission (FAM) which is a joint exercise involving United Nations High Commissioner for Refugees (UNHCR), WFP, and the local governing authority.

The decision who to give food aid to is partly dependent on how needs and vulnerability are viewed by the decision makers in the agencies or institutions involved. A biological view of famine focusing on the outcome of malnutrition would direct food rations at those with the most severe food deficits or the malnourished. Where resources are insufficient to provide everybody with rations, there is a strong argument to target the limited food supplies at those who show 'objective signs of starvation', or in other words to base food distribution on anthropometric assessment (Seaman and Rivers 1988). If however, a wider account of famine is assumed, that considers local responses and coping strategies, food distribution may be partly intended as an asset transfer. This broadens the scope of the targeting strategy to include those households who have vulnerable livelihoods and risk destitution (Jaspars and Young 1995a, 1995b).

There is currently a dispute over what constitutes an 'adequate' ration in terms of energy content. A minimum daily *per capita* energy requirement of 1900 kcal was recommended as a planning figure for emergency affected populations by Seaman and Rivers (1988). More recently many agencies, including Médecins Sans Frontières (MSF), WHO and the International Committee of the Red Cross (ICRC) have begun to advocate a higher planning figure. The basis of the controversy over planning figures for energy requirements is the allowance made for activity levels, but also the lack of allowances for other needs.

The debate has now moved on as it has recently been argued that no single working figure applies to all populations, because demographic composition, average body weight and ambient temperature vary widely between populations (Schofield and Mason 1996). These are the main parameters that determine the energy level for a specific population. Different values for these parameters give up to a twofold range in energy levels, for example a mainly female population has an energy requirement of 1782 kcal per person per day (medium activity levels, temperature 20–25°C), whereas a population consisting of mainly older children and adult males in the same environment, has an energy requirement of 2234 kcal per person per day. The age composition is also crucial; refugees in former Yugoslavia, for example, are predominantly elderly, whereas in most of Africa, the population is predominantly younger.

For a healthy population with a demographic composition typical of Africa, under normal nutritional conditions, and environmental temperature of 20°C, the average requirement is estimated as 1950–2210 kcal per person per day for light activity (1.55 Basal Metabolic Rate) (RNIS reports).

One of the major challenges in Africa remains how to respond appropriately and effectively to food insecurity and malnutrition in protracted or 'semi-permanent' emergencies. In the short-lived acute situation, the appropriate actions to save lives are clear, but these are neither sustainable nor appropriate in the long term. The emergency phase of a relief programme is often 'top-down' with decisions taken by outsiders and with little time for consultation or participation of the affected population. In contrast, phasing out food rations and changing the orientation of a relief programme must be planned with full consultation with representatives of the emergency affected population in order to ensure it is both timely and appropriate.

Food related income transfer programmes (food-for-work, cash-for-work, food stamps or vouchers)

Food related income transfers include food stamps or vouchers, which entitle the holder to a discount on selected food items purchased at private sector retail outlets, and food price subsidies, which lower the prices of selected foods below free market levels. These programmes are intended to raise the household's access to food in the market, thus to increase the household's food supply (Rogers 1995).

The distribution of vouchers, stamps or food in kind, may be in exchange for either work done (food-for-work programmes) or some other commodity the target group has available (see Box 9.9).

For the category of people defined as 'ultra-poor' by Lipton, who consume less than 80 per cent of calories required while spending more than 80 per cent of their income on food, income transfers translate directly into increased dietary adequacy.

Emergency livestock purchase in Wajir, North Kenya, in late 1996, enabled pastoralists to exchange some of their weakest goats for vouchers which they could then exchange for goods at local shops. Drought had caused pressure on available water supplies for watering livestock, a loss of pasture and thereby a deterioration in the condition of livestock. As a result livestock sales had led to a fall in prices to the detriment of livestock owners. This local initiative temporarily relieved the pressure livestock owners were under and was considered preferable to free food distribution by the relief agency involved and also by the local Pastoralist Associations involved (Oxfam 1997).

CONCLUSION: CHALLENGES FOR THE FUTURE

Despite the successes in recent years in combating the nutritional problems of our times, as the improvements in Latin America and Asia demonstrate, in Africa chronic malnutrition, or stunting, not only persists, but is getting worse in terms of numbers affected and total overall prevalance. Acute nutritional problems associated with emergencies are recurrent; as soon as the effects of one emergency subsides another takes its place.

Box 9.9   Food-for-work and drought relief in Zimbabwe, 1989–1992

In 1989 this programme was designed to supplant large-scale distributions of free food that had taken place annually since the 1981/82 drought. Over 2 million people depended on relief food for survival during the 1982–4 period. Ten years later, during the 1992 crisis, the number of people dependent on free food distribution had risen to 6 million. The government decided to suspend free food because of three problems: first, household targeting was thought to be inadequate, thereby spreading resources too thinly; second, there was sometimes poor targeting at a regional level; and third, criticism of the perceived dependency of recipients on free food.

In place of free food, drought relief was to be based on employment, or food-for-work. The programme was designed to operate from the bottom up, with projects identified by villagers themselves and provincial technicians assessing, approving and supervising appropriate plans. The largest number of projects in 1991 involved brick moulding and small building construction, activities generally completed without additional material inputs. Other activities included water control projects and construction and maintenance of feeder roads. Wages were set at 10 kg of maize *per capita* per month (supplemented where possible by beans, and dried meat or fish), but have varied. The numbers registered to participate rose from an average of 800 000 per month in 1991, to almost 3 million per month by mid-1992.

The availability of food-for-work through this programme was praised for preventing food shortages in 1990 escalating into a widespread famine in rural districts. However, it has proved difficult to expand the scale of the programme to meet emergency needs. The programme was highly effective in targeting poverty, as shown by selected indicators of poverty.

It was found that 95 per cent of the food received by food-for-work participants was consumed at home; in contrast to a cash-paying public works programme where only 35 per cent of the money received was spent on food.

Source: Webb 1995

As Richard Jolly, Chairman of the SCN, summarized at a symposium reviewing 'Effective Programmes in Africa for Improving Nutrition'

Nutrition is central to the human challenge in Africa today. With the long struggle in many countries against poverty, and with declining incomes and declines in the public services, it is not surprising, though it is still tragic, that we have seen evidence of deteriorating nutrition in many countries. We know why nutrition is deteriorating. Extreme poverty, severe drought, conflict and military spending. Africa is a continent where 179 soldiers exist on average for every 100 teachers or health workers. We also know that the underlying problems of chronic malnutrition are due to marginal access to food, seasonality problems, inadequate diet quality, and the chronic lack of basic services, health, water and education. But there are successes.

Richard Jolly, Chairman, SCN. Remarks in the Opening Ceremony, Accra, February 1996.

How far these successes can be built upon to reverse current trends is open to question. The underlying problems quoted above clearly require political solutions and commitment towards addressing malnutrition at every level of society. Advocacy towards that goal is a priority.

No doubt nutrition is recognized as important, but this does not necessarily lead to action. For example, in a review of the 23 Africa Region Poverty Assessments conducted by the World Bank, 19 mentioned malnutrition as a significant feature of poverty, eight found strong links between poverty and malnutrition, and ten had nutrition projects in the pipeline.

Policy makers and programme managers of the future need to reflect on our failures in Africa, and with humility and imagination seek new ways to address old problems. The knowledge and understanding of the extent of the problem and its causes is well established, much is also known about the options for addressing these problems. But as Berg (1993) has pointed out elsewhere, in Africa it is perhaps not only the 'what' but the 'how' that counts – *how* to implement effective programmes. Others have also concluded that how a programme is implemented may be as important, or in some cases more important, than the type of intervention (Kennedy 1991). Even in the most technical of nutritional interventions – rehabilitation of severely malnourished children in therapeutic feeding programmes – the practical constraints that limit the programme's effectiveness are frequently not technical, but managerial.

Tackling hunger and malnutrition is everybody's business and should be everybody's priority, including political leaders, policy makers, programme managers, service providers, NGOs, religious leaders, even consumer organizations. Combined and co-ordinated strategies are necessary to address the myriad of interconnecting causes of malnutrition, an important one of which is no doubt food security. However, it is not enough to recognize the multicausal nature of malnutrition and hope that a multisectoral approach will make all the difference. The reality is of course very different, and any approach will only work in the long term if those with the problem believe in the solution, in a true spirit of community participation, while others who recognize the need advocate for change.

CHAPTER TEN

Transfers and Safety Nets

Stephen Devereux

THIS CHAPTER IS organized around a series of simple questions:[1]

- *what* are transfers and safety nets?
- *why* are they needed? (the case for)
- *why not* implement them? (the case against)
- *who* should be targeted?
- *which* transfers and safety nets should be chosen?
- *how to evaluate* them?

The chapter begins by defining transfers and safety nets, looking at entitlement protection *versus* entitlement promotion, and identifying different categories of transfers (food, nutrition, income). The case for transfers and safety nets is disaggregated into 'moral' (humanitarian crises, equity), economic (market failure), and political rationales (public pressure and interest groups). The case against divides into financial constraints, logistical constraints, and political instability. Which specific option to choose depends on the objectives of the intervention and the capacity of the state and/or donors to implement it. Who should benefit from transfers and safety nets raises the difficult questions of targeting: how to identify beneficiaries; whether to adopt a targeted or untargeted approach; if the latter, whether to favour characteristic targeting, means testing, self-targeting or community targeting; and which targeting errors should be minimized (inclusion or exclusion). The next section considers actual applications of transfers and safety nets in Africa. These are grouped into food-based transfers (food-for-work, supplementary feeding, school feeding) and income-based transfer programmes (food price subsidies, food stamps, family income support such as social pensions and disability grants). The final question that this chapter attempts to answer is how to evaluate transfers and safety nets: using cost-effectiveness criteria, nutritional impact or some other criterion.

WHAT?

A transfer is any donation of cash or commodities that is given either for free or subsidized. *Private transfers* describe support to the poor that is provided informally within extended families and communities (remittances, charity). *Public transfers* describe formal (government, donor, NGO) redistribution of income, food and commodities towards the poor and vulnerable, ranging from *ad hoc* emergency relief interventions to permanent social welfare programmes.

Social *safety nets* can be defined as *income insurance* to help people through livelihood shocks and stresses, such as those caused by drought, illness, unemployment or displacement during a war. In the circus, a safety net catches someone who falls; its function being to prevent serious injury or death. So 'social safety nets' strictly applies only to situations of sudden income or consumption collapse. The 1990 World Development Report separates redistributive *income transfers* to chronically poor groups (e.g. 'the old or disabled') from systems of *income insurance* or *safety nets* for people who are 'acutely vulnerable to adverse events' (World Bank 1990, p. 90). So 'transfers' and 'safety nets' are seen as two distinct sets of interventions addressing two discrete sets of people: *transfers* are directed at 'those unable to participate in the growth process', while *safety nets* are intended to support 'those who may be temporarily in danger when events take an unfavourable turn' (World Bank 1990, p. 101).[2]

In the jargon of entitlements (Drèze and Sen 1989), social safety nets are 'entitlement protection' measures, since their objective is to prevent or ameliorate an *acute* decline in living standards following a livelihood shock in the short term – an example being famine relief during a drought. This contrasts with 'entitlement promotion' measures which aim at the enhancement of living standards to reduce *chronic* poverty and livelihood insecurity in the longer term – examples being sustainable employment creation or micro-credit programmes. The literature on 'linking relief and development'[3] highlights possible interconnections between the two categories: successful entitlement promotion will ultimately reduce the need for repeated entitlement protection interventions; and many responses to crisis (such as labour-intensive public works projects) embody both short term and longer term livelihood objectives.

The figures below illustrate these differences between alternative interventions. Recalling the four sources of entitlement as enumerated by Sen (1981) – production, trade, labour and transfers – Figure 10.1 illustrates a 'developmental' intervention which increases individual returns to agricultural production. A classic case in point is the 'Green Revolution' in India, or the more recent adoption of hybrid maize by smallholders in Malawi, which reduced food insecurity for successful adopters by raising their agricultural productivity. Assuming no offsetting reduction in other sources of entitlement, the diagram shows schematically how this intervention can allow chronically poor farming households to escape from poverty.

Figure 10.2 illustrates a conventional case of 'social welfare' transfers to the chronically poor. As in Figure 10.1, this individual is initially unable to

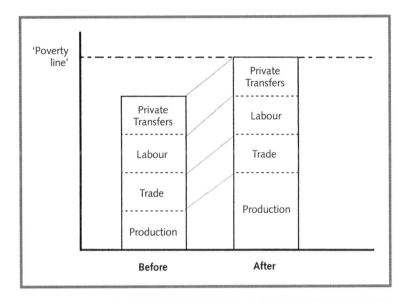

Figure 10.1   Entitlement promotion (poverty reduction)

attain even a minimum standard of living as represented by the 'poverty line' (which might be defined in terms of a 'basic food basket', say, or 'a dollar a day') through returns to his or her efforts in terms of production, trade, and labour. This person also lacks support in the form of private transfers, and therefore subsists in poverty. A welfarist intervention such as food aid

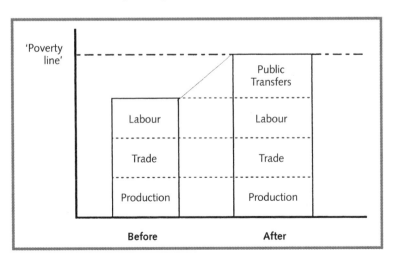

Figure 10.2   Entitlement protection (poverty alleviation)

or a cash grant will allow this beneficiary to bridge their consumption deficit for as long as the transfer programme continues. However, in contrast to Figure 10.1, this welfare transfer will not reduce poverty sustainably, because it has no impact on productivity – it is not a livelihood enhancing intervention.

Social safety nets are compensatory 'social insurance' mechanisms that restore lost income – e.g. food aid during droughts, pensions following retirement, unemployment benefit for retrenched workers – rather than 'social assistance' mechanisms that lift the chronically poor out of poverty or at least reduce the severity of their poverty. Safety nets can have either 'entitlement protecting' or 'entitlement promoting' outcomes – or both, as in the case of public works which simultaneously transfer income or food and create public assets (such as roads or dams) that should help to enhance future livelihoods. But the key distinguishing feature of safety nets is not their impact but the prior position of the beneficiary. Figure 10.3 shows a household whose livelihood system includes farming ('production entitlement'), petty trading ('trade entitlement') and remittances from an employed relative ('transfer entitlement'). Initially this household survives at the poverty line, but it is acutely vulnerable to a collapse in income – say, a drought which reduces food crop production by 50 per cent. The final column in Figure 10.3 shows how the introduction of public works projects following a drought acts as a safety net for farmers, by creating labour-based entitlements to compensate farmers for their lost agricultural production and income.

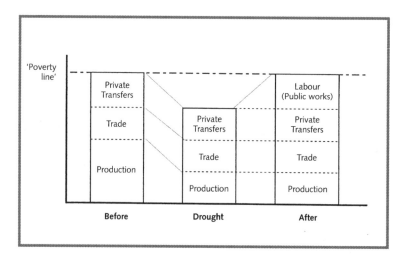

Figure 10.3   Social safety nets: public works projects

WHY?

Transfers and safety nets are needed for moral, economic and political reasons. The moral or humanitarian justification is 'the removal or reduction of deprivation or vulnerability' (Burgess and Stern 1991, p. 42). In normal times, the aim of redistribution within any society is to reduce inequality and relative poverty. In emergency contexts the objective of redistributive public action is more fundamental – to save lives.

Economic justifications for transfers and safety net interventions in poor countries focus on several kinds of market failure.

- *Commodity (food and asset) markets.* Emergency interventions (famine relief) are needed because of poverty and the inability of markets, especially in isolated rural areas, either to deliver food to drought- or flood-affected people at reasonable cost, or to offer reasonable prices for those assets (such as livestock) that poor people can sell to buy food.
- *Labour markets* are weak in developing countries because of the seasonality of labour demand in rural areas and limited formal employment opportunities in both rural and urban areas, which channels people into the informal sector and self-employment. Employment-based safety nets (public works) attempt to address this category of market failure.
- *Capital markets*, such as borrowing and savings facilities, transfer income between time periods for consumption smoothing purposes. They are virtually non-existent in poor rural areas because of low average incomes, lack of creditworthiness (no collateral where land is communally owned) and high administrative costs (dispersed and illiterate populations).
- *Insurance markets* such as crop and unemployment insurance protect people against the consequences of livelihood shocks. Again, insurance markets are absent in most developing countries because of poverty, monitoring problems, and covariate risk (a severe drought would require insurance payouts to thousands of farmers).

A final set of justifications for transfers and safety nets is political. Powerful pressure groups, such as the urban middle class, the military or bureaucrats can pressurize governments into introducing food subsidies and other policies that benefit these groups as much as – or more than – the poor and vulnerable. Alternatively, the government may come into power with an explicit mandate to redress historical injustices, so that poverty reduction is one of its policy priorities (an example is India's 'anti-famine contract', as discussed in Chapter 5).

WHY NOT?

Although the case for providing safety net transfers, such as free food distribution, is rarely contested in emergency contexts,[4] there is less widespread support for the establishment of comprehensive, formal social security systems to alleviate poverty in low-income countries. The 'case against' rests on feasibility rather than ideology – although most development practitioners believe that social security systems would be desirable, they also assert that these are not feasible in poor countries because of financial, logistical and political constraints.

In most African countries, it is argued that limited government budgets make universal state-funded social security interventions unaffordable, since social welfare programmes require a sizeable fiscal base and significant income inequality as preconditions for redistribution from rich to poor. Only a few middle-income African countries (such as South Africa, Namibia and Botswana, which have introduced state-funded 'social pensions') meet these preconditions. For desperately poor countries like Ethiopia and Sudan, a nationwide social pension system is simply out of the question. (Against this assertion, one might ask how even the poorest governments somehow manage to raise revenues for standing armies and national airlines, and foreign exchange to import armaments and aeroplanes.) As for donors, most have short-term planning horizons – three-year project cycles are typical – so it is difficult to secure a commitment for long-term financial support from external funders.

Logistical constraints include limited administrative resources (including personnel) and weak infrastructure (communications, roads), which make implementing social security programmes operationally difficult. Even in Namibia, with its well developed road network, the social pension reached just 60 per cent of the eligible population until the Department of Social Services privatized the delivery mechanism in 1995, since when cash dispensing machines accompanied by armed guards have toured the entire country every month and coverage has risen to 83 per cent. Finally, political instability – civil strife and insecurity, or frequent changes of government – undermines the planning and delivery of institutionalized social security programmes.

Transfers and safety net programmes can be implemented permanently (e.g. social security systems), seasonally (e.g. counterseasonal food price stabilization), or during food crises (emergency relief). In practice, for the reasons discussed above, most interventions in Africa tend to be short term and reactive responses to shocks – episodes of acute food insecurity – rather than institutionalized programmes to alleviate chronic poverty. The *ad hoc* nature of such interventions means that the African poor have no guaranteed safety net to rely on – unlike, for instance, the Employment Guarantee Scheme in Maharashtra, India, which until 1988 provided low-paid employment on public works projects to anyone who needed work.

WHO?

Key questions for decision makers concerned with transferring resources or establishing safety net programmes for food insecure households include:

- *How many* people are food insecure?
- *Who are* the food insecure? What are their characteristics – geographic (location), demographic (age and gender), and economic (income level, occupation)?
- *How to reach them* with appropriate and cost-effective food security interventions?

Defining and estimating the numbers of intended beneficiaries for a safety net programme is generally straightforward: drought-affected farmers, the poor (e.g. people living on less than a dollar a day), or the 'ultra-poor' (people who consume less than 80 per cent of RDA – recommended daily allowance – despite spending more than 80 per cent of their income on food). More problematic than defining the target group in theory is identifying them in practice. This raises the issue of targeting, which can be defined as any mechanism for identifying 'needy' individuals and screening out the 'non-needy', typically by defining eligibility criteria. But this is expensive, and explains why targeted interventions generally carry higher administrative costs than untargeted interventions (or lower 'alpha-ratios', defined as the proportion of any programme's budget that is directly transferred to beneficiaries). As Rogers (1995, p. 211) observes: 'The objective of targeting is to reduce leakage of program benefits so as to reduce costs and improve cost-effectiveness. … But targeting itself entails costs'.

Targeting introduces two types of error: *exclusion* – failing to reach all those in need of assistance – and *inclusion* – leakages to the non-needy.[5] In practice, there is often a trade-off between the two categories: with untargeted interventions (e.g. food price subsidies) inclusion errors are high and exclusion errors are very low; but as targeting increases, inclusion errors fall but exclusion errors rise. Because the welfare costs of failing to reach the poor are so high, Cornia and Stewart (1993) have argued that exclusion errors should be given greater weight than inclusion errors; but in practice policy makers tend to expend great effort in designing targeting mechanisms that minimize leakages.

Following Grosh (1995), targeting mechanisms can be classified into three broad categories: those based on *individual assessment* of need (e.g. means testing or nutrition status), those that use *group characteristics* as proxy indicators of need (an individual's age, sex, disability or geographic location), and *self-targeting* (where needy individuals select themselves). Each approach has its strengths and weaknesses.

Individual assessment is the most objective and accurate targeting mechanism in theory, but the most difficult and expensive to implement in practice. Individual assessment (or 'means testing') requires measuring every potential beneficiary's income or nutrition status and comparing this against a minimum standard (e.g. the national poverty line, or anthropometric reference tables). If the applicant's income or nutrition status is found to be inadequate it is supplemented by publicly funded transfers of cash or food. The 'moral hazard' problems are obvious – applicants have incentives to conceal their incomes or exaggerate their hunger – and for these reasons close monitoring is essential, which is not needed under untargeted or self-targeted programmes. Besley and Kanbur (1993, p. 71) suggest that the administrative costs of any targeting mechanism rise 'at an increasing rate' as targeting accuracy increases, which introduces a difficult trade-off. On the one hand, it is important for efficiency and equity reasons to minimize leakages to the non-needy; on the other hand, higher administrative costs reduce available transfer resources, again creating efficiency and equity losses.

Identifying common *characteristics* of poor people or 'vulnerable groups' as proxy indicators of need is simpler and cheaper than individual assessment and is less susceptible to distortion – an individual's age or sex is more readily observable, and more difficult to conceal or change – than their income or food consumption. But this approach is only as good as the specific proxy selected, and is highly susceptible to both types of targeting error. Nonetheless, when resources are limited or time is short, it is common practice for transfers – such as emergency food aid during a drought – to be distributed on the basis of proxy indicators of vulnerability. Instead of evaluating each individual case, every person displaying the required characteristics is declared eligible for assistance. This method allows for rapid and inexpensive identification of large numbers of beneficiaries at the cost of an acceptable degree of leakage to the non-needy.

Proxy indicators used during emergencies are often *geographic* ('disaster zones') or *demographic* (sub-groups of the population are isolated in terms of personal characteristics such as age, sex, or disability). During recent African droughts, governments and donors have adopted a combination of geographic and demographic proxies: typically, food-for-work for able-bodied adults in designated drought-affected areas, plus free food distribution to 'vulnerable groups' such as female-headed households, children under five, and the elderly.

Self-targeting is popular with designers of transfer programmes because it is cheaper and more accurate than alternative mechanisms. Instead of identifying beneficiaries by costly individual assessments or crude proxy indicators, programme designers get the poor to select themselves. The method is to raise the cost of accessing the resource transferred relative to its benefit, in one of two ways: either the *value of the transfer* is so low that it discourages all but the poorest from applying for it, or the *costs of accessing the transfer* are prohibitively high for the non-poor. A mild form of self-targeting is to introduce price subsidies on less preferred food items, such as yellow maize (which is considered 'poor people's food' throughout Africa), to discourage the rich from buying it. Public works projects exploit self-targeting by adjusting both elements, since participants are required to work for the transfer – a significant 'access cost' in terms of time and energy expenditure – and its value (in cash wages or food rations) is typically set below local wage rates. Potential workers make implicit cost/benefit calculations before deciding whether it is worth while to apply for this employment.

On the other hand, access costs also make self-targeting prone to significant exclusion errors. Imposing a work requirement, as in public works projects, should discourage the wealthy and those who are already employed from applying. The disadvantage is that it also screens out many categories of poor and vulnerable people who do not have the physical strength required, such as the very old, the very young and the disabled. These people may be in greatest need of public assistance, yet they are unable to participate. For this reason, as noted above, public works projects for those able to perform manual labour are often supplemented by free transfers to designated vulnerable groups who cannot work.

WHICH?

Selecting an appropriate intervention depends on the objectives of the intervention and the capacity of the country to implement it. If the objective is to keep people alive during famines, then food aid is an obvious and often essential intervention. If instead, in a non-emergency context, the objective of a national food security and nutrition policy is to reduce vitamin A deficiency, then micronutrient supplementation is the logical approach. Table 10.1 tabulates many common types of food, income and nutrition transfer programmes, categorized by their targeting mechanism.

The choice of intervention should also be matched to the country's capacity to implement it, which is a function of several factors, including:

- *Cash and food* resources available (including donor support).
- *Social infrastructure.* For example, if there is a good primary health care system, clinics can be used to target supplementary feeding programmes.
- *Markets.* Food price interventions, which are administered through the market mechanism, can reach people in widely dispersed areas and are light on administrative personnel and physical infrastructure – but if the marketing system is weak outside urban centres, price subsidies are inappropriate.
- *Human resources.* Food stamps, for instance, require a good marketing system, a reliable banking system for redeeming the stamps, and confidence of traders that the system is sustainable – but determining eligibility also requires literate and numerate personnel.

Table 10.1   Food, income and nutrition transfers

Targeting	Food	Income	Nutrition
Targeted	Food stamps for the poor	Cash transfer 'safety nets' Unemployment benefits	Weaning foods for low-income families
	Food aid programmes Supplementary feeding for vulnerable groups	Disability grants Social pensions for the elderly	Vitamin and mineral supplements for specified groups
Untargeted	General food price subsidy Overvalued exchange rate for imported food	Universal child benefit	Water fluoridization
Self-targeted	Food-for-work programmes Price subsidy on inferior foods	Cash-for-work programmes	Iodization of salt

- There are invariably *political and social* considerations too – so technical criteria such as nutritional impact and cost-effectiveness are rarely the only criteria for selection.

This section will now consider alternative forms of safety net programmes, beginning with food transfers – food-for-work, supplementary feeding, and school feeding – then various income-based transfers – food price subsidies, social pensions and so on. Nutrition programmes are discussed in Chapter 9.

Food transfers[6]

Ever since its association in the 1950s and 1960s with the 'dumping' of North American and European food surpluses in developing countries, food aid has been a controversial instrument of aid – and foreign – policy.[7] Although food aid is commonly thought of as an emergency relief intervention, a significant proportion of food transfers to poor countries in sub-Saharan Africa and elsewhere is made in the form of programme support or food aid projects. Until the late 1980s, in fact, programme food aid was the dominant category of food aid provided worldwide (Shaw and Clay 1993), but emergency relief dominated in the 1990s because of the rising number of humanitarian crises involving large numbers of people. Even so, in 1998 as much as 44.5 per cent of all food aid delivered worldwide by the World Food Programme – 1.3 million out of 2.8 million tonnes – went towards non-emergency uses (WFP 1998a).

- *Emergency food aid* is provided by multilateral donors (such as the United Nations World Food Programme), bilateral donors (mainly Western governments) and international NGOs (such as Oxfam, CARE and the Red Cross/Red Crescent) for free distribution to victims of natural disasters (such as drought-induced famines), or to refugees and internally displaced people (during complex political emergencies).
- *Programme food aid* is the provision of food commodities directly to a government for sale ('monetization') on local markets, to provide either balance-of-payments support (by replacing commercial food imports) or budgetary support (from the proceeds of food sales) for processes of stabilization, adjustment and economic reform (Clay et al. 1996, p. 3), or to support national food security by stocking a strategic grain reserve.
- *Project food aid* is a mechanism for transferring income (in the form of food) to targeted 'vulnerable groups' among the poor in non-emergency 'normal' contexts, the most common mechanisms being supplementary feeding for mothers and young children, school feeding for learners, and food-for-work for underemployed adults.

Whereas emergency food aid is mobilized in response to food crises – episodes of acute but transitory food insecurity – programme food aid supports macroeconomic objectives at national level, and project food aid attempts to address problems of chronic poverty and food insecurity at the household or individual level. The remainder of this section focuses on various forms of project food aid, as this is the most direct food transfer made to individuals which has both immediate and longer term food security objectives. It is also controversial.

Supporters of project food aid justify its continuation on both positive and defensive grounds. The 'positive' argument is that project food aid can have powerful developmental impacts in stable (non-emergency) contexts.[8] The 'defensive' argument is that donors are generally more willing to provide food aid than cash transfers, and that food as an indirect form of income support to the poor is surely better than nothing.

The three main forms of project food aid that are currently operational throughout Africa – food-for-work, supplementary feeding, and school feeding – are now considered in turn.

Food-for-work[9]

Because food-for-work projects have two elements – 'food' and 'work' – they also have two objectives: to transfer food in the short term – an 'entitlement protection' aim – and to create lasting assets that have sustainable food security benefits – an 'entitlement promotion' aim. Public works can be implemented either in 'normal times' (as with Ethiopia's Employment

Generation Scheme) or during emergencies (as one component of a drought relief programme – see the Namibia case study in Box 10.1 below). Labour-intensive public works projects have provided employment for millions of poor people throughout Africa. Approximately 23 per cent of Botswana's total workforce was employed on the Labour-Based Relief Programme in 1986, while in Cape Verde in 1983 the figure was as high as 30 per cent (Drèze and Sen 1989). Public works projects have constructed or rehabilitated millions of dollars worth of infrastructure, mainly but not only in rural areas – feeder roads for transporting passengers and commodities; boreholes, pipelines and microdams for domestic water and irrigation; reafforestation for firewood and soil conservation. Three-quarters of Lesotho's road network was constructed through food-for-work schemes (Shaw and Clay 1993).

As a mechanism for transferring resources to the poor and food insecure, food- or cash-for-work is claimed to have several advantages over alternative mechanisms. First, as already noted, public works projects are *self-targeting*: by setting the ration or wage low enough to provide only for the basic needs of participants, people who do not need assistance will not apply. For this reason, in Burkina Faso in the early 1990s public works wages were set at one-third of the national minimum wage (von Braun et al. 1991). Second, public works are *cost-effective*: a general equilibrium model for India showed that public works were much better at reducing poverty than equivalent spending on direct food distribution.

Indirect benefits of public works include income stabilization, multiplier and insurance effects. The food or cash wages paid to workers help to stabilize income and food consumption after poor harvests or during the annual 'hungry season'. 'Multiplier effects' refer to the boost to workers' purchasing power created by the injection of food or cash into the local economy, which attracts traders and increases the general level of economic activity. 'Insurance effects' are achieved if poor households are confident that public works employment will be available to them when needed. For instance, the Employment Guarantee Scheme in Maharashtra, India, allows the poor to be more entrepreneurial: they can use resources tied up in precautionary savings (e.g. livestock) for investment in business or agricultural inputs. The availability of alternative incomes also protects people against the need to adopt damaging 'coping strategies' in times of stress, such as selling assets or becoming indebted to moneylenders.

The largest food-for-work project in Africa is WFP's Project Ethiopia 2488 – 'Rehabilitation and development of rural lands and infrastructure'.

The long-term objectives of the project are to stabilise land productivity, increase farmers' incomes and improve food security ... through the rehabilitation of degraded land, protection of the environment, and the development of infrastructure in selected communities of chronically and severely food-deficit areas (WFP 1997, p. 7).

By selecting projects – such as terracing, tree planting and microdams – that enhance agricultural productivity and reduce farmers' dependence on variable rains, the government and donors aim to raise food production towards self-sufficiency, thereby steadily reducing the need for food-for-work interventions.

There are also many problems with public works. It is often considered stigmatizing and demeaning to work for food – in Malawi, for instance, men tend to monopolize available cash-for-work employment while women dominate on food-for-work projects (Devereux 1999b, p. 54). Also, since infrastructure projects tend to involve physically demanding manual labour – in order to maximize employment, the use of capital equipment is minimized – anyone who is incapable of undertaking heavy labour is excluded. (In Ethiopia's Employment Generation Scheme, an '80: 20' rule of thumb is applied: at least 80 per cent of food aid should be distributed through food-for-work, with workers earning rations for their entire house-hold, since most of the non-able-bodied poor are living in families with able-bodied adults who can earn food for them.) On a related point, while gender quotas have been introduced on most public works schemes so that women and men can participate equally, women either remain excluded from certain strenuous activities or face implicit wage discrimination, because equal payment for piecework favours men who can complete arduous tasks faster. Moreover, women's domestic responsibilities are gen-erally greater than men's, so that working on public works projects might impose unfair additional burdens on their limited time and energy.

Another criticism of public works projects is that the poor often do not derive the benefits of the infrastructure they create – such as roads, dams, even airports – but that these benefits are enjoyed disproportionately by the non-poor. Project selection is important in this respect. If the aim is simply to transfer food or income, then 'second-round income effects' are an irrelevant consideration. But if the assets created by public works are to have sustainable impacts in terms of food security and poverty reduction for the people who work on these projects, they must be carefully selected and designed – preferably in consultation with the participants. This prin-ciple has been adopted by the World Food Programme in a recent policy shift from 'food-for-work' to 'food and assets for sustainable employment' (Tajgman 1997), which asserts that participants on food-for-work projects should derive direct benefits from any assets created.

On the other hand, evidence from several African countries suggests that attempts to achieve short-term and long-term benefits simultaneously have often failed, because of inevitable trade-offs between the two sets of objectives (Sijm 1997, p. 484). Well designed projects can realistically achieve poverty alleviation objectives, but probably not poverty reduction (entitlement protection rather than promotion). Because the work is mainly unskilled, there is little training or skills formation, so participants rarely 'graduate' to full-time employment. In cases where food-for-work supports income-generating activities (such as vegetable gardens) rather

Box 10.1   Case study: food-for-work in Namibia

Food-for-work started in Namibia during the southern African drought of 1992, as one of two food transfer components of the national Drought Relief Programme, the other being a Vulnerable Groups feeding programme (free food distribution to children under-five, pregnant and lactating women, disabled people and the elderly in drought-affected areas). By using complementary targeting rules – demographic characteristics for vulnerable groups and self-targeting for able-bodied adults – the programme hoped to minimize inclusion errors (since only the needy would register for food-for-work) as well as exclusion errors (since a broad range of criteria was devised to reach all vulnerable groups who were unable to work for food aid).

More than 500 food-for-work projects were initiated under the programme of 23 different types, from building teacher's houses to starting vegetable gardens to laying pipelines for improved community water supplies. The projects fell into two categories. Two-thirds were public works projects (PWPs), employing 71 people each on average and creating social and physical infrastructure. The remaining one-third were income-generating activities (IGAs), each employing just 22 people on average, but most of these collapsed once food deliveries were terminated after six months. This unsustainability suggests that accessing free food was the primary motivation for participants. In addition to food and non-food inputs, basic training was also provided on many projects, not only the technical skills necessary for project implementation (such as brick-making), but also bookkeeping and project management. The programme was successful in gender terms. Participation by women was high (over 50 per cent), and surveys suggested that their self-confidence and skills had been enhanced.

Notwithstanding these achievements, the food-for-work programme also faced severe problems. In terms of coverage it was much less successful than the Vulnerable Groups feeding programme, which reached 220 000 of its 250 000 targeted beneficiaries (88 per cent coverage). By contrast, only 27 000 out of 375 000 able-bodied adults targeted actually participated on food-for-work projects (7 per cent coverage). Two underlying problems explain this poor performance: a failure to appreciate that food-for-work involves a complex *employment creation* programme, not simply a food distribution programme, and the mistaken belief that food-for-work could be used to pursue *multiple goals* – not just immediate drought relief, but also sustainable long-term income generation in poor rural communities.

The programme experienced many administrative problems, including a centralized decision-making process (a Food-For-Work Committee sitting in the capital city assessed every project application nationwide, resulting in lengthy delays before project approval and implementation), and lack of previous experience with food-for-work, so there were no 'off the shelf' projects or guidelines for programme staff to draw on. Logistical constraints compounded these problems: the fact that written project proposals needed to be submitted resulted in leakages as literate community members such as teachers were written into projects intended to benefit the (mostly illiterate) poor. Also, Namibia being a large country with a dispersed population and well developed infrastructure meant that rural communities were too small to mobilize for large-scale employment; there were limited opportunities for labour-intensive public works such as roads; there were limited markets for IGA products; and it was difficult for programme staff to monitor projects and deliver food, training and non-food inputs.

An evaluation report concluded with two main recommendations:

■ If large-scale employment creation is the objective, public works projects are invariably better than income-generating projects.

■ One objective is better than many: for drought relief, large-scale short-term projects should be preferred; for linking relief and development, sustainable income generating activities should be encouraged, linked to provision of training.

Source: Devereux and Solomon 1994

than physical infrastructure, the scale of employment is considerably lower (see Box 10.1 for evidence from Namibia), and the cost of providing training and non-food inputs reduces the alpha-ratio (the proportion of project resources transferred directly to participants).

Maxwell (1993) summarizes the strengths and potential weaknesses of public works projects in tabular form, which is reproduced in Table 10.2.

Supplementary feeding

Supplementary feeding projects attempt to address the long-term problems caused by chronic food deficits, and are usually targeted at malnourished or at-risk children under five, expectant women and nursing mothers. The case for supplementary feeding having both an immediate and a lifelong beneficial impact has been succinctly expressed by Sen (1997, p. 36), drawing on evidence that 'investing' in women's health and nutrition is beneficial not just for the women themselves but also for their children:

> we have to look at the direct *impact of child and maternal undernourishment on future well-being (directly through health)* as well as the indirect *impact of today's deprivation on future well-being (through its influence on the ability to earn a income, to find a job, to be skilled and productive).*

Table 10.2   Best case and worst case scenarios for an employment-based safety net

	Best Case	Worst Case
Design	Shelf of well-designed projects ready in advance	Projects cobbled together when drought hits
Targeting and participation	All participants are poor and all poor who want and are able to participate do so	Many participants are not poor and/or some poor who wish to participate are excluded
Supervision and management	Adequate to guarantee technical quality of works and reasonable labour productivity	Inadequate leading to poor quality construction and very low labour productivity
Budget	Sufficient budget to provide all employment needed	Budget constraints mean employment has to be curtailed or rationed
Impact on markets	Works support labour market by providing employment of last resort	Works introduce distortions into labour market, by bidding up market wages to unreasonable levels, or because a dependency mentality is created
	Food or cash employment encourages development of local food markets, without creating either inflation or disincentives	Payments in cash cause inflation in food prices or, conversely, payment in food causes falls in food prices and disincentives to local production
Sustainability	Assets created can be and are maintained	Assets are allowed to deteriorate rapidly
Impact on income and employment	Assets created generate future employment and income, at times of year when labour is available	Assets create no new jobs, or jobs only at previous peak seasons
Impact on asset ownership	New assets belong proportionately or disproportionately to the poor	New assets belong disproportionately to the rich
Impact on the community	Works programme fosters community cohesion	Works programme undermines community cohesion and makes future self-help projects more difficult

Source: Maxwell 1993, pp. 105–106

Most evaluations of supplementary feeding have found evidence of increased attendance by mothers and children at day-care and health centres. Where the nutrition status of children is monitored, children who receive on-site supplementary feeding are found to derive measurable nutritional improvements for the duration of the feeding programme, though it is unclear whether these improvements are maintained after they leave the project. As a rule, the nutritional impact of any food transfer (whether to children or to pregnant women) is greater the more severely malnourished the individual. Rogers (1995, p. 207) reports on studies which found that:

> food supplements directed to pregnant women are effective in improving birth out-come and raising birth weight if they are provided to women who are thin, who show poor weight gain in pregnancy, and whose calorie intake is quite deficient.

The case against feeding programmes notes that they are generally targeted on the basis of poor nutritional status, so they reach only individuals who are already suffering some degree of malnutrition: indeed, irreversible damage to health may already have taken place. Also, such targeting may exclude individuals at high risk and therefore fail to *prevent* malnutrition. Moreover, since chronic malnutrition is typically a result of poverty, supplementary feeding programmes address only a symptom of the problem – they do not address the structural causes of malnutrition (Sijm 1997, p. 490).

Several evaluations of supplementary feeding programmes conducted during the 1990s have found their longer term nutritional impacts to be disappointingly limited, even negligible. Over a period of 38 years, for instance, USAID-sponsored supplementary feeding projects in the Sahel failed to achieve any lasting nutritional impacts on young children, and by the late 1980s most of these programmes were closed (USAID 1997, p. 2).[10] An evaluation of WFP's supplementary feeding programme in Malawi was equally negative (see Box 10.2).

School feeding

The benefits to the individual and to society of a sound basic education are uncontested, and school feeding programmes are justified as a means of attracting children from poor families to school and of increasing their cognitive abilities in class, since hungry children cannot concentrate or perform as effectively as well-nourished children. School feeding programmes are therefore intended to achieve longer term impacts on poverty reduction (through 'incentive effects' on child enrolment and school attendance, and on academic achievement) as well as immediate nutritional benefits – in fact, nutritional status is no longer even assessed in WFP's school feeding evaluations.[11]

The 'developmental' case for targeting food aid on learners in schools relies on evidence that rates of return to education worldwide are highest for primary education and for poor countries (Psacharopoulos 1994), so that encouraging attendance and improved performance at primary schools is likely to lead ultimately to higher household and national incomes. Other indirect benefits of basic education include positive effects

Box 10.2   Supplementary feeding in Malawi

An evaluation of WFP's impact in Malawi concluded that WFP's supplementary feeding programme had achieved little in over twenty years, either to reduce levels of undernutrition or to address the underlying causes of food insecurity (FSG 1994). As a result, WFP resolved to phase out supplementary feeding and related interventions by 1998, and to replace these programmes with developmental uses of food aid. Direct consumption support in the form of free food handouts would no longer be implemented, except during food crises such as drought. Several principles for WFP involvement in developmental food aid in Malawi for the 1995–2000 period are listed in the *Country Strategy Outline* prepared in 1994. Three of these principles are:

- Food aid should be used in ways which are 'developmentally beneficial'.
- Food-for-work should augment, not replace, existing rural employment opportunities, but should be implemented in areas of large-scale unemployment.
- Food aid should not be disruptive to the national or local economy: food should be purchased in-country whenever possible and delivered through existing market institutions, and should be 'provided as a wage payment for work done on projects identified according to village priorities' (FSG 1994, pp. 12–15).

Since 1994 WFP has experimented with different approaches to its food aid programming in Malawi. One initiative was an agricultural project targeted at female-headed households in rural areas, which delivered free maize meal for consumption, plus credit for farming inputs such as seeds and fertilizers. This project had food security rather than direct food consumption as its primary objective, and it signified a major shift in WFP-Malawi's thinking about how to address the problem of chronic food insecurity. Unfortunately, it was slow to get started, it reached relatively few households and the credit component suffered from high default rates.

More recently, WFP-Malawi has come round to the view that a more effective delivery mechanism might be to tie food aid to rural employment creation, through the delivery of food to public works projects, and WFP is currently supporting the Malawi Social Action Fund in precisely this way. In an attempt to maximize the impact of its food aid programme, WFP has also moved away from its historic practice of assisting vulnerable groups in all 24 districts of Malawi, focusing instead on 13 'most vulnerable' districts in 1996, which were reduced to eight districts in 1997 and just six 'chronically food deficit' districts by 1998. Following selection of these districts – on criteria which include food production levels, population density, health coverage, malnutrition and infant mortality rates, and the presence or absence of other donors and NGOs – WFP is committed to working with local communities for up to 10 years, in an effort to achieve sustained improvements in household food security.

Source: Devereux 1997

on population growth rates (because rising education levels are associated with lower fertility rates), and positive effects on income inequality (investing in primary education is progressive in terms of national income distribution, whereas investing in tertiary education is regressive). Since poor people in poor countries are disproportionately concentrated in agriculture, it is also worth noting evidence from southeast Asia that farmers achieve an average 10 per cent increase in farm output for every four years of education they receive, mainly through the adoption or more effective utilization of new technologies. Education also allows the poor to move more easily from low productivity activities (such as smallholder agriculture and the informal sector) into higher productivity activities (formal jobs in the private and public sectors).

In sub-Saharan Africa, the picture might be more complex than this 'conventional wisdom' suggests. Economic recession and falling quality of services have caused rates of return to education to decline, and they may now be higher for secondary than primary education, because a rapid expansion in basic literacy has been accompanied by high dropouts at secondary school level. Rates of return can also be biased by structural distortions in poor economies. In countries such as Ghana and Kenya, too many secondary school and university graduates were produced in the 1960s and 1970s to be absorbed into the formal sector workforce. Lack of waged employment opportunities means that actual returns to education (especially but not only higher education) are lower than potential or predicted returns.

Despite these reservations, school feeding remains a popular and generally positively evaluated form of project food aid. In Malawi in 1996, enrolment in one primary school rose by 26 per cent in one month following the introduction of a WFP-sponsored school feeding programme (Dil 1996, p. 18). An evaluation of a large USAID programme in Burkina Faso 'found evidence that this programme had a positive impact on children's nutrition, attendance, and academic achievement' (USAID 1997, p. 2). Attendance increased by 10–20 per cent, promotion rates were significantly higher and drop-out rates significantly lower, and pass rates in exams averaged 45 per cent in programme schools as compared with 38 per cent in non-programme schools. Of course, as with all targeted transfer programmes, targeting the poor through primary school children suffers from errors of exclusion: the poorest families often do not send their children to school (even with the inducement of a free meal), or withdraw them from school during difficult times, and many poor households (such as elderly couples or widows) do not have school-aged children, so these households do not benefit.

INCOME TRANSFERS

Income transfers can be made directly, in the form of cash handouts, or indirectly, in the form of price subsidies on goods and services. This section focuses on food-related income transfers: first, indirect income transfers (food price subsidies), then direct income transfers (social pensions to the elderly, cash grants to the destitute).

Food price subsidies

A price subsidy on selected food items has two positive effects on household food security: it reduces the price of the item relative to other food and non-food goods, and it increases the household's overall purchasing power. Prices of food crops (e.g. maize) or processed food items (e.g. bread) can be subsidized in several distinct ways:

1   the government can import food and sell it locally at lower prices;
2   the government can buy food locally and sell it at cost when prices rise;
3   the government can legislate 'ceiling prices', 'panterritorial pricing' or 'panseasonal pricing' for staple food crops.

The first option is mainly associated in Africa with the monetization of programme food aid. The second option is used mainly as a counter-seasonal price stabilization intervention in areas where prices fluctuate significantly from one season to the next, the idea being to compensate for weak and segmented markets. During the 1980s, Ghana's Food Distribution Corporation used to buy cereals cheaply after harvest, store them for 3–4 months, then release these stocks onto village markets in poor regions at cost (purchase price plus storage plus transport), which prevented local traders charging their typical 'hungry season' markup of 200–300 per cent. When the GFDC was 'reformed' and scaled down in the early 1990s, this practice was abandoned.

Untargeted price subsidies are usually applied to staple food items that are consumed more by the poor than the rich, for equity reasons. The effect on consumption of the subsidized food depends on its price elasticity of demand, while the effect on overall calorie and protein consumption depends on adjustments in consumption of other foods. A subsidy on chicken in the Dominican Republic actually led to *reduced* calorie and protein consumption because low-income consumers reduced their consumption of rice, beans and plantain in order to consume more chicken. A general food price subsidy in Egypt was found to be highly effective, since the value of the transfer amounted to 11 per cent of total expenditure by poor rural households, but it was also very expensive, accounting for 17 per cent of total public expenditure in the mid-1980s. Moreover, leakages were very high: while the rural poor benefited most proportionately, wealthy and urban Egyptians benefited most in absolute terms (World Bank 1990, p. 93).

Panterritorial and panseasonal prices were legislated in Tanzania and other African countries during the 1970s, in an attempt both to ensure reasonable selling prices for small farmers (the marketing parastatal paid all farmers in the country the same price for their crop, no matter how far they were located from roads and markets), and to prevent sharp seasonal price rises and consequent hunger and malnutrition. Eventually these policies became too expensive to sustain, and they were often undermined by private traders, so by the late 1980s they were phased out. In Malawi and other African countries, the shift away from fixed (subsidized) prices is being implemented through a process known as 'price banding': food prices are decompressed gradually, with lower floor and higher ceiling prices being announced by the government each agricultural marketing season.

Although food price subsidies have been used extensively in South America, the Caribbean, Asia and Africa, they have become unfashionable and are no longer used by most African governments. The ideological argument against all price subsidies is that they distort markets and therefore create inefficiencies and unsustainable demands on government budgets. The practical argument is that African economies are more open and less regulated now than ever before, as a consequence of economic liberalization measures, so that any attempt to subsidize food prices in one country will be subverted by traders who can simply buy up this artificially cheap food and sell it in neighbouring countries at market prices. For these reasons, price subsidies are no longer part of most governments' food policy toolbox. However, because of their popularity with key constituencies such as the urban middle class, the military and civil servants, removing food subsidies is politically controversial, and food riots occurred in many countries as prices rose, most recently in Zimbabwe and Malawi in the late 1990s.

Cash grants

It is not true, as the World Bank (1997, p. 56) asserts, that social assistance programmes in the form of cash transfers to the poor are 'nonexistent' in Africa; but they are certainly unusual. The reasons for this can be explained by briefly examining cash transfers using Grosh's (1993) 'five criteria for choosing among poverty programs'.

1   *Administrative feasibility.* Cash transfers to the poor are expensive, requiring a large fiscal base (i.e. a fairly wealthy economy) or a small population to make them feasible. In Africa's most food insecure countries (e.g. Ethiopia and Sudan) these conditions do not apply. Also, implementing cash transfers is administratively complex, requiring trained personnel and institutions (such as rural banks or post offices) which are often non-existent.

2   *Political feasibility.* Targeted cash transfers to the poor carry little political weight where (as in most of Africa) the poor are politically weak and governments are biased towards wealthier and more influential constituencies such as the urban middle classes.

3   *Collateral effects.* Cash transfers can have positive side-effects in terms of food security; for example, injecting cash into poor communities stimulates demand for food and other commodities and attracts traders to remote areas.

4   *Targeting* requires costly beneficiary identification mechanisms, such as means testing. Since cash handouts provide obvious inducements to corruption, close monitoring of both programme officials and beneficiaries is required. Nonetheless, leakages due to corruption or 'benefit fraud' on these programmes are invariably high.

5   *Tailoring solution to problem.* If they are well targeted and efficiently implemented, cash grants to the poor can be an effective mechanism for reducing poverty and food insecurity directly. But this depends on the coverage of the programme – often the majority of the poor are not reached – and the value of the transfer, which is often too small to raise household income significantly.

Among the rare examples of regular cash transfer programmes in sub-Saharan Africa, South Africa, Namibia and Botswana have non-contributory 'social pensions' for all their elderly citizens, while a programme called 'GAPVU' transfers cash to destitute families in urban Mozambique. The social pension is atypical and is unlikely to be replicated in other African countries in the near future. However, the cash transfer programme in Mozambique is similar to programmes implemented in Latin America and elsewhere, and has potential lessons for safety net interventions elsewhere in Africa. It is discussed in Box 10.3.

HOW TO EVALUATE?

Two factors should be considered when evaluating any transfer or safety net programme: did it achieve its goals (what was its nutritional, poverty or food security impact); and did it do so at reasonable cost (was it cost-effective)?

Box 10.3   Case study: 'GAPVU' in Mozambique

Despite being one of the world's poorest countries, Mozambique has implemented an ambitious social safety net programme since the late 1980s. Following the abolition of food price subsidies, the 'Office for Assistance to the Vulnerable Population' – known by its Portuguese acronym, GAPVU – was established in September 1990 in the Ministry for Social Action. GAPVU's aim was to increase the purchasing power of the 30 per cent of urban households classified as destitute in Mozambique's 13 towns and cities. Despite being a cash transfer, GAPVU was officially described as a 'food subsidy' because its aim was to provide income for food purchases to food insecure households: one eligibility criterion was households having malnourished children (other categories included the disabled, the chronically ill, the elderly living without support from relatives, and malnourished pregnant women).

Administration costs and the cash transfers paid to beneficiaries are financed from the state budget, with indirect donor support. Though expensive, costing about 2 per cent of government spending and 1.5 per cent of annual foreign aid inflows in the mid-1990s, GAPVU performed well in efficiency terms. The share of administration in total expenditure was 13 per cent in 1992 (so 87 per cent of the budget went in cash transfers to beneficiaries), and fell to just 3 per cent by 1995. GAPVU's supporters argued that alternatives such as food subsidies, direct food distribution and food vouchers are prone to higher administrative costs and leakages, and would not achieve such impressive cost-efficiency.

In terms of inclusion errors (leakages to the non-needy), GAPVU was at first very successful. An evaluation in 1993 found that 70 per cent of beneficiary households were 'destitute', while 20 per cent were 'absolutely poor' and only 10 per cent were neither poor nor destitute. A 1995 survey found that almost 50 per cent of GAPVU households had no income from employment, while among the old-age group, 60 per cent had no income at all, and only 27 per cent received assistance from their children – large numbers of whom were killed or disabled during the civil war. The 1993 survey found that households spent 82 per cent of their incomes on food before receiving the transfer, and 79 per cent afterwards. Despite its low value (about £1 *per capita* per month), GAPVU contributed 13 per cent to expenditure by beneficiary households. A comparison of the nutritional status of infants of beneficiaries and non-beneficiaries found that the transfer seemed to have a positive impact on birth weights and infant mortality rates.

GAPVU expanded rapidly and by 1996 had registered 92 000 beneficiaries. Unfortunately, it had by then become a victim of its own success. Because administrative overheads were so low, monitoring of the registration and disbursement process was minimal, and the programme was undermined by corruption by officials (e.g. registration of non-existent households) and (ineligible) beneficiaries. One ingenious case of fraud occurred when a woman whose malnourished child was registered for GAPVU 'lent' her child to six friends so that seven households registered and received the cash transfer. In December 1996 GAPVU was closed down and restructured: most officials (including the Director) were sacked, 34 000 beneficiaries were re-registered (the others were declared ineligible), new monitoring procedures were established and the name was changed to the National Institute for Social Action (INAS).

The shift from GAPVU to INAS also signified a new direction for social safety net programming in Mozambique. INAS has moved beyond GAPVU's residual welfarist objective (to provide subsistence support to the chronically poor) towards a more ambitious developmental goal: to raise beneficiaries above the poverty line on a sustainable basis. This is to be achieved by introducing cash-for-work projects that will create productive assets for participants, and to reach those unable to work through offering this employment to their able-bodied relatives, instead of through direct cash grants. As of late 2000, the implications for coverage, impact and cost-effectiveness of these radical changes had yet to be assessed.

Sources: Government of Mozambique 1995; Low et al. 1998; Devereux 1999a

Cost-effectiveness

Cost-effectiveness must be measured in terms of both direct and indirect costs. Direct costs of implementation include the value of the food or cash transferred, personnel, storage, transport and related administrative and logistical expenses. Indirect costs can also be broken down into several categories, including:

- *Opportunity cost.* How does the implemented programme compare with alternative possible uses of public (state or donor) resources?
- *Economic distortions.* For instance, food subsidies can contribute to inflation, and food aid is often accused of undermining the development of private trade;
- *Production disincentives.* Does the subsidization or free distribution of food reduce the market demand or profit for food producers and traders?
- *Disincentives to work.* Does the programme create a 'benefit trap'? In Britain, for example, critics of unemployment benefit argue that it encourages people to choose to remain unemployed.

One useful measure of transfer efficiency is the *alpha-ratio*, which is calculated as the total value of transfers made to beneficiaries as a proportion of the total cost of the programme ($0 < \alpha < 1$). A high alpha-ratio (close to 1) is considered to be good, while a low alpha-ratio (close to 0) means that the programme is relatively inefficient. However, a very high alpha-ratio may not always be ideal. The GAPVU programme in urban Mozambique, for example, found that its policy of restricting administrative overheads to just 4–5 per cent of total costs was too low. Poor monitoring and supervision meant that leakages were rising to unacceptably high levels. An optimal alpha-ratio is perhaps around 0.8, allowing up to 20 per cent of costs to go into managing the programme efficiently. In general, cost and cost-effectiveness are inversely related: it is easier to feed large numbers of malnourished people in refugee camps than to target food or cash assistance on a small number of poor individuals in a large population.

Nutritional impact

Most food-related interventions aim at direct improvements in the food security of the target population, usually measured in terms of anthropometric indicators. This is misguided. Nutrition interventions never achieve a 100 per cent impact, but this does not mean they have failed. Any transfer to a poor household, even if targeted on individual members such as children, can indirectly raise the nutritional status of other household members, and provide non-nutritional benefits because of its positive income effects. Possible reasons for limited nutritional impact include:

- *Environmental health conditions.* Undernutrition is not the only cause of high morbidity and mortality levels, especially among the poor. Egypt's food subsidy programme achieved substantial increases in food consumption, for instance, but had limited impact on infant mortality because of poor environmental hygiene, sanitation and health practices in poor communities.

- *'Engel's law'.* At lower levels of income, higher proportions of income are spent on food, since food is essential for life. This is the 'Engel's curve' effect. A review of several studies found that the income elasticity of demand for food in low-income households lies in the range of 0.6 to 0.8 (Alderman 1986), meaning that 60–80 per cent of any food or income transfer will be consumed as food. The elasticity of demand for calories is about half this, so the net increase in calorie intake would be 30–40 per cent. This is a more realistic target for food-related interventions to strive for than 100 per cent additionality in calorie consumption.

- *Fungibility of income.* Food-related income transfers are unlikely to achieve their full nutritional impact because of the fungibility of income, unless the household's priorities conform exactly to those of the nutrition programme. Any increase in household income – whether direct (cash transfer) or indirect (price subsidies) – will be allocated among various priorities. In very poor households the bulk will probably go towards food purchases, but some will almost certainly be allocated to health and education expenses, clothes, and various other basic living costs.

- *Fungibility of food.* Feeding programmes are equally unlikely to achieve 100 per cent impact, even though food is less fungible than cash. Food generally has a greater nutritional impact than cash, which still needs to be converted into food (at some transaction cost). Nonetheless, when individuals receive food directly, this allows the household to reallocate resources it would have expended on feeding that individual. In extreme cases, the free food might substitute entirely for the family's food, so that the net nutritional impact is zero. Studies of calorie substitution in food supplementation programmes found leakages of 37–53 per cent for on-site feeding and 46–82 per cent for take-home rations (Rogers 1995).

- *Reduction of other income.* Public transfers could crowd out private transfers (Cox and Jimenez 1990) – e.g. remittances from relatives to rural households in northern Namibia dried up after food aid was introduced during the 1991–2 drought, leaving some families worse off than before.

- *Differences in gender priorities.* The impact of an intervention is affected by who receives and controls the resource transferred. Resources transferred to women are more likely to be used for feeding children than resources given to men. The crude argument is that women have a higher propensity to care for their children ('mothers feed the children while fathers drink beer'). A subtler argument is that men and women have different preferences and priorities, so that a father might choose to spend additional income on looking for work – which could raise household nutrition in the long run – whereas a mother might be more concerned with ensuring that her child does not go to bed hungry tonight.

In summary, feeding programmes and food-related income transfers invariably suffer from high levels of *substitution* (household resources being transferred to other uses) and *leakages* (individuals other than the target group deriving benefits), which constrains their effectiveness. On the other hand, 'leakages' is not always as bad as it sounds. Some studies have shown that adults protect their children's nutrition during food crises by rationing their own consumption more severely. A feeding programme that targets children would release resources for the adults, with nutritional benefits for themselves and economic benefits for the family if their productivity increases. An evaluation which concluded that this feeding programme had failed because the nutritional impact on targeted children was negligible has simply failed to consider this important indirect or multiplier effect.

CONCLUSION

During the 1990s, targeted social safety nets became a popular policy response to the economic shocks that triggered and then followed the adoption of structural adjustment programmes in many African countries. In the face of intense fiscal austerity and donor conditionality, governments abolished universal price subsidies to food producers and consumers – often at great political cost – and replaced these with narrowly targeted food or cash transfers for specific 'vulnerable groups', or self-targeted public works projects for the rural poor. This chapter has identified several problems with this trend, including the costs and errors associated with alternative targeting mechanisms (e.g. the limited coverage of public works), the unsustainability of externally-funded safety net interventions, and the negligible impact on beneficiaries' nutritional status of transfers such as supplementary or school feeding programmes.

On the other hand, the contribution of even small transfers to the food security of recipients and their families cannot be underestimated. In the absence of comprehensive social security systems in low-income African countries, well designed safety nets can provide vital protection against transitory food insecurity. Moreover, the indirect benefits of these programmes – the assets created by public works, the improved attendance and performance of learners on school feeding programmes – can have positive impacts on food security in the longer term. Nonetheless, safety nets are no panacea, and these interventions should always be seen as complementing, not substituting for, more holistic and sustainable efforts to reduce household and national food insecurity.

CHAPTER ELEVEN

Organizational Issues in Food Security Planning

Simon Maxwell

A chapter on organizational issues in food security planning might seem superfluous. Surely, planning is a straightforward, professional process, and food security planning no exception to this rule? Planning ought to be a technical matter: about setting objectives, defining the incentive and regulatory environment, raising and distributing resources, writing projects, and providing a framework for monitoring and evaluation. Maybe so – but there are good theoretical reasons for expecting organizational problems of various kinds. More to the point, all our experience with the kind of multi-sectoral and multi-disciplinary planning required in food security tells us that many organizational problems do arise in practice.

We will start with experience, and come to the theory later. In reading about experience, however, it will be helpful at least to have in mind a checklist of themes that might be relevant. This is easily available from the extensive literature on organization and management. For example, the excellent introduction by Handy (1985) identifies the following topics as being relevant to the study of organizations:

- the motivation to work;
- roles and interactions between individuals;
- leadership;
- power and influence;
- the working of groups;
- cultures and structures;
- the management of difference.

Can this list be applied to practical cases?

To answer this question, consider a fictional – but, to many, an all too familiar – example, constructed from experience and observation in half a dozen different countries in sub-Saharan Africa (SSA). This is the story of Frederick and Judith, food security planners in a typical, low-income, drought-prone and aid-dependent African country. They each have a story to tell.

Judith's story

As Head of the Food Security Office, Judith was considering her future. Should she stay and fight? Or should she follow her instinct and ask for a transfer? Sectoral planning, perhaps, or even back to the Ministry of Health? Judith was worn out. Why was food security so difficult? And why wouldn't people cooperate?

Today had really been the last straw. She was struggling to put the final touches to the new, national Food Security Plan, and Frederick – she grimaced at the thought of his unrepentant male chauvinism – had announced a major new programme of food subsidies for the urban poor. Food subsidies! They weren't in the plan! And worse, the Ministry of Commerce and the Treasury had cooked this up on their own: neither Judith nor her staff had been consulted about the new proposals. What was the point of having a Food Security Office if it wasn't allowed to coordinate? And how could the Minister let Commerce push through a proposal like that without consulting her? That was what really hurt, Judith thought, the lack of support from her own boss.

In the beginning it had all been so different. The great drought had been a terrible affliction, but my goodness, they had worked hard during those years, and saved many lives: people from different ministries working together, central government sitting side by side with regional governments in special task forces, donor meetings every week, and the rewarding sight of the great food convoys setting off for the drought-affected areas. There was a spirit then, a real feeling that things could change.

The Government had felt it, too, she remembered – even the Minister. He had been enthusiastic when the World Financial Institution (WFI) had suggested setting up a project to prepare a national food security plan, and had welcomed her warmly to the Ministry as the national coordinator. He had really seemed to want a national strategy that would pull everything together and avoid another catastrophe.

It seemed only last week, Judith thought, though in reality it had been over three years ago. Setting up the office; welcoming the consultants from the WFI; the study tour to Sudan, Ethiopia and Zimbabwe. Of course, some of the consultants had been very inexperienced, but the work had been really intensive in those days. Judith remembered how they had 'pulled up the drawbridge' to the office and locked themselves inside, struggling to develop a conceptual model of food security, relevant to their own conditions. There had been so much to read, documents from the World Bank, the Food and Agriculture Organization (FAO), the United Nations Children's Fund and other institutions, as well as plans from other countries in Africa. Judith remembered the diagrams they had drawn to illustrate linkages in food security, the relationship between nutrition and food security and the role of different ministries. It had taken months, but finally they had produced a model – and there it was, she thought, pinned carefully to the wall above her desk, the colours slightly faded now, but still a powerful tool of analysis.

Then there had been the phase of developing plans to improve food security. The WFI had funded national and international consultants to prepare sectoral action plans. The office had seemed literally to hum with activity and Judith had spent long hours reading reports and correcting drafts. It was really a pity that the data were so poor, but still there were some good ideas, which went far beyond food security. They had had the makings not just of a plan for food security, but of a new agricultural strategy, a new rural development strategy, even a macroeconomic policy. How exciting that had been, Judith remembered; and what an effort they had put into producing their first draft of the national plan. How wide-ranging it was; how complete; how important for the different sectoral ministries.

At last, it had been time to reveal the ideas to the rest of the government, and Judith remembered the national workshop they had convened to launch the plan. She grimaced at the memory of the work that had had to be put into organization. For weeks, it had seemed that Judith's main job was to stand over a photocopier, producing copies of papers or invitations to receptions. Still, they had all come: ministers and ambassadors, technicians and aid officials. Not all for the whole time, it was true: most had left after the first plenary and had skipped the working groups. Still, at least they had all been informed about the plan. There had been many suggestions about how to improve it – in some ways almost too many. A report had been written and Judith and her staff had been able to set out to revise the draft.

Of course, that had been a bigger job than she had expected. In fact she had been at it for several months already. The change of government hadn't helped. Not only were there new ministers to brief, but the political orientation of the government had changed quite a bit. The new policy on self-sufficiency, for example, had quite serious implications for the plan; and the structural adjustment package agreed with the World Bank and the International Monetary Fund. Decentralization was an important theme, too, with authority being devolved to local government.

The trouble was that policy seemed to be changing so fast. Hardly a day went by without some new policy statement. And somehow the food security plan was no longer at the centre of affairs. At the beginning, after the drought, Judith had really felt that food security took centre stage in government policy making. But now?

So, should she give up, put it down to experience and go back to Health? It was difficult. Food security was a major problem, Judith was convinced. Over a quarter of all children in the country were malnourished. Drought was an ever-present threat. Surely, food security planning made sense. But if that was the case, why was it going so slowly? What had she done wrong?

Frederick's story

It was a day of achievement, a day of action. Earlier that morning, Frederick and his boss had announced a new, national programme of urban food subsidies. They were going to be a bit expensive, but they were going to be effective in reducing poverty, Frederick was sure. Equally important, they would take the political pressure off his boss. And, Frederick thought, managing the new programme could not be bad for his career. There was another advantage, too: if nothing else, Judith would be cross! In his mind's eye, Frederick could see her now, sitting in her office, devising yet another grandiose plan for food security.

It wasn't the idea of a plan that Frederick objected to so much: he was a planner himself. But when he thought about Judith, he couldn't suppress a feeling of irritation. What he remembered most clearly was the series of meetings he had been asked to attend (summoned more like) at the Ministry. Of course, he had gone, what else was he to do? But why should his Ministry, Commerce, be expected to share its ideas and submit to someone else's master plan? After all, his boss was in the Cabinet, just as Judith's was – and his Minister was at least as weighty a figure in the hierarchy as hers.

Getting across town for meetings was never easy, with the traffic and the road repairs. It was even harder when the Ministry vehicle was ten years old and stalled at every junction. And then to arrive and see Judith's brand new Peugeot sitting in the Ministry car park! And the air conditioning! And the photocopier! And the three computers, sitting neatly under plastic covers! Frederick grimaced at the thought. Didn't the WFI realise how badly his team at Commerce needed all those things?

The meetings themselves were an ordeal. Judith, of course, was in charge, but she would always have a technical specialist by her side, sometimes local, but more often a young, foreign consultant, new to the country, hopelessly inexperienced and earning far too much. Judith herself came from Health, Frederick knew, so you couldn't expect much: a fixation with nutrition, endless concern with mothers and young children, no idea about production, let alone trade, a romantic idea about mutual support in traditional communities.

Anyway, they'd all be there – half a dozen different Ministries, several autonomous agencies and sometimes some aid people – all waiting for Judith's latest bombshell. And sure enough, she'd call on her technical side-kick and out would come some half-baked proposal that they had dreamed up behind closed doors, but which always meant somebody else taking on the burden of implementation. Not only that, but the proposal would be weighed down with endless committees and task forces, responsible for everything from detailed planning to post-project evaluation: and always with someone from Judith's office in the chair. It was like being in a police state, Frederick had thought, as if no one could be trusted to do anything on their own. Judith would probably call it coordination, he thought; he himself would simply call it bureaucratic.

Well, of course, Frederick was an experienced enough civil servant to deal with meetings like that. He'd always be very polite, the idea was wonderful, definitely worth thinking about. His special congratulations to the WFI for supporting this fascinating work. There were one or two small points that needed further discussion, but Frederick was sure they could be sorted out. What was needed was very careful study by the national, technical specialists (these words said with especial emphasis) and he would guarantee to undertake detailed scrutiny at the Ministry of Commerce. And with a bit of luck, that was that: he would take the proposal back to the office, boot it down to a group of junior people and forget all about it. If Judith rang, well, they were on the job, this was a very delicate area and he would get back to her as soon as he could.

Poor Judith. But she had to learn. Food trade and food pricing were his responsibility. It was no use her pushing for a decision in these meetings. She couldn't be authoritarian with him, or tell him what to do. After all, who had dreamed up the idea of food subsidies? And who had persuaded the Cabinet to accept the idea? Frederick didn't need a Food Security Office, did he?

And with that, Frederick's smile returned and he turned back to his desk. Time to write a memo to the WFI, asking them to support the new food subsidy programme. A Peugeot, perhaps, or would a Land Cruiser be better?

A THEORETICAL PERSPECTIVE

Frederick's and Judith's stories are fictional, but the problems they face are not. The stories will resonate in different ways for different readers. Some will recognize particularly the inter-ministerial conflict, others the shifts in political climate, others still the gender conflict or the dominant role of outside aid agencies. All these are real issues in the real world. It is worth asking then how far Handy's checklist of topics can help us to understand what is going on. How can an organizational analysis help us to put food security planning in the country back onto the right track? Equally, how can an appreciation of these issues help us to avoid similar problems in other countries? Much has been written on different aspects of policy and planning: the pretensions of planning to objectivity and impartiality have long been questioned (Clay and Shaffer 1984; Gillespie and McNeill 1992). However, two particular pieces of organization theory appear relevant to these questions. They deal respectively with organizational culture and with the performance of groups.

ORGANIZATIONAL CULTURE

It is obvious that Judith's food security planning frame is both multi-sectoral and multi-disciplinary. It involves productive sectors, like agriculture, but also infrastructural and social sectors – roads, health, education and the like. By the same token, the plan cannot be written by specialists in one discipline acting in isolation – it needs input by nutritionists, agriculturalists, engineers, economists and others. Food security planning is necessarily collaborative and integrative, with all the scope for competition and conflict that statement implies.

One way to illustrate the problem is to examine Table 11.1, which defines various levels of integration, from 'disciplinary' or 'sectoral' at one extreme to 'trans-disciplinary' or 'trans-sectoral' at the other. At the top of the table, 'disciplinary' or 'sectoral' planning eschews integration altogether, and relies on casual interaction for the whole to be greater than the sum of the parts. At the other extreme, 'trans-disciplinary' or 'trans-sectoral' planning requires the creation of a new cognitive paradigm. It is very ambitious and probably unattainable. In between the two extremes are two variants of cross-disciplinary, or cross-sectoral, planning which are more likely to be found in the real world, and which sound like plausible paths for Judith. The first is 'multi-disciplinary', or 'multi-sectoral', and the second 'inter-disciplinary' or 'inter-sectoral': the first involves common goals but relies on individual action; and the second takes integration one step further, with co-operative goal definition and collaborative action. Note that both of these require collaboration in new ways between groups of people who have traditionally worked in separate compartments.

Table 11.1 Types of cross-disciplinary and cross-sectoral planning

Disciplinary or sectoral	Independent planning and communication, leading to influence
Multi-disciplinary or multi-sectoral	Common goals, independent planning
Inter-disciplinary or inter-sectoral	Systematic integration, leading to co-operative goal definition, planning and action
Trans-disciplinary or trans-sectoral	Transcend individual skills and disciplines, leading to a new common, cognitive map

Source: Adapted from Flynn and Denning 1982

The different ways of working can be understood as different organizational 'cultures', illustrated diagrammatically in Figure 11.1. There are four of these, respectively a 'power' culture, a 'role' culture, a 'task' culture and a 'person' culture. A power culture is highly personalized, with a strong individual at the centre and lines of authority radiating outwards. A role culture is more hierarchical, with interactions characterized by rules and regulations. A task culture is focused on the job in hand, with teams

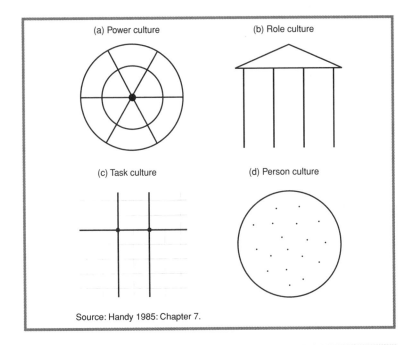

(a) Power culture

(b) Role culture

(c) Task culture

(d) Person culture

Source: Handy 1985: Chapter 7.

Figure 11.1 Four organizational cultures

forming and re-forming as the task changes. And, finally, a person culture is characterized by the pre-eminence of individual aspirations and priorities, with the organization existing only to support the individuals.

A typical example of a power culture might be a new non-governmental organization (NGO), formed by a charismatic and dominating individual. A typical example of a role culture would be a government department. A task culture might be found in a research department. A university is often cited as a typical example of a person culture.

It would be wrong to say that one culture is better or worse than another. Organizational cultures are formed by history and experience, and often conform to the type of work being undertaken. For example, an NGO might start off with a charismatic leader in a power culture, but then evolve into a role culture when growing size means that informal and personalized ways of operating can no longer be sustained, and have to be replaced with rules and procedures. Of course, the process of change is often very painful for the organization and the individuals concerned. Similarly, a person culture in a university department might prove to be unsustainable when funding cuts mean that individual independence has to be sacrificed to some common fund-raising strategy. By the same token, some types of culture are better suited to certain kinds of work: for example, a government department handling large volumes of routine work, perhaps processing vehicle licensing applications, will probably be characterized by a role culture.

Now, Frederick and Judith are civil servants. Their normal experience will be in a 'role' culture, diagram (b) in Figure 11.1. The role culture, of course, is the classic Weberian bureaucracy. Handy (1985, p. 190) suggests that its patron god is Apollo, the god of reason. He adds that:

> the work of the pillars, and the interaction between the pillars, is controlled by procedures for roles (e.g. job descriptions), procedures for communication and rules for settlement of disputes.

The role culture offers security and predictability and it works well in a stable environment. The Ministers are at the top of their respective pillars, providing leadership and a source of power. Both Frederick's and Judith's ministers are 'barons' in this respect.

The problem is that the role culture is not flexible, does not adapt well to change and is not suited to multi-sectoral projects which link the pillars. The task culture, by contrast, is well suited to new forms of collaboration. As Handy (1985, p. 193) describes it, the task culture is a:

> team culture, where the outcome, the result, the product of the team's work tends to be the common enemy, obliterating individual objectives and most status and style differences.

The task culture will have a different form of leadership, more supportive and less directive. It will often be found in the innovative parts of organizations, including research and sometimes planning. It sounds like the right culture for Frederick and Judith.

Organizational problems will arise if the organizational culture is wrong. Group dynamics will fail, conflict will grow, leadership will become embattled and personal motivation will disappear. Practical programmes will be lost to bureaucratic infighting. Handy (1985, p. 208), again, summarizes the likely outcome of trying to establish creative multi-disciplinary or multi-sectoral units within a role culture:

> *The management of steady state activities should properly be concerned with rules, procedures, regulations and formal controls. Apply these to the innovation arms of the organisation and they will suffocate.*

It is easy to see that Frederick and Judith are close to suffocating. This simple but powerful piece of theory suggests that a key source of their problems is that they were operating within the wrong organizational culture. Trapped in a role culture, they would have been far more productive in a task culture.

The answer is obvious – change the culture. Unfortunately, this is easier said than done. After all, both Frederick and Judith are small cogs in a large government machine. How can they change the whole civil service? The answer is, of course, that they can't. Nevertheless, it may be possible to do something within the narrower confines of their own smaller world. The secret, it seems, may lie in the working of groups.

GROUPS

The inter-ministerial planning team established by Judith constitutes a group, and there is now a considerable theory about how groups work. At best, groups become self-managing, mutual responsibility teams, which approximate to task cultures. Judith's problem, then, is how to create a team that really works – how to change Frederick from a saboteur to a full member with shared objectives.

A first stab at understanding how groups work is to recognize that all groups go through a sequence of stages: forming–storming–norming–performing. When a group is formed, there are always teething problems, because people come to groups with different expectations and ways of doing things. The relationship between group members can be stormy. Eventually, things settle down and the group learns to work together: new norms are established for settling disputes, and the group can then begin to perform. Judith's group, unfortunately, seems never to have reached this stage.

The working of groups can be presented in a more complete way. Table 11.2 offers five stages of group development, beginning with a simple 'membership' group and working through to a 'shared-responsibility' group. The stages differ in the characteristics listed down the left-hand

Table 11.2   Common operating characteristics of the stages of task-group development

Behavioural or skill area	Stage of group development				
	Membership	Sub-grouping	Confrontation	Differentiation	Shared responsibility
Atmosphere and relationships	Cautious, feelings suppressed, low conflict, few outbursts	Increasing closeness within sub-groups, cross-group criticism, false unanimity	Hostility between sub-groups	Confident, satisfied, open, honest, differences	Supportive, open, expressive, varied; disagreement resolved promptly
Goal understanding and acceptance	Low, fuzzy	Increasing clarity, misperceptions	Up for grabs, fought over	Agreed on by most	Commitment to overarching goal
Listening and information sharing	Intense, but high distortion and low disclosure	Similarities within sub-groups not as great as perceived	Poor	Reasonably good	Excellent, rapid, direct
Decision making	Dominated by active members	Fragmented, deadlocks, to the boss by default	Dominated by most powerful, loudest	Based on individual expertise, often by the boss in consultation with subordinates	By consensus, collective when all resources needed, individual when one is expert (not necessarily the boss)
Reaction to leadership	Tested by members tentative	Resisted, often covertly	Power struggles, jockeying for position	General support, individual differences in influence	Highly supportive but free to disagree on issues
Attention to way group is working	Ignored	Noticed but avoided, discussed outside meetings in small groups	Used as weapon against opponents	Alternates between uncritical or overcompulsive discussion	Discussed as needed, to aid work accomplishment; anyone can initiate

Source: Bradford and Cohen 1997, p.189

side of the table: atmosphere, acceptance of goals, information sharing, decision making, reaction to leadership, and attention to the way the group is working. In a membership group, commitment to goals is low, leadership is weak, and conflict is frequent, if often implicit – this sounds very much like Judith's meetings. In a shared-responsibility group, by contrast, everyone is committed to the goal, internal communications are good, and decisions are reached quickly and collectively. Clearly, this is Judith's goal. A shared-responsibility group would provide her with exactly the kind of task culture she needs for her multi-sectoral and multi-disciplinary enterprise.

What, then, should Judith do differently to move her team forward? Bradford and Cohen (1997) suggest that the key is to abandon a heroic style of leadership, in which the leader carries all the burden of motivation and decision taking (the Lone Ranger style), in favour of a 'post-heroic' style in which the manager devolves responsibility and acts as more of a 'developer'. Thus:

> the Developer must work concurrently on three separate but related areas: to increase systematically the importance of the problems the team deals with; to move from a consultative to a consensual joint decision-making style as problems increase in importance; and to change the norms and develop members' skills to succeed in their expanded responsibility (Bradford and Cohen 1997, p. 196).

In this model, the developer's task is to analyse the state of development of the group, and help it move forward to the next stage illustrated in Table 11.2. Group development is a key management function – and one which Judith effectively ignored.

Now, of course, no one would pretend that changing the character of Judith's and Frederick's group would be straightforward. There are many deep-seated problems of status, gender and professional pride underlying their conflict. Nevertheless, these problems are not unique, and the theory suggests that changes in personal style and in the management of the group dynamic can make a material difference to the performance of a planning team.

LESSONS OF EXPERIENCE

The last statement, about the scope for change, requires a 'reality check'. The next step in our analysis, therefore, is to look back at other examples of multi-sectoral and multi-disciplinary planning, and see what can be learned. There is material in the literatures on: integrated rural development; multi-sectoral nutrition planning; farming systems research; national food security planning; poverty planning; and industrial development. In all these cases, we are looking not just at questions of culture, or group dynamics, but more generally at how organizations work. One particular question to address is what happens after the planning is complete, when implementation begins?

INTEGRATED RURAL DEVELOPMENT

The history of rural development over the past thirty years can be divided schematically into four phases.

- A period during which issues of poverty and unemployment gradually came to the fore, culminating in Robert McNamara's Nairobi speech of 1973 which committed the World Bank to a new poverty focus. This period was marked by a shift in rural development away from production-oriented programmes, often targeted to high potential areas, towards programmes aimed specifically at poor people.
- A period marked by the realization that the symptoms and causes of rural poverty were multi-dimensional, resulting in theories of basic needs and in systematic attempts to integrate the various components of rural development programmes. This period, broadly the second half of the 1970s, marked the high point of integrated rural development (IRD) and of the large-scale, top-down projects through which IRD philosophies were implemented.
- A gradual disenchantment and retrenchment, caused by the difficulty of financing the high recurrent costs of IRD programmes after the second oil shock of 1979, as well as by the many organizational problems of IRD.
- A search for new models of rural development, which resulted in the rejection of old-style 'blueprint' methods in favour of new, flexible, decentralized and high participative 'process' modes, often implemented by NGOs.

We are not concerned here with objections to the underlying model of rural development, pretty well common to all four phases, notably the common assumptions about the desirability and feasibility of targeting, the tendency to ignore macroeconomic imperatives and, at least in the first three phases, a limited view of participation (see, however, Heyer et al. 1981). Our concern here is rather with the organizational problems of IRD and with the attempts to overcome them.

The organizational problems of rural development have been a common theme of the literature. A good example is the review of IRD by Crener et al. in 1984. This lists seven reasons for the failure of IRD, of which two are clearly to do with organization.

- projects were conceived in a rigid manner, due to an overly idealized economic, political and institutional environment; and
- both newly created and existing organizational structures did not foster effective and efficient project management (Crener et al.1984, p. 40ff).

What these criticisms mean in practice is that the technical departments involved in the implementation of IRD were often in conflict, so that decisions were constantly being postponed and a global approach was lost; that responsibilities and decision-making powers were dispersed throughout the relevant government structures; that technical assistance was frequently called on to assume management responsibilities; and that autonomous project management units created to overcome these problems disintegrated when external funding was removed. The underlying problems reflect the failure of IRD to build on local institutional structures or to recognize conflicts of interest between institutions and individuals (Crener et al. 1984, p. 43).

A similar diagnosis stems from Birgegard's 1987 analysis of IRD. He points out that the characteristics of the task and the environment typical of IRD require management which is:

> flexible, adaptable, willing to experiment, to learn and to accept mistakes. Managers need to have bargaining and negotiating skills to reconcile conflicting interests [and] placate influential demands at different levels ... and have the ability to explore and to understand the dynamic informal processes between conflicting interests in the project environment (Birgegard 1987, p. 6). ... Sadly, the 'control-oriented', compartmentalised government bureaucracies with centralised decision-making hardly match the prerequisites of effective management of IRD projects' (Birgegard 1987, p. 7).

A number of different problems surface in these analyses, and in many others on the same theme. Crener et al. offer one set of solutions. They put forward five general principles for a new-style IRD, all of which in some way or other influence organizational design:

- simple or medium-term interventions on an initially limited scale at the outset;
- constant interaction between planning, execution and evaluation;
- dynamic analysis and more in-depth comprehension of the milieu;
- increased participation on the part of target groups in decision making, implementation and evaluation;
- diversification and strengthening of the support given to local capacity for institutional organization.

The organizational implications are far-reaching: much greater simplicity in planning and implementation, with less ambitious goals and less overt integration; open-ended planning and greater flexibility; genuine participation in decision making; and the strengthening of decentralized institutions in rural areas. There are interesting implications here for Judith's planning process, which was very centralized and very detailed – in the sense of preparing a meticulous and time-consuming plan before launching any initiatives on the ground.

Table 11.3 The blueprint and learning process approaches in rural development contrasted

	Blueprint	Learning process
Idea originates in	Capital city	Village
First steps	Data collection and plan	Awareness and action
Design	Static, by experts	Evolving, people involved
Supporting organization	Existing, or built top down	Built bottom up, with lateral spread
Main resources	Central funds and technicians	Local people and their assets
Staff development	Classroom, didactic	Field-based action learning
Implementation	Rapid, widespread	Gradual, local, at people's pace
Management focus	Spending budgets, Completing projects on time	Sustained improvement and performance
Content of action	Standardized	Diverse
Communication	Vertical: orders down, reports up	Lateral: mutual learning and sharing experience
Leadership	Positional, changing	Personal, sustained
Evaluation	External, intermittent	Internal, continuous
Error	Buried	Embraced
Effects	Dependency creating	Empowering
Associated with	Normal professionalism	New professionalism

Source: Chambers 1993, p. 12

Crener et al.'s five principles encapsulate the new approach to rural development planning, styled 'process approaches', in contrast to earlier 'blueprint' models. Chambers has summarized the alternative approaches (see Table 11.3) and it is clear from this that process planning embodies a very different organizational culture to blueprint planning. Thus, blueprint planning uses technical specialists to devise a scientific plan in the capital city, which is then implemented according to a rigid timetable; process planning, by contrast, is bottom-up in nature, organic, flexible and action-oriented.

Whether these principles work in practice is another matter. In NGOs, they probably do (Fowler 1988). In government agencies, success is much less likely. Birgegard reviews the evidence on the government side, tracing a shift from independent project management units to lead agency arrangements, with one ministry, designated as the 'project owner', subcontracting to others. This is a very partial move towards a simplified mode of operation, but Birgegard concludes that the outcome is not ideal even in these cases, with management and co-ordination problems continuing to plague rural development projects (Fowler 1988, p. 8). This is true even in

Sri Lanka, which is often cited as having one of the most successful government-sponsored IRD programmes. Birgegard concludes, as do others, that the solution may be to abandon IRD in favour of a much more modest approach: integrated planning but not integrated implementation (Fowler 1988, p. 14ff). Are there lessons here for Judith?

MULTI-SECTORAL NUTRITION PLANNING

The history of multi-sectoral nutrition planning (MSNP) is rather harder to interpret than that of integrated rural development. On one view, it 'experienced a meteoric rise and an equally meteoric fall in the 1970s' (Field 1987, p. 19). On another, its key elements remain intact and its influence can be seen in food security studies, adjustment with a human face and many other dimensions of poverty planning (Berg 1987).

What all would agree, however, is that large-scale and systems-oriented multi-sectoral nutrition planning did benefit from a boom in the 1970s, at a time roughly corresponding to the second phase of the IRD history outlined in the previous section. It fell out of favour for some of the same reasons as large-scale IRD, and at about the same time. However, there were also special factors which applied to MSNP.

MSNP suffered from familiar problems of large data requirements. In addition, Field has identified seven 'intellectual flaws' which 'derailed' MSNP (Field 1987, p. 23ff):

- MSNP was largely oblivious to problems of implementation as 'an inherently pluralistic, often conflictual process that is uncertain, even precarious ...';
- the programmatic features of MSNP were 'devastating to effective implementation', with ambitious goals, long chains of causality and multiple-decision points;
- organizational overload, with a 'premium placed on inter-ministerial co-ordination [that] was neither [sic] realistic, desirable nor necessary';
- naivety about political economy and illusions about technocratic omnipotence;
- political conservatism and disregard of broader social, economic and political relationships;
- neglect of wider development linkages;
- MSNP fell between sectoral stools and suffered from an identity crisis.

Despite disagreement on details, this diagnosis is confirmed by others, especially with regard to the large-scale multi-sectoral systems analysis projects of the 1970s (Berg 1987; Levinson 1995). There are also a number of common themes with the analysis of IRD, especially with regard to the disproportionate importance given to planning and the difficulties of implementation. Again, there are many parallels to the experience of food security planning described by Frederick and Judith.

The response of the nutrition community to these criticisms has been to follow two complementary paths, which again parallel the routes taken by IRD. One path has been explicitly to seek better ways of managing MSNP, which broadly correspond to the process approach of IRD. The other has been to stage a strategic retreat and focus on inserting nutritional insights into more general debates on food security and structural adjustment: this broadly corresponds to the IRD solution of 'integrated planning but not integrated implementation'.

Following the first path, Field (1987, p. 26ff) has identified eleven lessons for the future of MSNP. These introduce a process dimension to nutrition planning, with increased emphasis on beneficiary participation and 'backward mapping'. They also downgrade the importance of planning, emphasize the need for simplicity, subordinate analysis to action, and focus on the implementing role of the existing sectoral ministries. This is a list which is familiar from the IRD process model, except that it applies the lessons to questions of national planning rather than to project implementation: indeed, there is a marked overlap in the academic material on which these two sets of prescriptions are based.

Field does not provide evidence on the extent to which his prescriptions have been followed. In his reply to Field, however, Berg (1987) cites Zimbabwe, Indonesia, Tamil Nadu and a dozen other countries or regions as places where part of the new agenda is already to be found, by implication with success.

Berg goes on to make the case for the alternative, almost covert route to multi-sectoriality. MSNP may not have the prominence once hoped for in the 1970s, but 'slowly, with the advent of nutrition planning, respect for nutrition has grown in some development circles and it has become a legitimate subject for inclusion in the policy discussions of planning councils of many governments ...' (Berg 1987, p. 375). Evidence for the truth of this statement can be found in the growth of nutrition advocacy and of nutrition programmes in developing countries (Gillespie and McNeill 1992; FAO/WHO 1992; Levinson 1995).

FARMING SYSTEMS RESEARCH

As a way of organizing agricultural research and generating new technology, farming systems research (FSR) provides a contrasting case to the others considered: here the problems are largely confined to individual research stations and the organizational issues arise between specialists in different disciplines, rather than between the agricultural and other sectors. Nevertheless, the issues and the solutions follow a similar pattern; furthermore, the smaller scale of the problem makes it easier to see solutions.

FSR has had no less a turbulent history than either IRD or MSNP. It emerged in the late 1970s, in response to growing dissatisfaction with the failure of traditional agricultural research to tailor technologies to the needs of small farmers. It introduced the idea of a holistic, multi-disciplinary diagnosis of farming systems, followed by a coordinated research programme and mutually supporting recommendations. There are again many variants (Merrill-Sands 1986).

FSR became the dominant agricultural research paradigm of the 1980s, overcoming a good deal of resistance on the way, both in the international research system of the Consultative Group on International Agricultural Research (CGIAR) and in national research organizations. It was then challenged by 'complementary' farmer-first paradigms, which laid more stress on the diversity of traditional agriculture and the need for flexibility in technology design (Richards 1985; Chambers and Jiggins 1986). At the extreme, the alternative approaches could be presented as radical departures, bearing the same relationship to FSR as process planning did to blueprint planning (Chambers et al. 1989). Alternatively, and perhaps more constructively, they could be seen as evolutionary developments in a broadly farmer-oriented approach (Tripp 1989).

Irrespective of whether we are dealing here with one paradigm or two, agricultural research has come to place unprecedented demands on interdisciplinary collaboration and institutional flexibility. These demands have not always been successfully met and institutional friction has been a theme of the literature (Flynn and Denning 1982; Biggs and Clay 1983). Maxwell (1986) described the institutional difficulties of research stations and attempted to explain them. He concluded that there were five underlying factors:

- personal inadequacy, meaning that the individuals concerned were unable to work together;
- communication problems between disciplines, particularly between natural scientists and social scientists (Chambers 1983, p. 33: natural scientists are trained to act, social scientists are trained to criticize);
- poor and poorly managed group dynamics, exacerbated by poor conflict resolution and the wrong leadership styles;
- inappropriate organizational cultures, particularly clinging to a role culture when a task culture would be more appropriate;
- power struggles between different disciplines and different individuals.

Maxwell noted that institutional disruption was usually attributed to the behavioural characteristics of particular individuals, but suggested that cultural and structural issues usually provided more powerful explanations. This conclusion was certainly consistent with later work, for example by the Institute for Strengthening Agricultural Research (ISNAR), which was concerned with the effective management of on-farm, client-oriented research. Merrill-Sands and McAllister concluded, for example, that conflict was frequent between on-farm and on-station research: 'divergent goals and attitudes lead, in turn, to disputes over more concrete issues, such as resource allocation, priorities in planning and programming of research, or the validity and interpretation of results' (1988, p. 4). Conflict could be avoided if scientists shared a common approach to research, agreed on the benefits of collaboration and had adequate opportunities for collaboration.

There are suggestions as to how this desirable outcome can be brought about, in the earlier literature, in the writings on complementary paradigms and in the work by ISNAR. Pulling the various themes together, there are a dozen practical steps to take, grouped into three main areas: organization; training; and work practice (Maxwell 1986).

In the sphere of organization, the main recommendations are for the introduction of a task culture, for participative leadership and for rewards and sanctions which encourage collaborative work. These should provide the conditions within which collaborative work can flourish.

With regard to training, the literature suggests special attention to communication skills, to the techniques of conflict management and to the basic concepts and skills of the other disciplines in a multi-disciplinary team. Taken together, these recommendations should overcome problems of behaviour and build greater team spirit.

Finally, with regard to work practice, the prescriptions are to start on a small scale with practical actions rather than philosophies, to undertake collaborative fieldwork, and to build a larger programme slowly over time as attitudes begin to change: in fact, a process approach.

NATIONAL FOOD SECURITY PLANNING

National food security planning went through an initial phase of popularity in the 1980s. There were many different approaches, with the World Bank, the FAO and the European Commission all sponsoring their own approaches and with country experience throwing up new variants, especially in SSA (Maxwell 1990a). Familiar problems arose, however. For example, Belshaw (1990) describes communication problems between government departments in Ethiopia, and Maxwell (1991) discusses the difficulties of donor coordination on food security in Sudan. Similarly, Kennes (1990) analyses the question of dialogue between governments and donors and the difficulty for donors of integrating instruments in pursuit of food security. Davies (1994) reviews the institutional problems of trying to link relief and development in the field of food security, including questions of capacity, flexibility and sustainability.

How, then, can the ideal of promoting food security as an 'organizing principle' (Hindle 1990) be carried into practice? FAO has pioneered planning methods which involve workshop sessions to develop and analyse multiple criteria tables for ranking and choosing food security interventions – a good example of building mutual responsibility (Huddleston 1990). More generally, an approach to food security planning has been proposed which draws on the lessons of previous experience:

integrated planning but independent implementation ('no super ministries'); the importance of a bias to action over planning ('start small and grow'); the value of risk-taking and innovation ('pilot projects'); and the importance of addressing explicitly the need for new modes of organisation in multi-disciplinary team work ('task cultures not role cultures') (Maxwell 1990b, p. 6).

These, again, are familiar themes. Davies (1994) suggests caution, however, citing Moore (1993) to the effect that many African countries may need to (re)create a public service which meets minimal Weberian requirements to establish overall competence and accountability, before more complex and appropriate systems can be achieved. 'Paradoxically', she concludes, 'overcoming institutional constraints. . . may therefore necessitate the establishment of a minimal level of apparently old-style bureaucracies before these can then be reformed to respond to the complex needs of linking relief and development' (Moore 1993, p. 52). This need not be inconsistent with the development of team working, however.

POVERTY PLANNING

A further example comes from the wave of work on poverty which followed the publication of the 1990 *World Development Report* (World Bank 1990), and which has resulted in a large number of poverty assessments (PAs) and poverty reduction strategies. A review of World Bank work in this area in SSA, carried out in 1994 (IDS/IUED 1994), identified two main areas of weakness which are relevant to a discussion of organizational issues.

The first was a lack of inter-disciplinary analysis of poverty, and particularly the lack of political and social analysis: the poverty assessments reviewed had concentrated on collecting economic data on levels of consumption, and had neglected analysis of underlying social processes. Summarizing the results of the study, Toye and Jackson (1996, pp. 58–9) commented that:

the analysis of the process of poverty … has been the major weak point of the Bank's poverty assessment efforts to date … it is a critical area of weakness, given the boldness and ambition of the new poverty agenda.

The second weakness was the lack of linkage between poverty assessments and other instruments of planning and policy. Poverty reduction strategies were designed to influence policy across the board, but it often seemed that they had little influence. Toye and Jackson (1996, p. 60) again commented that:

At present there seems to be little connection between the processes of preparing the new Poverty Assessments and other tasks of country documentation, including the preparation of Public Expenditure Reviews … without any particular sensitivity to the logical links between the attempt to achieve a new anti-poverty emphasis in country policies and the implications of this for changes in their public expenditure management.

Implicit in these criticisms is a model of preparing poverty assessments which entrusts the task to a small group which may or may not consult as widely as it should, and whose report is thrown into a competitive arena with other sectoral or thematic special interests. Once again, this sounds like a familiar problem from our case study.

The World Bank has been aware of the problems, and its response throws further light on how to approach multi-sectoral planning. A task force report is remarkably frank about the difficulties of integrating poverty assessments into country assistance strategies and lending programmes, and concludes that although:

> PAs have done a reasonably good job of identifying the policy and strategy options that will assist the poor to become more active participants in the growth process, these options, typically, are not being reflected in the Bank's assistance strategies or operations (World Bank 1996, p. 102).

Various reasons are cited for the shortcomings, including inadequate information, complacent attitudes by governments, a willingness by Bank management to compromise on poverty in the interest of good country relations and, importantly for our purposes, the fact that 'operational interests tend to be made based more on sectoral interests and less on the understanding that poverty reduction requires a multi-sectoral, integrated approach' (World Bank 1996, p. 110).

The solutions offered by the task force are to strengthen linkage between the poverty assessment, the country assistance strategy and the lending programme, and to achieve this by taking, *inter alia*, the following actions (World Bank 1996, pp. 1111–12) (italics added):

1   Establishing poverty reduction as the pervasive organizing principle, 'through the *leadership* of managers and the actions of staff';
2   Establishing a strengthened *process* for preparing country assistance strategies, working with country teams, governments, donors and other stakeholders;
3   Introducing *procedures* such that country business plans set out in detail how the poverty reduction strategy will feed into the Bank's work programme;
4   New *training* and *incentives* for staff; and, finally,
5   Rigorous *monitoring* of how well a new poverty strategy is being implemented.

INDUSTRIAL ORGANIZATION

A final example comes from the world of industrial organization, where the dominant paradigm is of 'post-Fordism', characterized by a move away from repetitive routines on a production line, towards more flexible and responsive team working. Many of the precepts of process planning – participation, a bias to action, decentralization – will be familiar to students of task-oriented 'post-Fordism' in industrial organization and to what Murray calls the 'new managerialism' (Murray 1992; Peters and Waterman 1982; Peters 1987). It is interesting, for example, to compare Chambers' description of process planning in Table 11.3 with a description of contrasting corporate business cultures, summarized in Table 11.4: the two are entirely complementary.

CONCLUSION

The initiatives reviewed differ in important respects:

- some are concerned just with planning, others with both planning and implementation;
- FSR is essentially a question of multi-disciplinarity, where the others combine multi-disciplinarity with multi-sectorality;
- FSR and the story on industrial organization are also mostly concerned with relations within one institution, where IRD is focused on more complex institutional structures at the district or regional level and the others start at least with a national perspective.

Nevertheless, our brief review of the organizational issues in these very different fields suggests that there are important commonalities. If this is true, there is certainly potential for learning across programmes.

The first point to make is that institutional analysis has played a major part in the assessment of each of these multi-dimensional initiatives. The very least this suggests is that institutional issues deserve much greater attention whenever disciplines and sectors come together.

A second point is that organizational culture and structure seem to be at the heart of the problem, whether the theme is planning or implementation and whether the level of analysis is national, regional or institutional. Culture and structure are, in a sense, catch-all notions, which encompass such issues as motivation, leadership, conflict and the nature of interaction between individuals and groups. This, however, is precisely what makes them powerful: they are metaphors for the stance an organization takes, internally and externally.

The message from all our examples is that a traditional role culture is not well suited to these new, holistic programmes. In all the cases, different departments are thrown into conflict over priorities and resources, decision making is disrupted, and short-term organizational solutions prove to be ephemeral. Particular strain is placed on managers, who are ill-equipped to handle new pressures and new levels of complexity.

If all the experiments examined have run into problems of organizational

Table 11.4 Contrasting models of corporate organization

	Mechanistic		**Organic**
Closed system:	Adapting Internally oriented Passive consumers Arm's length suppliers Competitive	Open system:	Adaptive Interplay of internal/external User centred Close, long-term supplier relations Collaborative networks
Planning:	Pre-planning Concentrated at centre Detailed targets Imposed by centre	Strategy:	Feedback from action Participative process Adjustable range of target within constraints consensus

Organization:	Multi-layered pyramid
	Vertical flow of
	  information and
	  command
	Unitary segmented
	  organization
	Departmental
	  specialization
	Role culture
	Organograms/job
	  descriptions
	Centralization of
	  operating
	  responsibility/rules
	  and manuals
	Management role:
	  planning, organization
	  command, co-
	  ordination, control
	Organization as instrument
		Network:	Flat hierarchies
			Horizontal connectedness,
			  through project teams, task
			  forces, matrix methods
			Decomposed system
			Functional redundancy/
			  duplication
			Task culture
			Clusters/project goals
			Workplace autonomy
			Management role: boundary
			  management system
			  adjustment, enabling,
			  supporting, educating,
			  monitoring
			Organization as learning

Labour:	Labour as cost
	Incentives through pay
	Strict hierarchies
	Rate for the job
	High turnover
	Taylorized: fragmented,
	  de-skilled
	Division of mental and
	  manual work
		Staff:	Labour as asset
			Incentives through quality of
			  work
			Less inequality
			Incremental pay
			Lower turnover
			Multi-skilling – 'requisite
			  variety'/group working

Source: Murray 1992, p. 81

culture and structure, none has really managed to define and implement an alternative model, at least for public sector agencies. Nevertheless, there is a striking similarity of approach in searching for new models along a continuum labelled blueprint–process. This is most clearly found in IRD, but is also evident in MSNP and contributions to agricultural research, as well as industrial development. The striking feature of process approaches is that they correspond closely to a task culture approach. The key features of a task culture – innovation, flexibility, participatory leadership, result-orientation – are all found in process models.

The key question, then, is how to bring about the shift from a role culture to a task culture, or from a blueprint approach to a process approach. Here, the theory on the development of groups seems to offer a way forward. The different areas reviewed also contain a wealth of suggestions for practical action to be taken by individuals, programme managers and policy makers. Specifically, and supplementary to Davies' concern for minimal bureaucratic soundness, there are ten main lessons to be drawn.

- On planning:
    - set clear, short-term goals and work towards them; focus on the task;
    - train the team to work together, with training in communication, conflict resolution and multi-disciplinary skills;
    - build team cohesion, through collaborative fieldwork, participative leadership;
    - stay close to the customer, build in participation.

- On implementation:
    - build in a bias to action; start small and grow;
    - take risks and innovate; embrace error;
    - downgrade overt integration – integrated planning but independent implementation.

- On evaluation and public relations:
    - constant iteration between planning, execution and evaluation; be flexible;
    - monitor progress; be publicly accountable for targets;
    - raise the profile of the topic; raise consciousness.

In conclusion, it is worth emphasizing that if food security planning survives, it is not just because of vested interests in Ministries of Planning and donor offices. It is because the problems with which planning is concerned are at the heart of governance. In particular, the state cannot efficiently set the incentive and regulatory framework, nor raise and distribute resources, without attention to the main steps in planning: setting objectives, identifying and selecting alternatives, monitoring impact, and so on. This remains true however market-based economies become, and however political the policy process appears to be (Clay and Schaffer 1984). To be successful, however, planning needs to be done in new ways.

References

INTRODUCTION

Administrative Committee on Coordination: Sub-Committee on Nutrition (ACC/SCN) (2000), *4th Report on the World Nutrition Situation*. Geneva: United Nations ACC Sub-Committee on Nutrition. January.

Conway G. (1997), *The Doubly Green Revolution: Food for all in the 21st Century*. London: Penguin.

FAO (1999), *The State of Food Insecurity in the World. Food Insecurity: When people must live with hunger and fear starvation*. Rome: FAO.

Pinstrup-Andersen, P, R. Pandya-Lorch and M.W. Rosegrant (1999), 'World food prospects: critical issues for the early twenty-first century', *IPFRI Food Policy Report*. Washington DC: IFPRI.

United Nations (1996), *World Population Prospects*. New York: United Nations Population Fund.

United States Department of Agriculture (USDA) (1999), 'Food security assessment', *GFA-11*. Washington DC: USDA, December.

World Bank (2000), *World Development Report 2000/1: Attacking Poverty*. Washington DC: World Bank, January.

CHAPTER 1

ACC/SCN (1991), 'Some options for improving nutrition in the 90s', *SCN News*, **7**, Geneva: ACC/SCN.

Alamgir, M. and P. Arora (1991), *Providing Food Security for All*, New York: New York University Press, International Fund for Agricultural Development.

Barraclough, S.L. (1991), *An End to Hunger? The Social Origins of Food Strategies*, London: Zed Books Ltd.

Barraclough, S.L. and P. Utting (1987), 'Food security trends and prospects in Latin America', *Working Paper*, **99**, Helen Kellog Institute for International Studies, University of Notre Dame, USA.

Bayliss-Smith, T. (1991), 'Food security and agricultural sustainability in the New Guinea Highlands: vulnerable people, vulnerable places', *IDS Bulletin*, **22** (3), 5–11.

Benson, C., E.J. Clay and R.H. Green (1986), 'Food security in Sub-Saharan Africa', paper presented for The Other Economic Summit, Brighton: IDS, University of Sussex.

Berg, A. (1973), *The Nutrition Factor*, Washington DC: The Brookings Institute.

Blaikie, P. and H. Brookfield (1987), *Land Degradation and Society*, London and New York: Methuen.

Bryceson, D.F. (1990), *Food Insecurity and the Social Division of Labour in Tanzania 1919–85*, Oxford: Macmillan.

Chambers, R. (ed.) (1979), *Rural Development: Whose Knowledge Counts?, IDS Bulletin,* **10** (2), Brighton: Institute of Development Studies.

Chambers, R. (1988a), 'Poverty in India: concepts, research and reality', *Discussion Paper,* **241,** January, Brighton: Institute of Development Studies.

Chambers, R. (1988b), 'Sustainable rural livelihoods: a key strategy for people, environment and development', in C. Conroy and M. Litvinoff (eds), *The Greening of Aid,* London: Earthscan.

Chambers, R. (1989), 'Editorial introduction: vulnerability, coping and policy', *IDS Bulletin,* **20** (2), 1–7.

Chambers, R. (1997), *Whose Reality Counts?: Putting the First Last,* London: Intermediate Technology Publications.

Chenery, H.B., I. Bowan and B.J. Svikhart (1974), *Redistribution with growth: policies to improve income distribution in developing countries in the context of economic growth University of Sussex,* London: Oxford University Press.

Corbett, J.E.M. (1988), 'Famine and household coping strategies', *World Development,* **16** (9), 1099–1112.

Cornia, G.A., R. Jolly and F. Stewart (eds) (1987), *Adjustment with a Human Face,* Oxford: Clarendon.

Davies, S. (1993), 'Are coping strategies a cop out?', in J. Swift (ed.), 'New approaches to famine', *IDS Bulletin,* **24** (4), October, 60–72.

Davies, S. (1996), *Adaptable Livelihoods: Coping with Food Insecurity in the Malian Sahel,* Oxford: Macmillan.

de Waal, A. (1991), 'Emergency food security in Western Sudan: what is it for?', in S. Maxwell (ed.), *To Cure all Hunger: Food Policy and Food Security in Sudan,* London: Intermediate Technology.

Drèze, J. and A. Sen (1989), *Hunger and Public Action,* Oxford: Clarendon Press.

EC (1988), 'Food security policy: examination of recent experiences in Sub-Saharan Africa', *Commission Staff Paper,* SEC (88) 1076.

Eide, W.B. (1990), 'Proceedings of the Agriculture-Nutrition Linkage Workshop', **1,** February, Virginia.

Eide, W.B., G. Holmboe-Ottesen, A. Oshaug, M. Wandel, D. Perera and S. Tilakaratna, (1985), 'Introducing nutritional considerations into rural development programmes with focus on agriculture: towards practice', *Development of Methodology for the Evaluation of Nutritional Impact of Development Programmes Research Report,* **1,** Institute for Nutrition Research, University of Oslo, June.

Eide, W.B., G. Holmboe-Ottesen, A. Oshaug, M. Wandel, D. Perera and S. Tilakaratna (1986), 'Introducing nutritional considerations into rural development programmes with focus on agriculture: a theoretical contribution', *Development of Methodology for the Evaluation of Nutritional Impact of Development Programmes Research Report,* **2,** Institute for Nutrition Research, University of Oslo, March.

Evans, A. (1991), 'Gender issues in rural household economics', *IDS Bulletin,* **22** (1), 51–59.

Falcon, W.P., C.T. Kurien, F. Monckeberg, A.P. Okeyo, S.O. Olayide, F. Rabar and W. Tims (1987), 'The world food and hunger problem: changing perspectives and possibilities, 1974–1984', in J.P. Gittinger, J. Leslie and C. Hoisington (eds), *Food Policy: Integrating Supply, Distribution and Consumption,* Baltimore and London: John Hopkins University Press.

FAO (1983), 'World food security: a reappraisal of the concepts and approaches', *Director-General's Report,* Rome: FAO.

FAO (1996a), *Rome Declaration on World Food Security and World Food Summit Plan of Action,* November, Rome: FAO.

FAO (1996b), *World Food Summit: Synthesis of the Technical Background Documents,* Rome: FAO.

FAO/WHO (1992), 'World declaration and plan of action for nutrition', International Conference on Nutrition, December, Rome.

Frankenberger, T.R. (1992), 'Indicators and data collection methods for assessing household food security', in S. Maxwell and T. R. Frankenburger (eds), *Household Food Security: Concepts, Indicators, Measurements: A Technical Review*, New York and Rome: UNICEF and IFAD.

Frankenberger, T.R. and D.M. Goldstein (1991), 'Food security, coping strategies and environmental degradation', *Arid Lands Newsletter*, **30**, 21–7, Office of Arid Land Studies, University of Arizona

Gillespie, S. and J. Mason (1991), 'Nutrition-relevant actions: some experience from the eighties and lessons for the nineties', *Nutrition Policy Discussion Paper*, **10**, Geneva: ACC/SCN.

Gittinger, J., S. Chernick, N.R. Hosenstein and K. Saiter (1990), 'Household food security and the role of women', *World Bank Discussion Paper*, **96**, Washington DC: The World Bank.

Hart, G.A. (1986), *Power, Labour and Livelihood. Processes of Change in Rural Java*, California: California Press.

Heald, C. and M. Lipton (1984), 'African food strategies and the EEC's role: an interim review', *IDS Commissioned Study*, **6**, Brighton: Institute of Development Studies.

Hindle, R.E. (1990), 'The World Bank approach to food security analysis', *IDS Bulletin*, **21** (3), 62–66.

Hopkins, R.F. (1986), 'Food security, policy options and the evolution of state responsibility', in F.L. Tullis and W.L. Hollist (eds), *Food, the State and International Political Economy: Dilemmas of Developing Countries*, Lincoln and London: University of Nebraska Press.

Huddleston, B. (1990), 'FAO's overall approach and methodology for formulating national food security programmes in developing countries', *IDS Bulletin*, **21** (3), July, 72–80.

Jonsson, U. and D. Toole (1991), 'Household food security and nutrition: a conceptual analysis', mimeo, New York: UNICEF.

Joy, L. (1973), 'Food and nutrition planning', *Journal of Agricultural Economics*, **XXIV** (1), January, 165–192.

Kabeer, N. (1988), 'Monitoring poverty as if gender mattered: a methodology for rural Bangladesh', *Discussion Paper*, **255**, Brighton: Institute of Development Studies.

Kabeer, N. (1991), 'Gender, production and well-being: rethinking the household economy', *Discussion Paper*, **288**, Brighton: Institute of Development Studies.

Kabeer, N. (1995), 'Necessary, sufficient or irrelevant?: women, wages and intra-household power relations in urban Bangladesh', *IDS Working Paper*, **25**, Brighton: Institute of Development Studies.

Kennes, W. (1990), 'The European Community and food security', *IDS Bulletin*, **21** (3), July, 67–71.

Kielman, A.A., et al. (1977), 'The Narangwal nutrition study: a summary review', Department of International Health, mimeo, School of Hygiene and Public Health, Baltimore: John Hopkins University.

Kracht, U. (1981), 'Food security for people in the 1980s', paper presented for discussion at the North-South Food Roundtable Meeting, Washington.

Levinson, F.J. (1974), '"Morinda": an economic analysis of malnutrition among young children in rural India', Cornell-MIT International, Massachusetts: Nutrition Policy Series.

Maslow, A. (1954), *Motivation and Personality*, Harper and Row.

Maxwell, S. (1988), 'National food security planning: first thoughts from Sudan', paper presented to workshop on food security in the Sudan, Brighton: Institute of Development Studies.

Maxwell, S. (1991), *To Cure all Hunger: Food Policy and Food Security in Sudan*, London: Intermediate Technology Publications.

Maxwell, S. (1992), 'Food security in Africa: priorities for reducing hunger', *Briefing Paper*, 6, Africa Recovery, New York: United Nations.

Maxwell, S. (1996) 'Food security: a post-modern perspective', *Food Policy*, 21 (2), 155–170.

Maxwell, S. and M. Smith (1992), 'Household food security: a conceptual review', in S. Maxwell and T. Frankenburger (eds), 'Household Food Security: Concepts, Indicators, Measurements: A Technical Review', Monograph, New York and Rome: UNICEF and IFAD.

Mellor, J. (1990), 'Global food balances and food security', in C.K. Eicher and J.M. Staatz (eds), *Agricultural Development in the Third World*, 2nd Edition, Baltimore: John Hopkins University Press.

ODI (1997), 'Global hunger and food security after the World Food Summit', *Briefing Paper*, 1, February.

Oomen, Ir. A. (1988), 'Food security: experiences and prospects', in *From Beyond Adjustment SDA*, Africa Seminar, Maastricht.

Oshaug, A. (1985), 'The composite concept of food security', in W. B. Eide, et al., (eds), 'Introducing nutritional considerations into rural development programmes with focus on agriculture: a theoretical contribution', *Development of Methodology for the Evaluation of Nutritional Impact of Development Programmes Report*, 1, Institute of Nutrition Research, University of Oslo.

Pacey, A. and P. Payne (1985), *Agricultural Development and Nutrition*, Hutchinson, by arrangement with FAO and UNICEF.

Payne, P. (1990), 'Measuring malnutrition', *IDS Bulletin*, 21 (3), July, 14–30.

Payne, P. and M. Lipton with R. Longhurst, J. North and S. Treagust (1994), 'How third world rural households adapt to dietary energy stress: the evidence and the issues', *IFPRI Food Policy Review*, Washington DC: International Food Policy Research Institute.

Philips, T. and D. Taylor (1990), 'Optimal control of food insecurity: a conceptual framework', *American Journal of Agricultural Economics*, 72 (5), 1304–1310, December.

Radimer, K.L., C.M. Olson, J.C. Green, C.C. Campbell and J-P. Habicht (1992), 'Understanding hunger and developing indicators to assess it in women and children', *Journal of Nutrition Education*, 24 (1), supplement, 36–44.

Reardon, T. and P. Matlon (1989), 'Seasonal food insecurity and vulnerability in drought-affected regions of Burkina-Faso', in D.E. Sahn (ed.), *Seasonal Variability in Third World Agriculture: The Consequences for Food Security*, Baltimore and London: John Hopkins University Press.

Reutlinger, S. (1982), 'Policies for food security in food-importing developing countries', in A.H. Chisholm and R. Tyers (eds), *Food Security: Theory, Policy, and Perspectives from Asia and the Pacific Rim*, Massachusetts: Lexington Books.

Reutlinger, S. (1985), 'Food security and poverty in LDCs', *Finance and Development*, 22 (4), 7–11.

Reutlinger, S. and K. Knapp (1980), 'Food security in food deficit countries', *World Bank Staff Working Paper*, 393, Washington DC: World Bank.

Sahn, D.E. (1989), 'A conceptual framework for examining the seasonal aspects of household food security', in D. E. Sahn (ed.), *Seasonal Variability in Third World Agriculture: The Consequences for Food Security*, Baltimore and London: John Hopkins University Press.

Sarris, A.H. (1989), 'Food security and international security', *Discussion Paper*, 301, May, London: Centre for Economic Policy Research.

Sen, A.K. (1981), *Poverty and Famines: An Essay on Entitlement and Deprivation*, Oxford: Clarendon Press.

Siamwalla, A. and A. Valdes, (1980), 'Food insecurity in developing countries', *Food Policy*, 5 (4), November.

Smith, M., J. Pointing and S. Maxwell (1993), 'Household food security, concepts and definitions: an annotated bibliography', *Development Bibliography*, 8, Institute of Development Studies, February.

Staatz, J. (1990), 'Food security and agricultural policy: summary', *Proceedings of the Agriculture-Nutrition Linkage Workshop*, 1, Virginia, February.

Swift, J.J. (1989), 'Why are rural people vulnerable to famine?', *IDS Bulletin*, 20 (2), 8–15.

Tannehill, R. (1988), *Food in History*, London: Penguin.

Thomas, D. (1991), 'Gender differences in household resource allocation', Population and Human Resources Department, Living Standards Measurement Study, *Working Paper*, 79, Washington DC: World Bank.

Townsend, P. (1974), 'Poverty as relative deprivation: resources and styles of living', in D. Wedderburn (ed.), *Poverty, Inequality and Class Structure*, Cambridge University Press.

UN (1975), 'Report of the World Food Conference', New York, 5–16 November 1974, Rome.

UN (1988), 'Towards sustainable food security: critical issues', Report by the Secretariat, World Food Council, Fourteenth Ministerial Session, 23–26 May 1988, Nicosia, Cyprus.

UNICEF (1990), 'Strategy of improved nutrition of children and women in developing countries', A UNICEF Policy Review, New York: UNICEF.

Valdes, A. (ed.) (1981), *Food Security in Developing Countries*, Boulder: Westview Press.

Valdes, A. and P. Konandreas (1981), 'Assessing food insecurity based on national aggregates in developing countries' in A. Valdes (ed.), *Food Security in Developing Countries*, Boulder: Westview Press.

von Braun, J. (1991), 'Policy agenda for famine prevention in Africa', *Food Policy Report*, Washington DC: International Food Policy Research Institute.

von Braun, J., H. Bouis and R. Pandya-Lorch (1992), *Improving Food Security of the Poor: Concept, Policy and Programmes*, Washington: IFPRI.

Weber, M.T. and T.S. Jayne (1991), 'Food security and its relationship to technology, institutions, policies and human capital' in G. Johnson et al. (eds), *Social Science Agricultural Agendas and Strategies*, East Lansing: Michigan State University.

World Bank (1986), 'Poverty and hunger: issues and options for food security in developing countries', *World Bank Policy Study*, Washington DC.

World Bank (1988), *The Challenge of Hunger in Africa*, Washington DC: World Bank.

World Bank (1990), *World Development Report*, Washington DC: World Bank.

World Bank (1993), *Poverty Reduction Handbook*, Washington DC: World Bank.

Zipperer, S. (1987), *Food Security and Agricultural Policy and Hunger*, Harare: Zimbabwe Foundation for Education with Production.

CHAPTER 2

Alexandratos, N. (ed.) (1995), *World Agriculture: Towards 2010: An FAO Study*, Chichester: John Wiley.

Belshaw, D. (1990), 'Food strategy formulation and development planning in Ethiopia', *IDS Bulletin*, 21 (3), 31–43.

Brown, L.R. and H. Kane (1994), *Full House: Reassessing the Earth's Population Carrying Capacity*, Worldwatch Institute, London: Earthscan.

Buchanan-Smith, M. and S. Maxwell (eds) (1994), 'Linking relief and development', *IDS Bulletin*, 25 (4), Brighton: Institute of Development Studies.

Chambers, R. and B.P. Ghildyal (1985), 'Agricultural research for resource poor farmers: the farmer-first and last model', *IDS Discussion Paper*, **203**, Brighton: Institute of Development Studies.

Chenery, H. et al. (1974), *Redistribution with Growth: Policies to Improve Income Distribution in Developing Countries in the Context of Economic Growth; a Joint Study by the World Bank's Development Research Center and the IDS*, London: Oxford University Press.

Conway, G.R. et al. (1994), 'Sustainable agriculture for a food secure world: a vision for international agricultural research', July, Washington DC: CGIAR.

Conway, G. (1997), *The Doubly Green Revolution: Food for all in the Twenty-First Century*, London: Penguin.

Cornia, G.A. et al. (1987), *Adjustment with a Human Face*, UNICEF, Oxford: Clarendon Press.

Crosson, P. and J. Anderson (1992), 'Achieving a sustainable agricultural system in Sub-Saharan Africa: 1990–2025', *A Post-UNCED Series Paper*, Washington DC: World Bank.

Delgado, C.L. (1995), 'Africa's changing agricultural development strategies: past and present paradigms as a guide to the future', *Food, Agriculture, and the Environment Discussion Paper*, **3**, Washington DC: International Food Policy Research Institute.

Dyson, T. (1996), *Population and Food: Global Trends and Future Prospects*, ESRC Global Environmental Change Programme, London: Routledge.

Ellis, F. (1988), 'Small-farm sugar production in Fiji: employment and distribution aspects', *IDS Bulletin*, **19** (2).

FAO (1995), *Investment in Agriculture: Evolution and Prospects*, Rome: Food and Agriculture Organization of the United Nations.

FAO (1996), *The World Food Summit*, Rome: FAO.

FAO (1998), *The State of Food and Agriculture*, Rome: FAO.

George, S. (1976), *How the Other Half Dies: The Real Reason for World Hunger*, London: Penguin Books.

Heald, C. and M. Lipton (1984), 'African food strategies and the EEC's role: an interim review', *IDS Commissioned Study*, **6**, Brighton: Institute of Development Studies.

Holdcroft, L.E. (1984), 'The rise and fall of community development, 1950–65, a critical assessment', in C. Eicher and J. Staatz (eds), *Agricultural Development in the Third World*, Baltimore: Johns Hopkins University Press.

Islam, N. (1995), 'Population and food in the early twenty-first century: meeting future food demands of an increasing population', *IFPRI Occasional Papers*, Washington DC: IFPRI.

Jamal, V. and J. Weeks (1993), *Africa Misunderstood, or, Whatever Happened to the Rural – Urban Gap?*, World Employment Programme, The Macmillan series of ILO studies, Basingstoke: Macmillan.

Johnston, B.F. (1970), 'Agriculture and structural transformation in developing countries: a survey of research', *Journal of Economic Literature*, **3** (2), 369–404.

Johnston, B.F. and J.W. Mellor (1961), 'The role of agriculture in economic development', *American Economic Review*, **51** (4): 556–93.

Lappe, F.M. and J. Collins (1979), *World Hunger: Ten Myths*, San Francisco: Institute for Food and Development Policy.

Lappe, F.M. and J. Collins (1986), *World Hunger: Twelve Myths*, New York: Grove Press.

Leonard, H.T. (1989), *Environment and the Poor: Development Strategies for a Common Agenda*, New Brunswick: Oxford.

Lipton, M. (1977), *Why Do Poor People Stay Poor: A Study on Urban Bias in World Development*, London: Temple Smith.

Longhurst, R. (1988), 'Cash crops, household food security and nutrition', *IDS Bulletin*, **19** (2), Brighton: Institute of Development Studies, April.

Maxwell, S. (1996), 'Walking on two legs, but with one leg longer than the other: a strategy for the World Food Summit', *Forum Valutanzione*, **9**, 89–103, Viezzoli, M. (ed.), Edizioni Associate Editrice Internazionale, Rome.

Maxwell, S. and A. Fernando (1989), 'Cash crops in developing countries: the issues, the facts, the policies', *World Development*, **17** (11), 1677–1708.

Maxwell, S. and A. Lirenso (1994), 'Linking relief and development: an Ethiopian case study', *IDS Bulletin*, **25** (4), 65–76.

Mellor, J. (1976), *The New Economics of Growth: A Strategy for India and the Developing World*, Ithaca: Cornell University Press.

Mellor, J.W. (ed.) (1995), *Agriculture on the Road to Industrialization*, Baltimore: John Hopkins University Press for the International Food Policy Research Institute.

Mitchell, D.O. and M.D. Ingco (1993), 'How EC 1992 and reforms of the Common Agricultural Policy would affect developing countries' grain trade, international trade', *Policy Research Working Paper*, **848**, Washington DC: World Bank.

Mosher, A.T. (1966), *Getting Agriculture Moving: Essentials for Development and Modernization*, New York: Praeger.

Nicholls, W. (1964), 'The place of agriculture in economic development', in C. Eicher and L. Witt (eds), *Agriculture in Economic Development*, New York: McGraw-Hill, pp. 11–44.

Pearson, L.B., et al. (1969), *Partners in Development: Report of the Commission on International Development*, New York: Praeger.

Pinstrup-Anderson, P., et al. (1999), 'World food prospects: critical issues for the early 21st century', *IFPRI 2020 Vision Food Policy Report*, Washington DC: IFPRI.

Pretty, J. (1995), *Regenerating Agriculture: Policies and Practice for Sustainability and Self-Reliance*, London: Earthscan Publications.

Pretty, J., J. Thompson and F. Hinchcliffe (1996), 'Sustainable agriculture: impacts on food production and challenges for food security', *Gatekeeper Series*, **60**, London: International Institute for Environment and Development, Sustainable Agriculture Programme.

Rosegrant, M.W., et al. (1995), 'Global food projections to 2020: implications for investment, food, agriculture and the environment', *Discussion Paper*, Washington DC: IFPRI.

Ruthenberg, H. (1980), *Farming Systems in the Tropics*, Oxford: Clarendon Press, 3rd Edition.

Spooner, N. (1988) 'Does the World Bank Inhibit Smallholder Cash Cropping? The Case of Malawi', *IDS Bulletin*, **19** (2), 66–70.

Thrupp, L-A. (1995), *Bittersweet Harvests for Global Supermarkets: Challenges in Latin America's Agricultural Boom*, Washington DC: World Resources Institute.

UNDP (1990), *Human Development Report*, New York: United Nations Development Programme.

von Braun, J. and E. Kennedy (eds) (1994), *Agricultural Commercialization, Economic Development, and Nutrition*, Baltimore: John Hopkins University Press.

World Bank (1990), *World Development Report: Poverty*, Washington DC: World Bank.

World Bank (1994), *World Development Report: Infrastructure for Development*, Washington DC: World Bank.

World Bank (1998), *World Development Report: Knowledge for Development*, Washington DC: World Bank.

CHAPTER 3

Behnke, R.H., I. Scoones, C. Kerven (eds) (1993), *Range Ecology at Disequilibrium: New Models of Natural Variability and Pastoral Adaptation in African Savannas*, London: Overseas Development Institute and Commonwealth Secretariat.

Brock, K., and N. Coulibaly (1999), 'Sustainable rural livelihoods in Mali', *IDS Research Report* 35, Brighton: Institute of Development Studies.

Bryceson, D.F. (1999), 'African rural labour, income diversification and livelihood approaches: a long term development perspective', *Review of African Political Economy*, **80**, 171–189.

Carney, D. (1998), *Sustainable Rural Livelihoods: What Contribution can we Make?*, London: Department for International Development.

Carney, D. (1999), 'Approaches to sustainable livelihoods for the rural poor', *ODI Poverty Briefing* 2, January, London: Overseas Development Institute.

Carswell, G., A. de Haan, D. Dea, A. Konde, H. Seba, A. Shankland and A. Sinclair (2000), 'Sustainable livelihoods in Ethiopia', *IDS Research Report*, forthcoming, Brighton: Institute of Development Studies.

Cliffe, L. and R. Luckham (1999), 'Complex political emergencies and the state: failure and the fate of the state', *Third World Quarterly*, **20** (1), 27–50.

Davies, S. (1996), *Adaptable Livelihoods: Coping with Food Insecurity in the Malian Sahel*, Basingstoke: Macmillan.

Devereux, S. (1993a), *Theories of Famine*, London: Harvester Wheatsheaf.

Devereux, S. (1993b), 'Goats before ploughs: dilemmas of household response sequencing during food shortages', *IDS Bulletin*, **24** (4), 52–59.

de Waal, A. (1989) *Famine that Kills: Darfur, Sudan 1984–1985*, Oxford: Clarendon Press.

de Waal. A. (1996), 'Contemporary warfare in Africa: changing context, changing strategies', *IDS Bulletin*, **27** (3), 6–16.

Downing, T., K.W. Gitu and C.M. Kamau (1989), *Coping with Drought in Kenya: national and local strategies*, Boulder, Colorado: Lynne Rienner.

Drescher, A.W. (1999), 'Urban agriculture in the seasonal tropics: the case of Lusaka, Zambia.' in M. Koc, R. MacRae, L.J.A. Mougeot (eds), *For Hunger-Proof Cities: Sustainable Urban Food Systems*, Ottawa: IDRC.

Drèze, J., A. Hussain and A. Sen (1995), *The Political Economy of Hunger: Selected Essays*, World Institute for Development Economics Research, Oxford: Clarendon Press.

Ellis, F. (1998), 'Household strategies and rural livelihood diversification', *Journal of Development Studies*, **35** (1), 1–38.

Ellis, F. (1999), 'Rural livelihood diversity in developing countries: evidence and policy implications', *ODI Natural Resources Perspectives* 40, London: Overseas Development Institute.

Farrington, J., D. Carney, C. Ashley and C. Turton (1999), 'Sustainable livelihoods in practice: early applications of concepts in rural areas', *ODI Natural Resource Perspectives* 42, London: Overseas Development Institute.

Johnson, C. (1997), 'Rules, norms and the pursuit of sustainable livelihoods', *IDS Working Paper* 52, Brighton: Institute of Development Studies.

Kamete, A.M. (1998), 'Interlocking livelihoods: farm and small town in Zimbabwe', *Environment and Urbanisation*, **10** (1), 23–34.

Keen, D. (1997), *The Benefits of Famine: A Political Economy of Famine in South-Western Sudan 1983–1989*, Princeton NJ: Princeton University Press.

Kratli, S. and J. Swift (1999), *Understanding and Managing Pastoral Conflict in Kenya*, Brighton: Institute of Development Studies.

Leybourne, S.L. and M. Grant (1999), 'Bottlenecks in the informal food transportation network of Harare, Zimbabwe', in M. Koc, R. MacRae, L.J.A.

Mougeot (eds), *For Hunger-Proof Cities: Sustainable Urban Food Systems*, Ottawa: IDRC.

McCabe, J.Y. (1990), 'Success and failure: the breakdown of traditional drought coping institutions among the pastoral Turkana of Kenya', *Journal of African and Asian Studies*, **25** (3–4).

Maxwell, D.G. (1998), 'The political economy of urban food security in Sub-Saharan Africa', *IFPRI Discussion Paper* **41**, Washington DC: IFPRI.

Maxwell, D.G. (1999), 'Urban food security in sub-Saharan Africa', in M. Koc, R. MacRae, L.J.A. Mougeot (eds), *For Hunger-Proof Cities: Sustainable Urban Food Systems*, Ottawa: IDRC.

Maxwell, D.G., C. Levin and J. Csete (1998), 'Does urban agriculture help prevent malnutrition? Evidence from Kampala', *IFPRI FCND Discussion Paper* **45**, Washington DC: IFPRI.

Maxwell, D.G., C. Levin, M. Armar-Klemesu, M. Ruel, S. Morris and C. Ahiadeke (2000), 'Urban livelihoods and food and nutrition security in greater Accra, Ghana', *IFPRI Research Report* **112**, Washington DC: IFPRI.

Ruel, M.T., J.L. Garrett, S.S. Morris, D. Maxwell, A. Oshaug, P. Engle, P. Menon, A. Slack and L. Haddad (1998), 'Urban challenges to food and nutrition security: a review of food security, health and caregiving in the cities', *IFPRI FCND Discussion Paper* **51**, Washington DC: IFPRI.

Scoones, I., (ed.) (1995), *Living with Uncertainty: New Directions in Pastoral Development in Africa*, London: Intermediate Technology Publications.

Scoones, I. (1998), 'Sustainable rural livelihoods: a framework for analysis', *IDS Working Paper* **72**, Brighton: Institute of Development Studies.

Sen, A. (1981), *Poverty and Famines: An Essay on Entitlement and Deprivation*, Oxford: Clarendon Press.

Streiffeler, F. (2000), 'Urban Agriculture in Africa with Special Reference to the Former Zaire: Social, Ecological Land Use Aspects', in U. Kracht and M. Schulz (eds), *Food Security and Nutrition: The Global Challenge*, New York: St Martin's Press.

Swift, J. (1989a), 'Why are rural people vulnerable to famine?', *IDS Bulletin*, **20** (2), 8–15.

Swift, J. (1989b), 'Planning against drought and famine in Turkana: A district famine contingency plan', in T. Downing, K. Gitu and C. Kamau (eds), *Coping with Drought in Kenya: National and Local Strategies*, Boulder, Colorado and London: Lynne Rienner, 306–328.

Swift, J. (ed.) (1996), *War and Rural Development in Africa*, IDS Bulletin **27** (3).

Swift, J. (1998), 'Factors influencing the dynamics of livelihood diversification and rural non-farm employment in space and time', Chatham: Natural Resources Institute.

Swift, J., C. Toulmin and S. Chatting (1990), *Providing Services for Nomadic People: A Review of the Literature and Annotated Bibliography*, UNICEF Staff Working Paper No. 8, New York: WHO/UNICEF Nutrition Support Programme, UNICEF.

Tacoli, C. (1998), 'Bridging the divide: rural-urban interactions and livelihood strategies', *Gatekeeper Series* **77**, London: IIED Sustainable Agriculture and Rural Livelihoods Programme.

CHAPTER 4

Bayliss-Smith, T. (1991), 'Food security and agricultural sustainability in the New Guinea highlands: vulnerable people, vulnerable places', *IDS Bulletin*, **22** (3), 5–11.

Blaikie, P. and H. Brookfield (1987), *Land Degradation and Society*, London: Methuen.

Brock, K. and A. Coulibaly (1999), 'Sustainable rural livelihoods in Mali', *IDS Research Report*, No.36, Brighton: Institute of Development Studies.

Cannon, T. (1991), 'Hunger and famine: using a food systems model to analyse vulnerability', in H.G. Bohle, T. Cannon, G. Hugo and F.N. Ibrahim (eds), *Famine and Food Security in Africa and Asia: Indigenous Response and External Intervention to Avoid Hunger, Bayreuther Geowissenschaftliche Arbeiten*, **15**.

Carney, D. (1999), 'Approaches to sustainable livelihoods for the rural poor', *ODI Poverty Briefing*, **2**, January, London: Overseas Development Institute.

Carswell, G., A. de Haan, D. Dea, A. Konde, H. Seba, A. Shankland and A. Sinclair (1991), 'Sustainable livelihoods in Southern Ethiopia', *IDS Research Report*, No. 44, Brighton: Institute of Development Studies.

Chambers, R. and G. Conway (1992), 'Sustainable rural livelihoods: practical concepts for the 21ˢᵗ century', *IDS Discussion Paper*, **296**, Brighton: Institute of Development Studies.

Chen, R.S. and R.W. Kates (eds) (1994), 'Special issue: climate change and world food security', *Global Environmental Change*, **4** (1).

Cohen, J.E. (1995), *How Many People Can the Earth Support?*, New York: Norton.

Conway, G. (1997), *The Doubly Green Revolution: Food for All in the 21ˢᵗ Century*, Harmondsworth: Penguin.

Conway, G. and E.G. Barbier (1990), *After the Green Revolution: Sustainable Agriculture for Development*, London: Earthscan.

Davies, S. and M. Leach (1991a), 'Editorial: food security and the environment', *IDS Bulletin*, **22** (3), 1-4.

Davies, S., and M. Leach (1991b), 'Globalism versus villagism: food security and environment at national and international levels', *IDS Bulletin*, **22** (3), 43–50.

Davies, S., M. Leach and R. David (1991), 'Food security and the environment conflict or complementarily?', *IDS Discussion Paper*, **285**, Brighton: Institute of Development Studies.

Devereux, S., M. Rimmer, D. LeBeau and W. Pendleton (1993), 'The 1992/3 drought in Namibia: an evaluation of its socio-economic impact on affected households', *SSD Research Report*, **7**, Windhoek: University of Namibia, Social Sciences Division.

Downing, T. (1991), 'Vulnerability to hunger in Africa', *Global Environmental Change*, December 1 (5), 365–80.

Drinkwater, M. and M.A. McEwan (1994), 'Household food security and environmental sustainability in farming systems research: developing sustainable livelihoods', *Journal for Farming Systems Research-Extension*, **4** (2), 111–26.

Dyson, T. (1994), 'Population growth and food production recent global and regional trends', *Population and Development Review*, **20** (2), 397–412.

Fairhead, J. and M. Leach (1996), *Misreading the African Landscape: Society and Ecology in a Forest-Savanna Mosaic*, Cambridge: Cambridge University Press.

FAO, 1996, *State of Food and Agriculture 1996*, Rome: Food and Agriculture Organization of the United Nations (diskette).

Frankenberger, T.R and D.M. Goldstein (1990), 'Food security, coping strategies and environmental degradation', *Arid Lands Newsletter*, **30**.

Ghai, D. (1994), 'Environment, livelihood and empowerment', *Development and Change*, **25** (1), 1–12.

Hardin, G. (1968), 'The tragedy of the commons', *Science*, **162**, 1243–49.

Hoben, A. (1996), 'The cultural construction of environmental policy: paradigms and politics in Ethiopia', in M. Leach and R Mearns (eds), op. cit. Ch. 11.

IIED, (1994), 'Whose Eden? An overview of community approaches to wildlife management', report to the Overseas Development Administration, London: International Institute for Environment and Development.

IUCN, (1987), *Conservation with Equity: Strategies for Sustainable Development, Proceedings of the Conference on Conservation and Development: Implementing the World Conservation Strategy*, Gland: International Union for the Conservation of Nature and Natural Resources.

Lado, C. (1993), 'A note of the environmental and socio-economic insecurity in the Sudan', *Eastern and Southern African Geographical Journal*, **4** (1).

Leach, M. and R. Mearns (1991), *Poverty and Environment in Developing Countries: An Overview Study*, report to ESRC, Global Environmental Change Programme, and Overseas Development Administration, Swindon: ESRC.

Leach, M. and R. Mearns (eds) (1996a), *The Lie of the Land*, The International African Institute with Oxford: James Currey, and Portsmouth N.H.: Heinemann.

Leach, M. and R. Mearns (1996b), 'Environmental change and policy: challenging receive wisdom in Africa', in M. Leach and R Mearns (eds), op. cit. Ch. 1.

Leach, M., R. Mearns and I. Scoones (1997), 'Environmental entitlements: a framework for understanding the institutional dynamics of environmental change', *IDS Discussion Paper*, No. 359, Brighton: Institute of Development Studies.

Leach, M., R. Mearns and I. Scoones (1999), 'Environmental entitlements: Dynamics and Institutions in Community-Based Natural Resource Management', *World Development*, **27** (2), 225–247.

Lindblade, K.A., G. Carswell and J.K. Tumuhairwe (1998), 'Mitigating the relationship between population growth and land degradation', *Ambio*, **27** (7), 565–71.

Maxwell, S. and M. Buchanan-Smith (eds) (1994), 'Linking relief and development', *IDS Bulletin*, **25** (4), Brighton: Institute of Development Studies.

Murton, J. (1997), 'Sustainable livelihoods in marginal African environments? The social and economic impacts of agricultural intensification in Makueni District, Kenya', Draft paper presented to the ESRC conference on Sustainable Livelihoods in Marginal African Environments, Sheffield University, 10–11th April 1997.

Mwaka, V.M. (1991), 'The environment and food security in Uganda', *Eastern and Southern Africa Geographical Journal*, **2** (1).

Norse, D. (1994), 'Multiple threats to regional food production environment, economy, population?', *Food Policy*, **19** (2), 133–48.

Paarlberg, R. (1999), 'Agrobiotechnology Choices in Developing Countries', *Science, Technology and Innovation Discussion Paper*, **1**, Centre for International Development, Harvard University, Cambridge, MA, USA.

Payne, P. and M. Lipton (1994), 'How Third World rural households adapt to dietary energy stress: the evidence and the issues', *Food Policy Review*, **2**, Washington DC: IFPRI.

Peet, R. and M. Watts (1996), 'Liberation ecology: development, sustainability and environment in an age of market triumphalism', in R. Peet and M. Watts (eds), *Liberation Ecologies: Environment, Development, Social Movements*, London and New York: Routledge.

Scoones, I. (1995), 'New directions in pastoral development in Africa', in I. Scoones (ed.), *Living with Uncertainty: New Directions in Pastoral Development in Africa*, London: Intermediate Technology Publications.

Scoones, I. (1998), 'Sustainable Rural Livelihoods: A Framework for Analysis', *IDS Working Paper*, **72**, Brighton: Institute of Development Studies.

Sen, A. (1981), *Poverty and Famines: An Essay on Entitlement and Deprivation*, Oxford: Clarendon Press.

Swift, J. (1996), 'Desertification narratives, winners and losers', in M. Leach and R. Mearns (eds), op. cit. Ch. 4.

Tiffen, M. and M. Mortimore (1994), 'Malthus controverted the role of capital and technology in growth and environment recovery in Kenya', *World Development*, **22** (7), 997–1010.

Tiffen, M., M. Mortimore and F. Gichuki (1994), *More People, Less Erosion: Environmental Recovery in Kenya*, Chichester: John Wiley.

WCED, 1987, *Our Common Future,* World Commission on Environment and Development, Oxford: Oxford University Press.

CHAPTER 5

Adams (1993), 'Food insecurity in Mali: exploring the role of the moral economy', *IDS Bulletin*, **24**(4), 41–51.

Africa Watch (1991), *Evil Days: 30 Days of War and Famine in Ethiopia*, Washington DC: Human Rights Watch.

Ahmed, I. and R. Green (1999), 'The heritage of war and state collapse in Somalia and Somaliland: Local-level effects, external interventions and reconstruction', *Third World Quarterly*, **20**(1), 113–127.

Boserup, E. (1983), 'The impact of scarcity and plenty on development', in R. Rotberg and T. Rabb (eds), *Hunger and History*, Cambridge: Cambridge University Press.

Brown, L. (1995), *Who Will Feed China? Wake-up Call for a Small Planet*, New York: W.W. Norton.

Bryceson, D. (1990), *Food Insecurity and the Social Division of Labour in Tanzania, 1919–85*, London: Macmillan.

Buchanan-Smith, M. and S. Maxwell (eds) (1994), *Linking Relief and Development*, *IDS Bulletin*, **25**(4), Brighton: Institute of Development Studies.

Caldwell, J. and P. Caldwell (1992), 'Famine in Africa: A global perspective', in E. van de Walle, G. Pison and M. Sala-Diakanda (eds), *Mortality and Society in Sub-Saharan Africa*, Oxford: Clarendon Press.

Cannon, T. (1991) 'Hunger and famine: using a food systems model to analyse vulnerability', in H. Bohle, T. Cannon, G. Hugo and F. Ibrahim (eds), *Famine and Food Security in Africa and Asia: Indigenous Response and External Intervention to Avoid Hunger*, Bayreuth: Bayreuther Geowissenschaftliche Arbeiten.

Corbett, J. (1988), 'Famine and household coping strategies', *World Development*, **16**(9), 1099–1112.

Dando, W. (1980), *The Geography of Famine*, London: Edward Arnold.

Davies, S. (1996), *Adaptable Livelihoods: Coping with Food Insecurity in the Malian Sahel*, London: Macmillan.

de Waal, A. (1989), *Famine That Kills: Darfur, Sudan, 1984–1985*, Oxford: Clarendon Press.

de Waal, A. (1997), *Famine Crimes: Politics and the Disaster Relief Industry in Africa*, Oxford: James Currey.

Deng, L. (1999) 'The 1998 Famine in the Sudan: Causes, Preparedness and Response', *IDS Discussion Paper* **369**, Brighton: Institute of Development Studies.

Devereux, S. (1988), 'Entitlements, availability and famine: a revisionist view of Wollo, 1972–74', *Food Policy*, **13**, 270–282.

Devereux, S. (1993a), *Theories of Famine*, Hemel Hempstead: Harvester Wheatsheaf.

Devereux, S. (1993b), 'Goats before ploughs: Dilemmas of household response sequencing during food shortages', *IDS Bulletin*, **24**(4), 52–59.

Devereux, S. (1999), '"Making less last longer": Informal safety nets in Malawi', *IDS Discussion Paper* **373**, Brighton: Institute of Development Studies.

Devereux, S. (2000), 'Famine in the twentieth century', *IDS Working Paper* **105**, Brighton: Institute of Development Studies.

Duffield, M. (1993), 'NGOs, disaster relief and asset transfer in the Horn: Political survival in a permanent emergency', *Development and Change*, **24**, 131–157.

Field, J. (1993), 'Understanding famine', in J. Field (ed.), *The Challenge of Famine: Recent Experience, Lessons Learned*, West Hartford, Conn.: Kumarian Press.

Franke, R. and B. Chasin (1980), *Seeds of Famine: Ecological destruction and the development dilemma in the West African Sahel.* Monclair: Allanheld and Osmun.

Iliffe, J. (1979), *A Modern History of Tanganyika*, Cambridge: Cambridge University Press.

Iliffe, J. (1987), *The African Poor: A History*, Cambridge: Cambridge University Press.

Iliffe, J. (1990), *Famine in Zimbabwe: 1890–1960*, Harare: Mambo Press.

Keen, D. (1994), *The Benefits of Famine: A Political Economy of Famine and Relief in Southwestern Sudan, 1983–1989*, Princeton: Princeton University Press.

Kumar, B. (1990), 'Ethiopian famines 1973–1985: A case study', in J. Drèze and A. Sen (eds), *The Political Economy of Hunger, Vol. 2: Famine Prevention*, Oxford: Clarendon Press, Chapter 3.

Meillassoux, C. (1974), 'Development or exploitation: Is the Sahel famine good business?', *Review of African Political Economy*, **1**, 27–33.

Moore, P., A. Marfin, L. Quenemoen, B. Gessner, Y. Ayub, D. Miller, K. Sullivan and M. Toole (1993), 'Mortality rates in displaced and resident populations of central Somalia during 1992 famine', *The Lancet*, **341**, 935–938.

Mortimore, M. (1989), *Adapting to Drought: Farmers, famines and desertification in West Africa*, Cambridge: Cambridge University Press.

Pankhurst, R. (1989), 'The History of Famine in Ethiopia', in A. Lemma and P. Malaska (eds), *Africa Beyond Famine: A Report to the Club of Rome*, London: Tycooly Publishing, Chapter 7.

Ravallion, M. (1987), *Markets and Famines*, Oxford: Oxford University Press.

Raynault, C. (1977), 'Lessons of a crisis', in D. Dalby, R. Church and F. Bezzaz (eds), *Drought in Africa 2*, London: International African Institute.

Scott, J. (1976), *The Moral Economy of the Peasant*, New Haven: Yale University Press.

Seaman, J. (1993), 'Famine mortality in Africa', *IDS Bulletin*, **24**(4), 27–32.

Seaman, J. and J. Holt (1980), 'Markets and famines in the Third World', *Disasters*, **4**(3), 283–297.

Sen, A. (1981), *Poverty and Famines*, Oxford: Clarendon Press.

Sen, A. (1986), 'Food, economics and entitlements', *Lloyds Bank Review*, April.

Shepherd, J. (1993), ''Some tragic errors': American policy and the Ethiopian famine, 1981–85', in J. Field (ed.), *The Challenge of Famine: Recent Experience, Lessons Learned*, West Hartford, Conn.: Kumarian Press.

Swift, J. (1989), 'Why are rural people vulnerable to famine?', *IDS Bulletin*, **20**(2), 8–15.

Swift, J. (1993), 'Understanding and preventing famine and famine mortality', *IDS Bulletin*, **24**(4), 1–16.

Vaughan, M. (1987), *The Story of an African Famine: Gender and famine in twentieth-century Malawi*, Cambridge: Cambridge University Press.

von Braun, J., T. Teklu and P. Webb (1998), *Famine in Africa: Causes, Responses, and Prevention*, Baltimore: Johns Hopkins University Press.

Walker, P. (1989), *Famine Early Warning Systems: Victims and Destitution*, London: Earthscan.

Watts, M. (1983), *Silent Violence: Food, Famine and Peasantry in Northern Nigeria*, Berkeley: University of California Press.

Webb, P. and von Braun, J. (1994), *Famine and Food Security in Ethiopia: Lessons for Africa*, Chichester: John Wiley.

White, H. with S. Kayizzi-Mugerwa, T. Killick and M-A. Savane (2000), *Africa Poverty Status Report 1999*, Report to the SPA, Washington DC: World Bank.

Wolde-Mariam, Mesfin (1986), *Rural Vulnerability to Famine in Ethiopia: 1958–1977*, London: Intermediate Technology Publications.

CHAPTER 6

Abbott, J.C. (1987), *Agricultural Marketing Enterprises for Developing World*, New York: Cambridge University Press.

Bates, R. (1981), *Markets and States in Tropical Africa: The Political Basis of Agricultural Policies*, California: University of California Press.

Bevan, D., P. Collier and J.W. Gunning (1993), 'Agriculture and the policy environment: Tanzania and Kenya', Development Centre Studies, Organisation for Economic Cooperation and Development.

Beynon, J., S. Jones and S. Yao (1992), 'Market reform and private trade in Eastern and Southern Africa', *Food Policy*, 17 (6): 399-408.

Bryceson, D.F. (1993), 'Urban bias revisited: staple food pricing in Tanzania', in C.H. de Alcantara (ed.) *Real Markets: Social and Political Issues of Food Policy Reform*, London: Frank Cass.

Coulter, J. and P. Golob (1992), 'Cereal marketing liberalization in Tanzania', *Food Policy*, 17 (6): 420-430.

Gordon, H.F. (1994), 'Grain marketing performance and public policy in Tanzania', PhD Thesis, Fletcher School of Law and Diplomacy.

IBRD (1994), 'Tanzania: agriculture', *World Bank Country Study*, Washington DC: World Bank.

Jones, S. (1994), *Agricultural Marketing in Africa: Privatisation and Policy Reform*, Queen Elizabeth House, University of Oxford: Food Studies Group.

Monke, E., S.R. Pearson and B. Baulch (1997), 'Potential tradeables and price stabilization policy: rice in Indonesia', mimeo, Department of Agricultural and Resource Economics, University of Arizona.

Norton, G.W. and J. Alwang (1993), *Introduction to Economics of Agricultural Development*, Singapore: McGraw-Hill.

Santorum, A. and A. Tibaijuka (1992), 'Trading responses to food market liberalization in Tanzania', *Food Policy*, 17 (6): 431-442.

Southworth, V.R. (1981), 'Food crop marketing in Atebubu District, Ghana', Ph.D. dissertation, Stanford University.

Timmer, P. (1989), 'Food price policy: the rationale for government intervention', *Food Policy* 14(1): 17–27.

Timmer, P., W.P. Falcon and S.R. Pearson (1983), *Food Policy Analysis*, Baltimore and London: Johns Hopkins University Press.

CHAPTER 7

Eurostat (1991), *EEC external trade (Nimexe) 1976–1987*, Supplement 1/1991, Luxembourg: Statistical Office of the European Communities.

Eurostat (1997), *Intra- and extra-EU trade (annual data – Combined Nomenclature)*, Supplement 2, Luxembourg: Statistical Office of the European Communities.

Eurostat (1998), *Intra- and extra-EU trade (annual data – Combined Nomenclature)*, Supplement 2, Luxembourg: Statistical Office of the European Communities.

FAO (1999) *FAOSTAT Databases* [website: http://apps.fao.org/default.htm], Rome: Food and Agriculture Organization of the United Nations.

FSG (1996), *Global Cereal Markets and Food Security*, Oxford, UK: Queen Elizabeth House, University of Oxford, Food Studies Group.

GATT (1994), *The Results of the Uruguay Round of Multilateral Trade Negotiations*, Geneva: GATT Secretariat.

Mitchell, D.O. and M.D. Ingco (1993), *World Food Outlook*, Cambridge: Cambridge University Press.

Swinbank, A. (1996), 'Capping the CAP? Implementation of the Uruguay Round Agreement by the European Union', *Food Policy*, Guildford, UK.

UNDP (1998), *Human Development Report 1998*, New York and Oxford: Oxford University Press for the United Nations Development Program.

UNDP (1999), *Human Development Report 1999*, New York and Oxford: Oxford University Press for the United Nations Development Program.

World Bank (1995), 'The Uruguay Round and the developing economies', *World Bank Discussion Paper*, **307**, Washington DC: The World Bank.

WTO (1996), *The Results of the Uraguay Round* (CD-Rom), Geneva: World Trade Organization.

CHAPTER 8

Boudreau, T. (1998), 'The food economy approach: a framework for understanding rural livelihoods', *ODI Relief and Rehabilitation Network Paper*, **26**, May, London: Overseas Development Institute.

Buchanan-Smith, M. and S. Davies (1995), *Famine Early Warning and Response: The Missing Link*, London: Intermediate Technology Publications.

Chambers, R. (1993), *Challenging the Professions: Frontiers for Rural Development*, London: Intermediate Technology Publications.

Club du Sahel (1994), 'Assessment of the application of the Food Aid Charter in the Sahel', *Report on the Meeting of the Network for the Prevention of Food Crises in the Sahel*, Paris: OECD.

Davies, S. (1994), 'Information, knowledge and power', *IDS Bulletin*, **25** (2), 1–13.

Devereux, S. and T. Næraa (1996), 'Drought and survival in rural Namibia', *Journal of Southern African Studies*, **22** (3), 421–440.

Drèze, J. and A. Sen (1989), *Hunger and Public Action*, Oxford: Clarendon Press.

Food and Agriculture Organization (1985), *Committee on World Food Security: Tenth Session, 10–17 April 1985*, Rome: FAO.

Food and Agriculture Organization (1989), *Committee on World Food Security: Fourteenth Session, 3–7 April 1989*, Rome: FAO.

Food and Agriculture Organization (1996), *The Sixth World Food Survey*, Rome: FAO.

Food and Agriculture Organization (1997), *Committee on World Food Security: Twenty-third session, 14–18 April 1997*, Rome: FAO.

Geier, G. (1995), *Food Security Policy in Africa Between Disaster Relief and Structural Adjustment: Reflections on the Conception and Effectiveness of Policies: The Case of Tanzania*, London: Frank Cass.

Government of Ethiopia (1997), *Market Information Bulletin: July 1997*, Addis Ababa: Grain Market Research Project, Ministry of Economic Development and Cooperation.

Government of Somaliland (1995), *Market Prices and Trade Bulletin: July/October 1995*, Djibouti: Nutrition Unit, Somaliland Ministry of Health.

Helder, J. and J. Nijhoff (1995), *Technical Handbook: Market Information for Early Warning*, Harare: SADC/FAO Early Warning System.

Maimbo, F., A. Huijsman, D. Mulwanda, and B. Lof (1996), *Opportunities for Western Province: An agro-economic reconnaissance study*, Amsterdam: Royal Tropical Institute.

Manarolla, J. (1991), 'The food security index', *Mimeo*, Washington DC: USAID.

Mudimu, G. and R. Mabeza-Chimeda (eds) (1996), *Agricultural Competitiveness, Market Forces, and Policy Choice: Eastern and Southern Africa Perspectives and Case Studies*, Hamburg: Lit Verlag Munster-Hamburg.

Namibian Institute of Social and Economic Research (NISER) (1993), *Namibia Household Food Security Report: September 1993*, Windhoek: University of Namibia.

SADC (1997), *Food Security Quarterly Bulletin: Jan/Feb 1997*, Harare: SADC Regional Early Warning Unit.

Seaman, J. (1996), 'The food economy approach to Vulnerability Assessment and the RiskMap Computer Programme', in FAO, *Second Informal Meeting on Methodology for Vulnerability Assessment: Summary Report*, Rome: FAO.

Seaman, J. and J. Holt (1980), 'Markets and famines in the Third World', *Disasters*, **4** (3).

Sen, A. (1981), *Poverty and Famines*, Oxford: Clarendon Press.

Shepherd, A. (1997), 'Market information services: theory and practice', *FAO Agricultural Services Bulletin*, **125**, Rome: Food and Agriculture Organization.

Smith, L. (1998), 'Can FAO's measure of chronic undernourishment be strengthened?', *Food Policy*, **23** (5), 425–445.

Stephenson, R. and P. Anderson (1997), 'Disasters and the information technology revolution', *Disasters*, **21** (4), 305–334.

United Nations (1975), *Report of the World Food Conference: Rome 5–16 November 1974*, New York: United Nations.

Wood, D., R. van Otterdijk and T. Muthana (1998), *Aide Memoire: Assessment of Zambia's Food Security for the 1998/1999 Agricultural Marketing Season*, Lusaka.

World Food Programme (1996), *Zambia Vulnerability Assessment and Mapping Project: Analyses of normal and current food security conditions*, Lusaka: WFP.

World Food Programme (1997), *Senegal Vulnerability Analysis*, Dakar: WFP.

World Food Summit (1996), *Rome Declaration on World Food Security and World Food Summit Plan of Action*, Rome: World Food Summit.

Wyeth, J. (1992), 'The measurement of market integration and applications to food security policies', *IDS Discussion Paper*, **314**, Brighton: Institute of Development Studies.

CHAPTER 9

ACC/SCN (1993), *Second Report on the World Nutrition Situation*, Geneva: Administrative Committee on Co-ordination – Sub-Committee on Nutrition of the United Nations.

ACC/SCN (1994), 'Controlling vitamin A deficiency', ACC/SCN State-of-the-Art Series, *Nutrition Policy Discussion Paper*, **14**, United Nations Administrative Committee on Co-ordination – Sub-Committee on Nutrition, January.

ACC/SCN (1997), *Third Report on the World Nutrition Situation*. Geneva: Administrative Committee on Co-ordination – Sub-Committee on Nutrition of the United Nations.

ACC/SCN (2000), *Fourth Report on the World Nutrition Situation*, Geneva: Administrative Committee on Co-ordination – Sub-Committee on Nutrition of the United Nations.

Ashworth, A. and S. Khanum (1997), 'Cost-effective treatment for severely malnourished children: what is the best approach?', *Health Policy and Planning*, **12**(2).

Ashworth, A., A. Jackson, S. Khanum and C. Schofield (1996), *Ten Steps to Recovery – Ten Steps to Manage Severely Malnourished Children*, Child Health Dialogue.

Bailey, K. and A. Ferro-Luzzi (1995), 'Use of body mass index of adults in assessing individual and community nutritional status', *Bulletin of the World Health Organization*, **73**(5), 673–680.

Beaton, G.H. (1993), 'Nutritional issues in food aid', Papers from the ACC/SCN 19th Session, April, 37–55.

Berg, Alan (1993), 'Sliding toward nutrition malpractice; time to reconsider and redeploy', *American Journal of Clinical Nutrition*, **57**, 3–7.

Breslin, D., P. Delius and C. Madrid et al. (1997), 'Strengthening institutional safety nets in South Africa: sharing Operation Hunger's insights and experiences',

Development Southern Africa, **14**(1), 21–41, Development Bank of Southern Africa.

Briend, A. and M.H.N. Golden (1993), 'Treatment of severe child malnutrition in refugee camps', *European Journal of Clinical Nutrition*, **47**, 750–754.

Centers for Disease Control (1992), 'Famine affected, refugee, and displaced populations: Recommendations for public health issues', *Centers for Disease Control, Morbidity and Mortality Weekly Report (MMWR)* **41**(RR-13).

Collins, S. (1995), 'The limit of human adaptation to starvation', *Nature Medicine*, **1**(8), 810–814.

Curdy, A. (1994), 'The relevance of supplementary feeding programmes for refugees, displaced or otherwise affected populations', Paper presented at a workshop on the Improvement of the Nutrition of Refugees and Displaced People in Africa, Machakos, Kenya, 5 December 1994, Geneva: ACC/SCN.

Curtis, Patrice (1995), 'Urban household coping strategies during war: Bosnia Hercegovina', *Disasters Journal*, **19**(1), 68–73.

Cutler, P. (1984), 'The measurement of poverty, a review of attempts to quantify the poor with special reference to India' *World Development*, **12**(11/12), 1119–30.

de Onis, M. and J-P. Habicht (1996), 'Anthropometric reference data for international use: recommendations from a World Health Organization Expert Committee', *American Journal of Clinical Nutrition*, **64**, 650–658.

de Onis, M., R. Yip and Z. Mei (1997), 'The development of MUAC-for-age reference data recommended by a WHO Expert Committee', *Bulletin of the World Health Organization*, **75**(1), 11–18.

Djikhuizen, P. (1997), 'Postscript; production of pre-cooked fortified blended foods in Kenya: a success story', *The Field Exchange*, **2**, 7.

Engle, P. (1992), 'Care and child nutrition', Paper for the International Conference on Nutrition, New York: UNICEF.

FAO Codex Alimentarius Commission (1991), Second edition, 'Guidelines: formulated supplementary foods for older infants and children', in Volume 4, *Foods for Special Dietary Uses (Including Foods for Infants and Children), Part 2 – Foods for Infants and Children*, CAC/GL 8–1991,

FAO (1993), *Food Aid in Figures, Vol II*, Rome: Food and Agriculture Organization of the United Nations.

FAO/GIEWS (1997), *Food Outlook*, May/June

Fincham, R. (1997), Nutrition surveillance and intervention, South Africa, *SCN News* **15**(8).

Gillespie, S. and J. Mason (1991), *Nutrition-Relevant Actions, Some Experiences from the Eighties and Lessons for the Nineties*, Geneva: Administrative Committee on Co-ordination – Sub-Committee on Nutrition, October.

Golden, M.H.N. (1991) 'The nature of nutritional deficiency in relation to growth failure and poverty', *Acta Paediatr Scand Suppl*, **374**, 95–110.

Golden, M.H.N. (1996), 'Severe malnutrition', in D.J. Wetherall, et al. (eds), *Oxford Textbook of Medicine*, Oxford: Oxford University Press, pp. 1278–1296.

Gorstein, J., K. Sullivan, R. Yip, M. de Onis, F. Trowbridge, P. Fajans, and G. Clugston (1994), 'Issues in the assessment of nutritional status using anthropometry', *Bulletin of the World Health Organization*, **72**(2), 273–83.

Graitcer, P. L. and E.M. Gentry (1981), 'Measuring children: one reference for all', *The Lancet*, **2**, 297–299.

Habicht, J-P., R. Martorell, C. Yarborough, R.M. Malina and R.E. Klein (1974), 'Height and weight standards for pre-school children, how relevant are ethnic differences in growth potential?', *The Lancet*, **1**, 611–615.

Hertz, G. (1997), 'Production of pre-cooked fortified blended foods in Kenya: a success story', *ENN Field Exchange*, **Aug**(2), 6.

ICCIDD (1996), 'Conference on the Sustainable Elimination of Iodine Deficiency Disorders in Africa by the year 2000', Annual ICCIDD Board Meeting, Zimbabwe,

Harare International Conference Centre, Zimbabwe/Africa., 22–24 April 1996. International Council for the Control of Iodine Deficiency Disorders.

Jaspars, S. and H. Young (1995a), 'General food distribution in emergencies: from nutritional needs to political priorities' *Good Practice Review*, **3**, London: Relief and Rehabilitation Network, Overseas Development Institute, December.

Jaspars, S. and H. Young (1995b), 'Malnutrition and poverty in the early stages of famine: North Darfur, 1988–90', *Disasters Journal*, **12**(3), 198–215.

JNSP (1989), *The Joint WHO/UNICEF Nutrition Support Programme in Iringa, Tanzania, 1983–1988 Evaluation Report*, Dar es Salaam, Tanzania: Government of the United Republic of Tanzania, World Health Organization, United Nations Children's Fund.

Kennedy, E. (1991), *Successful Nutrition Programmes in Africa, What Makes Them Work?*, World Bank, Population and Human Resources Department.

Levinson, F. James (1991), 'Addressing malnutrition in Africa: low cost program possibilities for government agencies and donors', *Social Dimensions of Adjustment in Sub-Saharan Africa, Working Paper No. 13*, Washington, DC: World Bank.

Lipton, M. (1983), 'Poverty, undernutrition and hunger', *World Bank Staff Working Paper*, Washington, DC: World Bank.

Longhurst, R. and A. Tomkins (1995), 'The role of care in nutrition - a neglected essential ingredient', *SCN News*, **12**, 1–5.

Lorri, W. (1997), 'Nutrition programmes in Tanzania', *SCN News*, **15**, 6.

Macrae, J. and A. Zwi (1994) 'Famine, Complex Emergencies and International Policy in Africa: An Overview' in *War and Hunger: Rethinking international responses to complex emergencies*, London: Zed Books, 6–36.

Mears, C. and S. Chowdhury (1994), 'Health care for refugees and displaced people', *Oxfam Practical Guide*, **9**, Oxford: Oxfam.

Mears, C., and H. Young (1998), 'The acceptability and use of cereal based foods. Case-studies from Nepal, Ethiopia and Tanzania', *Oxfam Working Paper*, Oxford: Oxfam.

Oxfam (1997), 'Evaluation of the 1996 Turkana Food Distribution Programme', draft, Oxford: Oxfam.

Pacey, A., and P. Payne (eds) (1985), *Agricultural Development and Nutrition*, Hutchinson, by arrangement with FAO and UNICEF.

Parlato, M., and P. Gottert (1996), 'Promoting Vitamin A in rural Niger: Strategies for adverse conditions', in *Strategies for Promoting Vitamin A Production, Consumption and Supplementation. Four Case-Studies*, Washington: The Academy for Educational Development.

Rogers, B. (1995), 'Feeding programs and food-related income transfers' in P. Pinstrup-Anderson, D. Pelletier and H. Alderman (eds), *Child Growth and Nutrition in Developing Countries: Priorities for Action*, Ithaca: Cornell University Press, Chapter 11.

Schofield, C. and A. Ashworth (1996), 'Why have mortality rates for severe malnutrition remained so high?' *Bulletin of the World Health Organization* **74**(2): 223–229.

Schofield, C. and J. Mason (1996), 'Setting and evaluating the energy content of emergency rations', *Disasters Journal*, **20**(3), 248–260.

Seaman, J., and J. Rivers (1988), 'Strategies for the distribution of relief food', *Journal of the Royal Statistical Society*, Series A, **151**(3), 464–72.

Sen, A. (1981), *Poverty and Famines, An Essay on Entitlement and Deprivation*, Oxford: Clarendon Press.

Shoham, J. (1995), *Emergency Supplementary Feeding Programmes*, Good Practice Review **2**, London: Overseas Development Institute, Relief and Rehabilitation Network.

Tomkins, A. and F. Watson (1989), 'Malnutrition and infection', ACC/SCN State-of-the-Art Series, *Nutrition Policy Discussion Paper*, 5, United Nations Administrative Committee on Co-ordination – Sub-Committee on Nutrition, October.

UNICEF (1990), *Strategy for Improved Nutrition of Children and Women in Developing Countries. A UNICEF Policy Review*, New York: UNICEF.

Van Nieuwenhuyse, C. (1995), 'Getting food to victims of man-made disasters, food mobilization and logistics constraints', Paper presented at UNHCR Workshop on Tools and Strategies for Nutritional Needs Assessment and the Management of Food and Nutrition Programmes for Refugees and Displaced Populations, Addis Ababa, October 15–21 1995.

Waterlow, J.C. (1992), *Protein Energy Malnutrition*, (low priced edition), London: Edward Arnold.

Webb, P. (1995) 'Employment programs for food security in rural and urban Africa: Experiences in Niger and Zimbabwe', in *Employment for Poverty Reduction and Food Security*, Washington, DC: International Food Policy Research Institute.

WHO Working Group (1986), 'Use and interpretation of anthropometric indicators of nutritional status', *Bulletin of the World Health Organization* 64(6), 929–941.

WHO (1995), *Management of Severe Malnutrition, a Manual for Physicians and Other Senior Health Workers*, draft, Geneva: WHO.

Young, H. and S. Jaspars (1995), *Nutrition Matters – People, Food and Famine*, London: Intermediate Technology Publications.

CHAPTER 10

Alderman, H. (1986), *The Effect of Food Price and Income Changes on the Acquisition of Food by Low-income Households*, Washington DC: International Food Policy Research Institute.

Ball, R. and C. Johnson (1996), 'Political, economic and humanitarian motivations for PL 480 food aid: evidence from Africa', *Economic Development and Cultural Change*, 44 (3), 515–537.

Besley, T. and R. Kanbur (1993), 'The principles of targeting', Chapter 3 in M. Lipton and J. van der Gaag (eds), *Including the Poor*, Washington DC: The World Bank.

Buchanan-Smith, M. and S. Maxwell (eds) (1994), 'Linking relief and development', *IDS Bulletin*, 25 (4), Brighton: Institute of Development Studies.

Burgess, R. and N. Stern (1991), 'Social security in developing countries: what, who, why and how?', in E. Ahmed et al. (eds), *Social Security in Developing Countries*, Oxford: Clarendon Press.

Clay, E., S. Dhiri and C. Benson (1996), *Joint Evaluation of European Union Programme Food Aid: Synthesis Report*, London: Overseas Development Institute.

Cornia, G. and F. Stewart (1993), 'Two errors of targeting', *Journal of International Development*, 5 (5), 459–496.

Cox, D. and E. Jimenez (1990), 'Achieving social objectives through private transfers', *World Bank Research Observer*, 5 (2), 205–218.

Devereux, S. (1997), 'Household Food Security in Malawi', *IDS Discussion Paper*, 362, Brighton: Institute of Development Studies.

Devereux, S. (1998), 'The impact of WFP development assistance: effective approaches for food aid interventions', in *Time for Change: Food Aid and Development*, Rome: World Food Programme.

Devereux, S. (1999a), 'Targeting Transfers: Innovative solutions to familiar problems', *IDS Bulletin*, 30 (2), 61–74.

Devereux, S. (1999b), 'Making Less Last Longer: Informal safety nets in Malawi', *IDS Discussion Paper*, 373. Brighton: Institute of Development Studies.

Devereux, S. and C. Solomon (1994), 'Food-For-Work in Namibia: A review of the

1992/93 food-for-work programme', *SSD Research Report*, **18**. Windhoek: UNICEF-Namibia and Social Sciences Division, University of Namibia.

de Waal, A. (1997), *Famine Crimes: Politics and the Disaster Relief Industry in Africa*, Oxford: James Currey.

Dil, L. (1996), *Rural Appraisal: Primary Schools, Vulnerable Group Feeding, and Food for Work as Channels of Maize Distribution*, Lilongwe: World Food Programme.

Drèze, J. and A. Sen (1989), *Hunger and Public Action*, Oxford: Clarendon Press.

Food Studies Group (FSG) (1994), *Country Strategy Outline: World Food Programme – Malawi*, Lilongwe: World Food Programme.

Friedmann, H. (1990), 'The origins of Third World food dependence', in H. Bernstein, B. Crow, M. Mackintosh and C. Martin (eds), *The Food Question: Profits Versus People?*, London: Earthscan.

Government of Mozambique (1995), 'Impact evaluation of the GAPVU program', Maputo: Ministry of Planning and Finance, Poverty Alleviation Unit.

Grosh, M. (1993), 'Five criteria for choosing among poverty progams', *Policy Research Working Papers*, Washington DC: World Bank.

Grosh, M. (1995), 'Toward quantifying the trade-off: administrative costs and incidence in targeted programs in Latin America', Chapter 16 in D. van de Walle and K. Nead (eds), *Public Spending and the Poor*, Baltimore: Johns Hopkins University Press.

Hay, R. (1986), 'Food Aid and Relief-Development Strategies', *Occasional Paper*, **8**, Rome: World Food Programme.

Holzmann, R. and S. Jørgensen (2000), 'Social risk manaagement: a new conceptual framework for social protection, and beyond', *Social Protection Discussion Paper*, **6**, Washington DC: World Bank.

Low, J., J. Garrett, and V. Ginja (1998), 'Formal Safety Nets in an Urban Setting: Lessons from a cash transfer program in Mozambique', in Ministry of Planning and Finance, et al., *Understanding Poverty and Well-Being in Mozambique: The First National Assessment (1996–97)*, Maputo: Government of Mozambique.

Macrae, J. (1998), 'The death of humanitarianism? An anatomy of the attack', *Disasters*, **22** (4), 309–317.

Maxwell, S. (1993), 'Can a cloudless sky have a silver lining? The scope for an employment-based safety net in Ethiopia', in H. Thrimm and H. Hahn (eds), *Regional Food Security and Rural Infrastructure*, Hamburg: Lit Verlag Munster-Hamburg.

Psacharopoulos, G. (1994), 'Returns to investment in education: a global update', *World Development*, **22** (9), 1325–1344.

Rogers, B. (1995), 'Feeding programs and food-related income transfers', Chapter 11 in P. Pinstrup-Andersen, D. Pelletier, and H. Alderman (eds), *Child Growth and Nutrition in Developing Countries: Priorities for Action*, Ithaca: Cornell University Press.

Sen, A. (1981), *Poverty and Famines*, Oxford: Clarendon Press.

Sen, A. (1997), 'Entitlement perspectives of hunger', in *Ending the Inheritance of Hunger*, Rome: World Food Programme.

Shaw, J. and E. Clay (eds) (1993), *World Food Aid: Experiences of Recipients and Donors*, Rome: World Food Programme and London: James Currey and Heinemann.

Sijm, J. (1997), *Food Security and Policy Interventions in Sub-Saharan Africa: Lessons from the Past Two Decades*, Amsterdam: Thesis Publishers.

Subbarao, K., A. Bonnerjee, J. Braithwaite, S. Carvalho, K. Ezemenari, C. Graham and A. Thompson (1996), *Social Assistance and Poverty-targeted Programs*, Washington DC: World Bank Poverty and Social Policy Department.

Tajgman, D. (1997), *Food for Thought: A Guide for Moving from Food for Work (FFW) to Food for Assets and Sustainable Employment (FASE)*, Aarhus, Denmark: Labour in Development.

USAID (1997), 'Food aid in the Sahel', *Impact Evaluation Number 8*, Washington D.C.: United States Agency for International Development.

von Braun, J., T. Teklu and P. Webb (1991), 'Labour-intensive public works for food security: Experience in Africa', *Working Paper on Food Subsidies*, **6**. Washington DC: International Food Policy Research Institute.

World Bank (1990), *World Development Report: 1990: Poverty*, Washington DC: Oxford University Press.

World Bank (1997), *World Development Report 1997: The State in a Changing World*, Washington DC: Oxford University Press.

World Food Programme (1995), *Operational Guidelines for WFP Assistance to Education*, Rome: World Food Programme.

World Food Programme (1997), *WFP Interventions in the Field of Natural Resources: Ethiopia – Food Assistance to Rehabilitation of Rural Lands and Infrastructure*, Rome: World Food Programme.

World Food Programme (1998a), http://www.wfp.org/reports/wfpstats/98/, Rome: World Food Programme.

World Food Programme (1998b), *Time for Change: Food Aid and Development*, Rome: World Food Programme.

CHAPTER 11

Belshaw, D. (1990), 'Food strategy formulation and development planning in Ethiopia', *IDS Bulletin*, **21** (3), July, 31–43.

Berg, A. (1987), 'Nutrition planning is alive and well, thank you', *Food Policy*, **12** (4), November, 365–375.

Biggs, S.D. and E.J. Clay (1983), *Generation and Diffusion of Agricultural Technology: A Review of Theories and Experience*, report prepared for the Technology and Employment Branch, Technology and Employment Programme, Geneva: ILO.

Birgegard, L-E. (1987), 'A Review of experiences with integrated rural development', *Issue Paper*, **3**, March, Uppsala: International Rural Development Centre, Swedish University of Agricultural Sciences.

Bradford, D.L. and A.R. Cohen (1997), *Managing for Excellence: The Leadership Guide to Developing High Performance in Contemporary Organisations*, Chichester: Wiley.

Chambers, R. (1983), *Rural Development: Putting the Last First*, Harlow: Longman.

Chambers, R. (1993), *Challenging the Professions: Frontiers for Rural Development*, London: Intermediate Technology Publications.

Chambers, R. and J. Jiggins (1986), 'Agricultural research for resource-poor farmers: a parsimonious paradigm', *Discussion Paper*, **220**, Brighton: IDS.

Chambers, R., A. Pacey and L.A. Thrupp (eds) (1989), *Farmer First: Farmer Innovation and Agricultural Research*, London: Intermediate Technology Publications.

Clay, E.J., and B.B. Schaffer (eds) (1984), *Room for Manoeuvre: An Exploration of Public Policy in Agriculture and Rural Development*, London: Heinemann.

Crener, M.A., G. Leal, R. LeBlanc and B. Thebaud (1984), *Integrated Rural Development: State of the Art Review, 1983/84*, Ottawa: CIDA.

Davies, S. (1994), 'Public institutions, people, and famine mitigation', *IDS Bulletin*, **25** (4), October, 46–54.

FAO and WHO (1992), 'Incorporating nutrition objectives into development policies and programmes', Theme Paper No 8 in FAO/WHO, *Major Issues for Nutrition Strategies*, Rome: International Conference on Nutrition.

Field, J.O. (1987), 'Multi-sectoral nutrition planning: a post-mortem', *Food Policy*, **12** (1), February, 15–28.

Flynn, J.C. and G.L. Denning (1982), 'Interdisciplinary challenges and opportunities in international agricultural research', *IRRI Research Paper Series*, **82**, Manila: International Rice Research Institute.

Fowler, A. (1988), 'NGOs in Africa: achieving comparative advantage in relief and micro development', *Discussion Paper*, **249**, August, Brighton: IDS.

Gillespie, S. and G. McNeill (1992), *Food, Health and Survival in India and Developing Countries*, Delhi: Oxford University Press.

Handy, C.B. (1985), *Understanding Organisations*, (3rd edition), London: Penguin.

Heyer, J., P. Roberts and G. Williams (1981), *Rural Development in Tropical Africa*, London: Macmillan.

Hindle, R. (1990), 'The World Bank approach to food security analysis', *IDS Bulletin*, **21** (3), July, 62–66.

Huddleston, B. (1990), 'FAO's overall approach and methodology for formulating national food security programmes in developing countries', *IDS Bulletin*, **21** (3), July, 72–80.

IDS and IUED (1994), *Poverty Assessment and Public Expenditure: A Study for the SPA Working Group on Poverty and Social Policy*, September, Brighton: IDS.

Kennes, W. (1990), 'The European Community and food security', *IDS Bulletin*, **21** (3), July, 67–71.

Levinson, F.J. (1995), 'Multi-sectoral nutrition planning: a synthesis of experience', in P. Pinstrup-Andersen, D. Pelletier and H. Alderman (eds), *Child Growth and Nutrition in Developing Countries: Priorities for Action*, Ithaca: Cornell University Press.

Maxwell, S. (1986), 'The social scientist in farming systems research', *Journal of Agricultural Economics*, **XXXVII** (1), January, 25–35.

Maxwell, S. (ed.) (1990a), *Food Security in Developing Countries, IDS Bulletin*, **21** (3), July.

Maxwell, S. (1990b), 'Food security in developing countries: issues and options', *IDS Bulletin*, **21** (3), July, 2–13.

Maxwell, S. (1991), 'National food security planning: first thoughts from Sudan', in S. Maxwell (ed.), *To Cure all Hunger: Food Policy and Food Security in Sudan*, London: Intermediate Technology Publications.

Merrill-Sands, D. (1986), 'Farming systems research: clarification of terms and concepts', *Experimental Agriculture*, **22**, 87–104.

Merrill-Sands, D. and J. McAllister (1988), 'Strengthening the integration of on-farm client-oriented research and experiment station research in national agricultural research systems: management lessons from nine country case studies', *OFCOR Comparative Study*, **1**, September, The Hague: ISNAR.

Moore, M. (1993), 'Competition and pluralism in public bureaucracies', *IDS Bulletin*, **23** (4), 65–77.

Murray, R. (1992), 'Towards a flexible state', *IDS Bulletin*, **23** (4), October, 78–89.

Peters, T.J. (1987), *Thriving on Chaos*, London: Pan Books.

Peters, T.J. and R.H. Waterman (1982), *In Search of Excellence*, New York: Harper and Row.

Richards, P. (1985), *Indigenous Agricultural Revolution: Ecology and Food Production in West Africa*, London: Hutchinson.

Toye, J. and C. Jackson (1996), 'Public expenditure policy and poverty reduction: has the World Bank got it right?', *IDS Bulletin*, **27** (1), January, 56–66.

Tripp, R. (1989), 'Farmer participation in agricultural research: new directions or old problems?', *Discussion Paper*, **256**, February, Brighton: IDS.

World Bank (1990), *World Development Report 1990*, Washington: World Bank.

World Bank (1996), 'Taking action for poverty reduction in sub-Saharan Africa', *Report of an Africa Region Task Force*, **15575–AFR**, May, Washington: World Bank.

Notes

CHAPTER 1

1 This is a subset from nearly 200, collected by Smith et al. (1993).
2 Sen (1981) acknowledges the power of subjective analysis, but concentrates on objective entitlements.
3 Malthus, it will be recalled, argued that population increases in geometrical progression but food production only in arithmetic progression, leading to an increasing gap between population and food supply (see Chapter 5).

CHAPTER 4

1 Davies et al. (1991, p. 20). The links between nutrition and the environment are not explored in this short chapter: see Payne and Lipton (1994).
2 Chambers and Conway (1992, p. 13). They add to this the idea of preservation or enhancement of intangible assets, e.g. claims and access.
3 For further reading on food security and climate change see Chen and Kates (1994).
4 See Conway and Barbier (1990).
5 See Leach and Mearns (1991) for a discussion of poverty/environment linkages.
6 See Blaikie and Brookfield (1987) and, for a critique of political ecology, Peet and Watts (1996).
7 For a variety of studies about myths of environmental abuse and degradation, see Leach and Mearns (1996a). On desertification see Swift (1996) and on deforestation see Fairhead and Leach (1996).
8 See IIED (1994) for a discussion and examples of this shift in thinking.
9 See Hoben (1996) for a discussion of the impact of neo-Malthusian thinking on policy and practice in Ethiopia.
10 For a discussion of these issues see Maxwell and Buchanan-Smith (1994).

CHAPTER 5

1 Many other terms express this basic distinction, including: precipitating v. underlying factors, conjunctural v. structural causes, transitory v. chronic food insecurity, and shocks v. vulnerability.
2 Another example of the wealthy suffering famine during a war was the Netherlands in World War II, when 10 000 people died following a blockade by the Germans (Devereux 1993a).
3 For present purposes, 'political vulnerability' is narrowly defined to mean the

extent to which a government has neither the political will nor the capacity to intervene in food emergencies.

4   This line of argument was applied by radical French writers to the 1970s Sahelian famine – see Meillassoux (1974); Raynault (1977); also Franke and Chasin's *Seeds of Famine* (1980), which essentially blamed the famine on the expansion of groundnut cultivation during the colonial period.

5   This section draws on Devereux (1999).

CHAPTER 6

1   It is important to distinguish between transfer and transactions costs. Transactions costs include both the tangible transfer costs defined above and a number of, often notional, cost items, such as the time traders spend acquiring information or enforcing contracts.

2   See Abbott (1987) for a stimulating collection of practical case studies of agricultural marketing from around the world.

3   There are also some marketing boards, stabilization funds and advisory bodies, which have important price stabilization or market regulation roles, but do not engage in produce marketing on their own account (e.g. the Coffee and Cocoa Industry Boards in Papua New Guinea). Although such organizations have much to commend them, they will not be considered further here.

4   Pan-territorial pricing is when the food marketing parastatal pays one price to producers, wherever they are located in the country, and charges another price for grain distributed to consumers, again wherever they are located. Pricing is pan-seasonal when these parastatal purchase and sales prices are the same throughout the (crop) year.

5   Whether or not it makes sense for a country to rely on a buffer stock or a buffer fund in stabilizing food prices, depends on the commodity in question and transportation costs. International markets for some grains (such as white maize and – at least until a few years ago – *japonica* rice) are very 'thin', whereas for other grains (such as wheat) they are well developed. Futures and options contracts are one way in which food marketing parastatals in developing countries can protect themselves from sudden rises or falls in international grain prices. Furthermore, differences in transportation costs can differ dramatically between countries. International procurement of grain can be very costly for landlocked African countries such as Botswana or Malawi.

6   This is left to the interested reader as an 'exercise'!

7   See, for example, Norton and Alwang (1993, pp. 255–8).

8   Open market producer price data are not available. However, retail prices in the Southern Highlands provide a close approximation to producers' prices because transport costs within the Southern Highlands are low and the margin between producer and retail prices in this region is likely to be small.

CHAPTER 7

1   The FAO measures food security by the number malnourished while IFPRI measures the number of children undernourished.

CHAPTER 8

1   The 'Universal Declaration on the Eradication of Hunger and Malnutrition' followed Kissinger's appeal to governments and the international community

to 'accept the goal that within a decade no child will go to bed hungry, that no family will fear for its next day's bread and that no human being's future and capacities will be stunted by malnutrition' (United Nations 1975, p. 4).

2   Commitment Two – paragraph 20(a) – states that: 'governments, in partnership with all actors of civil society, as appropriate, will develop and periodically update, where necessary, a national food insecurity and vulnerability information and mapping system, indicating areas and populations, including at local level, affected by or at risk of hunger and malnutrition, and elements contributing to food insecurity, making maximum use of existing data and other information systems in order to avoid duplication of efforts' (World Food Summit 1996, p. 14).

3   Subsistence requirements are typically set at 167 kg, 200 kg or 220 kg per person *per annum*, or the calorie equivalent (e.g. 2200 kcal per person per day). Also, individuals are converted into 'adult equivalents' – e.g. children under 15 might count as half an adult in terms of consumption needs.

4   To be more precise – the food balance equation requires nine variables to be estimated, three measuring national *food supply* (domestic food production, net food imports or exports, and net change in year-end food stocks), and six indicators of *food utilization* (seed use, industrial non-food use, animal feed, on-farm and off-farm waste, losses in processing or extraction, and net food supply available for human consumption). The key final variable is a residual derived by subtracting the first five utilization variables from the total national food supply figure, and is expressed in per capita food availability terms (kilocalories and grams of protein).

5   FAO guidelines for food assessment missions explicitly stipulate that non-cereal crops should be assessed in terms of their capacity to offset shortfalls in cereal production. 'In particular, in cassava growing areas, the level of cassava reserves in the ground which could be utilized to meet cereal shortfalls should be estimated'. One reason for the neglect of cassava in official estimates may be that cassava in Zambia has historically been a non-tradeable crop which is rarely marketed through formal channels and so was never registered in parastatal records.

6   The UN Office for Coordination of Humanitarian Affairs defines a 'complex emergency' as 'a humanitarian crisis in a country, region or society where there is total or considerable breakdown of authority resulting from internal or external conflict and which requires an international response that goes beyond the mandate or capacity of any single agency'.

7   The clearest and most succinct statement emphasizing the importance of access to food (or effective demand) in addition to availability (or food supply) remains the opening sentences of Sen's 'Poverty and Famines' (1981, p. 1): 'Starvation is the characteristic of some people not *having* enough food to eat. It is not the characteristic of there *being* not enough food to eat. While the latter can be a cause of the former, it is but one of many *possible* causes.'

8   According to Smith (1998, p. 432), the correlation coefficient between the estimated prevalence of chronic undernourishment and national *per capita* DES is 0.91 ($P<0.001$), which suggests that the explanatory role of the distribution parameter is virtually redundant.

9   See Mudimu and Mabeza-Chimeda (1996) for a number of African case studies.

CHAPTER 9

1   'Underweight' is a shorthand term for a child with a particularly low value of the WFA index, as determined by internationally recognized reference cut-off values for the weights of children at different ages. The 'underweight' measure (WFA) is a composite of both stunting and wasting and is universally recognized as the most important summary indicator of a child's nutritional status.

2   Stunting refers to shortness that is a deficit, i.e. linear growth that has failed to reach genetic potential as a result of suboptimal health or nutrition conditions.

3   Malnutrition is clearly associated with poverty, but according to Golden (1991) this is not just a matter of a lack of staple food as such, rather a lack of variety of foods. As a family becomes poorer the luxury items are dropped first from the diet. Then the more expensive 'common' foods are consumed more and more rarely. With increasing poverty the diet becomes more and more restricted until, *in extremis,* only the staple food is being consumed.

4   Anaemia is the most widespread nutritional deficiency worldwide. It makes people tired and thereby reduces their ability to work and concentrate. Children have less energy for playing and learning and therefore may develop more slowly than other children. Vitamin A deficiency occurs mostly in pre-school children largely as a result of inadequate dietary intake, often exacerbated by protein energy malnutrition and/or infections – particularly measles. Children with vitamin A deficiency are more likely to get diarrhoea, respiratory and other infections and to die from them. Measles rapidly depletes the body's stores of vitamin A and contributes to post-illness malnutrition. In poor communities infants – often of low birth weight – are born with low liver stores of vitamin A due to maternal malnutrition. Iodine deficiencies lead to enlargement of the thyroid gland, reduced mental function, widespread lethargy, and increased rates of stillbirths and infant mortality. Children born to women who are deficient in iodine may suffer various degrees of irreversible mental impairment (cretinism).

5   See for example the many cases described in the *Journal of Refugee Studies,* Special Issue, 'The Nutrition Crisis among Refugees', 1992, Vol. 5, No 3/4.

6   Nutritional status may also be assessed by examining the adequacy of the diet, by measuring food intake and comparing the quality and quantity of food eaten with recommended levels (Recommended Daily Amounts). Two other methods include physical examination and biochemical analysis, which are not generally used for surveillance activities.

7   A standard implies the concept of a norm or target, that is, a value judgement (WHO Working Group, 1986). This concept has led to difficulty, since the international reference is widely used also as a standard. The justification for this is based on evidence collected by Habicht et al. (1974) and Graitcer and Gentry (1981). However, in view of significant technical drawbacks of the current NCHS/WHO reference an expert WHO committee has recommended the development of a new reference concerning weight and length/height for infants and children (de Onis and Habicht, 1996). Some of the difficulties are discussed by Gorstein et al. (1994).

8   Prevalence of low serum retinol of less than 10 per cent defines vitamin A deficiency as a public health problem (ACC/SCN 1997).

9   At a meeting on Supplementary Feeding in Dublin on 18 to 20 February 1997, convened by Concern, Ireland on behalf of an *ad hoc* group of nutritionists from NGOs and UN agencies, Professor Michael Golden of the University of Aberdeen summarized results of trials using these products (as yet

unpublished). The use of vitamin mineral pre-mix added to the high energy milk and also to a modified version of ORS significantly reduced the case fatality rate from 25.8 to 20.8. An important aspect of micronutrient supplementation was thought to be on anorexia.

10   When all children under a certain age group are included this is often referred to as 'blanket feeding'.

11   Jeremy Shoham (1995) has reviewed the experience of NGO supplementary feeding in emergencies.

CHAPTER 10

1   This structure was suggested by Burgess and Stern's (1991) review of 'Social security in developing countries: What, who, why and how?'.

2   More recently, the World Bank has shifted towards broader conceptualizations of social safety nets (Subbarao et al. 1996) and 'social risk management' (Holzmann and Jørgensen 2000), but for present purposes the original (1990) approach is preferred.

3   See Hay (1986); Buchanan-Smith and Maxwell (1994).

4   However, some observers have strongly critiqued the 'famine industry' – see de Waal (1997) and see Macrae (1999) for a defence of humanitarianism.

5   There are many other terms for this distinction, including: F-errors (failure to reach) or E-errors (excessive benefits), Type I or Type II errors, undercovergage or overcoverage, horizontal versus vertical inefficiency, and sensitivity or specificity errors.

6   This section draws on material presented more extensively in Devereux (1998). My thanks to Naomi Hossain for research assistance.

7   In an assessment of US food aid policy towards Africa, Ball and Johnson (1996) demonstrate that the aims of PL 480 ('Public Law') food aid clearly included the development of commercial food markets for American agricultural produce. Other critics have shown that allocations of American food aid reflected US strategic interests rather than the food security needs of recipient countries (Friedmann 1990).

8   Following a critical appraisal which recommended that all the World Food Programme's non-emergency food aid activities be closed down, WFP initiated an internal review process entitled 'Time for Change: Food Aid and Development' (WFP 1998b), for which a series of papers was commissioned presenting the case for the positive developmental impacts of project food aid.

9   Other terms include labour-intensive public works projects and 'employment-based safety nets' (Maxwell 1993). Payment on public works is not always in the form of food, but in Africa food-for-work is far more common than alternatives such as 'cash-for-work' or 'inputs-for-work'.

10   Of all American food aid delivered to the Sahel over the evaluation period (1960–97), 14 per cent was delivered through supplementary feeding programmes, 13 per cent through school feeding and 9 per cent through food-for-work, some of which was monetized.

11   In 1995 WFP effectively scrapped the nutritional improvement objective from its school feeding programmes in favour of the developmental objective, when a document titled 'Operational Guidelines for WFP Assistance to Education' (WFP 1995) concluded that future evaluations should assess only whether school feeding programmes improved school enrolment and attendance rates.

About the Contributors

Bob Baulch is an agricultural and development economist specializing in agricultural price analysis, the dynamics of rural poverty and the economics of food marketing. Before joining IDS in 1995 he was a staff member of the Natural Resources Institute and the Overseas Development Institute. His article on testing for food market integration in the *American Journal of Agricultural Economics* won the American Agricultural Economics Association's outstanding journal article award for 1997. He is currently on a secondment from IDS working with the World Bank in Vietnam.

Stephen Devereux is a development economist who joined IDS in 1996, following three years as a Senior Researcher at the University of Namibia. His research interests include famine theory, food security and anti-poverty interventions in Africa. His PhD thesis on food security in northern Ghana won the Africa Studies Association (UK) Dissertation Prize in 1993. He has lived and worked in Ghana, Namibia and South Africa and is currently undertaking research on safety nets and social protection programmes in Botswana, Ethiopia, Malawi, Mozambique and Zambia. His books include *Fieldwork in Developing Countries* (co-edited with John Hodinott) and *Theories of Famine*. In 1997 he was director of the IDS *Food Security in Africa* study course.

Kate Hamilton is studying for a DPhil at the Institute of Development Studies, where as a Research Assistant she has previously worked on a range of issues including sustainable livelihoods, participation, governance and civil society. Prior to Masters study, she worked for Oxfam UK & Ireland supporting emergency relief and community development programmes in Georgia, Armenia and Azerbaijan. She has also worked with rural NGOs in the far north and south of India, and is currently involved in setting up a community project in Brighton which aims to support local ecological livelihood initiatives and broaden participation in them.

Simon Maxwell is currently Director of the Overseas Development Institute (ODI) in London. He previously worked overseas for ten years, in Kenya, India and Bolivia; and from 1981–97 was a Fellow at the Institute of Development Studies, University of Sussex, latterly as Programme Manager for Poverty, Food Security and the Environment. He has published extensively on poverty, food security, agricultural development, farming systems research, and aid. In addition to conceptual and policy research on food security, he has advised governments, UN organizations and aid agencies on food security policy and planning; and has run many training programmes. In Africa, his main expertise is on the Greater Horn, especially

Ethiopia and Sudan. Publications include several books and over 50 journal articles and reports on food security issues.

Susanna Moorehead is Head of the Economic and Social Research Unit at the Department for International Development (DFID) in London. From 1992 to 1997 she was Deputy Director of IDS Sussex. She is the author of *Adaptable Livelihoods*, a study of vulnerability and resilience in northern Mali, and co-author with Margie Buchanan-Smith of *Famine Early Warning and Response: The Missing Link*, which assesses the effectiveness of early warning systems in five African countries. She was director of the IDS study course on Food Security in Africa in 1990 and 1995.

Christopher Stevens and **Jane Kennan** have worked together on many aspects of the external dimensions of food security in developing countries. These have included the effects of the GATT Uruguay Round and reform of the EU's Common Agricultural Policy (*Levelling the Field: Will CAP Reform Provide a Fair Deal for Developing Countries?*), the food security issues at stake in the current WTO renegotiations of the Agreement on Agriculture and the EU's post-Lomé trade regime with the ACP.

Jeremy Swift has written extensively on pastoralism, disaster planning and preparedness, famine, land tenure and common property resource management, and environmental impacts of alternative land use. He has field experience throughout the Sahel and the Horn of Africa, and is currently managing a major research programme at IDS on 'Sustainable Livelihoods', with research components in Ethiopia, Mali and Zimbabwe. He has edited IDS Bulletins on 'New Approaches to Famine' in 1992, and 'War and Rural Development in Africa' in 1996.

Helen Young is an Associate of the Feinstein International Famine Center, School of Nutrition Science and Policy, at Tufts University, where she teaches at Masters level, and is co-directing a global training initiative with the World Food Programme. She was formerly the Food and Nutrition Adviser in Oxfam's Emergency Department. Operational work has been with Oxfam (1985–9, and 1995–7) and with a range of UN agencies and non-governmental organizations undertaking short-term consultations in the Horn and East Africa. She has researched the role of nutrition in famine situations, at the Institute of Development Studies, and has published three books and several academic papers. Since 1998, she has been Co-Editor of the *Disasters Journal*, and since 1999 Technical Editor of the UN ACC/SCN Reports on the Nutrition Situation of Refugees and Displaced People (the RNIS). She holds a BSc from Oxford Polytechnic, and a PhD from the Council for National Academic Awards in the UK, qualifying in 1985.

William Wolmer is a PhD student in the Environment Group at the Institute of Development Studies, University of Sussex where he is conducting research on perceptions of landscape in southeastern Zimbabwe in relation to conservation and development policy. A geographer by training, he has previously worked on the dynamics of crop–livestock integration in Ethiopia, Mali and Zimbabwe.

Index